# Good Governance and Civil Society

# CGS Studies

Edited by

## Ralph Schattkowsky and Miloš Řezník

## Volume 3

# Good Governance and Civil Society: Selected Issues on the Relations between State, Economy and Society

Edited by

Adam Jarosz

CAMBRIDGE SCHOLARS

PUBLISHING

Good Governance and Civil Society:
Selected Issues on the Relations between State, Economy and Society
Edited by Adam Jarosz

Reviewed by:
Dr hab. Alfred Lutrzykowski, prof. UMK
Prof. dr hab. Katarzyna Żukrowska

This book first published 2014

Cambridge Scholars Publishing

Lady Stephenson Library, Newcastle upon Tyne, NE6 2PA, UK

British Library Cataloguing in Publication Data
A catalogue record for this book is available from the British Library



ISBN (10): 1-4438-7050-1, ISBN (13): 978-1-4438-7050-4

The publication has been financially supported by the
Visegrad Fund, City of Toruń and the Nicolaus Copernicus University in Toruń.

Visegrad Fund

Miasto Toruń

# TABLE OF CONTENTS

**Part Two: Communication and Self-Organisation as Elements of Regulation of Power and Society**



**Part Three: Quality of Regional and Local Identity as a Democratic Pattern of Efficacy of Civil Society**

# INTRODUCTION

## ADAM JAROSZ

The concept of governance is a key issue for public sector work at all possible levels. In the times of globalization and the growing significance of communication and participatory managing methods, public service provision and dialog with citizens have to be developed. The concept of governance seems to be an answer to these challenges. It combines cooperative forms of governing, involving private sector and social partners which can form networks to develop policies in different fields, good governance as an outcome of transparent and efficient way of governing, as well as multi-level governance where not only state but also other institutions (supranational institutions and organisations, local and regional governments) participate in the process of governing.

The political dimension is moving into a coordinative—instead of a hierarchical and ruling—mode of work. The private sector gains a much stronger position in the field of solving public issues than ever before due to its capacity to deliver services of high value at lower costs than the public subjects. It also has the necessary capital to invest in and maintain public infrastructure without increasing the public debt. The third party—society—becomes not only more conscious but also better organised as the concepts of civil society and self-organisation spread rapidly, together with the expectations for participation on different levels of decision-making. Nowadays, the demands for deliberative forms of democracy occur not only in the well-established Western democracies but also in the post-socialist and other countries facing democratic transition.

Democratic systems and the necessity of debate and deliberative forms push the political and other actors towards the development of communication on different levels, so that the cooperative forms have a chance to exist. In this context, the communication between different groups can have a regulatory character for the internationalizing and open societies, and the economic sector has an influence on the relations between society and state.

This book is the third volume of the Copernicus Graduate School Studies, and is devoted to these questions and research problems. Mostly young scientists examine different examples, issues and case studies considering different elements and aspects of the governance concept. This broad term needs interdisciplinary and multidimensional research to cover all the important issues related to it. The representatives of different disciplines develop various issues in the fields of politics, economy, society and communication on international, state and local levels.

The aim of the editors and authors, and the main objective of the volume, is to contribute to the discussion about governance, pointing out innovative fields of research which uncover interesting explanations and impulses regarding the formulation of innovative research questions on the matter. The concept of governance is very broad and refers to numerous spheres of public life. Therefore, a great deal of research is needed to uncover all of its aspects and interpretations.

# INITIAL REMARKS

# GOOD GOVERNANCE AND CIVIL SOCIETY: DEFINITIONS AND THE POLITICAL DIMENSION

RALPH SCHATTKOWSKY

The dynamics of changes resulting from globalization and the demise of a bipolar world order have been influencing every aspect of human existence. Taking into consideration the existential problems of humanity and consciously shaping the future for the general interest, one needs to pose fundamental questions on social functionality and state order once again. Traditional beliefs are more and more at one's disposal. As a central subject of this drive to change the relation between state and society appears, and an awareness of the need to newly arrange the relation between masses and authorities has been developing. This process involves the search for effective forms of social participation in decision-making as well as for adequate mechanisms of a transparent exercise of the state power. Nowadays, this process is expressed in the best way by the notions of Civil Society and Good Governance.

Good Governance is neither thinkable nor feasible without an adequate societal development, and depends on the existence and quality of Civil Society. It is a product of the arrangement for relations between state and society as a dynamic and permanent process of reciprocal influence meant as cooperation. Here is the essential new quality of governance. This connection is undisputable; however, it is rarely considered in research. One of the biggest potentials of this connection is that it describes both principal elements of a future-oriented organisation of human life, and above all examines where the fields of crucial dependence and coincidence are and how the communication between state and society is shaped.

Good Governance and Civil Society are not new in their characters; indeed, they are two of the great constants in the development of civilization in the European millennium. The search for and the claim on a merciful monarch has been a golden thread in the history of states, and has found its echo both in the education of princes in the Renaissance and

Romantic periods and in the belief in the "good father tsar." Since the discovery of the individual and the recognition of the existence of society in the modern European times, an appropriate form of organisation has been searched for. It is supposed to represent the interests of people in front of the authorities and to protect the individual from the authorities, the sovereign or the state, as well as to partner the authorities. This organisation form found its strongest articulation in the great European revolutions, whose most mature products are the parliamentary democracies of the nineteenth and twentieth centuries. However, something new that subjects these achievements to negotiation is that there has been a consensus about the notion of globalization in order to embrace those processes that have a transnational and worldwide impact, and they describe the powers that neither individual national states nor the existing, already widely eroded international systems are able to handle (such as capital flows, climate change and terror). In order to create a new international order, national forms of governance are also needed. Good Governance has the potential to implement international tasks on the national level. It also develops appropriate communication forms of a new international networking that combines the continuing national requirements with those of an international community and creates a bearable balance.

We have now come to the long-discussed point, the starting point of which seems to be the activity of the Club of Rome as well as Dennis Meadows' 1972 book *Beyond the Limits: Global Collapse or a Sustainable Future*. Even if Meadows concluded after 40 years of writing that "we are prisoners of the system" ("Süddeutsche Zeitung," January 2, 2013), one should not agree with him. The solution is found within the system in a proper combination of market and state. As a consequence, the state must play a greater role again which can be achieved in the interest of a functional democracy only by an arrangement of the state-society relation and by strengthening the Civil Society. A question that is crucial in reshaping that relation is "self-restraint," whereas to find a brand new approach to growth we are committed to a "revolutionary evolution."

In his 2011 book *Consumptionomics*, Chandran Nair, the founder of the Global Institute for Tomorrow, described the state of affairs and the tasks very consistently, following the logic of "the party is over!" The West has still not understood that economic liberalism, excessive consumption and accelerated urbanization are not solutions to upcoming problems. Nair refers to the necessity of setting new priorities in the twenty-first century. The right to individual freedom needs to give way to the provision of masses of population to secure their base of existence, which can be done only by a strong central power. It is an extremely risky assumption that needs to be thought about so that the notion of freedom is redefined.

Certainly, modernization processes are, first of all, always processes that increase the complexity and emergence of confusion known collectively in sociology as "functional differentiation." As we talk about limits of growth, we must accept that complexity can take a dimension that overcharges a community and creates uncontrollability out of confusion. This leads to a new order in terms of unbundling and distribution, possibly connected with a loss of a main societal perspective. The control of the society can no longer be comprehended by a simple nation-state model of the primacy of economy or politics, only by a qualitatively new ordered society. For this purpose, the concept of Civil Society was developed. The digital age, metaphorically paraphrased as the information and knowledge society, shows that the time has come. If we consider the realities of this world, it is a euphemism in its positive interpretation and is consciously used to calm us.

When we talk about Civil Society it is not about a self-organisation that exists outside the state but about an organisation other than that of the state. In this respect, Friedrich von Hayek gave the decisive hint that, exactly in a spontaneous appearance of order, the distributed knowledge of all people is implemented in a way that no planned construction would be able to achieve. He drew on the thinking model introduced by Adam Smith in his famous book *The Wealth of Nations* (1776), according to which the individual participant of the market is led by an "invisible hand" that promotes unintended societal objectives. That thinking model is based on a "system of natural freedom." If we translated it into present-day problems, it would lead us exactly towards the efforts aiming at an economic order beyond supply and demand.

To describe the relation between state and society, the German expert in constitutional law Ernst-Wolfgang Böckenförde's 1967 theory, known as the Böckenförde paradox, seems to be particularly appropriate: "The liberal secularized state lives on premises that it cannot guarantee by itself." These premises are "internal bonding forces" such as nation and religion that are increasingly being lost. Anyway, a community does not integrate itself solely out of the freedom of its members. It is exactly here that the Civil Society intervenes and defines its tasks out of this paradox.

The attitude of expectation built around Civil Society is very high, and is about nothing less than a search for and the determination of adequate forms of existence of modern society. They are supposed to live up to their emancipation character and their dynamics as well as be oriented towards the participation of the individual in decision-making. That participation establishes itself as a secure and enduring counterpart to the power of the state as well as a societal reassurance. This alone already marks the Civil Society as logical and necessary debate of the "century of the extreme" (Hobsbawm). The tendency to use Civil Society as a universal pebble tool in sociological research speaks undoubtedly in favour of a comprehensive effort aiming at a certain unambiguity of historical analysis and social findings about the nature of modern society. It assigned Europe a key role in world history and moreover is able to reveal social and political perspectives. The use of this "political signal concept" should not only distinguish between "good" and "bad" societies but also provide explanations about the relations between masses and authorities, state and society, as well as individual and group. Those explanations shall amount to the identification of the role of the individual in the societal process, and the individual's behaviour, motivations and perceptions. The individual is in fact reinvented as a motor of the history and his or her communication activity is examined in terms of virtues and core values of common human life. In search of a determining idea based on a functionality of the society, the Western canon of values—which includes democracy, freedom and a middle-class way of life labelling of society and separating it from the state and the exercise of power—is critically scrutinized as a blueprint for a future-oriented applicability. Thereby, the concept of Civil Society serves a double objective: "It helps us understand how in fact a certain society works and how it distinguishes itself from alternative forms of society. At the same time, the concept helps us come to a more clear conscience about our social norms, our values and reasons why they appeal to us" (Ernest Gellner).

The term "Good Governance" originally comes from the field of development aid and was used as a criterion of distribution of funds. In the last twenty years it has developed very dynamically. The questions of functionality and efficacy of traditional and proven Western government systems became subjects of wide debates, and influenced by the heavily changing world, the concept has significantly widened. Thus, it serves to describe effective, transparent and humane forms of government in general. Thereby, it is used both as a valuation standard for existing authority systems and as a claim for its creation or modification. In recent years, various concepts of Good Governance have been presented. In science, the notion has been considered from different perspectives according to interests, specialist focus or research paradigms. The basic content of Good Governance includes functioning state institutions, rule of law, respect for human rights and the principle of solidarity. It is a classical set of tools for the achievement of modern state objectives and not necessarily innovative elements of state policy. The actual impact is made by the universal usage of the concept. The question about the influence of the state is answered by the creation of its functionality with the help from stronger social participation. The penetration of national law standards by international law is regarded as indispensable. The creation of Good Governance is described as a common task that does not export any models, but that adapts itself to concrete circumstances (ownership). Related to the fact that the exercise of state power must be internationally credible, a market economy order is inherent to the logic of Good Governance. At the same time, an economic "recharge" of the concept related to the appearance of a new kind of "political economy" and the demand for an "economic statecraft" has taken place, further putting the economy into the commission of the state and its presence abroad (as requested by Hillary Clinton).

However, as a result of the processes of generalisation and widening, the concept has become less tangible and more abstract as an outline of statehood, or even an eschatological objective meant as a completeness of government. It ceased to be a concrete tool of state orientation for reshaping the relation between state and society. Thus, the concept is now subject to a heavy arbitrariness and serious doubts on its applicability and reasonableness are expressed (thus, the concept shares the fate of the term "Civil Society"). A comprehensive examination of its efficacy and implementation is therefore an important and so far unfulfilled task. Undoubtedly, we are now on the cusp of a re-evaluation of the concept, in which questions of its applicability and understanding are posed connected with the formulation of practical tasks for organisation of the relation between state and society in a global and transnational dimension.

The understanding of the concept of Good Governance is therefore a scientific desideratum. Not only it is worth considering and interesting as a research topic (regarding how the concept established oneself and became a paradigm of a basic orientation in politics and economy), but it is also worth asking how the concept redefines the relation between state and society, or else how it attempts to arrange the relation between the notions of "national" and "international" under conditions of globalization. Those questions can be answered successfully only with consideration of interdisciplinary approaches, in which politological, sociological and economic premises have priority. Not to a lesser degree, the work on the subject should also include historical experience and interpretation models. A particular challenge is to compare theoretical premises and arguments with their practical implementation or to examine their mutual influence and effects. The objectives of scientific cognition cannot be reached if relations between theory and practice are not taken into consideration. The cognition demands research which is close to the society and provides the practice with direct added value.

Therefore, we need to ask which processes or insights underlie the creation of the concept, in which degree its politicization has taken place, and which state and social powers have been working on the widening of the concept and if they draw direct consequences for their practical action. Furthermore, one needs to ask if a unification of perceptions can be derived from the development of the concept and the establishment of Good Governance on the international level, whether there are any reliable tendencies of practicing Good Governance, and finally if there are any truly practical conclusions for shaping Good Governance and Civil Society out of the endangerment of the civilization.

Certainly, the acceptance of this diagnosis is astonishingly large, and in any case what we have encountered so far in the analytical processing or the constructive showing of the right way is terrifying poor, oscillating between a flat criticism of capitalism, which is remote from the established analysis of society of the nineteenth century, and fatalistic expertise, which assumes that we will manage it because we have always managed it (i.e. the market will adjust everything). The society reacts with the "Attack" or "Occupy" movements as well as with the slogan "*Indignez-vous!*" (Stephane Hessel), ultimately a relatively helpless and disoriented one. Also, certainly well-meant appeals for a limitation of growth and a conscious living in the achieved welfare (as presented recently in Robert and Edward Skidelsky's *How Much is Enough?*) seem to be very naive in the face of dramatic problems. Notions such as post-modernity, late modernity or late capitalism are supposed to offer consolation and confirm vague expectations. However, they only point out the fact that the classical modern diagnoses no longer stand the test. Maybe the job of the scientist must be (again) to work up the courage to work in a less palatable way, to follow political correctness less and to serve the mainstream less, and should not confront the danger of being incomprehensible, awkward and working asymmetrically.

Most of all, the scientists should escape from the principle of general approval.

Ralph Schattkowsky is professor and head of the International Relations History Department at the Faculty for Political Sciences and International Studies at the Nicolaus University in Toruń (Poland). He is also head of the board of the Copernicus Graduate School and associated professor at the University of Rostock (Germany). His scientific interests concentrate on German-Polish relations, history of Central and Eastern Europe, nationalism and civil society.

# PART ONE

# INTERNATIONALIZATION OF GOVERNANCE AND SOCIETY

# CHAPTER ONE

# THE SIGNIFICANCE OF GOOD GOVERNANCE FOR SUSTAINABLE DEVELOPMENT: A THEORETICAL APPROACH

ROBERTA KAREIVAITĖ

## Introduction

In many developed countries good governance becomes an engine of the public management development, which empowers institutions to achieve a higher level of public services provided and satisfaction of citizens with the activity of the management system. The increase in economic problems under the influence of social groups, associations, the increasing of environmental requirements, the formation of global institutional networks, and the deepening of tensions between different interest groups have constituted assumptions for establishing other trends of compatibility of economic, social and environmental objectives—i.e. the concept of sustainable development, which has become an integral attribute of the contemporary democratic society and particularly a subject for scientific research.

The state and public administration should actively employ principles and techniques of good governance because they make an impact on sustainable development. Sustainable development is seen as a process of long-term economic growth, gradual social growth and rational use of environmental resources in the institutional-based system in a democratic society. Good governance should be perceived as an appropriate and necessary aspect of sustainability implementation based on institutions forming social, environmental and economic access and equal rights to public goods and resources, affecting different social groups and their interests.

The aim of this chapter is to reveal the significance of good governance for sustainable development from the theoretical approach. In this regard the following tasks were formulated: (1) present the concept of good governance, (2) identify sustainable development and its dimensions, (3) reveal the indicators of good governance, showing their impact on sustainable development. The following qualitative research methods were used: literature analysis, systematization, comparison generalization and synthesis.

## The Concept of Good Governance

The good governance concept is based on the position of international organisations (e.g. the World Bank, the International Monetary Fund, the United Nations Organisation), which say that "developing countries are facing economic and social problems due to the lack of good governance."[1] "Good governance is considered as synonymous for democratic governance, which stresses the interaction of governmental, private sector's and civil society's organisations in economic, political and administrative management areas."[2]

There are three key organisations which have promoted the refinement of the good governance idea. The World Bank represented the concept of good governance in 1992, identifying four aspects: accountability, rule of law, accessibility of a government's information, and transparency.[3] The Asian Development Bank identified the strategic objectives of good governance as poverty reduction and the effective ensuring of public financial resources (these are closely linked with objectives of sustainable development). Four elements—accountability, participation, predictability and transparency[4]—can also be adapted for the objective of sustainability. The International Monetary Fund specializes in three key areas of public management related to its role under the supervision of the macroeconomic management. Therefore, the focus is on the transparency of government accounts, the efficiency of public resource management,

---

[1] S. Pivoras, E. Visockytė, "Public Governance Concepts and their Use in Civil Service Reform Research," *Public Policy and Administration* 1 (10) (2011): 27–40.

[2] V. Domarkas, "Reflections on the Public Administration Paradigm Change in the Last Decade's Publications," *Public Policy and Administration* 1 (10) (2011): 9–16.

[3] V. Chhotray, G. Stoker, *Governance Theory and Practice* (Palgrave Macmillan, 2009), 312.

[4] *Asian Development Bank*, http://www.adb.org/themes/governance/overview (accessed May 7, 2013).

and the stability and transparency of the economic and legal environment in the private sector.[5]

Those three international organisations not only led to the emergence of the good governance concept, but also to its clarification. The evolution of the modern public management concept tolerated the changes of essential institutions' objectives, priorities and operating principles (working in the field of sustainable development). However, in view of the fact that good governance could ensure justification for the political, social and economic priorities using the inclusive public consensus, the good governance concept has to be directly linked to the principles declared in sustainable development.[6]

Good governance can be defined as one dimension of sustainable development. In the scientific literature it is mentioned that it has three main dimensions: economic, social and environmental. There are also many discussions about the fourth dimension, institutional, because institutions regulate economic, social and environmental dimensions and these have an impact on institutions. Therefore, it is very important to present the definition of sustainable development and its dimensions.

## Sustainable Development and its Dimensions

Since ancient times people have noticed that larger territories better provide people with work, income and welfare. However, many economists evaluated economic development differently, taking into account its beneficial and harmful consequences, amongst other things.

Some scientists are against further economic growth, basing their views on the fact that constantly growing populations and consumption are damaging ecosystems, depleting resources and destroying the basis of humanity's survival.[7] As a representative of Classical Economic Theory, A. Smith views progress as the constant insurance of continuous economic growth. Meanwhile, J. S. Mill in *Principles of Political Economy with*

---

[5] *Good Governance: The IMF's Role* http://www.imf.org/external/pubs/ft/exrp/govern/govern.pdf (accessed May 7, 2013).

[6] V. Juknevičienė, R. Kareivaitė, "Good Governance as the Instrument for the Implementation of the Sustainable Development's Conception," *Social Research* 3 (28) (2012): 28–42.

[7] A. Šileika, S. Žičkienė, "Sustainable Development: Conception and Debate" [in Lithuanian], *Environmental Research, Engineering and Management* 3 (17) (2001): 3–10.

*some of their Applications to Social Philosophy* (1848)[8] argues that the stationary state of economy is a natural state, because economic growth is possible only in a limited part of the world, and this is inevitably followed by stagnation. So, economic growth has not only physical but also moral restrictions, and the general macroeconomic goal must be oriented towards environmentally-friendly development, while at the same time achieving harmony between economic, environmental and social development.

While planning economic growth in the future, it is essential to assess the harm that our decisions can cause for current and future generations and to overcome the threats rising from stable development in a responsible and economical manner.[9] The management of such risks using progressive economic methods is currently becoming as important as the creation of new development opportunities.

After conducting the analysis of the scientific literature it can be noticed that economic development should be sustainable. Only then can the society achieve well-being, and the conditions for the economic development be created. Sustainable development can be defined as a process of developing land, cities, businesses and communities meeting our current needs without compromising the ability of future generations to meet theirs. It recognizes that social, economic and environmental issues are interconnected and that decisions must incorporate each of these aspects to be successful over the long term.[10]

Although the essence of the concept of sustainable development is clear enough, its exact interpretation and definition have caused broad discussions. It is possible that the terminology problem arises from the dual nature of the concept, covering development as well as sustainability.[11] Economic literature offers over one hundred definitions of sustainable development, mostly oriented towards separate sectors. We should take into consideration the fact that the concept of sustainable development may be difficult to understand and may have different meanings depending on the literature in which it is used.

---

[8] J. S. Mill, *Principles of Political Economy with some of their Applications to Social Philosophy*, W. J. Ashley (ed.), (London: Longmans, Green and Co., 1909, 7th ed.), 808.

[9] R. Čiegis, *Sustainable Economic Development* [in Lithuanian] (Šiauliai: Šiauliai University Publishing House, 2008), 206.

[10] *Environment Canada: Sustainability*, http://www.ec.gc.ca/default.asp?lang=En&n=354F26A4- (accessed May 7, 2013).

[11] R. Čiegis, *Economics and Environment: Sustainable Development Management* [in Lithuanian] (Kaunas: Vytautas Magnis University Publishing House, 2004), 551.

Sustainable development is a new term invented during the environmental movement development of 1970, at which time questions were raised concerning the Earth's resources and how to preserve them, considering how human decisions will influence the Earth's environment.[12]

The principles of sustainability require objective assessments on how society's actions in one of the three areas of economics, social life and the environment will potentially influence others in the long term. It is necessary to think and act in every direction, cautiously planning actions, seeking an optimal inter-balance and, most importantly, weighing intentions. The search for sustainability starts not only from environmental but also from social and economic concerns, and in their interaction and common impacts on the society.[13]

The definition of sustainable development requires that society sees the world as a system which connects both time and space.[14] When one thinks of the world above ground, one understands that the population of air space influences air quality, and that this in turn influences various things, e.g. people, fish and farming. Sustainable development can be characterized as economic development and growth which have environmental limits and ensure good health for the citizens. This kind of insurance is conducted through good administration and the responsible use of science.[15]

The concept of sustainable development is not only divided into three main dimensions (economic, social and environmental)—there is an additional dimension which is very important for achieving sustainability in a country and which is equal to the other main dimensions. This is the institutional dimension, and it is considered to be an equally important objective for implementing sustainability because it acts not only as a separate segment, but also runs deep into the other three parts of sustainable development as a policy or an implementation tool in strategic management, regulation, monitoring or control. Institutional aspects can

---

[12] R. W. Kates et al. "What is Sustainable Development? Goals, Indicators, Values and Practice," *Environment: Science and Policy for Sustainable Development* 3 (47) (2005): 8–21.

[13] *Regional Policy and Sustainable Development Principles* [in Lithuanian], http://svetikas.home.mruni.lt/wp-content/uploads/2008/11/21rp6.ppt (accessed May 7, 2013).

[14] D. Gagnier, *Guest View: Daniel Gagnier*, http://www.iisd.org/pdf/2009/com_guest_view_dan_gagnier.pdf (accessed May 7, 2013).

[15] O. Tahvonen, J. Kuuluvainen, "Economic Growth, Pollution and Renewable Resources," *Journal of Environmental Economics and Management* 2 (24) (1993): 101–118.

have an effect on stimulating or limiting the economic, natural and human resources. Institutional factors, such as corruption, property rights and rule of law can affect investment and production level. Similarly, financial institutions may have an impact on interest rates, investments or capital accumulation. All four dimensions are under the influence of good governance principles. It is evident that the biggest impact of good governance on sustainability is in the institutional dimension (and its development), which is using all available means for solving the various (economic, social, environmental and institutional) development issues. Thus, it becomes a major scientific research object in the context of sustainable development and good governance as an instrument to achieve sustainability.[16]

There are two opinions on the interaction between the institutional dimension and other sustainable development dimensions (economic, social and environmental). Some authors measure the institutional dimension as equal to others, while some consider that it cannot be equal because its regulation aspect makes it more important than the other dimensions (institutions regulate three sustainable development dimensions). Therefore, one direction of thinking we can call a "tetragon," and the other an "egg."

Fig 1.1. The "tetragon" principle of sustainable development

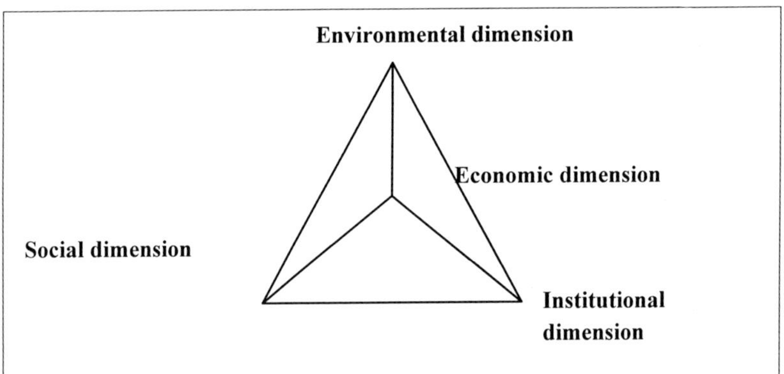


Source: Author's own research.

The framework objectives of sustainable development are to reconcile economic, social and environmental objectives so that development would

[16] V. Juknevičienė, R. Kareivaitė, *Good Governance as the Instrument*, 28–42.

not take place in any dimension, and to accept the equilateral "tetragon" formation which shows that there should be equal attention for all dimensions, emphasizing that development should not be based on an individual approach but on the whole system, i.e. an integrated system. If we give more attention to one dimension (e.g. institutional, economic, environmental or social), in this case it would only cover specific sustainability issues, and other areas of development would remain very weak.

Communication from the European Commission[17] on Rio+20 provides that there "is a need to reinforce and mainstream sustainable development governance within the UN system, *inter alia* by enhancing coherence and policy integration between the activities carried out under the economic, social and environmental pillars." Thus, the conception of sustainable development on four axes (dimensions) should give equal attention and weight to each of them. The United Nations[18] also states that sustainable development emphasizes a holistic, equitable and insightful approach to decision making at all levels.

## Indicators of Good Governance and their Impact on Sustainable Development

Every year the World Bank Group calculates and estimates the Worldwide Government Indicators, which comprise a long-standing research project to develop cross-country indicators of governance. They are based on several hundred variables obtained from thirty-one different data sources, capturing governance perceptions as reported by survey respondents, non-governmental organisations, commercial business information providers, and public sector organisations worldwide. Those indicators are:[19]

(1) Voice and Accountability (capture perceptions of the extent to which a country's citizens are able to participate in electing their government, as well as freedom of expression, association and media)

---

[17] *Communication from the Commission to the European Parliament, the Council, the European Economic and Social Committee and the Committee of the Regions*, http://eur-lex.europa.eu/LexUriServ/LexUriServ.do?uri=COM:2011:0363:FIN:EN:PDF (accessed April 20, 2013).

[18] *Rio+20*, http://www.uncsd2012.org/rio20/index.html (accessed April 20, 2013).

[19] *Worldwide Governance Indicators*, http://info.worldbank.org/governance/wgi/index.asp (accessed May 2, 2013).

(2) Political Stability and Absence of Violence/Terrorism (measure perceptions of the likelihood that the government will be destabilized or overthrown by unconstitutional or violent means, including politically-motivated violence and terrorism)
(3) Government Effectiveness (captures perceptions of the quality of public services, the quality of the civil service and the degree of its independence from political pressures, the quality of policy formulation and implementation, and the credibility of the government's commitment to such policies)
(4) Regulatory Quality (captures perceptions of the ability of the government to formulate and implement sound policies and regulations that permit and promote private sector development)
(5) Rule of Law (captures perceptions of the extent to which agents have confidence in and abide by the rules of society, and in particular the quality of contract enforcement, property rights, the police, and the courts, as well as the likelihood of crime and violence)
(6) Control of Corruption (capture perceptions of the extent to which public power is exercised for private gain, including both petty and grand forms of corruption, as well as capture of the state by elites and private interests).

The first two indicators present the process by which governments are selected, monitored and replaced, the third and the fourth discover the capacity of the government to effectively formulate and implement sound policies, and the final two indicators show the respect of citizens and the state for the institutions that govern economic and social interactions among them. The analysis of those six indicators is the most significant task for the research of the institutional dimension in the concept of sustainable development.[20] However, to reveal a more comprehensive view of the institutional development, another important indicator has been analyzed. This is the economic freedom index, calculated by the Fraser Institute.

The economic freedom index shows the country's political institutional and policy compatibility with the freedom of choice and exchange, free entry, competition and property rights protection. The country's economic freedom index consists of 42 indicators in five areas (these aspects are

[20] V. Juknevičienė, R. Kareivaitė, *Good Governance as the Instrument*, 28–42.

closely linked with all eight principles of good governance). Within the five major areas, there are 23 components in the index:[21]

(1) Size of Government—Expenditures, Taxes, and Enterprises (general government consumption spending as a percentage of total consumption; transfers and subsidies as a percentage of GDP; government enterprises and investment; top marginal tax rate).
(2) Legal Structure and Security of Property Rights (judicial independence; impartial courts; protection of property rights; military interference in the rule of law and the political process; integrity of the legal system; legal enforcement of contracts; regulatory restrictions on the sale of real property).
(3) Access to Sound Money (money growth; standard deviation of inflation; freedom to own foreign currency bank accounts).
(4) Freedom to Trade Internationally (taxes on international trade; regulatory trade barriers; size of trade sector related to expected; black-market exchange rates; international capital market controls).
(5) Regulation of Credit, Labour, and Business (credit market regulations; labour market regulations; business regulations).

Many of those components are themselves made up of several sub-components. In total, the index comprises 42 distinct variables. Table 1.1 below shows the relations between indicators from the institutional dimension of sustainable development (or good governance) and determinants of sustainable development.

**Table 1.1. Relationship between indicators of good governance and sustainable development**

| **Result** | **Institutional aspect** | **The determinants of sustainable development** |
|---|---|---|
| There is correlation | Institutions (in general) | Capital accumulation[22] |
| | | Foreign direct investment[23] |

[21] J. D. Gwartney et al., *Economic Freedom of the World: 2011 Annual Report*, http://www.freetheworld.com/2011/reports/world/EFW2011_complete.pdf (accessed April 20, 2013).
[22] S. Claessens et al., "Financial Frictions, Investment, and Institutions," *IMF Working Paper* 10 (231) (2010): 1–45.

| | | |
|---|---|---|
| | | Labour market[24] |
| | Corruption | The level of production[25] |
| | | Investment and government spending[26] |
| | Corruption | Environment, pollution levels[27] |
| | Protection of property rights | The level of production[28] |
| | Political freedom and Economic freedom | Productivity, human and physical capital accumulation, labour force growth[29] |
| | Freedom of investment and the size of government | Foreign direct investment[30] |

[23] A. Masron, H. Abdullah, "Institutional Quality as a Determinant for FDI Inflows: Evidence from ASEAN," *World Journal of Management* 2 (3) (2010): 115–128.

[24] O. Blanchard, J. Wolfers, "The Role of Shocks and Institutions in the Rise of European Unemployment: the Aggregate Evidence," *The Economic Journal* 110 (2000): C1–C33.

[25] H. Welsch, *Corruption, Growth, and the Environment: A Cross – Country Analysis*, http://econstor.eu/dspace/bitstream/10419/18117/1/dp357.pdf (accessed April 20, 2013).

[26] P. Mauro, *The Effects of Corruption on Growth, Investment, and Government Expenditure: A Cross Country Analysis*, http://www.adelinotorres.com/economia/Os%20efeitos%20da%20corrup%C3%A7%C3%A3o%20no%20mundo.pdf (accessed April 20, 2013).

[27] R. Damania et al., "Trade Liberalization, Corruption, and Environmental Policy Formation: Theory and Evidence," *Journal of Environmental Economics and Management* 46 (3) (2003): 490–512.

[28] K. Sonin, *Why the Rich May Favor Poor Protection of Property Rights*, http://deepblue.lib.umich.edu/bitstream/2027.42/39929/2/wp544.pdf (accessed April 20, 2013).

[29] M. Ulubasoglu, C. Doucouliagos, *Institutions and Economic Growth: A Systems Approach*, http://repec.org/esAUSM04/up.29323.1076501864.pdf (accessed April 20, 2013).

[30] J. Caetano, A. Galego, *FDI in European Union and Mena Countries: Institutional and Economic Determinants*, http://www.cefage.uevora.pt/en/content/download/1727/22514/version/1/file/2009_09.pdf (accessed April 20, 2013).

| | | |
|---|---|---|
| Correlation is not significant | Institutions (in general) | The unemployment rate[31] |
| | | Foreign direct investment[32] |
| | Corruption | Foreign direct investment[33] |
| | Protection of property rights | Foreign direct investment[34] |
| | Regulatory Quality | Foreign direct investment[35] |
| No correlation | Corruption | The level of production[36] [37] |
| | | Foreign direct investment[38] |

Source: Author's own research.

For the implementation of good governance principles, institutions are necessary to help citizens achieve sustainability by providing equal opportunities and ensuring social, economic and political access to resources. Public institutions make a significant contribution to the maintenance of human rights, environmental protection, stable

---

[31] E. Stockhammer, E. Klär, "Capital Accumulation, Labour Market Institutions and Unemployment in the Medium Run," *Cambridge Journal of Economics* (2010), available online at http://cje.oxfordjournals.org/content/early/2010/07/21/cje.beq020.full.pdf+html?sid=d3687392-0b70-4170-9582-4d6d44d5ed58 (accessed April 20, 2013).

[32] B. Anghel, *Do Institutions Affect Foreign Direct Investment?* (Barcelona: Universidad Autonoma de Barcelona, 2005), available online at http://idea.uab.es/abrindusa/research/paper_FDI_and_institutions.pdf (accessed April 20, 2013).

[33] J. Caetano, A. Galego, *FDI in European Union.*

[34] A. F. Ali et al., *Do Institutions Matter for Foreign Direct Investment?*, http://www.springerlink.com/content/c68lt0351k284572/fulltext.pdf (accessed April 20, 2013).

[35] B. Anghel, *Do Institutions Affect Foreign Direct Investment?*, http://idea.uab.es/abrindusa/research/paper_FDI_and_institutions.pdf (accessed April 20, 2013).

[36] J. Svensson, "Eight Questions about Corruption," *Journal of Economic Perspectives* 3 (19) (2005): 19–42.

[37] N. Mocan, *What Determines Corruption?*, http://econ.ucdenver.edu/beckman/Econ6410/mocan.pdf (accessed April 20, 2013).

[38] A. Al-Sadig, "The Effects of Corruption on FDI Inflows," *Cato Journal* 2 (29) (2009): 267–294.

macroeconomic conditions, support of health standards, mobilization of resources for essential public services, law enforcement and the formatting of the infrastructure design, assurance of the security, and social harmony. With an eye on the government and public sector, institutions properly perform their work for implementation of the sustainable development concept, and it is necessary to identify problems, develop agendas and create opportunities for individuals to act and work together, creating the open-government idea and formatting an appropriate public policy.[39] Therefore, it emphasizes the importance of the institutional dimension (especially formal institutions) in the implementation process of sustainable development.

However, despite the government systems, various economic, environmental and social features and varied experience (historical, geographical and political context, economic development, and resource limitations), all states must take into account the difficulties brought on by various institutional and social barriers to achieve the best response to the sustainable development's imperative.[40] Regarding this aim, the opportunities of the institutional networking should be used for the dissemination of the good governance principles in the context of sustainable development. This is the only way for the state or a group of them to achieve sustainability in the economic, social and environmental fields. Thus, interfaces between good governance and sustainability are reflected in the analysis of indicators from the fourth, institutional dimension. The enabling principles of good governance would significantly contribute to the improvement of sustainable development's situation in particular states, allowing for the improvement of the processes of sustainable development policy-making and implementation.[41]

## Conclusions

Sustainable development is not a choice between environmental protection and social progress, but is rather about striving for economic and social development that would be compatible with environmental protection. On

---

[39] D. West et al., *Innovation in Government: How to Make the Public Sector Faster, Smarter and More Connected*, http://www.brookings.edu/~/media/Files/events/2009/0617_government_innovation/20090617_innovation.pdf (accessed April 20, 2013).

[40] *Governance for Sustainable Human Development*, http://mirror.undp.org/magnet/policy/ (accessed April 20, 2013).

[41] V. Juknevičienė, R. Kareivaitė, *Good Governance as the Instrument*, 28–42.

the other hand, development, which is frequently understood as a synonym for progress, has become more acceptable since it was associated with "natural" limitations that were clearly identified in the concept of sustainability.

Making an assessment of sustainable development is important for following the equivalence of dimensions (i.e. the holistic principle) as its basic and essential aspect. Of course, the significance of weighting may change only if it is focused on a specific problem, or a specific strategy. Economic growth leads to democracy (a significant correlation). However, there are many other factors (investment and economic freedom, corruption, property rights and others) which are crucial for economic growth.

A too-rapid production growth may be affected by increasing government spending, or decreasing tax rates which increase the potential for a rise in corruption. The production level of variation may have an impact on economic freedom, property rights and bureaucracy since institutions may also affect the accumulation of capital investment. Therefore, the assessment of sustainable development is a very important institutional dimension.

Roberta Kareivaitė works as an assistant professor at the Šiauliai University. She holds a PhD degree in economics. Her areas of interest are regional economics, sustainable development and good governance.

# CHAPTER TWO

# THE GOVERNANCE OF POWER IN THE LATE-WESTPHALIAN INTERNATIONAL ENVIRONMENT

ADRIAN SZUMOWSKI

## Introduction

The contemporary international environment is becoming more sophisticated and elusive. The multilevel structure of international relations, intertwined and complex, poses a serious challenge to the governance capabilities of particular actors. The notion of power, understood primarily as a means of influencing an actor's surroundings and other objects,[1] seems to remain one of the primary features of its composition. However, the sheer complexity and fluidity of international relations pose a serious challenge for the traditional capabilities of constructing and executing power in international relations, which were once a backbone of both realist and neorealist theories.[2]

At first, after the sudden and unexpected conclusion of the Cold War and subsequent implosion of the Soviet Bloc, some optimistic scholars proclaimed "the end of history," which consisted of ultimate liberal democratic victory and the creation of a global utopia.[3] However, it turned out that the solution of tensions between West and East opened a new field of conflict along the north and south division. Moreover, during the 1990s the frozen processes gained momentum and initiated a quick transition

---

[1] K. W. Deutsh, *The Nerves of the Government* (New York: Free Press, 1966), 247.

[2] A. Wojciuk, *Dylemat potęgi: Praktyczna teoria stosunków międzynarodowych* (Warszawa: Wydawnictwo Uniwersytetu Warszawskiego, 2010), 24.

[3] F. Fukuyama, *Koniec historii* (Poznań: Zysk i S-ka Wydaw., cop., 1996) (original: *The End of History and the Last Man* [New York: Free Press, 1992], translated by T. Bieroń, M. Wichrowski).

toward a post-Westphalian international environment. Therefore, the contemporary international environment might be called late-Westphalian, because it is a sophisticated and complex hybrid composed of traditional and modern features and principles. The new shape of the international environment affects the majority of features and notions vital for international activity as well as creating a coherent international relations theory. One of the most prominent notions is that of power.

The main aim of this chapter is to present and analyze the evolution of a vital component of power in the international environment, which is the notion of governance of power.[4] This question refers not only to issues connected with tools and strategies commonly associated with utilizing power in international relations, but also primarily to a mode of governing resources and strategies required to display power in network-based as well as traditional societies. The contemporary international environment poses a serious challenge to politicians and strategists responsible for governing power in the international environment. A major influencing factor is the process of internal dynamization of power similar to Heisenberg's uncertainty principle,[5] which stated that the observer is unable to simultaneously designate the current state of affairs and the direction and pace of changes. The application of Heisenberg's principle in political science shows that the effectiveness of undertaken action requires constant attention and flexible patterns of reacting, and therefore requires a new quality of governance of power in the international environment.

---

[4] In this dimension, governance may be understood as "the use of institutions, structures of authority and even collaboration to allocate resources and coordinate or control activity in society or the economy," according to the definition of Stephen Bell, developed in the monograph S. Bell, *Economic governance & institutional dynamics* (Melbourne: Oxford University Press, 2002). In this case, governance is referred to as an activity in international relations.

[5] Heisenberg's Uncertainty Principle states that on a quantum mechanics level, there exist a certain pair of values which are unable to measure with the desired accuracy. The fact of measurement influences the reference system in this way, and that part of the information about second value is irreplaceably lost. This is a consequence of the dualistic, molecular and wave nature of matter. This principle was discovered by Warner Heisenberg in 1927. More information about his researches can be found in W. Heisenberg, *The Physical Principles of a Quantum Theory* (Chicago: Courier Dover Publications, 1949). This book was a point of reference for scientific debate and criticism, represented by D. Cassidy, *Beyond Uncertainity: Heisenberg Quantum Physics and the Bomb* (New York: Bellevue Literary Press 2009).

As may be noticed, the traditional thinking of power execution and application is becoming more and more ineffective. Scholars researching international relations, however, tend to focus on the identification of patterns, which would indicate a new recipe for success in international relations.[6] Some of them, however, pinpoint that a complex and sophisticated contemporary environment does not permit the existence of such a recipe. Therefore, instead of looking for one designated solution, contemporary power in international relations might be described and analyzed by a series of different and at first sight contradictory theories—from neorealist to critical theories—because today's complicated international environment requires the application of different theories for different challenges.[7]

To introduce order into further consideration, this chapter will be divided into three sections. The first is dedicated to a brief description and analysis of the nature of the late-Westphalian international environment. In this part, emphasis will be put on the features crucial for power in the international environment. The second consists of a deeper analysis of the dynamics of power introduced by the nature of the late-Westphalian international environment. This part is based on the research of John M. Rothgeb, supplemented by the remarks of subsequent researchers. The third part is dedicated to articulating principles for guiding construction and the execution of power in the international environment.

## Features of the Late-Westphalian International Environment

In 1648 the 30 Years War came to an end with the signing of peace treaties between the main belligerents—France, Sweden and the Holy Roman Empire. This date was accepted by the majority of scholars researching international relations as the beginning of the contemporary international system, primarily by adepts of the realist school of international relations. However, other traditions, like Liberal or Marxist, tend to place the genesis of the international system prior to or later than

---

[6] For instance J. S. Nye Jr, *Soft Power: Jak osiągnąć sukces w polityce światowej* (Warszawa: Wydawnictwa Akademickie i Profesjonalne, cop. 2007) (original: *Soft Power: The Means to Success in World Politics* [New York: Public Affairs 2004], translated by J. Zaborowski).

[7] The main thesis of publication by: M. Barnett, R. Duval, "Power in International Politics," *International Organization* 1 (winter) (59) (2005): 39–75.

that date.[8] Nevertheless, the notion of Westphalia has become a commonly accepted term for a particular set of international structures and guidelines and their functioning. However, the international system is similar to other physical and biological systems studied by science—in each the tendencies of continuation are mixed with the tendencies of change, and when the latter prevail, the system usually collapses and transforms into a new one. Such a transformation is occurring at the moment, and some scholars have coined the term "late-Westphalian international environment."[9]

A shift toward the late-Westphalian international environment began around the early 1990s, connected with a sudden ease of Cold War tensions, stabilizing the entire international environment by slowing down the tendencies of change, a situation that followed the extensive development of weapons of mass destruction by the superpowers. It underlined an urgent need to sustain tendencies on continuity in order to avoid the massive exchange of nuclear salvoes, and that required maintaining a delicate and precise balance which limited the development of tendencies of change. However, due to a slower but noticeable evolution, this balance became more expensive and less effective. As a result, the Cold War ended and an era of rapid change began.

The shift towards the late-Westphalian international environment was generated by the impact of so-called civilization megatrends of development. Those currents which guide transformation of every aspect of social activity were widely analyzed by Bolesław Balcerowicz[10]; however, the list and scope of every current are still open for an academic debate. However, two of the most important tendencies for the international environment, which heavily affect the international environment, can be identified.

First is the ongoing demographic revolution. As can be traced through history, the demographical tendencies shifted but were limited. However, in the nineteenth century the so-called demographic explosion occurred in Europe, generating a drastic quantitative rise of the European population. The shockwaves of this explosion slowly spread around globe, eventually

---

[8] L. Cruz, "Policy Point-Counterpoint: Is Westphalia a History?", *International Social Science Review* 3–4 (80) (2005): 152.

[9] A detailed description of the late-Westphalian international environment was an effect of a scientific project undertaken at the Political Science Faculty at the Marie Curie-Sklodowska University in Lublin. The publication embracing those researches was M. Pietraś, K. Marzęda (eds.), *Późnowestfalski ład międzynarodowy* (Lublin: Wydawnictwo UMCS, 2008).

[10] B. Balcerowicz, *Pokój i nie-pokój: Na progu XXI wieku* (Warszawa: "Bellona," 2002), 85–118.

reaching global peripheries such as Sub-Saharan Africa. However, this tendency is now reversing, and the demographic explosion is moving towards demographic implosion. The question is whether events in Europe will cause effects similar to the demographic explosion. If similarities occur—and UN forecasts predict this set of events, spread over time for different scenarios[11]—then within the next century the size of the global population will fall dramatically.

Second is the technological factor. To be precise, it must be pointed out that, despite common knowledge describing the contemporary situation as an ongoing progress, the beginning of the twenty-first century can be labelled as one of "technological stagnation."[12] In short, the number of cutting-edge technologies developed has fallen dramatically. On the other hand, research and development are compensated with two parallel factors. First is the shifting focus of major research and development centres on the aspect of adjusting existing technologies to consumer needs and finding new applications for existing ones. The second is the popularization of existing technologies from the developed centre toward the developing peripheries.[13] This transfer, primarily concerning IT technologies, is composed of legal technology transfer supplemented with corporate and governmental espionage. Those inventions, however, reshape the international environment with the creation of transnational social space, a new platform quality on which international relations are translated from traditional geopolitical, geo-economical and geo-cultural platforms.

The impact of those mega trends is shaping the late-Westphalian international environment as a hybrid construct combining principles, features and mechanisms of the traditional Westphalian environment and slowly evolving new quality of principles, features and mechanisms of the future post-Westphalian international environment. However, the late-

[11] Out of three scenarios—high, medium and low—high is the most optimistic and assumes the permanent development of the global population in the researched period. The remaining two underline a decline which will occur after a peak in 2050 (low) and 2075 (medium). In the former, the decline is sharp, resulting in a fall from 7.49 billion people to 2.31 billion. The latter underlines reaching the peak of 9.22 billion to 8.97 billion. The United Nations Secretariat, Department of Economic and Social Affairs, Population Division, *World Population to 2300* (New York: United Nations Publication, 2004), 14.

[12] G. Friedman, *Następna dekada: Gdzie byliśmy i dokąd zmierzamy* (Kraków: Wydawnictwo Literackie, cop., 2012), 275 (original: *The Next decade: Where We've Been ... and Where We're Going* [New York: Anchor Books, 2011], translated by Monika Wyrwas-Wiśniewska).

[13] Ibid., 284.

Westphalian international environment loosely resembles an internal structure of damascene steel, being composed of two layers of qualitatively different materials. One, as mentioned above, comprises remnants of the old generation of the international environment, embodied primarily through the notion of sovereignty, nation-state and balance of power. The other is the slowly originating future shape, which could be identified through the rise in non-state international actors and transnational post-sovereign space. However, the primary factor which decides the new quality of this particular environment is the set of unique institutions resembling unique microstructures created through the production process of damascene steel.[14] Therefore, the late-Westphalian situation is fitted with unique features that are qualitatively different from both generations of the environment.

Each consecutive generation of international environment is composed of three basic layers. First is the layer of fundamental principles which describes the basic parameters of the international environment. Second is the layer of space which describes the platform of international relations, its limitations, and features. Third is the layer of mechanisms which describes the structure, functions and capabilities of international relations. The main features of each layer are founded on Westphalian international environment features; however, they are modified by the influence of the aforementioned megatrends, introducing dynamization into international relations on an unprecedented scale.

First, the basic principles of the international environment are embracing fundamental values and institutions which serve as foundations of international relations, and from each stem more sophisticated and specialized institutions. The core principles of each generation of international environment are affected by global megatrends only to a small and limited degree. The core of the late-Westphalian international environment was transferred from the Westphalian international environment with only a few corrections, if any. Such institutions as sovereignty, territoriality and balance of power still serve as foundations of more complex and elusive processes in the international environment. However, it must be underlined that those principles are not immune to the influence of the global megatrends. The question for academic dispute concerns the extent of this influence. One of the most important and widely debated principles is sovereignty, strongly connected with the notion of nation-state, associated with certain features such as

[14] Such as microfibres and carbon tube structures responsible for the unique characteristics of damascene steel.

independence and self-governance. For instance, some scholars argue that the emergence of non-state actors, capable of battling the superpower on its own territory, means the issue of sovereignty has reached its demise. Others have stated that the nation-state still occupies a dominant position within the existing framework, indicating that sovereignty needs only a slight revision. A similar discussion is being waged about the role of territoriality, or geographical space in the late-Westphalian international environment. The discussion cycles between the two opposing posts of "the end of geopolitics" and the "return of geopolitics." In fact, those discussions point out that, despite the gradual shift induced by transformation, the core principles are only briefly affected by civilization megatrends.

Second are the guidelines stemming from basic foundations which regulate the shape, functions and space of the international environment. There are scores of principles which govern the particular features of international activity. The main problem is their correct identification due to the turbulent nature of the late-Westphalian international environment and the interference of randomizing factors, such as, for instance, the impact of super empowered individuals.[15] Those agents make the task of analyzing functional principles extremely difficult. However, this task is essential because those guidelines are connected with the understanding of power in international relations. For many scholars, power is the so-called "currency" of international relations, which makes undertaking every single international activity possible. This point of view is strongly connected with realism and related schools of international relations.[16] However, understanding power as a control seems to be a commonly accepted point of view among the majority of scholars researching international relations.[17] Therefore, regulations concerning the execution of control over the international environment and other actors are closely tied to functions of the international environment as a coherent system.

One of the most thoroughly conducted analyses of the functioning of the international environment was conducted by Phillip G. Cerny. In his

---

[15] J. Gryz, *NATO adaptacja do uwarunkowań środowiska bezpieczeństwa XXI wieku*, in M. Pietraś, J. Olchowski (eds.), *NATO w pozimnowojennym środowisku (nie)bezpieczeństwa* (Lublin: Wydawnictwo UMCS, 2011), 42.

[16] A. Wolfers, *Discord and Collaboration: Essays on International Politics* (Baltimore: Johns Hopkins Press 1962), 105.

[17] J. M. Rothgeb, *Defining Power. Influence and Force in the Contemporary International System* (New York: St. Martin's Press, 1993), 17.

work,[18] four basic sets of guidelines which shape contemporary international environment can be found. Each is researched from the perspective of change toward the late-Westphalian international environment. The main underlying factor is the melting down of state limits, which were dividing political sciences on the internal nation-state environment, researched primarily on the political science field; and the external, international environment, researched singularly by studies on international relations. The prerequisite assumption of Phillip G. Cerny is that the late-Westphalian international environment blurs this distinction, but not completely.[19] Therefore, each formerly separated system is gradually synchronizing and partially merging with another.

First is the lack of an overarching institution in the international environment, contrary to internal state environment in which the government is the ultimate level of decision making.[20] In the late-Westphalian environment, both international anarchy and national hierarchy are becoming more loosely organised. The national level is infected with a certain amount of anarchy, embodied by diluting the loyalty of large social groups for government[21] with the introduction of a certain amount of organisation on the international level, embodied in a system of international organisations and regimes generating legal constraints for undertaking international activity.[22] Second is the social legitimization of particular actors as legitimate power-wielders in the international environment. This principle refers to the legal entitlement for utilizing power. The Westphalian solution stated that legal issues should be submitted by precisely defined channels on the national level, described by the most important legal act, the constitution, and on the international level based on the nation-state consensus. The most important statement was that this is the only legitimate power-wielder on the national as well as international levels. The only exception to this rule was allowed on the basis of state consent. However, civilization developments are open for the international relations sector which cannot be controlled by the states, such as financial markets or the transnational space. Those areas on which

[18] P. G. Cerny, *Rethinking World Politics. A Theory of Transnational Neopluralism* (Oxford: Oxford University Press, 2010), 64–82.

[19] Ibid., 8.

[20] Ibid., 64–66.

[21] Multiple Futures Project. Navigating toward 2030. Final Report, April 2004, 21.

[22] The features and functions of international regimes were thoroughly investigated in M. Pietraś, *Międzynarodowy reżim zmian klimatu* (Toruń: Wydawnictwo Adam Marszałek, 2011).

states are not sovereign but one among other actors blur questions of legality of power usage.[23]

This may be exemplified by two international events. First was the NATO air and land operation against Serbian forces in Kosovo in 1999. Despite the regional powers' consensus supporting this enterprise, the lack of support from the global organisation, the UN and civil society actors, or even active opposition on their behalf, seriously undermined the capabilities of influencing the international environment by the allies. One of the most vivid critics of NATO's involvement was Noam Chomsky.[24] Second was the activity of al-Qaeda, which proved to be an effective opposition to state-centric security. Although this challenge is considered a short-term advantage, primarily by Stratfors chief George Friedman,[25] one thing should be pointed out. The non-state power wielders became capable of undertaking effective actions in the international environment outside of the state consensus. This also means that transnational organisations became important hubs of networks generating power, especially on a field of legal and cultural layers. Third is the set of principles which shapes the backbones of the international environment stemming from its foundations. The main concern connected with strategic issues is regulating activity in the international environment.

The structures of both spaces—the national as well as international—are gradually intertwining, distracting and twisting. A traditional, hierarchical and well-described in-nation system is being dissolved by the anarchic and fluid influences of the international environment, and in opposition are the elements of hierarchy and precisely described channels of communication. Therefore, classical strategic thought, which could be perceived as a set of guidelines for exploiting the international structure for power-wielding goals, becomes disputable.

There are three competing positions. The first states that strategic guidelines and consideration confronted with late-Westphalian international environment structures proved themselves obsolete, and as such need to be rejected completely.[26] The second points out that the qualitative

---

[23] P. G. Cerny, *Rethinking World Politics*, 67–68, 76–78.

[24] N. Chomsky, *The New Military Humanism: Lessons from Kosovo* (London: Pluto Press 1999).

[25] G. Friedman, *Następne sto lat: Prognozy na XXI wiek* (Warszawa: Andrzej Findeisen/AMF Plus Group, 2009), 46–66 (original: *The Next 100 Years: A Forecast for the 21st Century* [London: Allison & Busby, Limited, 2009], translated by M. Antosiewicz).

[26] A. K. Cebrowski, J. J. Garstka, "Network–Centric Warfare," *US Naval Institute Proceedings* 124/1 (January), (1998): 29.

transformation of international surroundings requires the adaptation of former thinkers, such as Clausewitz.[27] The third group, however, states that the recent development of the international environment proved that the strategic model delivered nothing more than illusions of control and was therefore impractical and damaging.[28] All positions disregard one important notion—the flexibility of the contemporary international environment, which will be proved and developed in subsequent sections of this chapter, and which rather suggests the actuality of the strategic question with a serious loss of the utilitarian value of strategic answers. The most visible evidence was the conduct of the "war on terror" in the first decade of the twenty-first century. During this set of conflicts and interventions a qualitative shift within the sphere of problem identification can be traced concerning non-state groups of Islamic fundamentalists, loosely connected under the umbrella of the al-Qaeda organisation. However, during the development of this struggle the strategy based on classical, Westphalian assumption proved to be ineffective, despite the skill in its implementation. U.S. President George W. Bush Jr.'s administration was unable to adapt when utilized resources and strategies proved ineffective or less effective than anticipated, especially because adaptation requires breaching classical strategic thinking with the preservation of classical strategic dilemmas, a combination which is a trademark of the late-Westphalian international environment. The fourth and final set of principles refers to resources which ought to be mobilized for undertaking actions in the late-Westphalian international environment. A similar combination of resources is also required for power implementation. The main difference is not the nature of resources, because they are similar—the main difference is the accents, granted differently on the national and international levels. The Westphalian international environment required a balanced mixture of qualitatively different resources, with the primary focus vested in military resources. The remaining resources were considered as support for aggressively implemented military power. On the other hand, the internal state environment is considered a pacified zone.

Therefore, resources connected with violence are strictly limited on three points. First, their only trustee is a state represented by a government and the people appointed by it. Secondly, those people are obliged to publicly display their prerogatives by certain signs of their functions,

---

[27] J. Keegan, *A History of Warfare* (New York: Knopf, 1993), 5.

[28] T. G. Mahnken, *Strategic Theory*, in J. Baylis et al., (eds.), *Strategy in the Contemporary World. An Introduction to Strategic Studies* (Oxford: Oxford University Press, 2007), 78.

respectively, uniform, identification document, and the open display of side arms.[29] Thirdly, the use of violence is strictly regulated by a set of instructions and regulations devoted primarily to the description of a situation in which they are to be used.

The transition toward the late-Westphalian international environment dilutes those precise divisions. On the one hand, military means both on national and the international level proved to be costly and of little efficiency. Therefore scholars, especially neoliberal thinkers such as Joseph S. Nye, underline the growing importance of non-military means of exercising power, such as cultural and normative elements, labelled soft power.[30] On the other hand, numerous events around the globe, such as the recent slaughter of an English soldier on the streets of London,[31] indicate that the use of violence might still be useful for acquiring certain political objectives.

Those principles form an intermediate layer between the core values of the international structure and the megatrends of civilization development, and such placement indicates their growing vulnerability on that evolution. Therefore, the impact of dynamization is felt more gravely. The primary factor of their evolution is the constantly progressing levelling of the meaning of nation-state borders, which in turn allow for the intertwining of the external, classical, Westphalian international environment with the internal nation-state environment.

Third, the development of civilization causes an internal fermentation of the international environment, a layer that was marginalized in previous generations. However, in the late-Westphalian international environment a massive surge in its meaning can be noticed. Two primary megatrends which have a grave impact on the shape of the international environment can be identified. First is the partial reversal of the demographic explosion of the Industrial Age. This is clearly visible in developed states; however, it seems that demographic implosion is already spreading to developing countries, even those considered to be the poorest and failing. Those changes impose the drastic reformation of the global society which will heavily affect the structure and functions of the late-Westphalian international environment, primarily through shattering massive entities known as modern societies on loosely connected smaller post-modern

---

[29] P. G. Cerny, *Rethinking World Politics*, 71–72.

[30] One of the greatest proponents of this notion is Joseph S. Nye.

[31] On Wednesday, May 22, 2013, a pair of local Muslim fundamentalists in London hit an English soldier with a car and subsequently decapitated him. This news stunned the international community, especially combined with frequent information of riots caused by immigrants.

societies. The main difference between them is the lessening cohesion among different sub-organisations as well as different generations. Those societies tend to embrace violence as a legal means of problem solving. Second is technological progress, or to be precise the spread of technologies developed during the Westphalian international environment. It seems that technological progress stalled, with most of the research and development centres focused primarily on upgrading existing technologies, the global technological base improving only thanks to replacing older technologies in developing countries. What is more important, however, is that the spread of modern technologies provides new and advanced capabilities for social groups, which in turn results in gaining access to resources previously belonging only to states or even regional powers. Those factors have introduced dynamism into the international environment structure, which disrupts and reorganises its connections along new and largely unknown patterns.

## Dynamics of Power

The structure of the international environment is a framework on which particular notions of international relations, such as notion of power, are developing. In this part, the notion of power stems from John M. Rothgeb's research, in which he states that the most valuable scientific perspective perceives power as a way to control other actors and tendencies in the international environment.[32] However, the ongoing evolution of power should be stressed. This takes place within the parameters generated by the international environment; therefore, investigating those subjects separately will not produce valuable results. Lack of such achievements is a primary concern for politicians as well as theoreticians.

A starting point in analyzing the notion of power is *Defining Power: Influence and Force in the Contemporary System* (1993), by John M. Rothgeb. This book is the result of one of the most thoroughly conducted analyses of this notion of power, but has one disadvantage—it was written at the beginning of the 1990s and therefore omits the bulk of power evolution connected with international events of the late 1990s and the first decade of the twenty-first century. Despite those drawbacks, Rothgeb's research is still valuable as a theoretical modulation of the internal composition of power.

---

[32] J. M. Rothgeb, *Defining Power*, 21–22.

According to this researcher, power in international relations, understood as a social control, can be seen as a social notion connected with an accurate perception rather than the physical possession of defined resources. More importantly, power is an internally diversified notion which could be described by the identification of four primary factors, which in conjunction are describing the capabilities of power execution in the international environment. There are four factors of power: domain, range, scope and weight.

First, the domain describes the quantity and diversity of objects an actor is capable of controlling.[33] A key criterion is the geographical distance between them—if it is short, the capabilities of influence grow larger, with the greatest capabilities in the direct vicinity of the actor. The domain refers primarily to the objectives of power use, and it is in this field that the majority of mistakes are made, primarily because of a misperception concerning the objectives of international activity being too ambitiously formulated. For instance, in Iraq, the U.S. George W. Bush administration undertook a wide agenda of transformation of the regional balance of power, disregarding the costs and effectiveness of such a process.[34] Therefore, those objectives were partially beyond the reach of the U.S.

Second, the range refers to the diversity of threat and the gains an actor may offer. This variable is closely connected with available resources—not only natural deposits and money, but also technology, information and culture, such as lifestyle. It is connected with the effective management of those resources. As may be seen, this factor is the only one strongly attached to the material aspect of power in international relations. However, this feature can only be partially measured by semi-physical tools, because even resources of power depend on the perception of an actor, as well as an object. For instance, the best described and measured military capabilities are questions of international and regional contexts. A middle power, such as Poland, in the context of Central and Eastern Europe, with the powerful armies of Germany and Russia at its borders, has less military power than the exact situation moved to Central Africa, where its potential would grant it the status of a regional power.

Third, the scope describes what behaviours of an object can be controlled by an actor. This factor focuses primarily on an object's reaction to the deployment of power in the international environment. Its most important field of analysis is the element of resistance which is

---

[33] Ibid., 38–44.

[34] G. Friedman, *Następne sto lat*, 82–88.

motivated by two assumptions. The first, of a theoretical nature, states that power in international relations occurs only in situations of conflict. The second, more practically, is that preserving the widest sphere of independence is the main paradigm of the foreign policy of various international actors. Of those two assumptions, the primary feature of scope is derived. The resistance hardens when actors try to control the deeper functions of an object. In a case of threat to fundamental identity, the resistance may reach an irrational level, as occurred in Iraq and Afghanistan.

Third, the weight describes the capability of an actor to convince an object to conduct the desired action. This factor embraces an important feature of power implementation, which is the cost and effect ratio, reflecting the effectiveness and governing skills of an actor. It also refers to the psycho-societal impact of power, which is the perception of power from the international community as well as the object. Summing up, every action concerning power in the international environment could be deconstructed by those four factors. However, due to the fact that international relations have evolved from the beginnings of the last decade of the twentieth century, those considerations have to be supplemented with three remarks.

The first was made by Phillip G. Cerny, who pointed out that with the development of processes of globalization, the thorough revision of neorealist assumptions is becoming essential.[35] Their preliminary assumption is that both kinds of environments—internal, the nation-state, and external, the international environment—have been breached. The reconstruction of a new, late-Westphalian international environment requires the parallel reconstruction of power. However, the main problem is that by mixing both structures together the traditional methods and understandings of power in international relations are rendered useless. The evolution of old schemes towards an unanticipated direction probably led to a new, non-Westphalian international environment and notion of power. However, in the meantime turbulence caused by the process of merging both structures gravely limits capabilities of managing, foreseeing and undertaking actions in the international environment. One of the most important consequences is progressing the transfer of power from nation states, which was a crucial element of the Westphalian international environment towards non-state actors present on the global and sub-national levels. Therefore, globalization and mixing both environments shift the nature of power from hazardous to uncertain.

---

[35] P. G. Cerny, *Rethinking World Politics*, 64–82.

The second remark was made by Joseph S. Nye, who was analyzing the situation in which U.S. foreign policy was trapped after the Iraqi invasion in 2003. He underlines the division of "hard" and "soft" power. The former, traditional notion of power was organised primarily on the military and economic plan of international relations according to a strategy of threats and use of violence. The role model, Bush's doctrine of pre-emptive strikes,[36] proved ineffective, not because of internal flaws but due to changes in the international surroundings. The second string of power is based on cultural and legal dimensions and is connected with strategies based on convincing the opponent on moral ground, and winning the hearts and minds of public opinion.[37] However, the internal logic of the late-Westphalian international environment blurred the division between those two, making a near-impossible identification of those strings. For instance, is the nuclear weapon of North Korea a "hard power" tool because it is a typical military object, or does it belong to "soft power" because it is used for gains on a legal basis?[38] These kinds of problems are multiplying.

The final remark concerns the urgent need to change assumptions in the research on power, similar to the change from Newtonian physics to quantum physics represented by the Heisenberg principle, which should underlay the unprecedented level of uncertainty augmented with every international action undertaken. Therefore, sudden and drastic changes in the late-Westphalian international environment, especially within the notion of power, require the abandoning of the assumption of the possibility of identification of precise prescription allowing victory every time it is applied. The best example could be a military power, which within a situation like the first Gulf War was extremely effective, but that during the second failed. This is the most important projection of dynamics of power. The growing impact of social constrictions responsible for the perception and identification of power tends to undermine attempts to create a single set of laws guiding the use of power. Each element of power is sometimes identified differently, even during the

[36] This doctrine was created as a US response to September 11, 2001 in September 2002 entitled *The National Security Strategy of the United States of America*, http://www.state.gov/documents/organization/63562.pdf (accessed June 2, 2013). It was amended by *The National Security Strategy of the United States of America* published in March 2006, http://georgewbush-whitehouse.archives.gov/nsc/nss/2006/index.html (accessed June 2, 2013).

[37] J. S. Nye, *Soft Power*, 77–88.

[38] G. Friedman, *Następne sto lat*, 90.

same action. Therefore, a key element of every application of power is synchronizing the perception of an actor and object. The unavoidable consequence is that each power implementation is unique and excludes the possibility of copying the scenarios and solutions.

## Challenges for Governance of Power

The evolution of the international environment, coupled with the evolution of the nature of power itself, tend to dilute the solid structures responsible for the repeatability of international relations. This challenge, especially for the governance of power, should be managed primarily through a shift in strategy. This movement ought to embrace a change in the governance of power from stiff planning and control of application, to managing power in the international environment by accepting the uncertainty level and constantly re-evaluating the effectiveness of the power execution. With the elimination of classical methods of power governance, the transition towards new notions started. This transformation favours the management of particular elements and strategies according to the effectiveness of the means used. This is a lesson learnt from the American war on terror. The George W. Bush administration proved unable to fluently shift the U.S. point of balance when the inability to achieve its objectives became apparent.[39]

The governance of power should incorporate two elements. First is the significant distance to assumed objectives which require thorough consideration and hierarchization. The management of objectives requires their constant juggling and their dropping beyond the reach of a particular actor. Second is understanding victory. With the inability to achieve the desired goals, the key element is "to freeze" the desired outcomes of power application. In contrast with the Westphalian International Environment, victory requires the constant attention of an actor or a proxy with common goals, as the U.S. planned to create in both Iraq and Afghanistan.

From the moment this shift became urgent there were few attempts to develop a new formula of governing power. One of the first undertaken to revise the traditional perception of power is the notion of "smart power."[40] Thus, this particular idea was developed by the joined initiative of Joseph S. Nye and his colleagues from the Center for Strategic and International

---

[39] Ibid., 74–82.

[40] This idea was developed in his recent publication J. S. Nye, *The Future of Power* (New York: Public Affairs, 2011).

Studies.[41] Their works' main aim was to undo the negative effects of an artificial division between "hard" and "soft" power. The objective of this project is to create a coherent and effective theory of power in international relations which could replace older, Westphalian paradigms. The fundamental principle is the combination of military, economic, diplomatic, legal and cultural means into a coherent strategy aiming at obtaining a particular objective defined by decision makers. However, this attempt met with criticism from neorealist thinkers as a simple contravention of the doctrine of pre-emptive strikes. Others, such as Ken Adelman, point out that the foundation of soft power has proved ineffective and difficult to manage.[42]

The next step was the creation of a codex of smart power application. It appears that the further development of smart power will encompass the utilization of traditional strategic thinking. At the core of this particular paradigm are five questions which describe individual power application. They are considered by Joseph Nye as comprising a key criterion transforming the traditional understanding of power.[43] The first question investigated was on the area of objectives. However, it did not focus only on enlisting the objectives, but primarily on putting them in the correct order and investigating the relations between them. In other words, does achieving a particular goal undermine others. Therefore, a crucial element is the identification and correct hierarchization of actor objectives to limit resource dispersion and entanglement in a futile effort to achieve too many equivalent targets. The second question refers to resources required for power use. The novelty of those considerations is the value of those resources, which changes along two lines. First is the social context of power, which determines the value of power resources and the possibility of their employment. For instance, the value of global trademarks such as Coca-Cola, which is considered a luxury brand in India,[44] while in Pakistan it has a very negative image. Second is the temporal availability

---

[41] The researches conducted during scientific project were published in R. L. Armitrage, J. S. Nye (eds.), *CSIS Commission on Smart Power: A Smarter, More Secure America* (Washington: The CSIS Press, 2007).
[42] K. Adelman, "Not-So-Smart Power. Go ahead, Congress, Cut Away at U.S. Foreign Aid," *Foreign Policy* April 18, 2011, http://www.foreignpolicy.com/articles/2011/04/18/not_so_smart_power?page=full, (accessed December 10, 2012).
[43] For more see J. S. Nye, *The Future*, chapter 7 "Smart Power."
[44] Statement made by the Ambassador of Republic of India to the Republic of Poland's Monika Kapil-Mohta during a lecture given at the Political Science Faculty at the Maria Curie-Skłodowska University in Lublin.

of particular resources. This question proved to be important with the growth of the financial crisis of 2008,[45] when the vast resources of the West collapsed within a short period without serious war.

The third question concerns the issue of positions and preferences of the objectives and their attempts at influence. The reaction of the object requires a flexible approach to a problem and underlines the oversight of power implementation and creativity during the adaptation of power implementation.

The fourth question concerns the correct application of power behaviour which has the highest probability of success, while the fifth question concerns the calculation of probability of success. The latter two questions seem to be the simplest to achieve, but are in fact the most elusive because the relative and processual perception of power requires the permanent evaluation of those variables. Therefore, managing power forces politicians and decision-makers to constantly and actively follow up different scenarios and estimate the desired outcomes.

Summing up the challenges of governance of power, the notion of smart power seems to be right direction for redefining this particular term. The questions which Joseph Nye stated repeat typical strategic thinking, but are refurbished with the incorporation of the internal dynamic of the late-Westphalian international environment. This interesting concept is an attempt to combine the political notion of power with the management technique called S.M.A.R.T., or even S.M.A.R.T.E.R.[46] (Specific, Measurable, Attainable, Relevant, Time bound, Evaluate, Re-evaluate). It is used primarily for undertaking activity in complex and fluid business environments; however, it could also be adapted for the needs of other social activities, including foreign policy. According to this slogan, governance of power ought to become more dynamic and softer than the stiff and hard government control of the Westphalian international environment, aimed primarily at checking and re-checking the effects of activity, and should be prepared for constant and somewhat radical changes. For instance, as George Friedman stated, the shift from conflict to cooperation between Iran and the U.S. should be conducted swiftly and as soon as other options are found to undermine the *raison d'état* of both

---

[45] The impact of the financial crisis on Western powers was researched in a scientific project conducted by Roman Kuźniar. Its results were published in R. Kuźniar (ed.), *Kryzys 2008 a międzynarodowa pozycja Zachodu* (Warszawa: Wydawnictwo Naukowe Scholar, 2011).

[46] P. J. Meyer, *Attitude Is Everything: If You Want to Succeed Above and Beyond* (Waco: Meyer Resource Group, Incorporated, 2003).

belligerents. The main reason for those transformations is that the social context is continuously changing and evolving.

Power is changing within the framework of the international environment, and its management is more demanding than it used to be. The application of power requires a complex mechanism combined with many actors from different categories. Those combinations and complex evaluations of power implementation comprise the main string of dynamics of power, which is becoming the predominant paradigm of the late-Westphalian international environment.

Adrian Szumowski, M.A., graduated from the Faculty of Political Science at the Maria Curie-Sklodowska University in Lublin, and is a PhD student in the Department of International Relations at the same university.

# CHAPTER THREE

# DEMOCRACY AND ITS DEFICIT IN THE EUROPEAN UNION

MAGDALENA ZAWALSKA

## Introduction

The democratic deficit is becoming a more and more popular topic while discussing the European Union, concerning both its present and future. EU structures are often criticized because of their allegedly undemocratic characters. The main goal of this chapter is to answer the question of whether the European Union actually suffers a democratic deficit. Is democratization in a system of democracies necessary?[1] What is democratic deficit? The most platitudinous definition says that democratic deficit is any situation in which there is a presumed lack of democratic accountability and control over the decision-making process. Further examination requires a more accurate construction of democratic deficit as a non-implemented model of procedural democracy or polyarchy. The category introduced by Robert Alan Dahl for qualifying states with a possibly high level of democratic procedures while having absolute democracy is an unattainable model (even for state level governance).[2]

According to the EU webpage dedicated to summaries of legislation, the democratic deficit in the Union in general and in its particular institutions is a result of the high level of complexity of EU structures.[3] The unique community character is undoubtedly a factor in making it

[1] D. N. Chryssochoou, *Democracy in the European Union* (New York: I. B. Tauris & Co, 2000), 47.
[2] R. A. Dahl, *A Preface to Democratic Theory* (Chicago: University of Chicago Press, 1956), 63.
[3] *Democratic Deficit* at http://europa.eu/legislation_summaries/glossary/democratic_deficit_en.htm (accessed August 20, 2013).

difficult to apply all pro-democratic solutions well known from state-level governance. What is more, according to the history of European integration, democracy was not even one of the main goals for integrated European structures. Thus, history is a major reason for the dereliction of democratization processes. What has to be noticed is that there are many initiatives pushing the EU towards the democratic model introduced.

A lack of democracy may be observed on various levels of the EU functioning, and this issue can concern the community institutional sphere or may be visible in people's (EU citizens) behaviours, beliefs and identities regarding EU structures and ideas. The purpose of this analysis is to explore the issue of democratic deficit and reveal on which levels of EU democracy a deficit exists, in which spheres democracy is being gradually consolidated, and what makes the total implementation of democracy rules impossible regarding a specific international community such as the EU.

## Procedural Democracy—Theoretical Foundations

The main theoretical bases for analysis are the concepts of two democracy thinkers who substantially influenced the concept of democracy in political science—Joseph A. Schumpeter and R. A. Dahl. What has to be mentioned here is the fact that both concepts of democracy were formulated according to nation states. Some general idea of what democracy and a democratic state are needs to be expanded for the European level to answer questions about the democratic deficit in the European Union.

J. A. Schumpeter is well known as an advocate of the procedural definition of democracy. This thinker skips ideals traditionally linked with democracy and focuses on the democratic method, i.e. election. The idea of the common good is excluded as an idea of people governance. Accordingly, "another theory of democracy"[4] is an institutional arrangement for political decisions taken by people in elections to realize the common good. Elites shape or formulate what common good means for them. During elections, people can choose only within competing elites, giving them (the chosen elites) political power and legitimization. Competition for political leadership is a key factor deciding a democratic

---

[4] J. A. Schumpeter, *Capitalism, Socialism and Democracy* (New York: Taylor & Francis e-Library, 2003), 269–273, http://digamo.free.fr/capisoc.pdf (accessed August 21, 2013).

(or non-democratic) system character.[5] Representatives are given prerogatives to influence people's lives to reach common goals set during elections. Elite power comes from competitive elections. In this model of democracy, society is more passive than active, and not informed enough to participate, making it an object of elite manipulation. Schumpeter calls his concept "another theory of democracy," allowing for the recognition of democratic systems according to one essential parameter—competition for ballots. Thus, Schumpeter's ideas are useful for analyzing political systems, but some more complex concepts should also be taken into consideration.

R. A. Dahl defines democracy as an ideal but utopian model. According to him, the system must fulfil a set of unreachable requirements to be called democratic. For countries, R. A. Dahl introduces a new category—polyarchy. There are five criteria that a system has to meet to be polyarchical. The first is effective participation, meaning that citizens must have equal and adequate opportunities to formulate their preferences and question the public agenda. At the decisive stage voting must be equal, which means that each voter must be assured that their judgments will be equally weighted with those of others. What is more, citizens of a polyarchy must have equal opportunities for discovering what choice would best serve their interests, and there must be an enlightened understanding in society. Demos must have the possibility to control the agenda, to decide what political matters are and which should be brought up for deliberation. The last requirement is the inclusiveness of the system, and all citizens within the state must have an equal stake within the political process. When the above requirements are met, and it has elected representatives, fair and free elections, rights to run for office, inclusive suffrage, freedom of expression and alternative information sources, the system is polyarchical.[6]

Summarizing procedural democratic concepts, democracy is an institutional system in which demos have the possibility of creation and control over the government. There must be competitive rivalry for leadership between politicians and potential voters must have equal rights and freedoms. Both concepts were created in relation to nation states, while the EU is not a state. Defining the EU in the categories of state or federation brings about doubts. The EU seems to *sui generis* have some characteristics typical for a state (a common legal system and executives) and others typical for international organisations (facultative membership,

---

[5] Ibid.

[6] R. A. Dahl, *Democracy and Its Critics* (New Heaven: Yale University Press, 1989), 221–222.

and an elaborate consultation system for the decision making process).[7] Also, the EU is still developing, which does not make analysis easier.

## Democracy towards the History of the Integration Process

According to the fact that most EU member countries (doubtless all of the founding countries) have rather strong democratic traditions and esteem for democratic values, the alleged deficit of democracy in EU structures may be an astonishing issue. As mentioned before, introducing democracy was not the EU founders' aim, as occurrences other than democratic values encouraged the biggest European countries to cooperate and integrate after World War II, which devastated international relations and the continent. The six founders of the contemporary EU (Belgium, France, Germany, Italy, Luxembourg and the Netherlands) initiated the processes of Western Europe integration to secure lasting peace in the Cold War reality and build structures for economic cooperation profitable for the European Coal and Steel Community (ECSC—established by the Treaty of Paris in 1951)[8] member states. Economic growth in cooperating countries initiated further integration and is extending spheres of common activities. The Treaty of Rome (1957)[9] created the European Economic Community and "Common Market" as well. The first fifteen years of integration were dominated by building a new order and appointing rules of economic cooperation. Initiating political debate involving citizens would lead to the failure of the integration idea and stop the process at its beginning. One of the Founding Fathers of the EU, Jean Monnet, realized that the excessive politicization of issues could result in the domination of public debate by national businesses and values in Europe. What he found important was the seriousness of unity and common European identity.[10] That matter had been understood in the 1970s and has acquired real shape since the 1980s, when integration became implied as a democratic

---

[7] D. N. Chryssochoou, *Democracy in the European Union.*

[8] *Treaty Establishing The European Coal and Steel Community* (April 18, 1951, Paris), http://www.proyectos.cchs.csic.es/euroconstitution/library/historic %20documents/Paris/TRAITES_1951_CECA.pdf (accessed August 21, 2013).

[9] *The Treaty of Rome* (March 25, 1957, Rome), http://ec.europa.eu/economy _finance/emu_history/documents/treaties/rometreaty2.pdf (accessed August 21, 2013).

[10] M. Burgess, *Monnet's Conception of Europe and its Political Implications*, in M. Cini (ed.), *European Union Politics* (New York: Oxford University Press, 2007), 77–80.

process.[11] Emphatically, at the beginning of the process, economic agents were determinant factors of integration.

The next decade (the 1960s) was a period of economic growth and developing new fields of collective activities. Applying a common policy according to agriculture and trade resulted in victual surpluses in member countries. The European Atomic Energy Community (Euratom or EAEC) pursued a policy towards the production and exploitation of nuclear energy. The funding of various institutions by the same member countries was a disadvantage. 1965 saw the signing of a treaty merging executives of three mentioned Communities (ECSC, EEC, EAEC). The European Community then became more complex than a political idea of economic cooperation.[12] The noticeable economic success attracted other European states to the integration concept. At first, France vetoed United Kingdom access to European structures which strained relations in the Community and diminished the level of confidence between member states. This situation resulted in an institutional crisis, and common executives took unfair advantage of their powers while national governments and state citizens were losing theirs. The Court of Justice of the European Communities (now known as the Court of Justice of the European Union) stated that countries accessing communities partially lost their independence and sovereignty, as one of the verdicts constituted:

> the Community constitutes a new legal order of international law for the benefit of which the states have limited their sovereign rights, albeit within limited fields, and the subjects of which comprise not only member states but also their nationals. Independently of the legislation of member states, community law therefore not only imposes obligations on individuals but is also intended to confer upon them rights which become part of their legal heritage. These rights arise not only where they are expressly granted by the treaty, but also by reason of obligations which the treaty imposes in a clearly defined way upon individuals as well as upon the member states and upon the institutions of the community.[13]

The following year, the sequential verdict of the CJEC classified a national legal order directly below Community Law:

---

[11] M. Gilbert, *Surpassing Realism: the Politics of European Integration since 1945* (Oxford: Rowman & Littlefield Publishers, 2003), 122.

[12] D. Lasok, *Zarys prawa Unii Europejskiej* (Toruń: Wydawnictwo TNOiK, 1998), 11–25.

[13] *Judgment of the Court of 5 February 1963—Van Gend en Los Case (26/62)*, http://eur-lex.europa.eu/LexUriServ/LexUriServ.do?uri=CELEX:61962CJ0026:EN:PDF (accessed August 21, 2013).

> by creating a Community of unlimited duration, having its own institutions, its own personality, its own legal capacity and capacity of representation on the international plane and, more particularly, real powers stemming from a limitation of sovereignty or a transfer of powers from the states to the Community, the member states have limited their sovereign rights, albeit within limited fields, and have thus created a body of law which binds both their nationals and themselves.[14]

At the turn of the decade, the Community became a great political project instead of a cooperation focused on economic issues. Increasing levels of competences and powers for Community executives brought new questions about the role of national states and power distribution in the ranges of states vs. the Community, and common executives vs state citizens, for example. Among other problems, those questions had to be consecutively answered in the following years. Finally, a number of new member countries emerged in 1973 as a result of the first enlargement, when Denmark, Ireland and the United Kingdom joined the Community. Horizontal expansion then meant that states applying for access, after fulfilling formal requirements, had to accept *acquis communautaire* (the hitherto accepted legal order), losing part of their own powers.

A key issue during the 1970s was the first election to European Parliament in 1979 when all citizens could, for the first time in integration history, elect their representatives directly.[15] The role and influence of the European Parliament, as most citizens' volition was dependent on EU institutions, are presented as relating to indirect democracy in the EU. Further enlargements took place at the beginning of the 1980s, firstly in 1981 when Greece joined and then five years later when Spain and Portugal accessed the Community. As a result of those two enlargements, the Community's power range broadened to southern Europe. On the one hand, this process demonstrated the growing influence of European structures across the continent, while on the other the accession of financially poorer states compelled the formatting and developing of new rules of cooperation towards supporting financial policies. During the 1980s an economic crisis occurred, and a recession caused a negative attitude with regard to the integration idea and the spread of Euroscepticism. The solution to the new difficulties was signing the Single European Act,

---

[14] *Judgment of the Court of 15 July 1964—Flanimo Costa v E.N.E.L. Case (6/64)*, http://eur-lex.europa.eu/LexUriServ/LexUriServ.do?uri=CELEX:61964CJ0006:EN:PDF (accessed August 21, 2013).

[15] K. Popowicz, *Historia integracji europejskiej* (Warszawa: Szkoła Główna Handlowa, 2006), 54–60.

which was a revision of the Treaty of Rome. Its primary innovation was the codification of the European Political Cooperation. The late 1980s brought about considerable changes in world geopolitics. German unification, the collapse of the USSR and the democratization processes in the post-Soviet states influenced further policy decisions in the Community. Executives of member states negotiated new forms of cooperation, and finally the Treaty on the European Union (known as the Maastricht Treaty)[16] was accepted. On this basis, a European Union consisting of three pillars arose. Regarding political issues, five matters were stressed during discussions:

- efficiency—necessity of increasing Community institution powers to build the Union
- expanding new fields of activity—social and economic cohesion, environment, healthcare, social problems, scientific research, infrastructure, energy and culture
- citizenship—rights of member state citizens towards the Community defined
- international relations and safety—stressing the necessity of institutional reform allowing for voting through majority rule
- democratic legitimization—increasing the powers of European Parliament (the only EU institution representing citizens and chosen by them in direct election).[17]

After editing and translation, the treaty was ratified by the twelve member states, but its final dispositions were not accepted without question by their societies. The relatively low results of referendums regarding treaty acceptance (difficulties in France) indicated that further integration without citizens' acceptance and engagement could be uncertain. Difficulties in introducing the European Union in a new form caused by common objections towards the treaty showed that society must be a relevant part of the Community-shaping processes. The necessity of persuading public opinion about the benefits of integration was exposed to executives. It had to be understood that building a great political project requires taking the will of the people into consideration and some democratic procedures had to be included.

[16] *Treaty on European Union*, July 29, 1992, http://eur-lex.europa.eu/pl/treaties/dat/11992M/htm/11992M.html (accessed August 21, 2013).
[17] K. Popowicz, *Historia integracji europejskiej*, 180–182.

During the 1990s three new countries joined the EU structures: Austria, Finland and Sweden. Many differences between these member states then resulted in a conflict of interests between them (for example, the prosperous north and the impecunious south). The next integration steps were taken and a common currency was planned and established in twelve of the fifteen member countries (1999 in non-cash transactions, and in 2002 paper money and coins were emitted). According to the democracy issue, the next enlargements were especially interesting. The 2004 enlargement was the biggest in the Community's history. What is more, countries which joined the EU had been under the political influence or were even elements of the USSR until the 1980s and 1990s. As mentioned above, the Community was developed in opposition to the USSR, making the accession of the Czech Republic, Estonia, Hungary, Latvia, Lithuania, Poland, Slovakia and Slovenia to the EU a great step towards integration. Two Mediterranean countries also joined the structures: Cyprus and Malta. Three years later the next eastern countries to join were Bulgaria and Romania, with Croatia joining in 2013.

Each enlargement influenced the decision-making process in the EU. The growing number of member states and, seemingly more important, the diversity of their interests did not facilitate governing. The number of policy fields controlled by common executives is still rising and the necessity of structure democratization is realized by the EU executives.

## Procedural Democracy in the EU

Discussion about the democratic deficit in the EU started in the 1970s when the Commission defined it in the Vedel Report.[18] This report revised issues of democracy and effectiveness in the EU and mentioned the need to increase the role of the European Parliament. As long as democratic legitimization in the EU was based on legitimization from the nation-state level, public opinion was not interested in affairs on the institutional level. Since the European Parliament has become the only institution chosen in direct elections, argumentation about increasing its influence on policy-making has gained more power and European discourse has focused on this point. The Parliament has the greatest democratic legitimacy, and election for the European Parliament is the fruition of Schumpeter's

---

[18] Commission of the European Communities, *Report of the Working Party Examining the Problem of the Enlargement of the Powers of the European Parliament. "Report Vedel,"* Brussels 1972, http://www.cvce.eu/content/publication/1999/4/7/a4f5b134-99b9-41b3-9715-41769dfea12a/publishable_en.pdf (accessed August 21, 2013).

democratic method towards the EU. The powers of the Parliament have been increasing since the Maastricht Treaty introduced the status of EU citizenship, granting EU citizens the right to vote, stand in elections for the European Parliament and municipal elections in their countries of residence, irrespective of nationality (subject to age and residency qualifications), and the legislative procedure known as the "co-decision procedure," giving the directly elected European Parliament the right to "co-decide" legislation on an equal footing with the Council of the European Union.[19] The Treaty of Lisbon, in confirming that the functioning of the EU should be founded on representative democracy, significantly reinforced powers of the European Parliament as the most democratic of EU institutions.[20]

According to the Treaty of Lisbon, the European Parliament is composed of directly chosen representatives of the Union's citizens, elected for five-year cadences by direct universal suffrage in secret and free ballots. The number of European Parliament members has increased and rules for their allocation are established (a proportional system with a minimum threshold of six members per state and a maximum limit of ninety-six members). The powers of the Parliament have also increased, and co-decision has become the "ordinary legislative procedure." The co-decision process has extended to more policy areas, and there are new legal bases where the co-decision procedure is used. The most significant fields of extension are Freedom, Security and Justice, the coordination of social security for migrant workers, structural funds, culture, and European administration. Co-decision was introduced to make EU decision-making more accountable, transparent and inclusive for citizens. Every citizen has the right to participate in the democratic life of the Union, and for that purpose EU decisions must be taken openly and as closely as possible to the citizens.

The European Parliament empowerment is a visible process but, according to Schumpeter's democratic method, EU Parliamentary elections should be treated as the substance of democracy towards the EU. Since 1979, elections have taken place in every member state every five years, but when a nation joins mid-term a by-election is held to elect their

---

[19] *Treaty on European Union*, July 29, 1992, http://eur-lex.europa.eu/pl/treaties/dat/11992M/htm/11992M.html (accessed August 21, 2013).

[20] J. Mayoral, *Democratic Improvements in the European Union under the Lisbon Treaty: Institutional Changes Regarding Democratic Government in the EU*, http://www.eui.eu/Projects/EUDO-Institutions/Documents/EUDOreport922011.pdf (accessed August 21, 2013).

representatives. To maintain proportionality, seats are allocated to states according to their population but no state can have more than ninety-nine, and no fewer than five. Those limitations mean that voting equality is not a given within the EU. Inclusiveness is essential for EU elections, and during those in 2009, the largest transnational simultaneous elections in history, nearly 380 million EU citizens had the right to vote. The average turnout was the lowest in history, with only 43% of those eligible to vote doing so. Such a decreasing turnout at the European elections is an indicator of the democratic gap in the EU. While the competences of the EU Parliament (the only direct representative of citizens) grow, people are less active in the essential democratic process of election. During the first elections in 1979 the turnout was almost 62% of those eligible to vote.

Fig. 3.1. Decreasing turnout in European Parliament Elections (1979–2009)

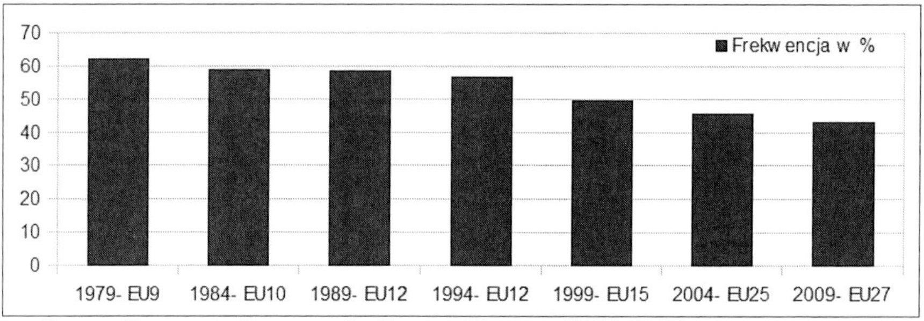


Source: *Turnout in European Parliament Elections (1979–2009)*, http://www.europarl.europa.eu/aboutparliament/en/000cdcd9d4/Frekwencja-(1979–2009).html (accessed August 22, 2013).

What could have influenced the decreasing turnout level was the fact that further enlargements involved countries without long-term, consolidated democratic systems, while at the beginning countries with democratic traditions were building the communities. In new member states turnout is much lower than in those countries that have belonged to the EU structures for longer, the exceptions being Malta, Latvia and Cyprus with turnouts higher than average for the EU.[21] The Bulgarian and Romanian elections brought two of the lowest turnouts for European elections, with just 28.6% and 28.3%, respectively. Steps are taken to engage EU citizens

[21] *Turnout in European Parliament Elections (1979–2009)*, http://www.europarl.europa.eu/aboutparliament/en/000cdcd9d4/Frekwencja-(1979–2009).html (accessed August 22, 2013).

in active participation during elections, but European issues are still not the main point of people's interest. Discussions in the public sphere, even during campaigns, are still dominated by matters of national states. Thus, EU citizens are not focused on pan-European ideas and goals. Citizens of EU member countries should be able to get information and knowledge about what I call "everyday EU life" easily. What EU institutions can do to improve this model of democracy is to persuade people about the importance of voting in EU Parliament elections because this is how this institution representing citizens gets democratic legitimacy. All processes should be more visible and transparent. Less than half of people asked answered that they know and understand how the European Union works, and what, in their opinion, creates low participation in political activities.[22] As long as people do not understand exactly how the EU works they should not be forced by the system to play an active role in its policy, even if they have the possibility to do so.

In order to facilitate participation in European civil society, the Treaties have established additional obligations for EU institutions to promote transparency, openness and the freedom of information. For the first time in integration history, citizens can directly influence or participate in the EU decision-making process by citizens' initiative, which give the opportunity to influence groups and associations, allowing for Dahl's effective participation and control of the agenda. The initiative should require the support of at least one million signatories from at least one quarter of all member states. The signatories and organisers have to be citizens of the Union and old enough to vote in EP elections. Initiative is an innovative mechanism of citizen participation, but few initiatives have been introduced. Ideas are brought by citizen committees, registered and later consulted via the internet. After collection and verification of statements of support, an initiative is submitted to the Commission, examined via public hearing in the European Parliament and, if accepted, legislative procedure puts it into motion, for example on media pluralism, voting, energy and environmental issues. Some initiatives have been withdrawn by organisers, and other initiatives which did not comply with formal conditions have been refused by EU structures. According to the EU webpage, no initiatives have yet been finalized. Thus, it is too early to estimate the efficiency of the new democratic tool towards the EU.[23]

---

[22] Eurobarometer 68, http://ec.europa.eu/public_opinion/archives/eb/eb68/eb_68_en.pdf (accessed August 22, 2013).
[23] *The European Citizens' Initiative. Official register*, http://ec.europa.eu/citizens-initiative/public/initiatives/finalised (accessed August 25, 2013).

Developed participative democracy seems to be not impossible within the European Union, but I think that it is too early to reach this goal.

Coming back to the main point of procedural democracy, which is representation chosen during election, the Treaty of Lisbon empowered national Parliaments as well as the European Parliament. National governments were given new rights in the field of information policy, meaning that they can receive information regarding EU legislative acts and programs directly from the EU institutions (and not only from their governments). On the grounds of subsidiarity, national parliaments have the right to object to EU acts, meaning that after receiving information concerning the draft of legislation, national parliaments have the opportunity to review the compliance of proposals with the principle of subsidiarity in fields not falling within the exclusive competence of the EU. There are two cooperative mechanisms for subsidiarity control: the "yellow card" mechanism and the "red card" mechanism. The "yellow card" mechanism is activated if such a reasoned opinion is submitted which represents one third of the total number of votes allocated to national parliaments. In that case, the Commission must review its proposal and give reasons explaining its decision to keep, change or withdraw the proposal. The "red card" mechanism is only applicable to co-decision proposals and is activated when a majority of national parliaments complain. The procedure is similar to the yellow card procedure, but the difference is that if the Commission wants to maintain the proposal it should send a justified opinion to the European Parliament and the Council. The proposal is not given further consideration if either the Council (by a majority of 55% of the members) or a majority in the European Parliament consider that the proposal is incompatible with the principle of subsidiarity.[24]

It should not be forgotten that the European Parliament and national parliaments are not the only carriers of democracy and democratic legitimization in the European Union. In parliamentary institutions other than the EU, nation-state governments represent their countries using EU institutions to articulate and reach their own aims or to satisfy preferences which cannot be satisfied on the national level. The main reason for the legitimization of other EU institutions (European Commission and Council of the European Union) is the same as on the national level. Governments are chosen by parliaments, not directly by citizens. Thus, they are legitimized on both levels, or one may say that national

---

[24] *Treaty of Lisbon*, December 13, 2007, http://eur-lex.europa.eu/JOHtml.do?uri=OJ:C:2007:306:SOM:EN:HTML (accessed August 22, 2013).

governments are not democratic. According to Moravcsik,[25] a supporter of the intergovernmental concept, European Union institutions work with issues in which direct participation is not needed. Issues which can focus public opinion are usually part of a nation-state government's policies. He puts more attention on the efficiency of the EU policy, which should be formulated and controlled by national democratic states and their representatives on the EU level. The possibilities for actively influencing EU policies by citizens exist but people do not use them, which is their choice.

According to Dahl's concept of polyarchy, most requirements are fulfilled. Since the introduction of the Lisbon Treaty there is an increasing number of possibilities for effective participation (mentioned above). Thus, according to the inter-governmental level, the EU does not suffer from a democratic deficit, but there are still some issues which should be improved. The most important is the transparency of institutions and the decision-making process in European Union structures. People, even if they do not play active roles in the policy-making process, should be able to know how this process is going.

Summarizing, as long as there is no European Demos,[26] this argumentation stressing the role of efficiency seems to be reasonable. People in Europe still have a stronger identity with the nation state than with Europe, and believe that nation state policies and aims influence European policies. According to Eurobarometer:

> Six out of ten Europeans consider that their country's voice counts in the European Union (61%). A majority of European citizens also consider that their country will become more influential in the EU in the future (43% versus 39% who take the opposite view). More than four out of ten people polled consider that they have a good understanding of how the European Union works (40% versus half of Europeans—51%—who take the opposite view), 38% consider that their country's interests are properly taken into account in the European Union (versus 46% who think the opposite), three out of ten Europeans agree with the statements that "my voice counts in the EU" (30% versus 61% who take the opposite view) and

[25] A. Moravcsik, "In Defence of the "Democratic Deficit": Reassessing Legitimacy in the European Union," *Journal of Common Market Studies* 4 (2002).

[26] M. J. Gabel, Ch. J. Anderson, "Exploring the European Demos (or Lack Thereof): the Structure of Citizen Attitudes and the European", *Political Space, CEuS Working Paper* 4 (2001), http://www.monnet-centre.uni-bremen.de/pdf/wp/2001-4-Gabel-Anderson.pdf (accessed August 21, 2013).

> a fifth of respondents feel very much involved in European affairs (20% versus 74% who disagree).[27]

The results of this public opinion poll seem to be empirical proof for the suitability of the theoretical inter-governmental concept of the present-day EU. They show that most people are satisfied with the level of democracy in the European Union and their countries' influence on its policies. According to the last Eurobarometer polls, 54% of EU member states' citizens asked declared themselves as very satisfied or fairly satisfied with democracy in the EU, while 32% are not very satisfied or not at all satisfied.[28] Thus, for now, democratic deficit is not a problem affecting European Union citizens. Building a pan-European democratic system was not an aim of the EU founders, as the structures are under the influence of the democratization process, and citizens are directly represented by the Members of European Parliament and indirectly by national governments. The requirements of the procedural democracy in the EU are fulfilled by EU institutions. On the other hand, there are gaps in participation but they are the result of a lack of European identity and a low level of consciousness towards the EU structures. Policies in those fields should be employed in building a participative democracy, as some further political integration believers wish.

Magdalena Zawalska is a PhD student in Political Sciences, has an M.A. in Political Science (Pedagogical University of Cracow), an M.A. in History (Högskolan Dalarna), and a B.A. in International Relations (Pedagogical University of Cracow). Her main fields of scientific interest are political theories according to democracy and democratization, political culture, the mediatization of politics, political news journalism, the media's effects on opinion formation process, and political public relations.

---

[27] Eurobarometer, 68.

[28] Eurobarometer, *How About the Way Democracy Works in the European Union?*, http://ec.europa.eu/public_opinion/cf/showtable.cfm?keyID=4&nationID=11,1,27,28,17,2,16,18,13,6,3,4,22,7,8,20,21,9,23,24,12,19,29,26,25,5,14,10,30,15,&startdate=2009.11&enddate=2009.11 (accessed August 21, 2013).

# CHAPTER FOUR

# EFFECTIVENESS OF THE POLITICAL SYSTEM AND GOVERNMENT EFFECTIVENESS (SELECTED ISSUES)

MARCIN ŁUKASZEWSKI

The issue of effectiveness is a relatively frequent topic of discussion for political science (especially with regard to the efficiency of financial operations and for organisation and management theory),[1] but reflections on the effectiveness of the political system are not the subject of many scientific studies. In the Polish literature, searching for papers which describe the problem of the effectiveness of the political system in a complementary way is almost fruitless. Often, researchers deal with only a very small portion of the effectiveness of the political reality, such as the election campaign, public relations or even military action. In the Anglo-Saxon literature, very often the effectiveness of the political system is identified with the efficiency of the government (government effectiveness) and thus outlines the performance criteria for this component of the political system. There are also attempts to study the effectiveness of various elements of the political system.[2]

---

[1] S. Elbanna, J. Child, "Influences on Strategic Decision Effectiveness: Development and Test of an Integrative Model," *Strategic Management Journal* 4 (28) (2007): 431–453.

[2] Many interesting questions are being asked by two authors trying to connect the two components of effectiveness and legislation, such as which legislators are especially effective at the job of law making, and what are the determinants of effectiveness? See G. Padró i Miquel, J. M. Snyder, "Legislative Effectiveness and Legislative Careers," *Legislative Studies Quarterly* 3 (31) (2006): 347–381.
W. Downs considers whether it is possible to build the *cordon sanitaire* as a remedy against extremist political parties (so here we have party system issues). See W. Downs, "How Effective is the Cordon Sanitaire? Lessons from Efforts to Contain the Far Right in Belgium, France, Denmark and Norway," *Journal für*

One of the most important factors inextricably linked to the political system, and which determines its choice, is its effectiveness. Of course, we cannot forget about other factors such as tradition or will of a causative agent in a country. But even the causative agent decides on the selection of a system that allows it to effectively exercise power. If the political system is no longer an effective sovereign (or other causative agent) this causes it to change. If this is in a legal way then we have to deal with constitutional revision, but if the change in the system is done in a manner contrary to the constitution there is a revolution, or a *coup d'état*.[3]

Hence, and interesting from a theoretical point of view, this is a matter of effectiveness and measurement. This chapter therefore shows the widely discussed and criticized points of view on the matters of effectiveness, the purpose of which is a brief look at the indicators adopted in science showing the problem of effectiveness in the literature and identifying problems that a researcher has to face in formulating indicators of the political system's effectiveness.

## Definitional Issues

This chapter uses a definition proposed by two representatives of the Poznań School of praxeology, Tadeusz Kotarbiński and Tadeusz Pszczołowski. According to this definition, effectiveness is a positive feature of actions which gives a positive result, regardless of whether it was intended or not.[4] In English we have both effectiveness and efficiency. Being effective means producing powerful effects, and being efficient means producing results with little wasted effort. Therefore, efficiency focuses on effort, time, process, aim and effectiveness, and mainly on a goal.[5]

---

*Konflikt und Gewaltforschung* 4 (1) (2002): 32–51; S. Rummens, K. Abts, "Defending Democracy: The Concentric Containment of Political Extremism," *Political Studies* 4 (58) (2010): 649–665.

[3] A. Hurrelmann et al., "Why the Democratic Nation-State is Still Legitimate: A Study of Media Discourses," *European Journal of Political Research* 4 (48) (2009): 499–500.

[4] T. Pszczołowski, *Mała encyklopedia prakseologii i teorii organizacji* (Wrocław: Ossolineum, 1978), 60.

[5] See A. Szpaderski, "Problemy efektywności działań w teorii organizacji i zarządzania i sugestie ich rozwiązywania w duchu prakseologii," in J. Michniak (ed.), *Efektywność kierowania (dowodzenia)* (Warszawa: AON, 2005), 43–53; E. Frøkjær et al., "Measuring Usability: are Effectiveness, Efficiency, and Satisfaction Really Correlated?," *CHI '00 Proceedings of the SIGCHI conference*

What must be noted is that we have both an *ex ante* and *ex post* cost-effectiveness analysis.[6] The effectiveness of *ex post* is defined as a relationship between the results and expenses incurred to obtain them. The *ex ante* effectiveness is seen as the relationship between the objectives of the action, and the anticipated resources necessary to achieve these objectives.[7]

The next problem we have to face is terminology. The question is, do effectiveness and performance mean the same thing? Soo-Young Lee and Andrew B. Whitford argue that the palette of solutions and answers to this question is too large, and this lack of consensus is a basic problem (because terminological problems are fundamental), as to take any further steps we have to agree that these terms mean the same.[8]

The following problem is the equalization of the terms "effectiveness of the political system" with "government effectiveness." The researcher has to face another question—are governmental effectiveness and effectiveness of the political system the same thing? According to Hossain Zillur Rahman and Mark Robinson, the effectiveness of a political system can be defined as the effectiveness of political institutions.[9] The answer to the question about equalization of governmental effectiveness and

---

*on Human Factors in Computing Systems* (New York: ACM, 2000), 345–352; D. Walters, "Effectiveness and Efficiency: the Role of Demand Chain Management," *The International Journal of Logistics Management* 1 (17) (2006): 75–94; A. Mazurkiewicz, "Sprawność działani—interpretacja teoretyczna pojęcia," in M. G. Woźniak (ed.), *Nierówności społeczne a wzrost gospodarczy, Zeszyt 20: Uwarunkowania sprawnego działania w przedsiębiorstwie i regionie* (Rzeszów: Wydawnictwo Uniwersytetu Rzeszowskiego, 2011), 47–57.

[6] What is obvious is that the effectiveness is connected with cost issues, so, for example, the government can provide a cost-effective environmental and climate policy or any other kind of policy. See A.T. Gullberg, T. Skodvin, "Cost Effectiveness and Target Group Influence in Norwegian Climate Policy," *Scandinavian Political Studies* 2 (34) (2011): 123–142.

[7] P. Bartkowiak, P. Niewiadomski, "Efektywne zarządzanie firmą rodzinną—kompetencyjne wyzwania sukcesji," in T. Dudycz et al., (eds.), *Efektywność—konceptualizacja i uwarunkowania* (Wrocław: Wydawnictwo Uniwersytetu Ekonomicznego we Wrocławiu, 2012), 13–15.

[8] S.-Young Lee, A. B. Whitford, "Government Effectiveness in the Comparative Perspective," *Journal of Comparative Policy Analysis: Research and Practice* 2 (11) (2009): 249–281.

See also S.-Young Lee, A. B. Whitford, "Disorder, Dictatorship and Government Effectiveness: Cross-National Evidence," *Journal of Public Policy* 1 (32) (2012): 5–31.

[9] H. Zillur Rahman, M. Robinson, "Governance and State Effectiveness in Asia," *DS Bulletin* 3 (37) (2006): 130.

effectiveness of the political system somehow depends on the methodological school used. If the political system means the same as the government, according to the traditional, institutional school of methodology, the answer is positive. But if the political system means more than the government, as other schools stand, the answer is negative.

It seems obvious that the issue of defining governance provides a number of problems. According to Kaufmann, Kraay & Mastruzzi, governance consists of the traditions and institutions by which authority in a country is exercised. This includes the process by which governments are selected, monitored and replaced—the capacity of the government to effectively formulate and implement sound policies, and the respect of citizens and the state for the institutions that govern economic and social interactions among them.[10]

## Effectiveness and the Political System

Effectiveness and the political system meet in many cases, mainly at the low level of effectiveness of both the political system and its environment. There are fundamental reasons for conducting political reforms or changing the system in an undemocratic manner.

Vivien A. Schmidt links governing effectiveness with Abraham Lincoln's famous dictum about democracy and normative definitions of legitimacy, in which democracy requires government by the people (political participation), of the people (citizen representation) and for the people (governing effectiveness), while the input-output terms themselves have been borrowed from systems theories. It is worth underlining that output legitimacy requires policies to work effectively while resonating with citizens' values and identity.[11]

E. Shils posits five kinds of "preconditions" to political development, the first of which are stability, coherence and effectiveness of the ruling elite.[12] Some examine government effectiveness by focusing on the effectiveness of policies.[13] M. Warren shows that creating the widely elected upper chambers in the UK and Canada will introduce effective

---

[10] D. Kaufmann et al., "The Worldwide Governance Indicators: Methodology and Analytical Issues," *The Hague Journal on the Rule of Law* 2 (3) (2011): 220–221.

[11] V.A. Schmidt, "Democracy and Legitimacy in the European Union Revisited: Input, Output and 'Throughput'," *Political Studies* 1 (61) (2013): 6–9.

[12] P. Coulter, "Democratic Political Development: A Systemic Model Based on Regulative Policy," *Development and Change* 1 (3) (1972): 29.

[13] P. Boekholt et al., *An International Review of Methods to Measure Relative Effectiveness of Technology Policy Instruments* (Amsterdam: Technopolis, 2001).

bicameralism and, according to Max Weber and Joseph Schumpeter, effective citizen participation is limited to choosing an elite in competitive elections.[14] P. Coulter links the level of political participation of the military (interventive, supportive and neutral) with the effectiveness of legislature (fully effective legislature is linked with neutral political participation by the military, etc.),[15] noticing that the centre of gravity of political decision-making must be, not in the party bureaucracy, but in parliament, in large part because popular esteem for parliament as an institution must be maintained and legislators must be able to act effectively.[16] In all cases, the effectiveness is one of many factors creating the perfect model of democracy.

## The Worldwide Governance Indicators (WGI) Project

Hossain Zillur Rahman and Mark Robinson, in their article "Governance and State Effectiveness in Asia," use the indicators of state effectiveness from the World Bank Institute (WBI). These variables are normalized to 0 and range from –2.5 to 2.5, with higher values indicating better performance. They are based on the aggregation of a range of governance surveys and indicators. Because the values are normalized from year to year, changes are not absolute changes but, instead, are measures of change relative to other countries.[17]

The WGI project reports aggregate and individual governance indicators for 215 economies over the period 1996–2011 for six dimensions of governance:

- Voice and Accountability
- Political Stability and Absence of Violence
- Government Effectiveness
- Regulatory Quality
- Rule of Law
- Control of Corruption.

[14] M. Warren, "Citizen Participation and Democratic Deficits: Considerations from the Perspective of Democratic Theory," in J. De Bardeleben, J. Pammet (eds.), *Activating the Citizen: Dilemmas of Participation in Europe and Canada* (Basingstoke, Houndsmill: Palgrave Macmillan, 2009), 14–40.

[15] P. Coulter, "Democratic Political Development: A Systemic Model Based on Regulative Policy," *Development and Change* 1 (3) (1972), 44.

[16] Ibid., 29.

[17] H. Zillur Rahman, M. Robinson, *Governance and State Effectiveness*, 145.

The WGI was created in 1996 by three authors: Daniel Kaufmann (Brookings Institution), Aart Kraay (World Bank Development Research Group) and Massimo Mastruzzi (World Bank Institute). The WGI has faced several critics but none were directly linked with government effectiveness.

According to the authors, government effectiveness is in capturing perceptions of the quality of public services, the quality of the civil service and the degree of its independence from political pressures, the quality of policy formulation and implementation, and the credibility of the government's commitment to such policies.[18]

The problem linked to measuring the effectiveness is the objectivity of sources used. One popular way of classifying performance measures has been the distinction between measures that are "objective" and those that are "subjective." What is obvious, but must be written down, is that we have to take the sources from both constructers: active participants (like pro-governmental politicians) in the political system, and its critics, like non-governmental organisations, media and politicians from opposition parties (even, or perhaps above all, extra-parliamentary parties). Objective measures are often unavailable, but we have to try and take the most objective ones we can. Kaufmann, Kraay & Mastruzzi distinguish between representative and non-representative sources (see Table 4.1 below).

**Table 4.1. One of the six aggregate measures of Worldwide Governance Indicators (Government Effectiveness)**

| CODE | CONCEPT MEASURED |
|---|---|
| **Representative Sources** | |
| **EIU** | Quality of bureaucracy / institutional effectiveness |
| | Excessive bureaucracy / red tape |
| **GCS** | Infrastructure |
| | Quality of primary education |
| **GWP** | Satisfaction with public transportation system |
| | Satisfaction with roads and highways |
| | Satisfaction with education system |
| **IPD** | Quality of the supply of public goods: education and basic health |
| | Capacity of political authorities to implement reforms |

[18] D. Kaufmann et al., *The Worldwide Governance*, 223–224.

| | |
|---|---|
| **PRS** | Bureaucratic Quality |
| **WMO** | Bureaucracy: An assessment of the quality of the country's bureaucracy. The better the bureaucracy the quicker decisions are made and the more easily foreign investors can go about their business. |
| | Policy consistency and forward planning. How confident businesses can be part of the continuity of economic policy stance—whether a change of government will entail major policy disruption, and whether the current government has pursued a coherent strategy. This factor also looks at the extent to which policy-making is far-sighted or conversely aimed at short-term economic advantage |
| **Non-representative Sources** | |
| **ADB** | Quality of public administration |
| | Quality of budgetary and financial management |
| | Efficiency of revenue mobilization |
| **AFR** | Government handling of public services (health, education) |
| **ASD** | Quality of public administration |
| | Efficiency of revenue mobilization |
| | Quality of budgetary & financial management |
| **BPS** | How problematic are telecommunications for the growth of your business? |
| | How problematic is electricity for the growth of your business? |
| | How problematic is transportation for the growth of your business? |
| **BTI** | Consensus Building (MI) |
| | Governance Capability (MI) |
| | Resource Efficiency (MI) |
| **IFD** | Allocation & management of public resources for rural development |
| **LBO** | Trust in Government |
| **PIA** | Quality of public administration |
| | Quality of budgetary and financial management |
| | Efficiency of revenue mobilization |
| **WCY** | Government economic policies do not adapt quickly to changes in the economy |
| | The public service is not independent from political interference |
| | Government decisions are not effectively implemented |
| | Bureaucracy hinders business activity |
| | The distribution infrastructure of goods and services is generally inefficient |
| | Policy direction is not consistent |

Source: *Government effectiveness*, http://info.worldbank.org/governance/wgi/pdf/ge.pdf (accessed May 10, 2013). See D. Kaufmann et al., *The Worldwide Governance.*

## Summary

Measuring the effectiveness of a political system and/or government effectiveness is a challenge for scientific research. One of the most valuable systems for measuring the effectiveness of a political system (to be more precise government effectiveness), but that is not without disadvantages, is created by three experts of the World Bank—Daniel Kaufmann, Aart Kraay and Massimo Mastruzzi. Undoubtedly, a very large methodological advantage of Government Effectiveness is basing the Index on a broad spectrum of indicators and sources. Therefore, the change of one indicator does not radically change the overall assessment of the effectiveness of the political system.[19] It is obvious that the effectiveness of the political system is a sum of components of the efficiency of the system, which means that the efficiency of one component of the system does not involve the effectiveness of another element, or even the system. A disadvantage of using the World Bank's Government Effectiveness Index, which researchers have to face, is the lack of data (there is no data in cases like San Marino and Monaco), but it is still one of the best ways to measure state effectiveness.

Marcin Łukaszewski, M.A. is a PhD student at the Faculty of Political Sciences and Journalism, the Adam Mickieiwcz University in Poznań, Poland. His research is focused mainly on political systems of European countries, in particular democratic so-called European microstates (such as Andorra, Liechtenstein, Monaco and San Marino).

[19] What is very interesting is the case of Singapore, which in 2011 had a Governance Score of +2.16, which was one of the best of all countries. Singapore is widely known as the partly free (incomplete democracy) and has a better rank than Switzerland or the USA. In view of the observation that the democratic system not always being a guarantee of an effective political system, creating a risky proposal may become the slogans of populist and extreme groups, which tend to rise in autocratic countries. In this respect, democracy is not the most effective political regime. *Freedom House Singapore*, http://www.freedomhouse.org/country/singapore (accessed May 16, 2013); *Statistical Table: Government Effectiveness, Comparison across selected countries—San Marino, Monaco*, http://info.worldbank.org/governance/wgi/mc_chart.asp (accessed May 16, 2013).

# CHAPTER FIVE

# STATE AS A PARTY TO INTERNATIONAL COMMERCIAL ARBITRATION

NĒRIKA LIZINSKA

## Introduction

Globalisation, development of international trade, and the evaluation of international trade law are the bases and main reasons why states can be involved in international commercial transactions. "In the course of the nineteenth century states appeared as commercial entrepreneurs on a considerable scale, creating monopolies in particular trades, and operating railway, shipping, and postal services."[1] At the present time, states can freely conclude international commercial contracts, and moreover it is internationally recognized that states can also freely conclude international arbitration agreements. This means that in cases of dispute arising under international arbitration agreement, a case will be heard in arbitration.[2]

First and foremost, arbitration is known as a method of dispute resolution for international traders. Merchants choose arbitration because this method has several advantages over court-based litigation (for example, speed of resolution, flexibility, confidentiality, neutrality and enforcement). In the author's opinion, neutrality and enforcement could be nominated as predominant.

---

[1] I. Brownlie, *Principles of Public International Law*, 7th ed. (Oxford University Press, 2008), 323.

[2] For example, according to the International Chamber of Commerce International Court of Arbitration (hereinafter – ICC Arbitration) statistics for the past three years, in 10% of cases at least one of the parties was a State or parastatal entity. *ICC Statistics*, http://www.iccwbo.org/Products-and-Services/Arbitration-and-ADR/Arbitration/Introduction-to-ICC-Arbitration/Statistics/ (accessed May 15, 2013). It should be noted that ICC Arbitration is one of several international commercial arbitrations where disputes may be heard.

> International arbitration is nationally neutral in the sense that there does not need to be a link between any party's place of incorporation or residence and the place of the arbitration. The parties can choose any place of arbitration, any applicable law, and any language for their arbitration. All of these elements can be neutral with respect to the parties.[3]

With respect to enforcement, it is particularly important in dealings with the state because that state can use its immunity from enforcement to avoid arbitral award.

In cases where the state is a party to arbitration, significant differences in the advantages of arbitration can be found.

> First, the very presence of a State as a party to the arbitration raises a public interest because the nationals and residents of that State have an interest in how the government acts during the arbitration and in the outcome of the arbitration. Moreover, the existence of this public interest has obvious implications for the conduct of the arbitration: according to principles of human rights law and good governance, government activities should be subject to basic requirements of transparency and public participation.[4]

As for the state, public interest is the main motive to concluding a commercial agreement in the first instance. This means that even if a state concludes international commercial agreements, this has been done without a view to making a profit, but instead for the common good. Hence, most advantages we can identify in the arbitration process (where both parties are merchants), will not be accessible where one of the parties is a state. Therefore, one may argue that the use of international commercial arbitration mainly brings benefits to the private companies and not the state. On the other hand, when a private company concludes international commercial contracts with the state, the state can use its legal instruments to avoid arbitration agreement, contract, or enforcement of the arbitral award. In dealings with the state, only arbitration can help to keep the balance in proceedings.

> The approach to State contracts in international commercial arbitration is characterized by its oscillation between two contrasting tendencies, one economic; the other political … The imperatives of the global economy

---

[3] *Introduction to ICC Arbitration*, http://www.iccwbo.org/products-and-services /arbitration-and-adr/arbitration/ (accessed May 15, 2013).

[4] International Institute for Sustainable Development, *Revising the UNCITRAL Arbitration Rules to Address State Arbitration*, http://www.iisd.org/pdf/2007 /investment_revising_uncitral_arbitration.pdf (accessed April 27, 2013).

> have given rise to expressions intended to ensure that State parties take part in arbitration and uphold the commitment they have made when consenting to an international commercial arbitration agreement.[5]

The question is whether the best way to protect the public (state) interests is to resolve international commercial disputes in the national court, and what international practice and regulation in this sphere are.

This chapter examines international regulations and exceptions, case law and the essence of the situation when a state concludes international commercial contracts with an arbitration clause, as well as legal instruments which the state uses to avoid the arbitration process or enforcement of arbitral awards.

## Legal Persons of Public Law

The 1961 European Convention on International Commercial Arbitration is the most significant commercial arbitration treaty (hereinafter European Convention) in this field. According to its preamble, the purpose of this convention is "as far as possible, removing certain difficulties that may impede the organisation and operation of international commercial arbitration in relations between physical or legal persons of different countries."[6] The European Convention entered into force in 1964, and more than 30 states[7] are currently party to it.

Pursuant to Article II of European Convention, legal persons considered by the law applicable to them as "legal persons of public law" have the right to conclude valid arbitration agreements.[8] "Article II validates both arbitration clauses and submission agreements entered into by 'legal persons of public law' with a view to placing them on the same

---

[5] E. S. Romero, "ICC Arbitration and State Contracts," *ICC International Court of Arbitration Bulletin* 1 (13) (2002): 59–60.

[6] *1961 European Convention on International Commercial Arbitration*, http://www.jus.uio.no/lm/europe.international.commercial.arbitration.convention.geneva.1961/ (accessed April 22, 2013).

[7] *European Convention Status*, available at http://treaties.un.org/Pages/ViewDetails.aspx?src=TREATY&mtdsg_no=XXII-2&chapter=22&lang=en (accessed June 1, 2013).

[8] According to the European Convention, Article I "arbitration agreements" shall mean either an arbitral clause in a contract or an arbitration agreement, the contract or arbitration agreement being signed by the parties, or contained in an exchange of letters, telegrams or in a communication by teleprinter and, in relations between States whose laws do not require that an arbitration agreement be made in writing, any arbitration agreement concluded in the form authorized by these laws.

footing as legal persons of private law."[9] As can be seen from the authentic text versions in English, French and Russian of this convention, they all contain the same legal subject—legal person of public law. Thus, the French version of the European Convention states that "*personnes morales de droit public*,"[10] and the Russian version that "*юридические лица публичного права*"[11] or "legal persons of public law" have a right to conclude valid arbitration agreements. In order to identify whether the entity has the right to enter into an arbitration agreement, applicable law to them should be analyzed. At the same time, "the expression 'legal persons of public law' should be interpreted in a broad way as to comprise not only public corporations but also States and any public agencies."[12] Thus, an "instrumentality," for example, "can be defined as an entity of the state which: (1) has its own legal personality; (2) was created by the State with a specific purpose …, and (3) is controlled by the state."[13]

In ICC case Svenska Petroleum Exploration AB v. Lithuania situation was following:

> the contract was entered into on the part of the State by AB Geonafta, a State corporation, but the contract was also signed by government officials and contained a statement above their signatures to the effect that the government approved the agreement and acknowledge[d] itself to be legally and contractually bound as if the Government were a signatory to the Agreement. The ICC tribunal found that the government was bound by the agreement.[14]

---

[9] A. J. Van Der Berg (ed.), "International Council for Commercial Arbitration," *Yearbook Commercial Arbitration* XX (1995): 1016.

[10] *Convention européenne sur l'arbitrage commercial international*, available at www.arbitrage.org/fr/presentation/texte_convention_euro.pdf (accessed May 20, 2013).

[11] *Европейская конвенция 1961 г. о внешнеторговом арбитраже*, available at www.law.edu.ru/norm/norm.asp?normID=1254444 (accessed May 20, 2013).

[12] D. Hascher, "Commentary on the European Convention on International Commercial Arbitration of 1961," *Yearbook Commercial Arbitration (Kluwer Law International)* XXXVI (2011): 516. Available also at http://www.arbitration-icca.org/media/1/13534204360520/hascher_commentary_on__the_european_convention_1961.pdf (accessed May 20, 2013).

[13] ICC Case No. 6465, August 15, 1991 Interim Award, cit. E. Gaillard, J. Younan, "State Entities in International Arbitration," *IAI Series on International Arbitration (Juris Publishing)*, 4 (2008): 36.

[14] V. Heisekanen, *State As A Private: The Participation of States in International Commercial Arbitration*, 7, cit. *Svenska Petroleum v. Lithuania*, (2006) APP.L.R. 11/13, 1.

Such a broad interpretation is related to the fact that the state, state entities, instrumentalities or other state organ acts are considered as a state act. Accordingly, if a legal subject concludes a valid arbitration agreement and it is possible to prove a "connection" or link with the state (as in the previous example, the contract was approved by the government, but the party was a state corporation), then the state will be bound by the arbitration agreement and it will be considered valid.

> The content of Article II met strong opposition from Civil Law countries where public entities are, generally, prohibited from resorting to arbitration. To accommodate these states, which otherwise would have not ratified the Convention, a second paragraph providing for the possibility of a reservation was added."[15]

The second paragraph of Article II of the European Convention states that "on signing, ratifying, or acceding to this Convention any State shall be entitled to declare that it limits the above faculty to such conditions as may be stated in its declaration."

## Two Different Approaches

As mentioned previously, more than 30 countries have joined the European Convention, and only two—Belgium and Latvia—have made a declaration.[16] The Belgian Government declared that in Belgium only the state has the faculty to conclude arbitration agreements. This declaration was made after the ad hoc award of Benteler v. Belgium on November 18, 1983.[17] This case, among the other aspects, concerns the main question of whether the state can rely on its national law which contains prohibition for the state to enter into an arbitration agreement with a private party to avoid an arbitration agreement to which it has freely entered. The "Benteler v. Belgium case provides further authority for the proposition that a commercial arbitration between a State and a private party cannot be avoided simply by the State's invoking a prohibition in its own law against

---

[15] D. Hascher, *Commentary on the European Convention*, 516.

[16] Both declarations to the European Convention are available at http://treaties.un.org/Pages/ViewDetails.aspx?src=TREATY&mtdsg_no=XXII-2&chapter=22&lang=en (accessed May 25, 2013).

[17] J. Paulsson, "May a State Invoke its Internal Law to Repudiate Consent to International Commercial Arbitration? Reflections on the Benteler v. Belgium Preliminary Award," *Arbitration International* 2 (2) (1986): 90–103.

arbitration by the State."[18] This principle is based on the following arguments:

First of all, Article 27 of the 1969 Vienna Convention on the Law of Treaties states that the "party may not invoke the provisions of its internal law as justification for its failure to perform a treaty."[19] "It denies that a State can invoke the provisions of its internal law to avoid responsibility for the observance of its treaty obligations and in particular to justify its failure to perform a treaty."[20] Moreover, "the provisions of internal law encompass provisions already in force as well as those which may be enacted subsequent to the treaty. The effective application of Article 27 obliges a State to ensure that all these provisions are compatible or brought into line with its internal obligations."[21]

In other words, if national law does not allow arbitration, but in the European convention the reservation has not been determined, then agreement will be in full effect in case a state concludes an international arbitration agreement. National law will not be considered as an argument to justify the invalidity of the contract. "The prevailing view is that it would be contrary to fundamental principles of good faith for a State party to an international contract, having freely accepted an arbitration clause, later to invoke its own legislation as grounds for contesting the validity of its agreement to arbitrate."[22] These findings are generally based on the fundamental principles of civil and international law *pacta sunt servanda* or "agreement must be kept,"[23] and the prohibition of *venire contra factum proprium*. It should be noted that this is one of the most important principles in the context of the issue.

---

[18] Ibid., 96.

[19] *1969 Vienna Convention on the Law of Treaties*, United Nations, 2005, http://untreaty.un.org/ilc/texts/instruments/english/conventions/1_1_1969.pdf (accessed May 27, 2013).

[20] M. E. Villiger, *Commentary on the 1969 Vienna Convention on the Law of Treaties* (Martinus Nijhoff Publishers, 2009), 371.

[21] Ibid., 372.

[22] J. Paulsson, "May a state invoke its internal law to repudiate consent to international commercial arbitration? Reflections on the Benteler v. Belgium Preliminary Award," *Arbitration International* 2 (2) (1986), 90.

[23] "*Pacta sunt servanda* generates not only the obligation of each party to a contract to fulfil its premises, but also the obligation to perform them in good faith, to compensate for the damage caused to the other party by their non-fulfilment, and not to terminate the contract unilaterally where such termination is not contractually or legally provided for." J. D. M. Lew, *Contemporary Problems in International Arbitration* (London: Springer, 1987), 115.

Contrary to the situation in Belgium, where the declaration was made only after the ad hoc case Benteler v. Belgium, Latvia, in accordance with its Article II when it joined European Convention,[24] declared that Latvian state authorities and government authorities have no right to conclude a valid arbitration agreement.

In 2009, the Ministry of Justice of the Republic of Latvia prepared a first draft[25] to annul the declaration to the European Convention.

> Declaration which Latvia has made joining the Convention, is in compliance with the principles of international trade and international arbitration practice ... Taking into account the intensity of international trade, not only for Latvian businesses, but also for Latvian state authorities it is necessary to agree on a neutral dispute settlement place, not a state court of general jurisdiction.[26]

This draft was supplemented and the faculty concluded arbitration agreements was retained only for state authorities. On the basis of the diversity of opinion, it was decided to not proceed with it further.

In 2011 the Ministry of Justice of the Republic of Latvia prepared a second draft (currently pending at the Parliament)[27] which is different from the previous one because it contains a special mechanism for local government authorities. It states that: "local government authorities before concluding the arbitration agreement shall transmit a draft to the Ministry of Environmental protection and regional development to obtain opinion from the State Chancellery that the arbitration agreement is in conformity with the state interest."[28] The questions in this case are on what the state interest (common good) is, how to determine it, and if it is possible to identify only from the content of the arbitration agreement whether the public interest will be protected.

The interest of the democratic state is to provide and develop a policy directed towards the common good. In order to establish whether the national interest is directed to the common good, it is first necessary to find out what the common good of society is. The main problem is that it is not possible to clearly define what constitutes the common good. First,

---

[24] Latvia joined European Convention on March 20, 2003, see note 16.

[25] Draft and annotation available at *www.mk.gov.lv/doc/2005 /TMAnot_190609_arbitration.2337.doc* (accessed May 12, 2013).

[26] Ibid.

[27] See more information on the Parliament of the Republic of Latvia (Saeima) website, http://titania.saeima.lv/LIVS11/SaeimaLIVS11.nsf/ (accessed May 2, 2013).

[28] Ibid.

the higher values are relative, and, second, different groups of individuals are defined and perceived differently. The main risk is that the notion of the "common good" can be filled with content that represents only the interests of the main political groups.[29] "The public interest is not simply the sum of the individual interests, but also the advance of a healthy and functional community, one where the search of private interests is balanced with the search of the community's interests."[30] Taking political decisions usually means that the decision is consistent with the public interest. "Many who deny that there is a 'public interest' assume that it must be either an interest or concern that all members of the public have or something in which all persons are actually interested … If it is in the public interest, it would appear that it must be in the interest of everyone."[31]

First, it should be noted that the public interest is primarily affected by the nature, purpose, terms and conditions contained in the contract and the parties' tactics during its execution. This means that the arbitration process can be considered as only a part of the aspects which have an effect on state interest. The outcome of the dispute will create a major impact on state interest, while the arbitration clause itself has no direct impact. This means that the arbitration clause may only secondarily affect the state interests.

"In many cases the legislator may find it very difficult or impossible to tell whether a piece of legislation is for the 'common good'."[32] Similarly, in this situation the arbitration clause (a mechanism for dispute resolution) affects only part of the final result. Therefore, it is problematical to ascertain whether and how the arbitration clause together with other factors will affect the state interest.

## State Immunity

The second fundamental principle developed in international commercial practice provides that if the state agrees to conclude an arbitration agreement then it waives its immunity.

---

[29] C. W. Cassinelli, "Some Reflections on the Concept of the Public Interest," *Ethics* 1 (69) (1958): 48–61.

[30] H. Ocampo S, "The Common Good, the Common Interest and the Decision Making Process," *International Management Review* 1 (6) (2010): 7.

[31] B. J. Diggs, "The Common Good as a Reason for Political Action," *Ethics* 4 (83) (1973): 286.

[32] Ibid., 290.

State immunity as a doctrine has experienced a long history of trials in its development. Besides the absolute state immunity doctrine, where the state has absolute immunity no matter the nature of transaction, the restrictive state immunity doctrine has developed which, in contradiction to the first, not only protects the state but also other parties of the contract. Restrictive state immunity can be compared to the scales of justice which, weighing the totality of criteria, decide to provide state immunity. This means that even if one of the parties is the state, both parties are treated equally, and in a case of the state concluding a contract, *acta iure gestionis* with arbitration clause, the state will not be able to claim its immunity.

> Questions of sovereign immunity must be considered at two levels—in relation to (1) jurisdiction and (2) execution. With respect to immunity from jurisdiction, in most cases, the agreement to arbitrate constitutes a waiver of that immunity—both in relation to the arbitral proceedings themselves and any ancillary proceedings in the national courts. However, with respect to enforcement, often neither the arbitration agreement itself nor the New York and ICSID Convention constitute a waiver of the right to immunity from execution. As a result, the incidence and success rate of State parties seeking to resist arbitral awards is higher compared with awards made against commercial entities.[33]

When a state engages in a commercial transaction with a private party and concludes an arbitration agreement, a waiver of immunity from jurisdiction can be proved, but regarding immunity from an execution situation can be more complicated. There are some cases where the court states that "the obligation entered into by the State by signing the arbitration agreement … implies a waiver of the States immunity from execution,"[34] but mainly waiver of this immunity must be proved.

In commercial transactions both parties should be treated equally. State immunity as a legal instrument on the one hand protects the state interests, but on the other creates a significant risk to the merchant. In dealings with the state, in the case of a dispute the private party cannot be secure on whether it will be possible to bring a case to court, and even if it is whether the judgement will be enforceable.

"The undertaking to arbitrate by a foreign State constitutes waiver of immunity from jurisdiction and probably also waiver of immunity from

[33] L. Chung, *Recent Trends in State Immunity*, http://kluwerarbitrationblog.com /blog/2013/04/25/recent-trends-in-state-immunity/ (accessed May 23, 2013).

[34] For example, case Creighton v. Qatar July 6, 2000, see E. Gaillard, "State Entities in International Arbitration," *IAI Series on International Arbitration (Juris Publishing)* 4 (2008): 179.

execution."[35] In order to ensure waiver from both immunities, "a party incorporating an arbitration agreement into a contract with a state party should include not just a reference to the relevant rules of arbitration, but additionally, specific requirements to the effect that immunity (i.e. from execution [author's note]) is waived."[36]

The above analysis shows a number of problematic aspects appearing in the arbitration process when the state is a party. Declaration to European convention, state immunity from jurisdiction and execution, and foremost the state interests are the main aspects which should be analyzed when a commercial party and the state conclude an international commercial agreement with an arbitration clause.

Nērika Lizinska is a doctoral student at the University of Latvia in Rīga.

---

[35] D. Chamlongrasdr, *Foreign State Immunity and Arbitration* (London: Cameron May, 2007), 79.

[36] N. Pengelley, "Waiver of Sovereign Immunity from Execution: Arbitration is Not Enough," *Journal of International Arbitration* 26 (6) (2009): 871.

# PART TWO

# COMMUNICATION AND SELF-ORGANISATION AS ELEMENTS OF REGULATION OF POWER AND SOCIETY

# CHAPTER SIX

# THE CONCEPTION OF THE FREE MARKETPLACE OF IDEAS AND FREEDOM OF POLITICAL SPEECH IN GERMANY: AN HISTORICAL INTRODUCTION

WIESŁAW WACŁAWCZYK

For years, Germany has been perceived as a country where freedom of expression is effectively protected. In the Press Freedom Index 2013, published by the French non-governmental organisation Reporters Without Borders (Reporters Sans Frontières), it was ranked 17 out of 179 countries; in the same ranking for the year 2014, Germany occupied the 14th place amongst 180 states. Although freedom of the press is not the same as freedom of expression, there is little doubt that the former may be regarded as the litmus test of the latter, as well as, to a great degree, the indicator of freedom in general. Does it mean, however, that the above-mentioned conception of a free marketplace of ideas has discovered fertile soil in Germany and finds good conditions for expansion there? Can this country be considered a staunch advocate of the conception under consideration? What is the presumptive evidence upon which one may answer "yes" to these questions, and what are the counterarguments?

This brief text aims at outlining how the conception of "free marketplace of ideas" has been developing in Germany until the present day. It is focused on speech referring to politics, that is to texts and expressions concerning the political relations in the country under consideration. At the same time, it leaves aside other forms of speech, for example texts and expressions pertaining specifically to religion, morals or commerce. Such an approach to the problem seems to be justified, considering the fact that the discussed conception has traditionally been perceived as being applicable, first and foremost, with reference to political speech.

The analysed problem is presented in a historical context. This perspective allows the author to point to the historical roots of the discussed conception and to stress the contribution made to its development by British and American writers, philosophers and jurists; it also helps show the historical differences between the Anglo-Saxon and German approaches to the idea of freedom of expression. It is at the same time a good way of bringing the reader's attention to the circumstances under which Germany began to adapt the conception of the "free marketplace of ideas." Finally, it helps explain why modern history, especially the events of World War II, has made it difficult for the Germans to accept an extremely broad conception of freedom of expression.

The text is not intended to be an in-depth analysis of the contemporary standards of freedom of expression in Germany. Instead, it is meant to be a short introduction to the history of free speech in this country.

## The Birth of the Conception of "Free Marketplace of Ideas"

Historically, the term "free marketplace of ideas" has usually been associated with British and American free speech theoreticians, first and foremost John Milton (1608–1674), John Stuart Mill (1806–1873), Oliver Wendell Holmes Jr. (1841–1935) and Louis Dembitz Brandeis (1856–1941). While Milton and Mill did not use this term literally when expanding on their theories of free speech, their views were rightly considered to be the spiritual inspiration for Justice Holmes, who coined the term under discussion, as well as for Justice Brandeis who, together with Holmes, decisively contributed to making the conception of the "free marketplace of ideas" probably the most influential theory in the free speech case law of the U.S. Supreme Court.

The central assumption of this theory is the assertion that freedom of expression constitutes the precondition of the search for truth. Therefore, only when all kinds of views may be freely expressed is the truth likely to win out. In the case of Abrams v. United States (1919), Holmes wrote in his dissenting opinion:

> … when men have realized that time has upset many fighting faiths they may come to believe even more than they believe the very foundations of their own conduct that the ultimate good desired is better reached by free trade in ideas—that the best test of truth is the power of the thought to get

> itself accepted in the competition of the market, and that truth is the only ground upon which their wishes safely can be carried out.[1]

It is to be remembered that although the conception of a free marketplace of ideas was put forward by Milton in his Areopagitica (1644) and developed by J. S. Mill in *On Liberty* (1859), it was another sixty years after Mill's famous essay appeared before Holmes tried to convert it into a legal doctrine, and another half a century before the U.S. Supreme Court adopted it as such in the case of Brandenburg v. Ohio (1969). It is also worth remembering that the whole idea remains challenging and controversial, especially outside the Anglo-Saxon world, and in Germany as well.

## Historical Premises of the Idea of Free Speech in Germany

While in England liberalism was already, albeit timidly, articulated in Milton's days, German states remained rather impervious to this idea at that time. The situation did not change in the nineteenth century. It is the irony of fate that the motto of *On Liberty* is the following words of the Prussian thinker, Wilhelm von Humboldt (1767–1835): "The grand, leading principle, towards which every argument unfolded in these pages directly converges, is the absolute and essential importance of human development in its richest diversity."[2]

Although the original version of the cited text, entitled *Ideen zu einem Versuch, die Grenzen der Wirksamkeit des Staats zu bestimmen*, was published in 1792, almost seven decades before *On Liberty*, it could not exert any influence on the standards of social life in Prussia, as it was only published in 1852. Apart from that, it is to be remembered that Prussia was not a country where freedom of expression could flourish. In his article entitled *Beantwortung der Frage: Was ist Aufklärung?* (*What is Enlightenment?*), published in 1784, Immanuel Kant (1724–1804) wrote:

---

[1] *Abrams v. United States (No. 316): Holmes, Jr., Dissenting Opinion, Supreme Court of the United States, 250 U.S. 216*, Legal Information Institute, http://www.law.cornell.edu/supct/html/historics/USSC_CR_0250_0616_ZD.html (accessed June 2, 2013).

[2] W. von Humboldt, *The Sphere and Duties of Government: The Limit of State Action* (London: John Chapman, 1854), The Online Library of Liberty http://oll.libertyfund.org/?option=com_staticxt&staticfile=show.php%3Ftitle=589&chapter=45490&layout=html&Itemid=27 (accessed June 2, 2013).

> The enlightenment requires nothing but freedom—and the most innocent of all that may be called "freedom": freedom to make public use of one's reason in all matters. Now I hear the cry from all sides: "Do not argue!" The officer says: "Do not argue—drill!" The tax collector: "Do not argue—pay!" The pastor: "Do not argue—believe!" Only one ruler in the world says: "Argue as much as you please, but obey!" We find restrictions on freedom everywhere. But which restriction is harmful to enlightenment? I reply: the public use of one's reason must be free at all times, and this alone can bring enlightenment to mankind.[3]

Although Kant stressed that discussion on public issues was curbed everywhere in his days, there is little doubt that, not only at that time, free speech limitations were stricter in Prussia and other German-speaking countries than in England. In the first half of the nineteenth century, the most fervent advocate of harsh censorship proved to be the Austrian Chancellor Klemens von Metternich, who regarded freedom of the media as the "scourge of the world."[4] Therefore, at the time under discussion, prior restraint, i.e. censorship before publication, became the norm in German-speaking countries. That was contrary to the ideas promulgated in "Britain, revolutionary America and France," where preventive censorship had been fought over on the premises that "the press should be limited only by the ordinary laws protecting public order, morality, and the rights of individuals, to be enforced by the courts."[5]

In the nineteenth century, the situation of the media in Austria and Germany was often compared to the relevant situation in Spain or Italy, and negatively juxtaposed with the relative freedom of the press in England. Here is how Robert J. Goldstein writes on this topic:

> With regard to the press, historian Frederick Artz notes that an English traveller's comments about the Spanish press in 1820 could have been equally said of that of Austria and Italy: they contained nothing but weather reports and "accounts of miracles wrought by different Virgins, lives of holy friars and sainted nuns, romances of marvelous conversations, libels against Jews, heretics and Freemasons, and histories of apparitions." The great Czech historian Frantisek Palacky complained in 1830, "I do not know how it will end when we cannot write about anything except cook-

[3] I. Kant, *What Is Enlightenment?*, Columbia University, http://www.columbia.edu/acis/ets/CCREAD/etscc/kant.html (accessed June 25, 2013).

[4] R. Lenman, *Germany*, in R. J. Goldstein (ed.), *The War for the Public Mind: Political Censorship in Nineteenth-Century Europe* (Westport: Praeger Publishers, 2000), 40.

[5] Ibid.

> books and prayer-books, fairy-tales and charades," and the Saxon journalist Robert Blum similarly lamented in the 1840s, "We must write pure nonsense or not be published at all." British observer William Howitt wrote in 1844 that the German press published nothing about "all those great questions which involve the political progress and development of a people," as "over all the heads of such journals hangs the iron pen of the censor and fills every writer with terror."[6]

All things considered, at the time under consideration freedom of speech and freedom of the media could not find fertile soil in German-speaking states. Only the wave of revolutions that rolled over Europe in 1848 brought a temporary betterment of the situation in this respect. Still, it proved to be short-lived. Admittedly, prior restraint was abolished and not reintroduced after 1849, yet "books and periodicals remained subject to a multitude of controls."[7] The 1850s turned out to be a decade of new repressions, which "soon had booksellers and publishers harking nostalgically to what they perceived as safer, more predictable conditions under prior censorship."[8]

At that time the media remained, as in 1819–1848, subject to both the individual state and federal legislation.[9] Amongst the most restricting regulations, adopted in the 1850s at both levels, were the federal "Reaction Resolution" of 1851, which encouraged the governments to restrict "atheistic, socialist, communist" as well as "antimonarchical" newspapers and journals; the Federal Press Law of 1854 (BPG), and the Prussian statute of May 12, 1851 (PrPG), which was a year later "supplemented by measures abolishing trial by jury for press offenders, reestablishing newspaper taxes, and making confiscation more effective."[10]

---

[6] R. J. Goldstein, "Introduction," in R. J. Goldstein (ed.), *The War for the Public Mind*, 27–28. The quotations come from O. Brockett, *History of the Theatre* (Boston: Allyn & Bacon, 1977), 369; M. Carlson, *The German Stage in the Nineteenth Century* (Metuchen: Scarecrow Press, 1972), 121; F. Artz, *Reaction and Revolution, 1814–1832* (New York: Harper & Row, 1934), 134–35; J. Zacek, *Metternich's Censors: The Case of Palacky*, in P. Brock, H. Skillings (eds.), *The Czech Renaissance of the Nineteenth Century* (Toronto: University of Toronto Press, 1970), 99; E. Newman, *Restoration Radical: Robert Blum and the Challenge of German Democracy* (Boston, 1974), 46; L. O'Boyle, "The Image of the Journalist in France, Germany and England, 1815–1848," *Comparative Studies in Society and History* 10 (1968): 305.

[7] Ibid., 50.

[8] Ibid., 50–51.

[9] Ibid., 51.

[10] Ibid.

Article 4 of the "*Grundrechte des Deutschen Volkes*" ("The Basic Rights of the German People"), which was part of the "*Verfassung des Deutschen Reiches*" ("The Constitution of the German Empire") of 1849, read: "[1] Every German has the right to freely express his opinions through word, writing, print and pictorial representation. [2] Freedom of the press shall be under no circumstances and in no way … restricted, suspended or cancelled."[11] But the relevant article of the Prussian constitution of 1850 stated: "Censorship shall not be cancelled" ("*Die Zensur darf nicht aufgehoben werden*").[12] The juxtaposition of these two provisions says volumes about the volatility of German free speech regulations in the period under discussion.

A characteristic feature of censorship in nineteenth-century Germany was the instrumental treatment of moral arguments, which were supposed to justify interference with the free-flow of ideas. The source of such an approach to the problem was to be looked for in the practice of theatre censorship.[13]

Also, the *Kaiserreich* could not be regarded as a country of free speech. The repressive censorship of that time proved to be strict and prompt in abridging various forms of expression. In the case of publishers and booksellers, amongst the most-often used means of repression were high recognisance fees (*Kautionszahlungen*), the obligation to present the evidence of dependability (*Zuverlässigkeitnachweis*) and the evidence of respectability (*Unbescholtenheitsnachweis*) as well as the obligation to deliver duty copies of books to the local police authorities.[14] The amendment of Germany's Reich Criminal Code of 1900 ("Lex Heinze") made it possible to introduce new means of restriction concerning literature and art. They contributed, first and foremost, to censoring theatre plays on the grounds of defending moral standards.[15]

---

[11] *Verfassung des Deutschen Reiches ("Frankfurter Reichsverfassung" bzw. Paulskirchen-Verfassung) vom 28. März 1849*; http://www.documentarchiv.de/nzjh/verfdr1848.htm (accessed June 26, 2013), transl. W. W. The original text "*[1] Jeder Deutsche hat das Recht, durch Wort, Schrift, Druck und bildliche Darstellung seine Meinung frei zu äußern. [2] Die Pressefreiheit darf unter keinen Umständen und in keiner Weise … beschränkt, suspendiert oder aufgehoben werden.*" Ibid.

[12] J. Lippmann, *Zensur in Deutschland von der 48er Revolution bis zum 1. Weltkrieg* (München: GRIN Verlag, 2002), 4.

[13] Cz. Karolak, *Wprowadzenie*, in Cz. Karolak (ed.), *Cenzura w Niemczech XX wieku* (Poznań: Wydawnictwo Poznańskie, 2000), 12.

[14] J. Lippmann, *Zensur in Deutschland*, 21.

[15] Ibid.

The Weimar Constitution of 1919 may be regarded as the first German fundamental law that provided an extensive catalogue of individual rights. Its Article 118 stated that "[e]very German is entitled, within the bounds set by general law, to express his opinion freely in word, writing, print, image or otherwise ...."[16] Apart from freedom of speech, the Weimar Constitution provided for such rights as equality before the law, freedom to move and settle down, the right to use a foreign language, freedom of private life or the right to privacy of correspondence.[17] Its Article 114 read: "The rights of the individual are inviolable. Limitation or deprivation of individual liberty is admissible only if based on a law."[18] One may say that the Weimar Constitution was, at least to some extent, the epitomisation of Humbold's ideas set forth in "*Ideen zu einem Versuch, die Grenzen der Wirksamkeit des Staats zu bestimmen.*"

## After World War II—Towards More Freedom of Expression

After the experiences of Nazism, Germany adopted in 1949 a constitution in which fundamental rights and freedoms were given their proper place. Article 5 of this constitution, named "Freedom of expression, arts and sciences," reads:

> (1) Every person shall have the right freely to express and disseminate his opinions in speech, writing and pictures, and to inform himself without hindrance from generally accessible sources. Freedom of the press and freedom of reporting by means of broadcasts and films shall be guaranteed. There shall be no censorship.
> (2) These rights shall find their limits in the provisions of general laws, in provisions for the protection of young persons, and in the right to personal honour.
> (3) Arts and sciences, research and teaching shall be free. The freedom of teaching shall not release any person from allegiance to the constitution.[19]

---

[16] *The Weimar Constitution of 1919*, http://www.global-ethic-now.de/gen-eng/0c_weltethos-und-politik/0c-02-menschenrechte/0c-02-138-weimarer-verfassung.php# (accessed June 28, 2013).
[17] Ibid.
[18] Ibid.
[19] *Basic Law for the Federal Republic of Germany*, https://www.btg-bestellservice.de/pdf/80201000.pdf (accessed June 29, 2013).

The influence of the experiences of Nazism on the content of the German Basic Law seems obvious in light of the provided article. The mentions of "protection of young persons," "the right to personal honour" or the duty of teachers to abide by the constitution clearly betray this influence. It is to be remembered that the constitution under discussion was framed in turbulent times, when the memory of war atrocities was still very fresh, the world stood at the threshold of the Cold War and it seemed obvious that media may exert a powerful, at times destructive impact on people's minds.

One thing is beyond doubt—Article 5 of the German Basic Law does not provide for absolute freedom of expression. When juxtaposed with the free speech clause of the First Amendment to the U.S. Constitution, which reads: "Congress shall make no law … abridging the freedom of speech, or of the press,"[20] the conception that the free marketplace of ideas could develop in the United States rather than in Germany seems understandable. Whereas the quoted clause of the First Amendment seems to absolutely protect freedom of speech and freedom of the media, Article 5 provides only for the limited protection of these freedoms.

Moreover, it is not only the article in question that makes free speech protection a qualified right in light of the German Constitution of 1949. Another is Article 1, named "Human dignity—Human rights—Legally binding force of basic rights." It reads:

> (1) Human dignity shall be inviolable. To respect and protect it shall be the duty of all state authority.
> (2) The German people therefore acknowledge inviolable and inalienable human rights as the basis of every community, of peace and of justice in the world.
> (3) The following basic rights shall bind the legislature, the executive and the judiciary as directly applicable law.[21]

This article obviously recalls the relevant part of the Universal Declaration of Human Rights, which was adopted only a few months earlier than the German Constitution of 1949. According to Article 1 of the Declaration: "All human beings are born free and equal in dignity and rights. They are endowed with reason and conscience and should act towards one another

---

[20] *U.S. Constitution: First Amendment*, http://www.law.cornell.edu/constitution/first_amendment (accessed June 29, 2013).

[21] *Basic Law for the Federal Republic of Germany.*

with a spirit of brotherhood."[22] Emphasis on human dignity in both documents may be regarded as the premise allowing some kinds of speech to be curbed. First and foremost, it seems to concern inflammatory speech, i.e. words or symbolic speech directed at persons that are not welcome in a certain community and may easily become subject to discrimination and victims of violence. Such kinds of speech are usually underpinned by discriminatory moods. Open or hidden reluctance or hatred to people who differ in their ethnic or national origin, religion, language, colour of skin, political views, etc. often lead to actions directed against stigmatized groups and pose the most serious challenge to the principle of the free marketplace of ideas.

Enshrining human dignity in a legal document, especially in its preamble or first article, has tangible consequences. In general, it legitimises individual rights and freedoms, while at the same time mitigating some of them, first and foremost freedom of speech and freedom of assembly. These two liberties, although very basic civil rights, may pose a danger to other rights, such as the right to private life, a good name, etc. The position of "human dignity" in the German Constitution is very strong. *Das Deutsche Grundgesetz* contains a number of guarantees, amongst which the term under discussion is of special importance. Here is how Jutta Limbach expands on this:

> (1) The basic freedoms of the constitution—such as democracy, the **rule of law**, the principle of the **social state**, **federalism**, respect of **human dignity**—may not be altered at all; not even by a constitutional amendment. The aim was to prevent the **enemies of democracy** from overturning it using its own instruments—like majority rule.
>
> (2) According to art. 1 (1) **human dignity** is the **unalterable foundation** of the constitutional order. The confession to the inviolability of human dignity and personality was and is a response to the perversion of law in the Third Reich and the mass murder in the shadow of this injustice. Therefore, the state is not only obliged to respect, but also to protect human dignity.

[22] *The Universal Declaration of Human Rights*, http://www.un.org/en/documents/udhr/ (accessed July 1, 2013).

> (3) Crowned by the principle of human dignity, the fundamental rights have legally binding force ....[23]

It so happened that the first seminal decision of the German Federal Constitutional Court (Bundesverfassungsgericht: BVerfG) concerned freedom of speech. In the Lüth case (1958), Erich Lüth, who headed the Press Association in Hamburg, publically called for a boycott of the film *Immortal Beloved*, directed by Veit Harlan. The latter was known in the Third Reich for his anti-Semitic movies. The producer and distributors of *Immortal Beloved* started a civil action against Lüth, ending with success as civil courts issued an injunction prohibiting him "from repeating his call for a boycott."[24] Later, Lüth filed a constitutional complaint in the Bundesverfassungsgericht, in which "he asserted that the civil courts had violated his constitutional rights of free expression."[25] The Bundesverfassungsgericht ruled that Lüth was right. The justices "found that constitutional rights exercised a very great 'influence' on cases of private law and that, in the process of balancing that the Court required for cases of this type, Lüth's rights of free expression outweighed the countervailing interests of the film distributors."[26]

The Lüth case is hailed today as a milestone in the case law of the Bundesverfassungsgericht. It is often looked upon as the case that introduced "the German model of rights adjudication" and that signified "both the foundation of a whole new 'paradigm of rights adjudication,' and the lasting influence of much older, deeply rooted Continental ideas about law and judicial lawmaking."[27] Comparing the American and German traditions of judicial balancing, the quoted author asserts that while the former is politicised, the latter shows "that judicial balancing in constitutional cases does not have to be politics, it can be law."[28]

---

[23] J. Limbach, *How a Constitution Can Safeguard Democracy: The German Experience*, http://www.law.hku.hk/ccpl/Docs/JuttaLimbach.pdf (accessed July 2, 2013).

[24] P. E. Quint, "A Return to Lüth," *Roger Williams University Law Review* 16 (1973): 75,
http://digitalcommons.law.umaryland.edu (accessed July 2, 2013).

[25] Ibid., 75–76.

[26] Ibid., 76.

[27] J. Bomhoff, "'Lüth's' 50th Anniversary: Some Contemporary Observations on the German Foundations of Judicial Balancing," *German Law Journal* 2 (9): 124, http://www.germanlawjournal.com/pdfs/Vol09No02/PDF_Vol_09_No_02_121-124_Articles_Bomhoff.pdf (accessed July 2, 2013).

[28] Ibid.

The Lüth case did not mean that the German Federal Constitutional Court was ready to give a free hand to any speaker who attempted to silence another. In the Blinkfüer case (1969), the same court ruled that a call for boycott made by the Springer company against a small, pro-communist weekly journal did not deserve constitutional protection. András Sajó comments on this case as follows:

> The Constitutional Court argued that the economic power of the Springer concern deprived the appellant of the opportunity for expression. The German position implies that the state has certain obligations to create conditions enabling the exercise of rights, for example, by protecting speech against private repression, including repression by more powerful speakers.[29]

The decision in the Blinkfüer case was a signal that, according to the Bundesverfassungsgericht, freedom of speech should not be seen as a privilege of the rich and mighty. On the other hand, neither in the Blinkfüer nor in the Lüth did the German Federal Constitutional Court rule that freedom of speech should have a privileged position amongst other civil liberties. Pursuant to the assumption taken by the Court, the Constitution of 1949 expresses "an objective hierarchy of values" which "centers upon dignity of the human personality developing freely within the social community," and which "must be looked upon as a fundamental constitutional decision affecting all spheres of law [public and private]."[30] Whereas the U.S. Supreme Court was, at least for some time, of the opinion that the First Amendment rights occupy a "preferred position,"[31] the Bundesverfassungsgericht assumed a more moderate course and stressed the binding force of "an objective hierarchy of values" and the value of judicial balancing.

The question is whether the German Constitutional Court consistently stuck to these principles. Bernd Rüthers stresses that freedom of the media and protection of personality rights are at odds, and that in Germany the former takes the upper hand over the latter. To justify his opinion, he points to a series of controversial decisions made by the Bundesfervassungsgericht. For example, Rüthers notes that according to one of these decisions (BverfG 86, 1, 11 ff) a handicapped retired officer of Bundeswehr must not be called "a cripple" (*Krüppel*) in a satirical journal, yet it was allowable to call him, regarding his military rank, "a

[29] A. Sajó, *Freedom of Expression* (Warsaw: Institute of Public Affairs, 2004), 59.
[30] Ibid., 58.
[31] R. L. Holsinger, *Media Law* (New York: Random House 1987), 26.

born murderer" ("*geb. Mörder*").[32] In congruence with another ruling of the same court (BverfG NJW 1994, 2943; BverGE 93, 266), a car sticker with the inscription "Soldiers are Murderers" ("*Soldaten sind Mörder*"), displayed by an opponent of military service, was regarded as a case of exercising the right to freedom of expression, and not as collective insult of Bundeswehr.[33] Referring to another of the mentioned decisions (BverGE 82, 43 und 272), Rüthers deplores that a democratically elected politician, Franz J. Strauss, the long-time minister-president of Bayern, could be described as a "friend of Nazis" ("*Faschistenfreund*") and a "forced democrat" ("*Zwangsdemokrat*").[34] Rüthers does not understand why the Bundesvassungsgericht pays no attention to the impropriety of the term "methods of Gestapo" ("*Gestapo-Methoden*") used to describe lawful means employed by a state institution (BverfG NJW 1992, 2815).[35] The reason for his indignation is also the German Federal Constitutional Court's indulgence for certain terms used by prisoners to insult employees of judicature. The terms in question are "hypocritical preachers of justice" (*verlogene Gerechtigketsprediger*) coined with reference to judges, "perverse" ("*pervers*"), "sadistic" ("*sadistisch*") and "morons" ("*Kretins*"), used with reference to prison service functionaries, and "the red mob" ("*rotes Dreckvolk*") applied with reference to prosecutors (Nachw. bei Tröndler/Fischer, StGB, 49. Aufl., § 193 Rdnr. 14 r.).[36]

Being convinced that Germany acquires the American legal standards of free speech protection, which are not compatible with the German Constitution, Rüthers asks rhetorically whether media law in Germany is in line with the Roman principle according to which "the law is the friend of the weak" ("*Das Gesetz ist ein Freund der Schwachen*").[37] To his mind, those who try to defend the personal honour ("*persönliche Ehre*") of the individual against the Fourth Estate, as the media are often referred to, fight a losing battle.

The question of which of the two is more important—freedom of expression or the protection of personal honour—is usually answered in

[32] B. Rüthers, "Medienfreiheit und Persönlichkeitsschutz im Konflikt: Erfahrungen und Grundsätze in Praxis und Lehre der Bundesrepublik Deutschland," in J. Krukowski, O. Theisen (eds.), *Materialen der 2. internationalen Tagung zum Thema Medienfreiheit: Lublin, 18.-19. Mai 2000* (Lublin: Towarzystwo Naukowe Katolickiego Uniwersytetu Lubelskiego 2002), 84.

[33] Ibid.

[34] Ibid.

[35] Ibid.

[36] Ibid.

[37] Ibid., 112.

favour of the former when "expression" is qualified as "political speech," i.e. speech that refers to political issues in the broad meaning of the term (basically, various forms of expression raising public concern). In this case, even extremely offensive speech is protected. Here is Bundesverfassungsgericht's stance on this issue, expressed in the Campaign Slur case (61 BVerfGE 1; 1982).

> This basic right guarantees to all persons the right to freedom of expression, without expressly distinguishing between a value judgment and a statement of fact. Everyone is at liberty to speak his mind freely whether or not he is able to furnish verifiable reasons for his judgment. At the same time the purpose of free speech is to form opinions, persuade, and exert an intellectual influence over other persons. This is why value judgments, always meant to convince others, are protected by Article 5 (1) [1] of the Basic Law. The basic right is designed primarily to protect the speaker's personal opinion. It is irrelevant whether an opinion is valuable or worthless, correct or false, or whether it is emotional or rational. If the opinion in question contributes to the intellectual struggle of opinions on an issue of public concern, it is presumed protected by the principle of free expression. Even caustic and exaggerated statements, particularly those uttered in the heat of an election campaign, are fundamentally within the protection of Article 5 (1) [1] ....[38]

Giving preference to political speech is, in general, a characteristic feature of the Western approach to freedom of expression. Regarded as a natural exponent of democracy, this approach emphasises the watchdog function of the media, and stresses that a free marketplace of political ideas is the indispensable precondition of the search for truth in public life. This assumption underpins the free speech case law of the U.S. Supreme Court and the European Court of Human Rights in Strasbourg. These two courts have exerted the greatest influence on the development of legal free speech standards in the Western world. In 1976, the European Court of Human Rights decided the case of Handyside v. United Kingdom and expressed the following view:

> The Court's supervisory functions oblige it to pay the utmost attention to the principles characterizing a "democratic society." Freedom of expression constitutes one of the essential foundations of such a society, one of the basic conditions for its progress and for the development of every man. Subject to paragraph 2 of Article 10 (art. 10-2), it is applicable not only to "information" or "ideas" that are favourably received or

[38] D. P. Kommers, *Constitutional Jurisprudence of the Federal Republic of Germany* (Durham: Duke University Press 1997), 379.

> regarded as inoffensive or as a matter of indifference, but also to those that offend, shock or disturb the State or any sector of the population. Such are the demands of that pluralism, tolerance and broadmindedness without which there is no "democratic society."[39]

In 1964, the US Supreme Court gave its verdict in the case of *The New York Times* v. Sullivan, which is often considered to be the greatest landmark decision concerning freedom of speech. The best-known excerpt from this decision reads: "[W]e consider this case against the background of a profound national commitment to the principle that debate on public issues should be uninhibited, robust, and wide-open, and that it may well include vehement, caustic, and sometimes unpleasantly sharp attacks on government and public officials."[40]

It is difficult not to notice that the above-cited decisions in the cases of Campaign Slur, Handyside and Sullivan have something in common. They all stress the importance of public debate with which the term "political speech" is strictly connected. It is also difficult to deny that the free speech case law of the U.S. Supreme Court has influenced, at least to some extent, the relevant case law of the European Court of Human Rights, which, in turn, exerted a significant impact on the adequate jurisprudence of the German Federal Constitutional Court.

The protection of freedom of political speech in Germany is strong but not absolute. According to Article 130 of the Strafgesetzbuch (German penal code), *Volksverhetzung*, i.e. "incitement of the people," is punishable; pursuant to Article 86a, using symbols of "unconstitutional

---

[39] *Case of Handyside v. The United Kingdom*, http://hudoc.echr.coe.int/sites/eng/pages/search.aspx?i=001-57499 (accessed July 6, 2013). The mentioned Article 10 of the European Convention of Human Rights reads as follows: "1. Everyone has the right to freedom of expression. This right shall include freedom to hold opinions and to receive and impart information and ideas without interference by public authority and regardless of frontiers. This Article (art. 10) shall not prevent States from requiring the licensing of broadcasting, television or cinema enterprises. 2. The exercise of these freedoms, since it carries with it duties and responsibilities, may be subject to such formalities, conditions, restrictions or penalties as are prescribed by law and are necessary in a democratic society, in the interests of national security, territorial integrity or public safety, for the prevention of disorder or crime, for the protection of health or morals, for the protection of the reputation or rights of others, for preventing the disclosure of information received in confidence, or for maintaining the authority and impartiality of the judiciary." Ibid.

[40] *New York Times Co. v. Sullivan*, http://www.bc.edu/bc_org/avp/cas/comm/free_speech/nytvsullivan.html (accessed July 6, 2013).

organisations" is outlawed (e.g. the Swastika, Nazi banners, uniforms, Nazi salute, etc.). In the Holocaust Denial case (90 Bverf GE 241; 1994), the Bundesfassungsgericht ruled that "a demonstrably untrue fact is not protected by the guarantee of freedom of expression."[41] The case under consideration concerned the question of the "Auschwitz Hoax" associated with the controversial historian David Irving. In the Flag Desecration case (81 BverfGE 278; 1990), the German Constitutional Court decided that the disparagement of national symbols must be criminalised. The position of the Bunderfassungsgericht, that the law ought to be used to protect the flag, is clearly different from the stance of the U.S. Supreme Court, which decided that burning a national flag is a protected form of expression (cases: Texas v. Johnson [1989], United States v. Eichman [1990]). Commenting on this issue, Ute Krüdewagen suggests that "the United States and Germany have different concepts of democracy," as "[w]hile the American concept is based on the spirit of popular sovereignty, the German concept is based on the notion that the democratic state needs to defend its own foundations."[42]

## Conclusions

Beyond doubt, present-day Germany subscribes to the concept of the free marketplace of ideas. Although the notion of human dignity has a uniquely strong position in the German Constitution, it does not undermine freedom of political speech in the country. It only moderates it, and rather selectively, for the practice of restricting speech concerns mainly questions such as "Holocaust denial," the "Auschwitz lie" or Nazi symbols. This content-based restriction may be, in turn, subject to criticism, as it is not in line with the idea of the free flow of political views. In fact, Germany is sometimes criticised "for dealing only with the very specific problem of banning hate speech directed at a single minority, which is seen as particularly deserving of protection given Germany's

---

[41] "Holocaust Denial Case, Germany (1994)," *Media Law and Freedom of Expression*, http://www.mlfoe.org/Article/Detail.aspx?ArticleUid=6a24251f-ed8b-4e9f-b4f0-8cb11c2884c0 (accessed July 7, 2013).

[42] U. Krüdewagen, "Political Symbols in Two Constitutional Orders: The Flag Desecration Decisions of the United States Supreme Court and the German Federal Constitutional Court," *Arizona Journal of International and Comparative Law* 2 (19) (2002): 704, http://www.ajicl.org/AJICL2002/vol192/Krudewagen.pdf (accessed July 7, 2013). Footnotes were omitted from the the quoted excerpt.

Nazi past."[43] In this connection, the "Holocaust denial" is perceived as "unworthy in the face of the dignity interest."[44]

To sum up, one may say that Germany can now be regarded as a country where freedom of political speech is the rule that rarely allows exceptions. Being a party to the European Convention of Human Rights and subject to the jurisdiction of the European Court of Human Rights, it abides, in general, by the standards of free speech protection worked out in the case law of the latter. It must be added, however, that the country's Nazi past still remains an important factor shaping its approach to the standards under discussion.

Wiesław Wacławczyk is a habilitated doctor of Political Science at the Nicolaus Copernicus University in Toruń. He specialises in human rights and mass communication issues.

[43] A. Sajó, *Freedom of Expression*, 66.
[44] Ibid.

# CHAPTER SEVEN

# PUBLIC SPEAKING: THE SOURCE IN RESEARCHING POLITICAL THOUGHT

TOMASZ WICHA

## Introduction

The art of public speaking was developed by ancient Greeks and since that time has played an important role in many spheres of human life. It can be perceived as a process, not just the final product of human actions. The core of public speaking is to make sure that the structure is compatible with the purpose of the speech. The functions of public speaking are worth considering if one wants to adjust the message properly to the target audience. The informative, persuasive and entertaining functions of public speaking are analysed in this chapter. The ability to speak in public is perceived as an art, as it is much more than the pure presentation of facts in sentences, which may wrongly lead the audience to think that the function of public speaking can be classified as advertising. Such understanding of public speaking is applicable in politics as it may serve as a source in researching political thought.

One may distinguish five general dimensions of public speaking which remain unchanged in the process of delivering a political speech. The aspect of who transfers a certain message to whom is of utmost importance if the process of communication exchange is to take place efficiently. Moreover, the medium of the communication process influences the transfer of the message which may have an impact on the effect of the whole process of coding and encoding the message. Finally, the purpose of the intercourse is crucial for the complete understanding of the process of exchanging information, as public speaking varies from telling a story to a child to political speeches.

## Speaking in Public

If one wants to make reference to the old English proverb that "talk is cheap," one ought to alter it, taking into account the fact that talking efficiently in a deliberate manner in twenty-first century is much more precious than ever before, especially in politics. Throughout history, one may find the occupations that aimed at traveling from one place to another with the purpose of entertaining or conveying information as channels for interpersonal communication were limited and there were few chances for delivering a message to the addressee in a faster way.[1]

There are people who consider the art of public speaking a natural and an inborn human capability. Others claim that the talent of speaking in public must be practiced if it is to be efficient. The speechmaking market is available in almost every field of human activity. A proficient speaker is able to attract thousands of people by a single speech, as it is a vital means of communication.[2]

The point of political public speaking is to make an outstanding impression through the use of one's talent and skills. It does not presuppose great modification which may aim at altering the life of the receiver. However, public speaking focuses on fulfilling the needs of the audience so that the receivers are ready to change their minds with regard to a particular situation or an event. Such an event links a topic of a public speech to the purpose of the meeting that actually takes place, which is mostly a persuasive one in political speeches.

Public speaking provides the opportunity to persuade people towards an option a speaker wishes the audience to choose. A speech may have an informative or entertaining purpose which focuses on the change of the attitude of the audience. An ordinary person spends as much as 30% of their daily life talking to others.[3] There are certain skills incorporated into the process of talking to other people in public.

The logical organisation of thoughts is the first step a speaker takes. Sometimes a direct statement cannot be made as it might be perceived as offensive to the receiver or not suitable as far as the tone of the utterance is concerned. The speaker, taking into account the fact that they want to be understood clearly, does not begin a speech with a final point or from the middle of an event that is described. The maximum impact effect is possible only when the story is built carefully and a tone of voice is

---

[1] J. Fast, *Body Language: Making Body Language Work in the Workplace* (New York: Viking 1991).

[2] S. Lucas, *The Art of Public Speaking* (Wisconsin: Random House, 1989), 4.

[3] Ibid., 5.

adjusted so that the best effect is achieved. The adaptation to the feedback of listeners is compulsory if one wants to benefit from one's own speech. Three kinds of reactions can be distinguished: (1) verbal (primarily during open meetings that promote equal rights of a speaker and an audience to participate in the process of a verbal exchange), (2) facial, and (3) physical reactions.

Training in public speaking provides a chance to make use of the skills taught in everyday encounters. Still, everyday conversations and public speaking are not alike.[4] Public speaking is structured in a clear way, with an exact timeframe assigned to a particular speaker as there are almost always time limitations which affect the process of an interaction between the speaker and the audience. Limited time makes the audience unable to ask questions or comment on the speech which somewhat impairs the process of getting to know the points presented. Moreover, the points of the speech are to be covered within the time assigned as there is sometimes no time for the discussion, which might act as the completion of what has not been said.[5] Some cognitive process takes place during the preparation of the speech as the speaker ought to take into account the queries that may arise in the audience regarding the facts or the situation presented with the use of the speech.[6] Finally, public speaking requires a more detailed plan. In contrast, everyday conversations are mainly unplanned and have no clear structure.

The analysis of the target audience is necessary for the process of efficient public speaking as it is often the case that the audience remains unknown to the speaker. Formal language with no jargon and bad grammar is one demand of public speaking. Even though the informality of many aspects of human activities is recommended, the audience generally reacts in a negative way to the speaker who does not use grammar carefully or does not polish the language of the speech. Public speaking needs to be somehow "special" in terms of the environment, the purpose of the speech and, consequently, grammar and lexis.

A different method of delivery is the final dissimilarity between a casual conversation and the one delivered in public. There is an exclusion of interjections in formal language and a special posture is adapted to the audience. Moreover, the tone of voice is stable and does not convey

---

[4] M. Corballis, *From Hand to Mouth: The Origins of Language* (Princeton: Princeton University Press, 2002).

[5] G. Brown, G. Yule, *Discourse Analysis* (Cambridge-New York: Cambridge University Press, 1983).

[6] N. Boothman, *How to Make People Like You in 90 Seconds or Less* (New York: Workman Publishing, 2000).

emotions to the extent that it does in everyday communication. Some verbal habits and mannerisms, which might be distracting to the audience, are to be condemned in public speaking, as opposed to informal conversations, which attract such aspects of communication.

Stage fright is one of the most important aspects inhibiting the communication process. It evokes great fear which can be won over by preparation and practice of speaking in public. Stage fright provokes anxiety no matter the age of the speaker. Still, those who are successful have learnt how to deal with nervousness as it is indispensable for success. Something unknown makes people nervous, but being nervous is claimed to be normal for those who aim at proficiency in public speaking.

Picking up the topics that the speaker cares about is one of the options for dealing with unavoidable stress.[7] Moreover, public speaking can be compared to a play and, similar to a performance, a speech needs to be polished if it aims to be attractive to the audience. Confidence increases with the process of thorough preparation. Studying the audience and many rehearsals are some promoted ways to deal with stage fright.

Positive thinking is one of the most important aspects one needs to build on to become a good speaker.[8] The visualisation of one's efficient speech helps to overcome stress and may lead to confidence and enable powerful delivery. Physical and mental preparation is indispensable for those who focus on proficiency in becoming a good speaker. Moreover, concentration must be promoted by the speaker, not by the audience, as hardly anyone will be interested in the topic if the speaker does not make an effort to make it attractive to the public.

Special attention has to be given to the introduction as it is claimed to serve as an incentive for the audience, but may affect the public in a negative way so that they are going to be lost at the beginning of the delivery. Building confidence at the beginning of one's speech may be beneficial for the whole process of a verbal exchange. Making eye contact that is not invasive towards the audience can be promoted as an individual approach, and is a sign of taking care of the receivers. Moreover, the use of visual aids can be helpful in emergency situations, although Lucas[9] pinpoints that they may act as distractions and thus should be used after thorough consideration.

---

[7] M. Corballis *From Hand to Mouth*, 8 and foll.

[8] N. Boothman, *How to Make People Like You*, 10 and foll.

[9] S. Lucas, *The Art of Public Speaking*, 35–116.

The perception of a mistake is yet another difference between casual conversation and public speaking.[10] Making mistakes in everyday interactions is normal, whereas in public speeches it can be perceived as a catastrophe. Still, it makes the speech more "human," as it is human to make mistakes. Lucas[11] recalls the case of Princess Diana who had problems with uttering the name of Prince Charles during her wedding ceremony.

## The Importance of Critical Thinking

Speaking in public implies the necessity for proper recognition of what critical thinking is. Lucas[12] calls it the ability to spot weaknesses in other people's arguments and the capability for dealing with them as soon as possible. Avoiding false arguments or improper suppositions is one of the core aspects a proficient speaker needs to take into account. Such understanding of logic involves the application of the correlated skills like distinguishing facts from opinions, the evaluation of what is true within the debate and judging the intention of the receivers.[13] Critical thinking focuses on the organised ability to think in a logical way. In its strict sense, the organisation of speech is not a pure mechanical activity as some other skills need to be incorporated within the process of encoding the information to the audience.

Regardless of the kind of the speech, one may distinguish seven elements of any communication process. The speaker is the first indispensable component if the process of delivering a speech is to take place. Obviously, there must be a message in the communication process otherwise the communication is pure nonsense. There is a special channel for a given exchange that is chosen after the analysis of the audience, the feedback (indirect or direct) and the listener. The communication process needs a particular situation and topic which lead to interaction.

Any speech begins with some intention the speaker has which is presented explicitly or remains unknown to the public. The speaker plays a

---

[10] C. Lavington, *You've Only Got Three Seconds: How to Make the Right Impression in Your Business and Social Life* (New York: Doubleday, 1997), 20–58.

[11] S. Lucas, *The Art of Public Speaking*, 13.

[12] Ibid., 14.

[13] D. Efron, S. van Veen, *Gesture and Environment: a Tentative Study of Some of the Spatio-temporal and "Linguistic" Aspects of the Gestural Behavior of Eastern Jews and Southern Italians in New York City, Living under Similar as Well as Different Environmental Conditions* (New York: Morningside Heigths, 1941).

double role in the process of speech communication as he or she is simultaneously the speaker and the listener in the encounter. The listener is active if some exchange is possible or remains passive in public speeches when the chance, if given, occurs after the delivery. Usually, public speeches occur with no interjection which might interrupt the process.[14] The success of the speech depends on the abilities of the speaker and their knowledge of the topic in its broader sense. The sensitivity to the audience and the responses is of utmost importance for the process of efficient communication.[15] Successful speaking is much more than pure technical activity. With no engagement and little enthusiasm, even a very well-prepared speech may turn out to be ineffective.

Whatever the speaker communicates to the audience is called the message. The notion of the message is sometimes spread to whatever the speaker wishes to deliver, even though sometimes not everything is spoken in an outright way. The message comprises a special tone of voice which might be evocative. A human being is able to convey some extra meaning to the message such as hesitation and reluctance, in particular when the message is delivered orally.

The goal of the message is to communicate the intended meaning. The intention may change within the process of delivering the speech and is natural. Both verbal and non-verbal aspects are to be taken into account in public speeches as it is not only what one says but how they do so. Some modification of the verbal organisation of the speech is necessary as there are limitations to speaking in public. Time is one of them, and narrowing the topic is therefore indispensable to conveying the meaning successfully.[16] Choosing the details that will support the thesis is yet another way to deal with the process of encoding the message in an efficient way.

Clear and appropriate register of the message increases the chances of its understanding. The language of the message ought to be neither sophisticated nor simplified. Sending the message does not limit itself to words, as non-verbal aspects of public communication are important for the process.[17]

The means by which the message is communicated comprise the channel. Channels may vary from a telephone to other technological

---

[14] S. Lucas, *The Art of Public Speaking*, 15.

[15] L. Holliday Willey, *Pretending to be Normal: Living with Asperger's Syndrome* (London-Philadelphia: Jessica Kingsley, 1999).

[16] D. McNeill, *Hand and Mind: What Gestures Reveal about Thought* (Chicago: University of Chicago Press, 1992), 10–65.

[17] J. Jacobi, *How to Say It with Your Voice* (New York: Paramus, 2000), 34–76.

devices available on the market. There is a distinction between a direct and indirect channel, assigned to such channels as radio that transfer the message with no visualization of the speaker.

The person that attempts to decode the message is called the listener or the receiver, and there are a great number of listeners in public speaking. The notion of the listener's frame of reference needs to be introduced at this stage, and enables some filtering of what has been said.[18] Such a process is individual as somebody's frame of reference is assigned to a particular person and comprises such aspects as life experience, understanding the intention of the speaker and sharing the values processed within the speech. The individual aspect of the frame implies some disparity between what has been said and what is received.

Testing one's frame of reference is possible at every stage of getting to know the audience. It is easily detected by asking the receivers to talk about a given issue. Some of the test subjects might have a similar opinion about the object, but this does not mean that it will be shared if some other object is under consideration. Such a situation does not imply the fact that people differ, but the necessity for adaptation to the message so that it can be understood by the majority of the audience.

Being audience-oriented ought to be the aim of the speaker in the communication process.[19] The speaker cannot be egoistic in setting the agenda of the speech, and being audience-centred is advisable at every stage of speaking in public. The assumption that the audience will be interested in what is said is wrong as delivering a speech with no involvement is barely possible. The knowledge of the audience is not limited to pure facts but their experience, walks of life and even getting to know the hobbies of the receivers might be beneficial for the process of exchanging information.

There are two aspects of communication that have to be taken into consideration: one-way and two-way communication. The fact that some politicians talk to the camera does not presuppose that this is one-way communication. Most situations involve two-way communication as there is not only the absorption of the message of the receiver but also the process of sending messages back, which is called feedback.

There are many aspects of feedback in verbal and nonverbal communication. The message which is sent by the reaction can be decoded

---

[18] A. Kendon, *How Can Gestures Become like Words?*, in F. Potoyas (ed.), *Cross-cultural Perspectives in Nonverbal Communication* (Toronto: Lewiston, 1988), 131–141.

[19] S. Davis, *Pragmatics: A Reader* (New York-Oxford: Oxford University Press, 1991), 23–56.

by the speaker, as he or she needs the response to make the speech more efficient. The notion of the personal frame of reference is applicable at this stage as well.[20] The extent to which feedback is affected by personal attitude towards the speaker cannot be assessed without context. Understanding the feedback enables the reaction that might be divergent, as there are some stages of feedback that the sender needs to take into account if he or she wants to process it in an efficient way.

Impediments that intrude into the process of communication are called interference. The fact that they impede public speaking may implicate wrong feedback.[21] The distraction from what is said might be the reason for misunderstanding. The majority of the interference comes from the audience who may speak or whisper during the speech. Holding the attention of the audience is crucial while dealing with interference.

## Conclusions

The situation of public interaction contains the place and the time in which communication takes place. There is no conversation without the environment affecting the process of communication. The situation is hardly ever neutral to the process of delivering the speech. Being alert to the situation is a necessity for the speaker as it affects the delivery of the message.

The physical setting of the speech is of utmost importance as well. There are certain implications that have to be thoroughly analysed while delivering a speech outdoors because there might be some unpredictable impediments, and making a speech indoors is considered to be safer for the speaker. Adjusting to the situation is a necessity for the speaker if the process of delivering a speech is to take place.[22]

The speechmaking process, as a powerful means, needs to be ethical if it aims to be informative, persuasive or entertaining. Being fair with oneself is the best bet not only for the speaker but also for the audience. Abusing the power of the speech may lead to disastrous effects if the ethical responsibilities are not met. Lucas[23] points out that Hitler was a great speaker who persuaded successfully but the tactics he undertook were despicable. Hitler and Stalin are examples of the necessity of the spoken word to be guided by integrity. The issue of integrity and ethics

---

[20] R. Kraut, R. Johnston, "Social and emotional images of smiling: An ethological approach," *Journal of Personality and Social Psychology* 42 (1979): 1529–1553.

[22] M. Hauser, *The Evolution of Communication* (Cambridge: MIT Press, 1996).

[23] S. Lucas, *The Art of Public Speaking*, 20.

cannot be separated from the goal of the speech, and the end does not always justify the means.

Over the years, scientists have set up some guidelines for speechmaking, the core of which is to become well informed about the topic and not deceive the audience. The obligation to explore the topic thoroughly does not link to the audience only but also, and first of all, to the speaker. The investigation of the story that takes into account both sides of a given issue and getting the facts is one of the issues the addressee needs to take into account. Being honest is another issue, as hardly any ethical communication takes place when false arguments are presented in a way that is disparate from the actual facts. Subjective opinions cannot be presented as exact evidence or final conclusions. The next step is the use of sound evidence, as the arguments that one depicts need some explanation and support. Qualified information and valid reasoning are promoted at any step of the process of delivering the speech.

Tomasz Wicha, M.A. is a PhD candidate at the Department of Political Science of the Maria Curie-Skłodowska University. His scientific interests concentrate on theory of politics and the political decision-making process.

# CHAPTER EIGHT

# ON SOME ASPECTS OF MEDIA COMMUNIQUÉ

HANNE-LORE BOBÁKOVÁ
AND JANUSZ KARPETA

## Introduction

This chapter deals with selected aspects of the modern media in the Czech Republic. The authors pay attention to the specifics of the terminology in the given field and point out the approaches taken by Czech and international scholars. Further, the details of the most commonly used instruments are referred to the examined aspects of the media such as participation, persuasiveness, credibility and so on. In particular, advertising and political elements of the media are described, and form the basis of the presented and examined examples.

The main aim of the chapter is to demonstrate that there is common ground as far as political and advertising media communiqués are concerned. In addition, it will show that there is a growing need to address the public by means of various morphological, lexical and syntax instruments with the view of making communiqués more attractive, catchy and persuasive, as well as integrating them into marketing and political communication.

Media belongs to the life of the individual and society and its importance continues to grow. The development of information technology is an unquestionable part of the growing influence of the media. Today's era of the information society vitally accelerates access to information and allows for achieving significantly better, mass effects on its recipients.

Media communication has attracted and still attracts the attention of many prominent Czech linguists. It is not possible to omit Hlavsa, who among other things gave attention to communication issues of the media, in particular from the point of view of the linguistic, sociological and psycho-linguistic aspects.[1] He also thoroughly studied persuasive means in Czech journalism.[2] In addition to the language aspects, he also researched non-verbal matters.[3]

## The Terminological Background

For the needs of this chapter we would like to briefly recall the terminology, based on social communication, as all media products are distributed through mass media. What we mean by mass communication is the process of transferring a statement from the communicator to the addressee. The communicator is a complex organisation employing professionals and using specialized technology to produce highly standardized statements intended for a large, disparate and thinly-spread audience.[4]

From the linguistic perspective the concepts of the fourth estate journalism are used. However, it is essential to designate different meanings of the terms and their connotations in journalism and linguistics.

In Czech linguistics the fourth estate is perceived as interpersonal communication which informs about current social and political events, and comments on them.[5] The style of the written fourth estate texts of all genres is traditionally known as the newspaper style, or journalism.

In journalism, the distinction between the informative, educational, entertaining and persuasive functions is made.[6] In this chapter, we use the term persuasion broadly. In the framework of the persuasive techniques we include within persuasion not only the functions of advocacy, acquisition and influencing, but also awareness raising, evaluative and challenging, along with informative ones. With the enumerations of the persuasive features of advocacy, acquisition, influencing, challenging,

---

[1] Z. Hlavsa, "K jazykovědné analýze komunikace v hromadných sdělovacích prostředcích," *Slovo a Slovestnost* 51 (1992): 124–129.

[2] Z. Hlavsa, "K persvazivním prostředkům české publicistiky," in *Spisovná čeština a jazyková kultura* (Praha: FF UK, 1995), 149–154.

[3] Z. Hlavsa, "K jazykovědné analýze komunikace," 124–129.

[4] I. Reifová et al., *The Dictionary of Media Communications* (Praha: Portál, 2004), 100

[5] M. Čechová, J. Chloupek, M. Krčmová, E. Minářová, *Stylistika současné češtiny*, (Prague, 1997).

[6] J. Bartošek, "Jazyk žurnalistiky," in F. Daneš et al. (eds.), *Český jazyk na přelomu tisíciletí* (Praha: Academia, 1997).

evaluating and awareness-raising,[7] we are deliberately expanding the informative dimension, which is, in our opinion, the priority one in terms of persuasion.

We proceed from the concept of a media product as a kind of a communication statement.[8] From different media products we will focus our attention on advertising and political communiqués in terms of persuasive elements. In our concept, the media communiqué is a result of communications events. Another consideration is the degree of persuasive techniques and their effect on the recipient.

## Participation

Political media product and advertising media product cause the subjective participation in the process of the adoption of the media content with recipients. McLuhan[9] described this process as participation. We have to admit that the concept of participation is not entirely unambiguous and specified. Most likely, it deals with a summary of communication links between human and medium, and this dichotomy is true both on the individual and collective levels.[10] This may raise a number of questions, in particular from the perspective of the use of participation in the persuasive media process. We see the problem especially in the fact that participation, as understood by McLuhan, is hard to quantify, since participation is in the process of perception, which is a highly individual matter, and is involved in a number of social, psychological and cultural factors. This means that adequate technology is not developed to quantify the degree of the effects of media products to the user.

## Persuasiveness of Media Communiqué

So that the media product is persuasive, influential and encouraging to further action, it has to meet the relevant criteria. Let us recall briefly the two requirements that are placed in the text so that the recipient can accept them along with achieving the persuasive effect:

---

[7] A. Jaklová, "Persvaze a její prostředky v současných žurnalistických textech," *Naše řeč* 4 (85) (2002): 169–176.

[8] J. Jirák, B. Köpplová, *Média a společnost* (Praha: Portál, 2003), 117.

[9] M. McLuhan, *Understanding media: The Extensions of Man* (New York: First MIT Press Edition, 1964).

[10] I. Reifová et al., *The Dictionary of Media Communications*, 133.

(1) Creating an intelligible text—as reported by Hlavsa,[11] if the recipient is to accept a journalistic text it has to be easily understood and unfocused. It assumes that its interpretation shall take place with no trouble at all levels.
(2) Credibility—as understood by Hlavsa, credibility means the sum of social norms (language, style, outer text presentation, non-verbal means, etc.).

The automatic adoption of ideas cannot be presumed. The recipient verifies the reality. However, it is often not possible to immediately verify the facts declared or verify them at all. Therefore, the media communiqués resort to the imperative mood. As an example, we are presenting the advertising communiqué for a new line of cosmetic products:

> Lancome
> SUPER SERUM
> High efficiency, immediately visible and demonstrable results.
> Try the new generation of Sera containing active substances and meet their immediately visible effects.

The recipient's distrust of the promotional product is eliminated by the notes of experts for use or characteristics of the product (see below for an example on anti-wrinkle Eucerin cream):

> Aesthetical surgeons consider filler injections with hyaluronic acid as the key in the fight against wrinkles. Eucerin has developed the first anti age treatment with hyaluronic acid and saponinum. **Intense filling HYALURON-FILLER creams immediately smooth the skin and return its young and fresh look.** Bioactive saponinum stimulates the production of hyaluronic acid in the deeper layers of the skin and can fill even the most prominent wrinkles.
> Clinically proven effectiveness with the maximum visual effect.
> 80% of women have confirmed a significant reduction of wrinkles after only four weeks.

With regard to the trust of the producer of the media communiqué, one cannot forget a hierarchical model of the impact on the content of a communication statement, an attempt at constructing a reality in the interest of fostering a pragmatic intention. Other equally important questions remain on the verge of mere conjectures:

---

[11] Z. Hlavsa, *K jazykovědné analýze komunikace*, 127.

(1) Is a common recipient competent enough to assess the fact that he or she is becoming the subject of persuasion?
(2) How can a common recipient ever assess the sources of information and the quality of the media?

The creators of advertising communiqués usually do not rely only on a single persuasive resource. The accumulation of more persuasive verbal resources is becoming the rule rather than the exception. The order of persuasive resources in communication, however, is changing. The structure of persuasion can look like the following from a text aspect:

(1) The opinion of experts on the stated matter
(2) The composition of the product
(3) The effect
(4) The verification of the effect
(5) The ultimate effect/best with numerical indication, by means of percentage representation, etc.

The structure of the persuasive text is different, is changing, and individual parts can be represented in a different order, while some components may not be present at all (see the following example for Kenwood):

> **Kenwood Cooking Chef MILES O70** is a unique kitchen robot that can even cook. The induction hob built directly under the bowl will ensure perfect temperature control with accuracy of two degrees. The temperature range is of 20–140 degrees C will allow a wide use in food preparation. Try the Italian risotto, meat ragout, sauces, veal in red wine sauce or whipped cream.

Let us return briefly to media imperatives. In the media world, they are infinitely rampant, and the current recipient is confronted with them on an almost daily basis. From the perspective of the producer a question of media imperatives is therefore very important. It turns out that this persuasive verbal form in the media product is paid due attention.

What is interesting then is the integration of imperative techniques in the media product, both in terms of the frequency of imperatives, as well as their inclusion in the structure of the text. The media imperative appears most frequently at the beginning and at the end of the communiqué. In some media products, imperativeness can appear twice (see the below advertising for the new product Elseve):

Discover now the right Elseve tailored to your type of hair!
New Elseve
Visit the online hair diagnosis at www.lorealparis.cz.

## Political Media Communiqué

As some of the most common features have been mentioned above as far as advertising media communiqué is concerned we can now turn our attention to the political media communiqué. On the face of it, it may variably contain a great number of the marketing features modern consumers are confronted with. According to the well-known principle of the "four Ps" in marketing we can denote the first visible feature of political media communiqué, i.e. the product (service), which is nicely packed and offered to the public by means of a set of well-thought through instruments supported additionally by price, place and promotion. In the process of communicating some political contents, as is often the case with psychology, one has to decode the message of political media communiqué as it requires both language and textual levels.

In our arguments we can have a closer look at some omnipresent and obvious features of modern political media communiqué. Firstly, the language used reflects the most direct and popular dialogue of a political party with a voter; secondly, it produces a successful discussion forum, and thirdly it convinces voters about the credibility and veracity of one's own political agenda by using the most modern techniques of media (internet, video, recorded election campaign materials).

Taking into account the aspect of the structure of political language one can find it in the following elements of harmonization: the image and the words, sound and spoken text, or in their combination. In other words, it is about the aspects most commonly used in the language of advertising or marketing. In accordance with political media communiqué, as well as the advertised product, it should sell the idea of a specific political party as efficiently as possible. For this purpose it uses and strengthens its action through rhetoric, persuasion, agitation, appeal or novelty. In addition to enlarging the effect on the recipient, one can mention the promise that the leaders of a political party shall submit any political media communiqué and its verification, which is achieved by verbal and non-verbal aspects such as sounds, atmosphere or graphic pictorial representations.

Another important factor is time and the role it has in creating political media communiqué. We know well that within a few minutes a maximum amount of information must be submitted to the public. The length of the average political media communiqué takes a few minutes. During such a short time, in accordance with the formulas of AIDA (attention-interest-desire-action), and DIPADA (definition-identification-proof-acceptance) used in marketing, it should act immediately on the recipient, thus penetrating into the memory.

Creators of political media communiqués realize, however, that without the repeatability of some of key words this effect would be minimal. Therefore, any political media communiqué reiterates several times the most important ideas or issues of a political party which it is trying to sell. Another extremely important aspect is its content, which is to attract attention and should be easy to remember. Further, it must meet the following criteria: accuracy, brevity, intelligibility, attractiveness, readability, easiness to remember, and originality. The language also needs to attract attention and become attractive. In doing so, texts support this idea by evoking impressions, applying non-verbal connotations and creating certain pictures of the reality. The topic should therefore make us interested along with addressing it to the recipient. In a political media communiqué we often hear appraisal, words of appreciation or even interest. Humour is another extremely important aspect and makes it even more attractive. Political media communiqués show signs of poetic language too, in which we can find various pieces of poetry, such as metaphor, metonymy and hyperbole. Suggestiveness is another important trait. It is known that some recipients are open to clear statements, while others respond to a categorized one. Everything is dependent on the perception of a sender and their credibility, as well as their prior attitude. The imperative nature is most often carried out through the use of modal adverbs, imperatives, quantifiers and intonation. Most statements such as these tend to be suggestive and conceal the functions of persuasive power.

The understandability of political media communiqués serves one primary goal—to influence the recipient. Information that is merely comprehensible and readable makes it more persuasive. For this purpose, the language uses individual words that evoke a desirable impression but do not need to create a coherent or even meaningful message. The recipient typically recognizes the attractive words. J. Bralczyk adds some further aspects: "other aspects of rationality are created by a legibility of the convention, and the ability to discern in communiqué not quite explicit allusions, jokes and quotes for the recipient, which can be very satisfying and enable him to feel unity with the sender."[12]

Another feature of political media communiqué is that it integrates visibly and now and then consciously the names of the political parties

---

[12] J. Bralczyk, *Język na sprzedaż* (Gdańsk: Gdańskie Wydawnictwo Psychologiczne, 2004).

into their message. This is what makes them sound and look different from others. For this purpose it abounds in all possible measures available, such as image, sound and graphics. They are indispensable in modern times, as recipients succumb to them easily and thus give way to persuasion and manipulation. The selection of certain words contributes to the creation of a "corporate culture" in politics as well as the image represented, creating slogans and other messages. In the language itself, the originality of political media communiqué comes with some apparent changes on the morphological, lexical and syntactical levels too.

## Conclusion

As presented above, media still lies at the heart of interest of plenty of modern scientists. In the Czech sphere, Hlavsa studies the aforementioned issues on the bases of linguistics, sociology and psycho-linguistics. Afterwards, the terminological background was clarified as for the different functions modern media currently play, along with persuasion. Shortly afterwards, the discussion succeeded in terms of understanding participation in this context as manifested by McLuhan. Based on that, the debate focused on the persuasiveness of media communiqué, which was supported by a number of examples from the advertising environment. This forms a logical link to political communiqué, detailing the necessary steps in making a political message more persuasive and attractive in the perspective of communication with the target group. Terms such as the four Ps, AIDA and DIPADA were applied to provide some tangible evidence of the aforementioned issues. This demonstrates a growing need to address the public by means of various morphological, lexical and syntax instruments with the view of making communiqués more attractive, catchy and persuasive, as well as integrating them into marketing and political communication.

Hanne-Lore Bobáková, PhD, is the Head of the Department of Foreign Languages and Communication at the School of Business Administration in Karvina of the Silesian University in Opava.

Janusz Karpeta, PhD, is the Deputy-Head of the Department of Foreign Languages and Communication at the School of Business Administration in Karvina of the Silesian University in Opava.

# Chapter Nine

# The Subjective Model of the Civil Society in Terms of Pope John Paul II

Ilona Balcerczyk

The idea of civil society outlined in the thought of Pope John Paul II is linked to the anthropocentric perspective of reality, and it fits into the overall idea of the civilization of love taught by this Pope. The civilization of love is an alternative to the civilization of consumption or civilization of indifference leading to totalitarianism, which the twentieth century experienced. The civilization of love is based on two pillars: human love for God and love between human beings. These two pillars are strong in the values that create them. Human love for God is highlighted in a number of ways. The first of these can be found in different religions that share a common core and common root.[1] The second can be found in human responsibility before God and the acknowledgement that God is the truth, and the life of the human being is full of an arduous search for the truth. The third clear visualization of human love for God is the respect for one's "I"—if a person is created in the image and likeness of God, respect should be paid to the "I," and responsibility for ourselves, our words and actions should be taken.

To sum up, the love of the human for God is manifested in fidelity to principles and universal values, in living in truth and in the constant pursuit of the truth. The human being is a person created in the image and likeness of God, and for all their activities is responsible before God. Love for God determines humanity, and shapes them as a person. Humans take responsibility for themselves, their actions and words, and do so only before God.

The second pillar on which the civilization of love is based is the love of human to human. Since our fellow creature is, as "I," created in the

[1] John Paul II, *Przekroczyć próg nadziei* (Lublin: Publishing Editor of the Catholic University of Lublin, 1994), 73.

image and likeness of God, one has to respect them in every aspect of their family, professional (work) and social lives. Another indicator of the love of the human is taking responsibility not only for the "I" but also for "you"—the responsibility for "you" and "we" is a necessary condition to avoid a civilization of indifference. Respect for the human being also extends to taking care after intellectual achievements, the products that the human being has created over the centuries following the drive to satisfy their needs of love, beauty, truth and usefulness. On this level comes recognition of and respect for national heritage, including language, culture and history of the nation.

Love for the human can be realized through the idea of brotherhood and solidarity with the other, through the creation of communities and making joint efforts to build the common good and peace. Indifference leads to the alienation of people, societies and nations. Indifference leads to totalitarianism like Nazism and Stalinism, and these lead to degradation, violation of the dignity of man, and the inevitable destruction of the human being as a person. Only the civilization of love has a chance to survive, because only that type is based on truth. Only truth is durable because it is a strong love for God and people, and every lie is temporary. All in all it generally does not matter whether the temporality lasts a year or decades—it always passes.

## Man as Subject

The key concepts for the civilization of love, and for understanding the idea of civil society proposed by Pope John Paul II, are subject and subjectivity. These result from the anthropocentrism of the Pope, are an integral element of social thought and can be found in almost all reflections of Karol Wojtyła, later Pope John Paul II, devoted to person, society, nation and state. Who is human? Who is a person? Around these questions the anthropological thought of Wojtyła seems to focus.[2] It is

---

[2] Answers to these questions can be sought in almost all works by Karol Wojtyła, later Pope John Paul II, see John Paul II, *Centesimus annus*, http://www.opoka.org.pl/biblioteka/W/WP/jan_pawel_ii/encykliki/centesimus_1.html (accessed February 14, 2012); K. Wojtyła, *Osoba i czyn oraz inne studia antropologiczne* (Lublin: Towarzystwo Naukowe KUL, 2000); John Paul II, *Dar i Tajemnica* (Kraków: Wydawnictwo Św. Stanisława BM Archidiecezji Krakowskiej, 2005); Enciclicals: *Dives In Misericordia*; *Dominum et Vivificantem*; *Laborem Exercens*; John Paul II, *Kochana młodzieży* (Warszawa: Wydawnictwo Amber, 2005); John Paul II, *Mężczyzną i niewiastą stworzył ich* (Lublin: Redakcja wydawnictw: KUL, 1998); John Paul II, *Pamięć i tożsamość* (Kraków:

through the prism of the human as a person that all aspects of society, including civil society, are looked at. To introduce the concept of the Pope's civil society, terms such as "person" and "subject/entity" must first be defined.

The human is a person created in the image and likeness of God. He or she is free, and can make their own choices. He or she creates their own world by making the Earth subject to them, is a producer, and also is treated as the bond connecting the Earth's natural resources with the work of the human. He or she creates a family that is a community of blood, the primary source of knowledge about the world, and the source of values. They create the societies which, just as the human, have free will and the right to make choices that shape the reality, and they may choose to live in truth, to hide or to live a lie. The human creates nations which are communities bonded by common language, history, culture and common heritage. He or she creates relationships between nations which can enrich each other or destroy and annihilate themselves. The human is the perpetrator who subjects the Earth, but also bears responsibility for it before another man and God. The human is an entity which visualizes them as a person in the act.

Wojtyła is not trying to justify in a phenomenological way that the human is a person, but he wants to see how the human is a person, and how the metaphysical structures which characterize their life are reflected in their conscious existence.[3] The human is a being that exists in the world alongside other beings like plants and animals.[4] "A person is—metaphysically speaking—both subject and object. It is a subjective being,

Wydwnictwo Znak, 2005); K. Wojtyła, "Podmiotowość i to, co nieredukowalne w człowieku," *Ethos* 2–3 (1988); K. Wojtyła, *U podstaw odnowy: Studium o realizacji Vaticanum II* (Kraków: UNUM, 2003) and the numerous speeches and homilies. See also J. Galarowicz, *Człowiek jest osobą* (Kraków: Wydawnictwo Naukowe Papieskiej Akademii Teologicznej, 1994).

[3] See R. Buttiglione, *Kilka uwag o sposobie czytania "Osoby i czynu,"* in K. Wojtyła, *Osoba i czyn oraz inne studia antropologiczne* (Lublin: Towarzystwo Naukowe KUL, 2000), 15.

[4] See "The man reveals himself simply as different and separate from the world of things in the immediate cognitive contact with that world. He sees directly, meaning he experiences, that by getting to know the real world of objects he is entirely different and absolutely irreducible to what is—and can be—studied by him, but cannot study on its own. What makes him so different from the world of things, in the same time makes him stand out among them. It causes that the man is apart and appears to be apart: 'differently' and 'above,' as if alone, lonely, and thanks to that 'loneliness' he is himself." T. Styczeń, *O antropologii Karola Wojtyły*, in K. Wojtyła, *Osoba i czyn*, 494.

meaning someone (existing as 'someone' in contrast to all other existing as a 'thing'), while at the same time it is *suppositum*, which exists as an entity ... In a person we find a synthesis of creation and subjectivity."[5]

The human as being made in the image and likeness of God, even though it exists in the world of things, has qualities that make them a subjective being. Only to the human belongs the mind and consciousness, action, personality, dignity and freedom to make choices, responsibility (for something and for someone), spirituality and happiness, as well as participation. Following Boethius and his works, Wojtyła considers the human to be an intelligent being ("*persona est rationalis naturea individua substantia*").[6] The mind (intellect) is a tool with which the human can get to know itself, meaning "I" and what is beyond the "I"—the world.[7] Exploring takes place through experiencing,[8] meaning the experience of the deliberate act by the human.[9]

---

[5] K. Wojtyła, *Osoba i czyn*, 158.

[6] Ibid., 122.

[7] Compare with the concept of "I" and "not-I" proposed by Havel, and his concept of civil society. More information about his civil society model can be found in V. Havel, *Citizen Vanek* (Pohorelice: CPI Moravia Books s.r.o., 2009); V. Havel, *Disturbing the Peace* (New York: Vintage Books, A Division of Random House, Inc., 1991); V. Havel, *Eseje polityczne, List do Husaka, Rozmowa z Lederem, Siła bezsilnych, Kundera o Havlu* (Warszawa: Wydawnictwo KRĄG, 1984); V. Havel, *Letters to Olga* (London, Faber and Faber, 1990); V. Havel, *Listy do Olgi (czerwiec 1979–wrzesień 1982) wybór* (Warszawa-Wrocław: Wydawnictwo Naukowe PWN, 1993); V. Havel, *Open Letters, Selected Writings 1965–1990* (New York: Vintage Books, A Division of Random House, Inc., 1992); V. Havel, *Siła bezsilnych i inne eseje* (Warszawa: Agora SA, 2011); V. Havel, *Summer meditatios* (New York: Vintage Books, A Division of Random House, Inc., 1993); V. Havel, *To the Castle and Back* (London: Portobello Books Ltd., 2009); V. Havel, *Tylko krótko, proszę. Rozmowa z Karalem Hvizzd'alą, zapiski, dokumenty* (Kraków: Wydawnictwo ZNAK, 2007); V. Havel, *Zaoczne przesłuchanie* (Warszawa: Niezależna Oficyna Wydawnicza, 1989).

[8] Compare I. Dec, *Transcendencja człowieka w przyrodzie* (Wrocław: Papieski Wydział Teologiczny, 2011).

[9] Compare "The interpretation of a man on the basis of experience demands the aspect of consciousness added to the analysis of being." K. Wojtyła, *Podmiotowość i to, co nieredukowalne w człowieku*, in K. Wojtyła, *Osoba i czyn*, 440; Compare "The man not only acts intentionally, but also is aware of his actions and of who is acting—so he is aware of the act and the person in their dynamic correlation. This awareness occurs simultaneously with the intentional action, accompanies it. It occurs also before and after it. It has its continuity and its identity, distinct from the constitution and the identity of each individual action. Each act stays in the awareness, forms and passes in relation with it, leaving

Awareness of itself does not have the cognitive function, rather a reflective one acting on all that the human comes into subjective contact with through acting (and is thus also cognitive), and all that "happens." The mechanism of reflection is possible through self-knowledge, and thanks to this the awareness reflects actions and their relation with the "I." Thanks to self-knowledge, the "I" of an acting object is cognitively recognized as a subject.[10] Because of this, self-knowledge is a kind of a link between the act and consciousness of a matter of cognition, involving both the person and their actions, as well as the awareness of actions and of the person: "I am aware of the act—that actually means, that through the act of self-knowledge I objectify my actions in relation to my person. I objectify the fact that it is a true action of my person, and not something that only happens in it ... All of that and the whole content of the act, objectified by the self-knowledge act, becomes the content of awareness."[11] Awareness fulfils another function—apart from exposing (reflecting) it shapes the experience. The human can experience the "I" and acts, thanks to which they can experience their own subjectivity.[12]

Through the contact with the "I" and with all that is beyond the "I," through the contact with "you," "we" and through communing with nature, intellectual heritage and the thoughts of great people, but above all through communion with God, the human becomes a person. That becoming should take place "in wisdom and grace."[13] However, it can

---

something like a trace of their presence. Awareness is accompanied by the act and reflects it when it is born, when it is fulfilled—and when it was met, even then it reflects it, but of course it is no longer associated by it." K. Wojtyła, *Osoba i czyn*, 79.

[10] "Awareness reflects the actions and their relation to their own "I" through self-knowledge. Without it, the awareness would be deprived of the semantic content relating to their own "I" of a man acting as the subject of direct cognizance, would find itself in a kind of vacuum." K. Wojtyła, *Osoba i czyn*, 85.

[11] K. Wojtyła, *Osoba i czyn*, 91

[12] Ibid. Compare "Thanks to the awareness man experiences himself as a subject. Experiences, so he is an entity in the strictest practical sense. Understanding grows here from the experience without any intermediate members, without reasoning. Man experiences his own actions, that he—the person—is the creator. That creation ... becomes obvious through the experience and so it appears to us in terms of consciousness. It is therefore necessary to approach to the experience—and to the man's subjectivity, which is his proper base—to capture the creativity as a fully experimental fact." K. Wojtyła, *Osoba i czyn*, 105.

[13] Compare "Growing up 'in years' refers to the natural human relationship with time: that growing up is a form of phase of 'ascending' the whole human passing. The physical and psychological development corresponds to it: growing of all that

occur due to the appropriate usage of freedom which, like dignity, is given and inflicted on a man at the same time.

## Participation

Analyzing the issue of community and society, Wojtyła introduces the concept of participation.[14] The human cooperates and participates in the community, and in the humanity of another human, who is their fellow creature. Sources of participation should be sought at the level of approximation of consciousness that comes from the experience of their own "I." The very broad understanding of the term "person" is not sufficient because of its generality and because it is not bringing a particular "I" to a specific "you":

> In the human experience, one of the other, as the second "I," is always a discreet choice concluded. Next is the selection of this particular man among others, as indeed comes down to the fact that this man among others is *hic et nunc*, or "given." Choice we speak about here, is that I accept his or her "I," in result affirm a person—in this way, I kind of "pick him in myself," or in my "I," because I do not have any other access to the other man as "myself" except through my "I."[15]

Acceptance of the "I" in "you" somehow determines the ability to participate, because the other represents here the subjective participation in humanity, and only by using this relation "I"-"you" ("I" and "you" as people created in the image and likeness of God) does the process of enrichment and human development take place. The relation between "I" and "you" is always a potential relation, as long as there is no internal impulse aspiring to its realization. The impulse in this case might be the commandment of love that requires a man to experience "you" as the other "I," that is, as a person: "Participation as a feature of a person is both a

---

energy, through which the normal human individuality is constituted. It is necessary that 'growing in wisdom and grace' corresponds to that process." John Paul II, *List do młodych całego świata (Parati Semper) Ojca Świętego z okazji międzynarodowego roku młodzieży*.
http://ekai.pl/biblioteka/dokumenty/x229/list-do-mlodych-calego-swiata/ (accessed March 16, 2013).

[14] There are works devoted to the issue of participation, like the whole fourth part of *Osoba i czyn* (*The Person and Act*), the encyclical *Centesimus annus* and numerous anthropological studies including: *Osoba: podmiot i wspólnota*, *Uczestnictwo czy alienacja* and others.

[15] K. Wojtyła, *Uczestnictwo czy alienacja*, 454.

specific *constitutivum* and essential trait of the community. With this characteristic, the person and the community adhere to each other, and they are not strangers or in opposition to each other, as it is demonstrated on the basis of individualistic and anti-individualistic way of thinking about a man."[16]

Participation is based on the occurrence of the subjective moment—that the human as a member of the community, by co-working and living with others, fulfils themselves with different actions. Those acts which he or she performs in different societies, communities or collectivities are at the same time the acts of a person.[17] They have a social character, and their sources should be sought in the personal character of the human: "The trait of the community—or social trait—is pressed on the human existence."[18] Only by the understanding the act and human action can the cooperation be properly interpreted. In the considerations directed to young people, John Paul II called for watchfulness and focusing on others, warning against closing off from the problems of others and being "in a cramped backyard of own interests, or even own judgments."[19]

The human fulfils themselves in love towards their fellow creatures, upon which fundamental human solidarity arises. Participation means taking responsibility for oneself, for another person and for the common heritage, which is society and nation. Participation leads to brotherhood, which becomes a source of strength for cooperation. Implanted human values such as love, kindness and respect for others constitute the human

---

[16] K. Wojtyła, *Osoba i czyn*, 316.
Compare "The man—a person is able not only to participate in the community, in being and acting as well as cooperating 'together with others,' but is able to participate in the humanity of 'the others.' Any participating in a community is based on that, and at the same time finds its personal sense through the ability to participate in the humanity of every person." Ibid., 331.

[17] Compare "The feature of participation shows that man acting in cooperation with others, preserves in that action his personalistic value of the act, and at the same time he embodies what results from the community action. You can also—turning the order—say that thanks to the participation man by acting with others retains all what evolves from the community of action, and at the same time thanks to it—understands the personalistic value of his own act." K. Wojtyła, *Osoba i czyn*, 309.

[18] K. Wojtyła, *Osoba i czyn*, 201.

[19] John Paul II, *Apel Jasnogórski: Rozważanie wygłoszone do młodzieży*, Częstochowa, June 18, 1983
http://ekai.pl/biblioteka/dokumenty/x511/apel-jasnogorski-rozwazanie-wygloszone-do-mlodziezy/
(accessed March 16, 2013).

as a person and at the same time generate their power. This strength empowers fighting evil and all that offends God, "with every injustice and exploitation, with all deceit and hypocrisy, with everything that hurts, humiliates, defiles human cohabitation and relation, with any crime against life—with every sin."[20]

The brotherhood arising from the subjective human personality defends them against alienation, which is a symbolic end to all human relationships based on values. Alienation first and foremost disturbs "I" to experience the humanity of "you." Referring to the history of the twentieth century, the tragedy of World War II, and concentration and labour camps, the Pope sees in alienation the causes of disintegration of brotherhood and participation in modern civilizations. In terms of everyday life, alienation is manifested by the isolation of interpersonal relations involving the disappearance of experiencing "you" as "I." Alienation also leads to the reduction of "I": "Because each of us celebrates his own humanity in proportion to how capable he is to participate in the humanity of others, to experience them as 'second 'I''."[21] Recalling the socio-political perspective raises the observation that alienation should be linked with the imperfect system solution, that is with imperfect social, economic, political and international regime. The repair of these system solutions however should begin with finding the reason for participation and its implementation. Wojtyła proposed a personalised approach to the problem, and the restoration of humanity to the human, and only after such a first step can the economic, political or sociological solutions take place.

## Community

Being based on a concept of the human as a suppositum and concept of action, in which the person is highlighted, Wojtyła introduces principles governing social existence and social activities. The human exists and works with others, and as a result matures as a person. More than one person forms a social community. The first principle within the society is the personalistic principle, involving the affirmation of the dignity of people as members of society. The main bond connecting community and society is the gift of love. We all live each day in the circle of people close to us. Gradually, the circle expands. More and more people are involved in our lives and we recognize the outlines of the community which connects us with them. Almost always, that community is differentiated in some

---

[20] John Paul II, *List do młodych całego świata*.
[21] K. Wojtyła, *Uczestnictwo czy alienacja*, 456.

way, based on the relations "I"-"you," "I"-"we," where "you" is an expression of connection rather than division.[22]

Through the relation of "I" with "you," the "I" is constituted. On the basis of this relation the process leading to the creation of the community can develop and the personal human subjectivity is revealed mutually. "We" is created from the human "I" contained in a plurality of entities acting jointly in relation to any one value, which thus becomes the common good. "We" is not only a multi-subjectivity, the multiplicity of entities of "I," but has a specific subjectivity:[23] "When we talk about the community, we do not think only about the multiplicity of entities, but the specific unity of that multiplicity."[24] When we talk about "we" we are talking about a set of people (community, society, social group) based on interpersonal relations. The superior role is attributed to these relations considering individuals that create a group. Community does not have a substantial being, only an accounted one.[25] The subjects that create it are the unity, which is based on shared values such as truth, love and the common good:

> Such fusion deserves to be called *communio* and *communio* is something more than a community (communitas). The Latin word *communio* suggests the only proper relation between people. It also points to the good which they bestow and which they give to each other and in the same time receive it in mutual relation.[26]

Being a subject in the community, a member of a set called a social group, is not a threat for the maintenance of the subjectivity of the individual.[27]

---

[22] John Paul II, *List do młodych całego świata.*

[23] K. Wojtyła, *Osoba i czyn*, 395–414.

[24] K. Wojtyła, *Osoba: podmiot i wspólnota*, 394.

[25] K. Wojtyła, *Uczestnictwo czy alienacja*, 457.

[26] K. Wojtyła, *U podstaw odnowy*, 53–54.

[27] Compare "Utilitarian anthropology and resulting from it ethics, present the assumption that a man generally tends to their own benefit and benefit of the group to which they belong. The final personal or collective benefit are their goals for acting." John Paul II, *Pamięć i tożsamość*, 43.
Compare "The appropriate state of human affairs and the moral health of the world cannot be guaranteed only through the structures, however they have a real value. Those structures are not only important but also necessary; they cannot and should not marginalize the human freedom. Even the best structures function properly only when in the society the convictions capable to motivate people to free taking the social order are alive. Freedom requires the belief; the belief does not exist on

On the contrary, through contact with "you" and "we" and the pursuit of a common goal, the human enriches its own "I" and thus develops their own humanity. Society is a collection of various communities based on values. These groups are autonomous from the state and have been in the process of self-organisation.[28] Józef Tischner emphasizes that the society is formed through two phases: "The first one results in the development from the monologue to the dialogue society, the second one from the dialogue to society of people, meaning legal entities."[29] That dialogue is the essence of the truth about the society: "The ultimate truth about social life does not drop from the clouds, like rain upon the earth, but grows from

its own, but still needs to be acquired through the community." Benedict XVI, *Encyclical Spe Salvi* (Libreria Editrice Vaticana, 2007), http://www.vatican.va /holy_father/benedict_xvi/encyclicals/documents/hf_ben-xvi_enc_20071130_spe-salvi_pl.html (accessed March 16, 2013).

[28] Jacek Kuroń assumes that the subjectivity of the Polish society began to wake up after the election of Karol Wojtyła as the Pope, in his opinion his pilgrimages to Poland and the socio-political thought of John Paul II were also important: "That was not a crowd anymore, they were organised and aware people. Fascinating. I looked at it and then I started to realize, that it was the moment when there was something great accomplished. The nation saw its power. We saw on the streets and squares, how many of us there is. All made alive by one spirit. These are not watchers, they came here intentionally to participate in something great." J. Kuroń, *Gwiezdny czas: „Wiary i winy" dalszy ciąg* (London: ANEKS 1991), 99.
"Subjectivity … of the move is based on the fact, that each participant is his host, every group of participants. We can make up the political line that we want, but if it is not accepted by all participants, it is simply ineffective because ignored …. If we want the move to be a self-organising revolution, if we want people to resign from various requests, we must remember that the truth for them is an extremely momentous moral satisfaction. Only for the prize of the truth they can agree for different concessions." Ibid., 161.
Compare "Through the term of 'the subjectivity of the society' John Paul II understands the autonomy of different social groups toward the state and therefore he thinks that 'the self-organisation of society' is a very positive phenomenon. It is a prerequisite for the preservation of his creativity and freedom." Pope John Paul II positively describes the process, in which different "intermediate communities 'start a kind of solidarity system' and 'strengthen the social structure, preventing its degradation, which is anonymous and impersonal massification.' The ideal is a vibrant, linked by numerous ties between people, self-organising society." Instytut Tertio Millenio, *Jan Paweł II i społeczeństwo obywatelskie*. Wyalienowane państwo,
http://www.tertio.pl/index/site/id/361/Jan_Pawel_II_i_spoleczenstwo_obywatelski e (accessed March 16, 2013).

[29] J. Tischner, *Mieć aby być*, in J. Tischner, *Etyka Solidarności* (Kraków: Znak, 2005), 147.

the depth of individual experiences and experimentations, from mutual understanding and agreements between people."[30] The society seeking maturity from fighting for things is on the level of fighting for rights. That is the way in which civil society develops, when the subjects of the social truth transform into subjects aware of law.[31] Social life and the shape of society depend on who is the human, and change at the level of governance depends on the changes at the level of cognition.[32]

## Summary

The concept of civil society proposed by Pope John Paul II should be considered on two levels: structural and organisational, as well as axiological. In the terms of the former, the Pope placed the civil society within the socio-economic approach next to the market and the state. All three actors are equally important and complementary. But while in the market the most popular are the tough rules of income and loss, the civil society is an area "of the gift of the logic without the compensation."[33] We

---

[30] Ibid., 149.

[31] Ibid, 157.

[32] Compare "You have to see a man in all aspects of his humanity. You cannot limit only to the extent of his material needs. You cannot measure the progress by the values of economy only. The spiritual dimension of that human must be in the right place. Man is themself through maturity of his spirit, conscience, his relation to God and to others. There will not be a better world or better social order, if that order does not give priority to the values of human spirit. All of you who so highly want changes for better and fairer society remember that—all you young people, who are expressing opposition to any harm, discrimination, violence, torture of people. Remember that order you desire is a moral order and you cannot achieve it without giving priority to what is the strength of the human spirit: justice, love, friendship." John Paul II, *Przemówienie do młodzieży*, Kraków, 8.06.1979, http://ekai.pl/biblioteka/dokumenty/x573/przemowienie-do-mlodziezy-nie-wygloszone/ (accessed March 16, 2013).

[33] Compare "My predecessor, John Paul II pointed to this issue, when in *Centesimus Annus* he drew the attention to the need for a system comprising three entities: the market, the state and the society" civil society (92). He considered civil society as an environment for economic gratuitousness and brotherhood in the strictest sense, but he was not going to deny it to the two that left. Today we can say that economic life must be understood as the reality of many dimensions: in all, in different extents and in a specific way the aspect of mutual brotherhood should be present. In the era of globalization, economic activity cannot abstract from gratuitousness, which promotes and strengthens solidarity and responsibility for justice, and common good in a variety of subjects as well as individuals who play major roles. Finally, reference is made about specific and complex forms of

can talk about the civil society when citizens, gathered together in the different communities, are free to create the social structure in such a way as to be able to seek the truth and live the truth:

> Next to the family they fulfill the essential role and they start a kind of solidarity system and other communities in between. They mature as real communities of people and they strengthen the social structure, preventing its degradation, which results in anonymity and impersonal massification, unfortunately common in today's society. The person is alive and the 'subjectivity of society' increases when the number of different relationships is mutually combined. Today very often the entity gets stuck between the two: the state and the market. Sometimes it seems like it exists only as a producer and buyer of the goods, or as an object of state administration and people tend to forget that neither the market nor the state are not the aim of interpersonal cohabitation, because it itself has a unique value which the state and the market serve to. Man is above all a being who seeks the truth, lives it and deepens it by the dialogue that covers past and future generations.[34]

We need, therefore, such legal regulations that provide voluntary and non-governmental activities for different organisations of public benefit.[35]

---

economic democracy. Solidarity means that we all feel the responsibility for all (93), and that this way it cannot be devoted only to the state. Yesterday you could state that you should seek justice first, and for her complementation with gratuitousness there will be time later. Today you need to say that without the gratuitousness there will be no justice. That way you need the market where freely, in terms of equal opportunities, companies will be able to operate and realize a variety of institutional goals. Next to the private company that is focused on profits and all kinds of public enterprises, manufacturing organisations designed for mutual assistance and social goals need to have a place for development and operation. From their mutual confrontation at the market, a specific type of "crossing" can be expected. Crossing of ways of doing business, and therefore of the care for civilization of economy. In this case, love in the truth means that you have to give organisational form and shape to these economic initiatives, which without negation of profit, are going to go beyond the logic of equal exchange and profit as a goal itself." Benedict XVI, *Caritas in Veritate*, III 37, http://www.vatican.va/holy_father/benedict_xvi/encyclicals/documents/hf_ben-xvi_enc_20090629_caritas-in-veritate_pl.html (accessed March 16, 2013).

[34] John Paul II, *Centesimus annus*, V 49.

[35] "Just as within different States you can and should create social economy, which will manage the functioning of the market so that it will benefit for common good, similarly proper interventions on the international level are needed. Therefore a huge effort of mutual understanding, knowing and awareness of consciences are needed as well. One can hope for such culture, which multiplies the belief in

In terms of the axiological point of view, the civil society is strong through the moral attitude of its citizens. The basis for this morality is first and foremost God, in addition to other important values such as awareness of the identity and national culture understood in the wider sense. Civil society is based on brotherhood and human solidarity, for which the foundations are truth, freedom and responsibility. Providing all of these values is the *conditio sine qua non* of maintaining human dignity and protecting civilization from indifference.[36] At the basis of the choices made by the human lies the system of values to which they adhere. The degree of awareness about the value varies depending on the effort put into work on themselves, understood as understanding their own decisions and behaviours. Following the considerations of Józef Tischner, our way of thinking determines our values because we do not descend to hideouts, as Kępiński would say, seeking safe shelter and escaping from the world, people, responsibility and freedom. Or, we choose the difficult path of living in the truth, refusing to place labels with the slogan "Workers of the world unite" in our grocery stores: "The way in which man experiences values is the crossroads leading towards the shelter or in the direction of the open space with hope."[37]

---

human potential of the poor, and therefore the ability to improve their situation through work, that is the positive contribution to the economic well-being. However, to accomplish this, the poor individual or nation has to have the conditions for it ensured. To create such conditions is a task for the global cooperation for the development, which involves sacrifices with regard to their income and power, which are the privilege for more developed economies." John Paul II, *Centesimus annus*, V 52.

[36] Compare "We are approaching the third millennium: it is you that will soon become the creators of the new societies, you will decide about the image of the world. But social harmony is not something, that can be 'fixed fast', improvised hastily, or imposed from outside: it develops from just, free, brotherly heart in which peace evolving from love lives. From now on, join all human beings, all peacemakers; unite your hearts and your efforts in a joint peace- building. Only by experiencing the love of God and by trying to realize the evangelic brotherhood you will be able to be true and happy architects of the civilization of love."
"The fall of ideology of the countries of Central and Eastern Europe has left (…) deep feeling of emptiness, feeling that they had been deceived, and the discouragement and fear of the future. Also in Western Europe many young people have lost their motivation to live (…). Passivity and lack of interest in all that what is happening around, happens to be a way of showing the sense of helplessness in the fight for good." John Paul II, *Kochana młodzieży*, 93, 101.

[37] J. Tischner, *Myślenie według wartości* (Kraków: Znak, 1993), 414.

In the encyclical *Caritas in veritate*, Pope Benedict XVI argues that the human, through the original sin, is an imperfect person, inclined to evil. Due to that weakness, the human is not able to establish a universal community understood as a brotherhood. He states that "the unity of the human race, fraternal communion beyond all divisions is born thanks to the invitation of the God word—Love."[38] It is impossible to establish a sustainable society without core values, such as internal (social) brotherhood, selflessness and trust: "The economic, social and political development, if it wants to be truly human, must respect the principle of selflessness as an expression of fraternity … Without internal forms of solidarity and mutual trust, the market cannot fulfil its economic function. Today we lack trust, and loss of trust is a serious loss."[39]

The civil society, above all, is a free society (not enslaved), responsible and autonomous towards the state which is created in the long process of changing of "old habits" (that is the process of changing the way of thinking through values) and changes in social structures. Pope John Paul II emphasizes that the development of civil society is a process extended in time,[40] which involves a gradual transition from values and "old habits"

---

[38] Benedict XVI, *Caritas in Veritate*, III 34.

[39] Ibid., III 35.

[40] We find a similar opinion in the considerations of Jacek Kuroń. The civil society woke up slowly, through the gradual release of awareness among citizens. The choice of Wojtyła for Pope was a huge impulse that triggered energy and strength of the nation, his pilgrimage to Poland and homilies, that added courage to the society and helped people to realize their collective power. The Pope appealed to human and national subjectivity. The subjective man is a free man in thinking, with autonomous actions and functioning within the society. The subjective man is a subjective citizen who acts consciously in society in the name of his freedom and the freedom of others. According to Kuroń, the self-organisation of the society was very important. The gradual subsidence of the system (1956, 1968, 1970, 1976, 1980 and finally 1989) moved structures of the society waking their subjectivity and unleashing hidden subjectivity potential. The subjectivity (potential) of citizens = subjectivity (potential) of the whole nation, a huge force that can move an avalanche. What the Workers' Defense Committee (Komitet Obrony Robotników) needed to make it work were:
—the awareness of the power that lies in the subjectivity of the society, discipline and self-organisation, cooperation and courage, and awareness that there is life without The New Belief was also important. Choosing the right matrix pill in the name of freedom, the painstaking work of those who washed the stairs and those who edited.
—the persistence to persevere despite the sticks of militia and breathing in the back from the outside, as well as the overall generational quarrel inside. The turn in 1989 did not come out of nowhere. It was prepared systematically both in the

to freedom, truth and common good: "The transition from an 'enslaved' society to the civil society, sovereign society, the Republic, sets for many new tasks. Against realization of them the old habits arise, and partly also the old structures which cannot be replaced overnight."[41] The transformation from an enslaved to civil society involves changes on many levels, including the political, economic and values, which is the basis for all other levels. Working on the construction of civil society is the way towards discovering the beauty in ourselves and in others.[42]

---

mental sphere (waking subjectivity of the society by the dissidents, opposition, Radio Free Europe, culture, the Pope) and the organisational sphere (forming structures independent from the government like KOR).
"Since mid-1979 it was not enough to develop the concept of self-organisation. I was convinced—I felt that our movement needs a new assignment. The type which will allow to expand the sphere of freedom visibly, dramatically reduce totalitarianism. I realized … that social tension is growing, that it will soon turn into open conflict with the communist regime. Then, if the independent social movements turn out to be strong enough, an agreement with the communist authorities will be reached, agreement which will ensure the conditions for the gradual establishment of public order and democratic sovereignty … When the time of social uprising will come, its program will be developed."
"For every society political struggle is better than war by tanks, bullets and gas, and from the division into the noble underground minority and indifferent majority living in the state during the war." J. Kuroń, *Gwiezdny czas*, 99, 100, 239.

[41] "You might get the impression that the complex processes caused by the globalization of the economy and the media gradually tend to make a man one of the elements of the market, a replaceable product or a meaningless factor for the most decisive elections. As a result, a man can feel destroyed by the global impersonal mechanisms and gradually lose his identity and dignity." John Paul II, *Wobec wyzwań globalizac*ji, September 8, 2001, Do członków Akademii Papieskich,
http://www.opoka.org.pl/biblioteka/W/WP/jan_pawel_ii/przemowienia/akadpap_08112001.html (accessed February 14, 2012).
"A man strives for good, but is also capable of evil; can rise above his immediate benefit, but remains attached to it. The social order will be more stable, the more it will take into consideration that fact and will not opposite the personal interest to the interest of the society as the whole, but rather will seek a way of fruitful coordination. In fact, where self-interest is violently suppressed, he is replaced by a hard bureaucratic system which deprives the man of initiative and creativity. When people think that they have gained the secret of perfect social organisation which eliminates evil, they also think that they can use all means of violence and deceit to make it real. Politics becomes 'a secular religion' which deludes itself that it builds a paradise on earth." John Paul II, *Centesimus annus*, II 25.

[42] "The generous work on the construction of the society seeking justice, harmony, solidarity and peace is the ideal, which reveals the richness of itself and the

The author of People and Action creates a subjective vision of civil society, whose main pillar is the autonomy of the individual as a person, and the autonomy of the community and society in relation to the state. The binder, combining various units that interact in various social groups, is the common good, understood in a personalistic way, as a superior value which enriches relationships. The cooperation of individuals should be allowed under the relevant state regulations and supranational structures in such a way that the citizens feel themselves the hosts of the communities to which they belong.[43]

Ilona Balcerczyk is a university teacher and coach for personal development. She works in the Department of Science and the Quality of Education at the University of Humanities and Economics in Łódź. She graduated from the Faculty of Law and Administration at the University of Łódź, and is now a PhD student at that university. She is interested in the questions of civil society and the political thought of Václav Havel, particularly in the subject of the doctrinal reasons for the formation of civil society.

richness of its personal service. The ideal that everyone carries in themselves. In cooperation for building the brotherhood between people among nations, in a generous helping the poor a man can discover the beauty of life." John Paul II, *Kochana młodzieży*, 102.

[43] Compare "Human subjectivity achieved through the participation in organised community life is an eternal dream of the left. Social cooperation—without the proper organisation of the subjectivity of individuals becomes an illusion in the blink of an eye." J. Kuroń, *Gwiezdny czas*, 161, 242.

"From the Christian concept of a person the right vision of the society stems. According to *Rerum novarum* and the whole social doctrine of the Church, the state is not the only way of expression of the social nature of a man, but also various intermediate groups from families to economic, social, political and cultural communities which as a manifestation of that human nature have—always in the frame of common good—their own autonomy. That is what I have called 'subjectivity' of the society, which together with the subjectivity of individuals was destroyed by a 'real socialism'." John Paul II, *Centesimus annus*, II 13.

# CHAPTER TEN

# HELP IS THEIR BUSINESS: INTERNATIONAL SERVICE CLUBS IN GERMANY

ANNA RYDEL

## Introduction

This chapter will examine the role of service clubs, focusing on the Federal Republic of Germany. All of the examined service clubs were created in the U.S., but the idea proved to be universal. Most focus on the Rotary Club as the first service club in the world, but in my opinion it is necessary to take a broader look and examine the influence of other organisations of this type. Joseph Nye, co-founder of the Complex Interdependence Theory, distinguishes between "hard" and "soft" state power. The first category is the potential of geopolitical and economic factors; the second is the ability to attract allies and gain influence. While only states can compete in the geopolitical and economic categories, soft power is open to transnational corporations, international financial institutions and, most importantly for this study, international non-governmental organisations.[1]

Service clubs are an interesting type of non-governmental organisations because of their structure and membership benefits. Nowadays, non-state actors have a bigger role in the creation of the world order than fifty years ago, which causes changing goals in world politics. Relationships become equal to or even more important than traditional attributes of power. That is why states are interested in having good relations with non-governmental organisations.[2] The world's three biggest

[1] J. Nye, *Soft Power: The Means to Success in World Politics* (New York: Public Affairs, 2004), 1–33.
[2] J. Nye, "Soft Power," *Foreign Policy* 80 (1990): 153–170.

service clubs (Rotary, Kiwanis and Lions) have some common features: business people or professionals rendering humanitarian assistance, promoting high ethical standards, and peace in the world.

It is useful to see how American ideas work in the economically strongest country of the European Union. Germany is an interesting case study because of the historical context. Two world wars, the Weimar instability and Nazi dictatorship could not destroy the will to help others, even when parts of the country were separated and citizens had to live on either side of the Iron Curtain. To see if these events have implications for the engagement of citizens in voluntary work, it is necessary to examine the available government reports. This lack of sources at this time makes it impossible to conduct a complete study on the work of service clubs as an area of engagement in previous years in German society. This chapter can give rise to a discussion about the role of these types of organisations in Germany during the twentieth century. The methods used in this study will be statistical and comparative.

## Why Do People Help Each Other?

"People are never so poor that they cannot afford to share their goods with others."[3] Therefore, it can be assumed that a person is predisposed to do good, regardless of his or her social or economic status. Characteristic of the human species is the ability to change the world and themselves. Gogol's quote includes the intuition that there is always something we can offer to another, something to share, so we direct our will and action towards relieving another's poverty. If we always have something to offer another, it does not help to keep this something only for ourselves.

Many German citizens older than 14 are involved in voluntary associations because they want to do something for society. According to a report from 2010, in 2009 61% of respondents declared civic engagement as their full motivation for volunteering, and the next 34% said that it is a partial motivation. This can be interpreted as a lack of confidence in federal policy leading many people to focus their public commitment to manageable fields. The subject is nevertheless still clearly visible and includes almost all those committed (not just 6% of those involved). The second most popular motivation was spending time with other people, which was the full motivation for 60% of respondents, and partial for 36%. Raising qualifications motivated 64% of responders

---

[3] K. Nowak, *Leksykon złotych myśli* (Warszawa: Książka i Wiedza, Warszawa 1998, 12.

(including 34% partially). Helping others was also an opportunity for gaining prestige and influence in local community (full motivation for 12% people, partially for 42%). Voluntary service as a means to improve career prospects was the motivation for 29% of responders (including 10% as full motivation).[4]

Based on the data collected, it appears that contemporary German society has recognized the need to help others (84% of the respondents indicated helping others as being an important or very important part of their lives),[5] but it is expected that service will be rewarded. The figures, however, paint a very optimistic picture; in the Gensicke and Geiss study, 36% of respondents identified themselves as involved in helping others, which for Germany is more than 25 million people (according to the German population at the end of 2012).[6]

## The Idea of Service Clubs

It is necessary to distinguish between volunteering and "civic engagement," which is a democratic republican tradition and thus suggests a context of active participation in political, social and community life. Since the unification of Germany, especially at the local level, there has been a long tradition of civic engagement. Civic engagement was always in the shadow of an authoritarian state to a considerable extent, and unlike France, the U.K. or the U.S., service clubs have chosen a third way—every one of these organisations has its own mission and is focused on different groups of society. They are based on the voluntary work of participants grouped by region. Membership also brings some benefits, such as social occasions, networking, and personal growth opportunities.[7] According to Flanagan, who focused on the young generation, it could be said that civic engagement helps strengthen democratic values in society and develop social allegiances. Therefore, it is a broader term than volunteerism.[8]

---

[4] T.Gensicke, S.Geiss, *Hauptbericht des Freiwilligensurveys. Zivilgesellschaft, soziales Kapital und freiwilliges Engagement in Deutschland 1999–2004–2009* (München: TNS Infratest Sozialforschung , 2010), 117.

[5] Ibid., 108.

[6] www.indexmundi.com (accessed August 10, 2013).

[7] A. Zimmer, *Vom Ehrenamt zum Bürgerschaftlichen Engagement; Einführung in den Stand der Debatte* (Stuttgart: Lucius & Lucius, 2005), 30–31.

[8] C. Flanagan, "Volunteerism, Leadership, Political Socialization, and Civic Engagement," *Handbook of Adolescent Psychology* 2 (2004): 731–740.

According to social scientist Anette Zimmer, citizens are not rational actors; they are strongly influenced by preferences, values and norms. Their engagement is an important basis of a functioning social integration and a prosperous economy. Modern societies and market economies highly interact and depend on each other. Democratic traditions also have a big influence on creating new forms of civil society because of their social-political cohesion.[9]

The success of the Rotary Club, which within six years of its foundation had a branch in every major American city, shows its effectiveness at organising in a time of economic development parallel to personal development and falling inequality. The new type of club was an answer to the emergence of businessmen service clubs. Organisations grounded in the previous century, like Odd-Fellows, Redmen, and the Noble Woodmen, were focused more on the affirmation of symbolic brotherhood through secret rituals, rather than including members from the working class and professionals.[10] The creation of service clubs was a consequence of strengthening the role of the middle class and expanding their values, creating a hybrid form between the old style of clubs and contemporary volunteering. Paul Harris, the founder of Rotary, did so with his club idea in America—a "service" movement that took place in the period between 1915 and 1920. University of Illinois professor Jeffrey Charles argues that the service movement began because it is not easy to help others outside of an organisation. The service concept does not pass from one person to another but must be organised by a medium, such as that offered by the service clubs.[11]

## Service Clubs in the U.S.

Since the creation of the Rotary Club in 1905, many organisations in the world started working in a similar way. This chapter will present the three biggest service clubs, which were all grounded in the U.S. but worked worldwide. All have rules and duties necessary to protect and develop the web of clubs. One of the rules of the service club is that it is impossible to apply for membership—only members can suggest new candidates. Regular meetings are practiced by every club. In the absence of a member, that person will be asked for an oral or written apology. Friendships

---

[9] A. Zimmer, *Vom Ehrenamt zum Bürgerschaftlichen Engagement: Einführung in den Stand der Debatte* (Stuttgart, Lucius & Lucius, 2005), 35–36.

[10] J. Charles, *Service Clubs in American Society: Rotary, Kiwanis and Lions* (University of Illinois Press, 1993), 10.

[11] Ibid., 8–29.

between clubs will be maintained and problems will be fixed. The intensity of social ties, as mentioned above, coupled with the frequency of the members' meetings, equals a greater possibility to establish new friendships and make existing relations deepen.

**Table 10.1. Comparison of the basic information about service clubs**

| Criteria/Club | Rotary | Kiwanis | Lions |
|---|---|---|---|
| Emblem | | | |
| Motto | "Service Above Self" | "Serving the Children of the World" | "We Serve" |
| Grounding | 1905, Chicago, IL | 1915, Detroit, MI | 1917, Chicago, IL |
| Present headquarters | Evanston, IL | Indianapolis, IN | Oakbrook, IL |
| Participants:<br>World<br>Germany (ca.) | <br>1.214.714<br>42.600 | <br>275.000<br>2.900 | <br>1.363.683<br>43.300 |
| Gender | Mixed | Mixed | Mixed |
| Professions principle | Yes | Yes | Yes |
| Presentation rule | Yes | Yes | Yes |
| Meetings | Four times per month | Two times per month | Two times per month |

Source: Author's own research.

Service clubs are international organisations *per se*. They form ethical goals which are important for areas where the participants come from and work. Moreover, is it possible to mark out the international components wherein the person should serve not only alone, with their knowledge, but to also try to get to know other people and their cultures to bring peace to the world. All of the clubs create possibilities for their members to cooperate abroad. This became especially relevant after the Second World War in uniting the Western world in the voluntary aspect.[12]

## Rotary Club

According to the definition from 1976, "Rotary is an organisation of business and professional persons united worldwide who provide humanitarian service, encourage high ethical standards in all vocations, and help build goodwill and peace on the world."[13] Their objectives are encouraging and fostering services as a basis of worldly enterprise. Their ethics are based on four questions: (1) Is it the truth? (2) Is it fair to all concerned? (3) Will it build goodwill and better friendships? (4) Will it be beneficial to all concerned? Paul Harris was the founder and first president of Rotary International, but not the first president of the Rotary Club, as the founding members chose Silvester Schiele. In 1910, sixteen Rotary Clubs existed and it was decided to create an organisation called the National Association of Rotary Clubs. After joining clubs from Canada, England, Ireland and Scotland the organisation changed its name to Rotary International in 1922.[14]

In 1985 Rotary International started the campaign Polio Plus against Poliomyelitis. This disease was unknown before the late nineteenth century, but became one of the most dreaded childhood diseases of the twentieth century, causing paralysis and death. Epidemics, which left thousands of children and adults paralyzed, provided the impetus for a "Great Race" towards the development of a vaccine. Developed in the 1950s, polio vaccines have reduced the global number of cases per year from many hundreds of thousands to under a thousand. The joint forces of Rotary International, the World Health Organization and UNICEF made the world 99% polio free. Recently, through great efforts, it was possible to eliminate polio endemic in India. In 2012 to 2013 the private sector, including Rotary International, provided more than 20% of the total contribution for the elimination of polio.[15]

---

[12] M.C. Potthoff, "Traditionelle Bürgerlichkeit im internationalen Kontext: Rotary und Lions Club nach 1945," in G. Budde et al., (eds.), *Bürgertum nach dem bürgerlichen Zeitalter: Leitbilder und Praxis seit 1945* (Göttingen:Vandenhoeck & Ruprecht, 2010), 92–98.
[13] C. Dochterman, *The ABCs of Rotary* (Evanston: Rotary International, 2006), 1.
[14] Ibid., 4–5.
[15] "Just Add Your Voice," *The Rotarian*, February 2013 (January 22, 2013): 60–66.

The biggest problem of Rotary International is the lack of new members. They try to explain this as an effect of modern life, because after growing steadily from the 1940s to the mid-1990s the membership levelled off. The economy does not help; in the United States between the years 2010 and 2012, 15,493 people left the club. The organisation sees that it is time for changes, and that is why they seek current and potential members with new propositions to make the club more interesting. Some of such propositions are lower dues, a focus on fun or inviting an expert for meetings. The coming year will show if the assumptions for making the Rotary Club more friendly are working.[16]

## Kiwanis

"Serving the children of the world" is the motto of Kiwanis International, a global organisation of volunteers dedicated to improving the world, the life of one child and one community at a time. The Kiwanis name comes from the Indian language and means "to help others with your skills." Today, Kiwanis International is more than 8,000-clubs strong with 265,000 volunteers in 96 countries. It is one of the world's largest charitable organisations that focuses primarily on the support and development of children and youths around the world through activities like promoting literacy or supporting sports. Kiwanis' members volunteer about two hours each month for projects involving children or persons in need. The Kiwanis family includes organisations for people of every age, which are sponsored by clubs and the Kiwanis International Foundation. It includes K-Kids at the elementary level, Builders Clubs at the middle school level, Action Clubs for people living with a disability, Kiwanis Junior for young adults in Europe between the ages of 18 and 32, Key Clubs at the high school level, and Circle K Clubs at the college level, providing youths with the opportunity to help others, become personally involved in their community, and build a positive future for themselves.[17]

Beginning in 2010, Kiwanis joined forces with UNICEF in a global campaign for children to virtually eliminate iodine deficiency disorders (IDD). Kiwanis raised and leveraged more than $1,426,826, which helped change lives in 103 countries. The number of households estimated to be consuming iodized salt has jumped from less than 20% in 1990 to more

---

[16] K. Lisagor, "Starting Fresh: to Get New Members, Launch New Clubs," *The Rotarian*, January 2013 (January 3, 2013): 29–31.

[17] http://www.kiwanis.org/docs/default-source/about-kiwanis/kiwanis-history/history-outline.pdf?sfvrsn=16 (accessed August 04, 2013).

than 70%, and the effort has been heralded as one of the most successful health initiatives in the world. Financial support from UNICEF was approximately $991,000.[18] Since 1999, UNICEF and its partners have immunized nearly 100 million women in 50 countries with two or more doses of the vaccine, and have eliminated the disease in 29 countries. Countries that have recently validated the elimination of Maternal/Neonatal Tetanus MNT include Turkey, Burundi and the Democratic Republic of the Congo. As of January 29, 2013 these countries had achieved MNT elimination, leaving 30 countries that have not yet eliminated the disease.[19]

## Lions Club

The Lions was the first to become an international service club. In 1920 the first club in Canada was established, and Mexico followed in 1927. In the 1950s and 1960s the international growth accelerated, with new clubs appearing in Europe, Asia and Africa. In 1945 it was one of the first non-governmental organisations invited to assist in the drafting of the United Nations Charter and has supported the work of the UN since its beginning. The mission of the Lions Clubs is to empower volunteers to serve their communities, meet humanitarian needs, encourage peace and promote international understanding.[20]

Lions Clubs International pays special attention to the autonomy of the clubs at the international level. "Every club has the right to regulate club life and domestic affairs. It is autonomous as long as the obligations under applicable statutory law of Lions Club International is met to further the goals and principles of the Lions actions." A certain autonomy promotes self-motivation for the regional clubs, so that clubs in accordance with active aid projects can contribute. "The Lions Club, a group of friends from many professions, is the main active unit in Lionism. It is a non-legally binding association and is governed by a board with a 'president' as top officials of the club."[21]

Their international humanitarian programs are focused in four main areas. The first is Preserving Sight. Since 1990, SightFirst has been

---

[18] http://sites.kiwanis.org/Kiwanis/en/theELIMINATEproject/Progress/Kiwanis familyfundraisingtotals.aspx) (accessed August 10, 2013).

[19] http://sites.kiwanis.org/Kiwanis/en/theELIMINATEproject/MNT/UNICEFMNT .aspx (accessed August 10, 2013).

[20] http://www.lionsclubs.org/EN/about-lions/mission-and-history/our-history /index.php (accessed August 10, 2013).

[21] D. Bergener, *Lions was ist das? Zahlen, Daten, Fakten: Das Handbuch für Lions in Taschenformat* (Troisdorf: District MD 111 Rheinland, 2004), 19.

making quality eye care accessible to those who most need it. SightFirst has made it possible for more than 30 million people to have improved or restored vision. The second is Supporting Youth. Over the past 25 years, 12 million young people in 78 countries have benefited through Lions Quest. Their youth development program covers children from kindergarten through to twelfth grade. The third is Providing Disaster Relief. In times of disaster, Lions meet immediate needs such as food, water and shelter with funds from the Lions Club International Foundation. For larger-scale disasters, the Foundation remains committed to helping communities rebuild into the future. The last is Meeting Humanitarian Needs. The Lions Foundation is active in a variety of international humanitarian efforts, such as supporting the construction of homes for the disabled, providing vision screenings to Special Olympics athletes and combating measles.[22] The four programs mentioned have so far spent $811 million on such initiatives. The organisation also helps people individually through giving grants, and only last year it was able to award 513 grants totalling $55.5 million. These international grants are helping thousands of people to have a better life. Some of its accomplishments include: 70,850 people helped through 200 Emergency grants totalling $1.69 million; 1,141,837 people helped through 136 Standard grants totalling $6.17 million; more than 75,777 people were helped through 28 International Assistance grants that provided clean water and access to health care through medical missions totalling $377,026; 2,064,829 people improved their vision through 45 SightFirst grants totalling $12.39 million.[23]

## Service Clubs in Germany

Germany is a country with a well-developed social care system, created by Otto von Bismarck in the second half of the nineteenth century. Aid in the workplace or the community was well known in earlier German states and found a perfect place to thrive. During the regime of the "Iron Chancellor," prosperity was recognized as an obligation to the state, and moreover citizens were not to be left to fend for themselves against adversities. Therefore, in 1883 the state introduced compulsory health insurance for employees, and a year later insurance against accidents. Social policy was clearly oriented to the proletariat, and even became a model for other states. The hidden goal was to drag the interest of the

[22] http://www.lcif.org/EN/our-programs/index.php (accessed August 11, 2013).
[23] http://www.lcif.org/EN/_files/pdfs/lcif30_10-11.pdf (accessed August 11, 2013).

workers away from the socialist party. Bismarck defined it as a "bribe" for the working class "to perceive the state as a social creation that exists for her [working class] and cares about her welfare."[24]

Unstable times during the Weimar Republic were accompanied by concern for the survival of the social system in an era of rampant inflation, expanding the scope of social insurance but imposing restrictions on the socio-political interests of certain groups mobilized against the state. Increasingly higher costs generated by this system were not stopped by national socialism, which expanded the circle of people entitled to use it. However, there was no increase in benefits, despite an increase in income due to the expansion of the armaments sector. In addition, social policy was used in political struggle, and enemies of the state were excluded from protection or oppressed.[25] Twisted roots and a sense of exclusion of certain social groups intensified their conviction of the need to engage in extra-state social care system. Service clubs, although elite in essence, provided what the state could not offer. Help for the needy became a goal in itself, not a system of dependence based on a fee.

The first service Club taken to Germany was the Rotary Club, with the first local community being Hamburg in 1927.[26] The Second World War was an acid test for service clubs in all of Europe, especially in Germany. Only in the late 1930s did the Nazi regime close the 42 clubs in the Third Reich. Between 1945 and 1967, the United States, because of its strong position in politics, influenced the social life in Western Europe by bringing back other organisations of this type. Participation started to be seen as a civic responsibility due to these clubs' strengthening of the reputation and relationships in the local community. The situation looked different on the east side of the Iron Curtain, where Stalinism refused all non–governmental organisations, so there were none in East Germany, Poland, Romania and Czechoslovakia. In contrast to the Rotary, other service clubs were not interested in expanding during the early periods of their existence. Wilke points out that the clubs did not want to be seen as agents for the promotion of American values abroad.[27] The first German Lions Club was created in

---

[24] L. Jodkowska, *Państwo opiekuńcze w Polsce i w Niemczech* (Warszawa: Difin, 2009), 46–49.
[25] V. Ziegelmayer, *Państwo socjalne w Niemczech. Zmiana systemu?*, in K. Kraus et al. (eds.), *Państwo socjalne w Europie. Historia-rozwój-perspektywy* (Toruń: Wydawnictwo Uniwersytetu Mikołaja Kopernika, 2005), 85–92.
[26] http://rotary.de/was_ist_rotary/index.php (accessed August 11, 2013).
[27] T. Wikle, "International Expansion of the American-Style Service Clubs," *Journal of American Culture* 22 (1999): 42–52.

Düsseldorf in 1951.[28] To be part of the Kiwanis Club, people in the Federal Republic of Germany had to wait until 1963 when the first club was founded in Frankfurt am Main.[29] The collapse of the Soviet Union brought with it the reactivation of service clubs in many countries. According to data from 1997, the only places in Europe where service clubs do not exist are Moldova, Svalbard Island (a territory dependent of Norway, halfway between Norway's mainland and the North Pole), and Vatican City.

## Rotary Club

As mentioned above, the history of the Rotary in Germany started in 1927. In Germany today there are nearly 50,000 members.[30] Rotary in Germany is divided into 15 districts and 1,023 Clubs. Fig 10.1 below shows the location of all 15 districts in Germany.

Fig. 10.1. Rotary districts in Germany

Source: http://rotary.de/clubs/images/distrikte_ab072013.jpg (accessed August 23, 2013).

---

[28] https://www.lions.de/Ueber-Lions/Wer-sind-die-Lions.htm (accessed August 11, 2013).

[29] http://frankfurt-main.kiwanis.de/index.php?id=464 (accessed August 11, 2013).

[30] http://rotary.de/was_ist_rotary/index.php (accessed August 15, 2013).

Although districts in the western part of the country are smaller, there are more clubs because of the historical implications. The biggest number of clubs (107) is in district no.1,840 which is a part of Bayern, the only land in Germany with a roman-catholic majority, and which is also the richest part of Germany. Income in Bayern is approximately 13% higher than in other lands. The biggest is district no. 1,800 (East Lower Saxony and Saxony-Anhalt), where the number of Rotary participants reaches nearly 3,800 women and men in 76 clubs (July 2012).

Service in the Rotary has many levels. The first is Club Service that focus on strengthening fellowship and ensuring that the club can fulfil its duties. In this area, the Rotary uses the work of volunteers who can share their knowledge and experiences and also promote the project. Through their active engagement in the service branches, volunteers contribute to the Rotary's mission. In transferring donations, it is important that the donor club works closely with the goods-receiving club.[31] Vocational Service involves Rotarians, their professional expertise, how they contribute to the development of ethical standards, and how they inspire others through their commitment. As a group of successful people from different branches, Rotary will use this potential to organise educational programs in kindergartens and training for students to help start their careers. The exchange program of Rotary International—comprising Group Study Exchange and New Generation—is the highlight of the international professional service.

The promotion of youth is one of the most important goals set by Rotarians worldwide. The Rotary International Exchange Program, with new annual members ranging from 8,000 to 10,000 young people worldwide, has opened the opportunity of international meetings for its members. Under the protection of the Rotary Club, young people can move abroad. The program is open for children of Rotary members and non-members alike. With these exchanges, the Rotarians seek to contribute to cultural exchange and thus to international understanding and peace. Its objectives are learning about other lifestyles and the depth of experience of different cultures, and, more generally, the extension of one's field of vision and the development of their personality. There are three possibilities when looking at this international travel opportunity: the first is a one-year trip to one of 40 countries offered by Rotary Club Germany. More than 650 students from Germany choose this form of engagement every year. Two other possibilities are short-time exchanges,

---

[31] http://www.rotary.org/de/ServiceAndFellowship/StartAProject/Resources/Pages/ridefault.aspx (accessed August 15, 2013).

such as summer camps or family exchanges. The summer camps each have a special theme with age limits specified by the camp organisers. Camps are staffed internationally, as only one or two participants will be invited per country. This year, camps will be organised in most countries of the European Union, Norway, Turkey, Israel and the U.S. The Rotary also offers the opportunity to live with families in a host country for 3 to 6 weeks. Those who live with a host family should know that both families will receive, for the same length of stay, an international guest. The goals of their vacation, or "family-to-family" exchange, are to promote international understanding and goodwill through the expansion of international communication at the personal level. The only country which does not participate in this program is the United Kingdom.[32]

Each of the Rotary Districts in Germany has a Chairman of International Service. He or she is a member of the Chair District of the German Section of that Intercountry Committee. All of the German Rotary Clubs are linked to more than 1,200 Contact Clubs abroad. The best connection with Clubs in the United States is district no. 1,950, with partner clubs in Athens (GA), Gastonia, and Hickory (NC). Together, German Rotary Clubs have 14 Contact Clubs in the United States.[33]

Some actions supported by Rotary Club Germany are help for disabled people in Badacin, Romania. During the Ceausescu dictatorship period, disabled people could not belong to the society. Children and adolescents, sometimes with severe disabilities, lived in anguish in unheated, bare rooms, and many did not survive the inhumane conditions. With the help of special pedagogic professionals it was possible to create a special place to take care of people with physical and mental disabilities, improving the quality of life for residents in many areas. People who work there are trained and motivated to perform many different promotional offers regularly, enabling the development potential of the residents. At the nursing home management level, as well as the superior governmental agencies, there is a greater desire for individuals to help others with chores around the home, including those persons with disabilities as they too benefit from such participation. This type of engagement is slowly starting to grow.[34]

---

[32] http://www.rotary-jugenddienst.de/jugenddienst/ (accessed August 15, 2013).
[33] http://w4.rotary.de/international_service/index.php (accessed August 15, 2013).
[34] http://de.rotary.de/rdg/abgewickelte_projekte/MG73149_Rumaenien.php (accessed August 15, 2013).

## Kiwanis

Fig. 10.2. Kiwanis districts in Germany

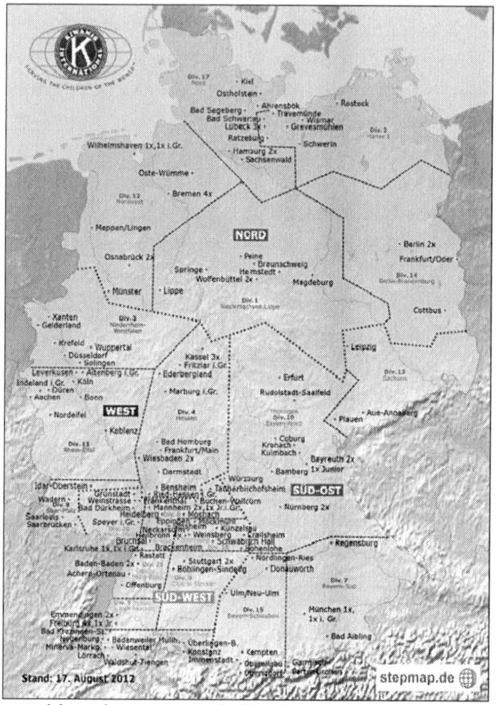


Source: http://www.kiwanis-germany.de/distrikt/ (accessed August 20, 2013).

Kiwanis is the youngest of the worldwide service clubs working in Germany. In Germany, Kiwanis comprised one district composed of four regions—North, West, South-East, South-West—divided into twenty-one divisions. Most of the divisions are in the smallest district, the South-West (seven). In 2012, 145 Kiwanis Clubs existed with 3,300 participants.

The main project of German Kiwanis is supporting "Bethanien Dorf" (Bethany Village), where pedagogs live together with children. Sometimes there are also couples that serve as Children's Village parents. This village living is designed for children and adolescents who do not want to live with their families, or cannot and need a place to escape to. These young people live together in a group home with educators, and adult educators take turns in their service. Relationships are important here too, and students always have the same teachers. In addition, there are many different ways of living with or caring for children and adolescents. These include certain days when the children go back to their parents in the evening. Around three hundred youths are cared for in the three German children's villages in rural families, residential, or day groups. It was necessary to make a major overhaul of houses in Eltville costing 85,000 euros. The Kiwanis Foundation paid 40,000 euros for this.[35]

Another project supported by Kiwanis Germany was the community of Eichof, a village built for people with mental disabilities. It was founded by a community of parents who wanted to create a special place in which their children's capabilities would be best fostered and where each person would be viewed as an individual, each with their own personal strengths and weaknesses.[36]

Financial support allowed the club to provide workshops, build village shops, cafes and a Meeting House. Eichhof also released their own audiobook. Kiwanis Germany gave 100,000 euros for this goal.[37]

## Lions Club

The first German Lions Club was founded in 1951 in Düsseldorf. There are currently 51,032 members in over 1,157 clubs (96 women and 515 mixed clubs) in the Federal Republic of Germany for the community and people in need. Originally, the Lions movement in Germany was open only for men, but that has changed. Today, there are also many women's and mixed clubs. The Lions are in German Multi-District 111. Germany joined the International Association and is represented by the Chairman of the Governors Council (GVR).

Clubs in Ulm and Wiesbaden created in 1954 are the oldest in Germany. Every district is divided into Regions and Zones. The Headquarters of the German Lions is in Wiesbaden (Hesse).[38]

---

[35] http://www.bethanien-kinderdoerfer.de/bethanien/portrait/ (accessed August 17, 2013).
http://www.kiwanis.de/index.php?navid=foundation&subid=bethanien (accessed August 17, 2013).

[36] http://www.eichhof.org/ (accessed August 17, 2013).

[37] http://www.kiwanis.de/index.php?navid=projekte&subid=eichhof (accessed August 17, 2013).

[38] http://www.lions-club-wiesbaden.de/index.php?option=com_content&view =article&id=49&Itemid=66 (accessed August 18, 2013).

Fig. 10.3. Lions districts in Germany (2005)

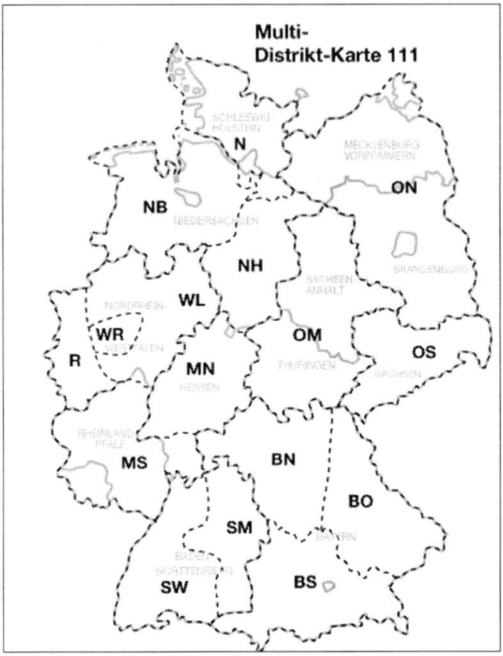


Source: http://www.lions-celle.de/fileadmin/user_upload/
Gesamt-Karte_LIONS_2007.gif (accessed August 20, 2013).

The agency of the German Lions (HDL—Hilfswerd der Deutsches Lions) is a service organisation of all German Lions Club. It is responsible for the management, counselling and, if necessary, financial support of major national and international projects of the club. It also ensures the implementation of the international Sight First program, the Lions Quest program "Growing Up" and the implementation of international youth work. Much of the aid flows into Lions charitable projects and the needy in Germany. In recent years, a majority of the help goes to the youth, the disabled and the elderly. For many years, the most severely injured children are taken from war and crisis zones to the Peace Village International in Oberhausen and treated. Organ donations save lives. The charity provides a donor card with the HDL logo and also Lions special attention for the support of cornea banks.

In November 2012, Lions Club Germany enforced successful action with the main German TV station, RTL, which this year was focused on children in Togo. Around one million euros raised in this project were spent on children's health care. In this project, RTL offered 500,000 euros through its foundation.[39]

The largest project that the German Lions implemented from 2000 to 2005 was the construction of four residential homes for children in the Peace Village in Oberhausen. Peace Village International was founded in 1967 for the care of injured children from war and crisis areas. In their homelands they are inadequately treated; in Germany, they have a chance to heal, and here they get the proper treatment and rehabilitation before returning home. To mark the anniversary of fifty years of Lions in Germany (2002), German Lions collected the sum of 1.5 million euros. In addition, the project was funded by grants from the Lions Clubs International Foundation (LCIF), giving 1.7 million euros along with the new buildings and improvements in the heating system and kitchens. Some Lions Clubs and friends are still involved in the Peace Village. Currently, the Peace Village is supporting children from war and crisis areas, bringing them to Germany, and constructing health and rehabilitation centres in those areas of conflict. Thus, the children can return to their homes and continue to be cared for reliably. Peace Villages led by Lions Germany exist in Vietnam, Cambodia, Angola, Afghanistan, Uzbekistan, Tajikistan, Sri Lanka and Romania.[40] Moreover, as a part of Lions International, Lions Germany helps victims of catastrophes, such as earthquakes in Haiti, floods in Pakistan, Hurricane Katrina in the U.S. and the tsunami in Japan.[41]

## Summary of Service Clubs' Work

According to David Horton Smith, non-governmental organisations are more effective when they develop a significant internal organisational capacity to accomplish their goals. It is possible to make a set of characteristics for successful organisations to foster a sense of local community, justify the group's activities in terms of broader values and ideology, generate cohesiveness and solidarity among members (in part through the two foregoing activities), avoid factionalism that could stall or divide the group, utilize member or non-member expert personnel when needed, obtain external technical assistance without having control

---

[39] http://www.lions-hilfswerk.de/nationale_und_internationale_hilfsprojekte /weltweite_projekte_nach_laendern/weltweite_projekte_im_ueberblick/t/togo /rtl_spendenmarathon_2012_lichtblicke_fuer_kinder_in_togo.html (accessed August 18, 2013).

[40] https://www.friedensdorf.de/ (accessed August 18, 2013).

[41] https://www.lions.de/Unser-Handeln/3257.htm (accessed August 18, 2013).

attached, develop an international web of contacts, and acquire sufficient material resources.[42] Mentioned in this article, all service clubs fulfil these criteria. High effectiveness also brings greater prestige for the organisation, more social, recreational and entertainment meetings, less internal conflicts, and primary goals that serve the general welfare.[43]

Besides helping others, service clubs are making an impression of solidarity, responding to the damage caused by the industrialization of living and working conditions. The inward-looking self-help relates to the internal conditions of the club. Internal orientation refers entirely to tackling the issues of members. A combination of the approaches of Durkheim and Brown would lead to a breakdown of solidarity. For one, the "internal solidarity" supports the self-interest of the members, and second there is the "external solidarity" that supports the interests of others.[44]

The trend in Germany is surprising. It might be initially thought that this shift to more traditional, morally particular, demanding commitment patterns would decrease mainly due to the now much larger weight of engaged elders in the voluntary sector. Despite this, it confirmed that the public interest orientation is typical for older individuals rather than younger ones. The public welfare is still the most important factor of volunteer engagement in this age group, however between 1999 and 2009 percentage rates dropped from 41% to 38%. The second important reason of civic engagement became personal interest, which saw a rise from 24% in 1999 to 35% in 2009. The youngest group (up to 14 years old) saw public welfare becoming an important reason to volunteer, with the rate increasing from 18% in 1999 to 30% in 2009. They also did not do it for social reasons as often as the children in 1999. Socialising was a main reason of volunteering for 43% of children, while in 2009 it was just 30%; 2009 also saw private interest becoming the main motivation of civic engagement (40% polled).[45]

---

[42] D. H. Smith, "The Effective Grassroots Association II: Organizational Factors That Produce External Impact," *Nonprofit Management and Leadership* 10 (1999): 104–106.

[43] Ibid., 109.

[44] K. Radtke, "Die Entgrenzung der Solidarität. Hilfe in einer globalisierten Welt," *Aus Politik und Zeitgeschichte* 21 (2008): 27–32.

[45] T. Gensicke, S. Geiss, *Hauptbericht des Freiwilligensurveys. Zivilgesellschaft, soziales Kapital und freiwilliges Engagement in Deutschland 1999–2004–2009* (München: TNS Infratest Sozialforschung , 2010), 123–126.

## Perspectives for Service Clubs

Concurrency between service clubs are nowadays bigger than before, primarily because of globalisation. They have made more effort to gain new members, which can bring organisational changes. There is a big incentive because rich societies still see the necessity of helping others, even if the ideas were born on the other side of the Atlantic Ocean. The progressive commercialisation of the charity sector opens a new space for service clubs but also brings market rules which have to fit with the reality of every country where the clubs exist and work.[46]

A negative, backward-looking orientation is encountered in many American Service clubs, but fortunately has no equivalent in Germany. On the contrary, the service clubs here are still on the rise. Nevertheless, service clubs should play a more active role in social life. Citizens of the twenty-first century are living in a turbulent period of social, political and especially economic development. The classic dependencies between political community and the nation-state have become less important. Also, in the individual area of our world we are confronted with major changes.

Living conditions are changing rapidly, and this applies particularly to the economy. No phenomenon of recent years in science, politics and the general public has been so violent and controversial as the globalization of the economy. Against this background, the globalization and internationalization of the service idea could play a central role. Similarly, one hundred years ago service clubs offered a bond with their local communities, in particular their expertise in economic issues, locally an important resource for social change.[47]

The growing disproportion in global density can cause problems in the working of service clubs in the coming years. The so-called "rich north" is depopulating and aging; moreover, the level of its wealth fell through the unfavourable economic situation. In this case, service clubs will have difficulty fighting the growing social disparities as effectively as before. A partnership with the big religions of the world is risky but is, in Rademacher's opinion, a good way to create a global society and strengthen the service club's position between NGOs. In today's world it is necessary for clubs, beyond being oriented for human poverty, to become interested in a market economy. To work better they have to

[46] S. Fleßa, "Karitative Nonprofit-Organisationen als Betriebstyp," *Zeitschrift für öffentliche und gemeinwirtschaftliche Unternehmen* 25 (1) (2002): 78–86.

[47] A. Zimmer, "Service Clubs heute—Traditionen und Perspektiven," *Münsteraner Diskussionspapiere zum Nonprofit-Sektor* 18 (2002): 1–10.

observe global growth processes, innovations, technological advances and improved resource productivity.[48]

Especially in the combination of local bonds, economic competence and innovation in the network are great opportunities for service clubs today. This is an opportunity to use the clubs and combine expertise of business, science and social knowhow at the service of their communities and municipalities. The greatest obstacle to reform in Germany is in small-scale departmental thinking. Troubleshooting in modern network structures requires cooperation between the economy and society. Unfortunately, this usually fails because of a lack of communication between them.[49]

The service clubs offer a unique opportunity for multidisciplinary discourse in the service of a practical consensus that points exactly to the needs of the region, community, city or district in which they are based. The globalisation era gives them the possibility to be serious alternatives for NGOs if they overcome their internal problems.

Anna Rydel, B.A. is an M.A. student of International Relations at the Nicolaus Copernicus University in Toruń. She is a holder of the Freda and Leonard T. Zawadzki Scholarship at Southern Oregon University. Her research interests are the history of Central and Eastern Europe, and the foreign policy and party system of the Federal Republic of Germany.

[48] F. J. Radermacher, "Globalisierung, Bevölkerungsentwicklung und Nachhaltigkeit: Herausforderungen für die Gesellschaft und die Rolle von Rotary," in B. Lindsay et al. (eds.), *Sustainability, Human Dignity and the Population Issue*: *Zinser für die IFP&D-UNFPA conference*, New York, May 8, 1999.

[49] A. Zimmer, "Service Clubs heute—Traditionen und Perspektiven," *Münsteraner Diskussionspapiere zum Nonprofit-Sektor* 18 (2002): 1–10.

# CHAPTER ELEVEN

# THE POLISH "SUBTITLES SCENE" IN THE CONTEXT OF POSTMODERN CIVIL SOCIETY

KAMIL ŁUCZAJ
AND MAGDALENA HOŁY-ŁUCZAJ

This chapter presents the results of research into one of the newest phenomena within popular culture—the "subtitles scene." This term refers to creating free subtitles for foreign language films and TV series that Poles, usually illegally, download from the internet. The presented data come from an online survey conducted by the authors between January and March 2013. An extensive questionnaire concerned the basic socio-demographic characteristics of respondents, their motivations to create the subtitles, the ways in which they do it, as well as a number of questions about the use of new technologies in this environment. This group is especially interesting in the context of civil society. This chapter proposes to perceive the "subtitlers" as postmodern creators of this phenomenon.

It consists of seven parts. The first specifies our understanding of the term "subtitles scene" and provides theoretical reflection on sharing the files for free on the internet. The second discusses the methodology of research. The third concerns the socio-demographic profile of respondents. The fourth concentrates on their participation in culture. The fifth is dedicated to methods employed in creating Polish-language subtitles. The sixth is focused on the motivation driving respondents to do it for free, and the last recapitulates the results of research and clarifies the relation between this cultural phenomenon and civil society.

## Content Circulation on the Internet— Collective Intelligence, Civil Society, Internet Altruism or the Cult of the Amateur?

Social research on altruistic behaviour on the Internet is intensively developing. Until now, scholars have analyzed such phenomena as exchange of knowledge on forums and Wikipedia, motivation to write consumer reviews, or making entertainment content for free.[1] The least-known phenomenon in this field remains the so-called "subtitles scene," which is typical for non-English-speaking countries.[2] The creators of free subtitles, who translate dialogue in films, respond to the vivid needs of users of illegal copies of films and TV series distributed online.

Subtitling is strongly connected with illegal online file sharing. Although this phenomenon is not the subject of our analysis, it is worth presenting its scale and significance in Poland. It is so because the occurrence of the subtitles scene results directly from the unofficial "circulation" of films. The research carried out by Mirosław Filiciak and his team confirms that this is a widespread phenomenon in Poland, with three quarters of respondents declaring participation in file sharing.[3] The answers concerning the reasons for participating in the content circulation turned out to be very interesting. The largest group, covering almost half of active internet users, claimed that the content circulation is simply "expanding their horizons." The key factor according to them is the possibility to "know more" thanks to it, and not the fact that it provides a

---

[1] See A. Halfaker et al., "The Rise and Decline of an Open Collaboration System: How Wikipedia's Reaction to Popularity Is Causing Its Decline," *American Behavioral Scientist* 5(57) (2013): 664–688; S. Utz, "Egoboo vs. Altruism: the Role of Reputation in Online Consumer Communities," *Media & Society* 11 (3) (2009): 357–374; H. Jenkins et al., *Spreadable Media: Creating Value and Meaning in a Networked Culture* (New York: New York University Press, 2013) (we used the Amazon Kindle edition of the book, which does not provide numbers of pages, so we refer to this publication in general).

[2] In English-speaking countries a similar phenomenon is "fansubbing," but it is related only to anime subtitles. See H. Jenkins et al., *Spreadable Media*; M. Ito, "Contributors vs. Leechers: Fansubbing Ethics and Hybrid Public Culture," in M. Ito et al., (eds.), *Fandom Unbound. Otaku Culture in a Connected World* (New Heaven 2012), 179–204; J. D. Cintas, "Funsubs: Audiovisual Translation in Amateur Environment," *Journal of Specialised Translation* 6 (2006): 37.

[3] M. Filiciak et al., *Obiegi kultury: Społeczna cyrkulacja treści: Raport z badań*, Warszawa 2012, http://creativecommons.pl/wp-content/uploads/2012/01/raport_obiegi_kultury.pdf, (accessed April 20, 2013).

free source of content.[4] It should be highlighted that illegal file sharing on the internet is characteristic for countries where the release of films or TV shows is delayed, or where this content is not distributed at all.[5] This diagnosis, in other European countries, has been confirmed by the research conducted by Hungarian scholars Bodó Balazs and Zoltán Lakatos, who analyzed which films are downloaded most frequently. Their results indicate that the people involved in file sharing in Hungary are mainly interested in films which are currently not shown in cinemas rather than those which are legally available.[6] Likewise, it appeared that Polish persons who participate in file sharing most intensively are at the same time those who reach out for payable cultural content most often, representing 32% who buy books, 51% music and 31% films.[7] These results suggest that the informal content circulation is not an alternative for the legal one, but that it supports the consumption of legally purchased cultural goods. All these facts incline to the revision of preconceived notions, according to which downloading movies from the internet is "piracy." Thereby, we share Jenkins, Ford and Green's opinion, who believe that "one of the problems of the current use of 'piracy' is that it shortcuts important conversations we should all be having about the economic and cultural impact of different types of media sharing."[8]

In this context, scholars employ such terms as "content circulation," "file sharing" or "spreadability" instead of "piracy."[9] These terms refer to the opportunity to share files found on the internet by its users, sometimes with the permission of the copyright holders, and sometimes against their will. In the same manner we recognize the creators of free Polish-language subtitles (members of the "subtitles scene"). Our chapter describes this community, thanks to which access to foreign films and TV series has significantly increased. Quite often, these are works that were not officially translated into Polish because they were not officially distributed in Poland. However, watching films in the original version requires language proficiency which many people interested in the particular content lack. Therefore, we would like to answer the two following

---

[4] Ibid., 7.

[5] See H. Jenkins et al., *Spreadable Media*; A. De Kosnik, *Piracy is the Future of Television* (Berkeley: University of California, 2010), http://boletines.prisadigital.com/piracy_future_television-full.pdf (accessed April 20, 2013).

[6] M. Filiciak et al., *Obiegi kultury*, 18.

[7] Ibid., 39–41.

[8] H. Jenkins et al., *Spreadable Media*.

[9] See M. Filiciak et al., *Obiegi kultury*; Jenkins et al., *Spreadable Media*.

questions: (1) who are the people making Polish-language subtitles for free, and (2) what motivates them to do it.

In the theoretical reflection there are two attempts to answer this second question. The first is based on the notion of "collective intelligence." This term, according to Jean-François Noubel, refers to "the capability for a group of people to collaborate in order to achieve goals in a complex context."[10] Its basic form is "original collective intelligence," which is usually represented by a group of 10 to 20 people. Its functioning is based on the following principles: transparency, collective consciousness, polymorphic structure, high learning ability, the convergence of individual and social interests and the logic involved in the gift economy.[11] A new type of social organisation, "Global Collective Intelligence," is, as Noubel claims, built on the same fundaments as its original form. What differs is a lack of member limit and necessity of physical contact in the Global Collective Intelligence.[12] The individuals who participate in the process of exchange do not have to be related in any closer way, or know each other. They can be (and most often are) anonymous. However, it does not prevent them from achieving their goal (creating something), which constitutes the actual link between them.[13] The occurrence of collective intelligence seems like a full realization of the idea of civil society. When we define the former, in a popular and widely accepted way, as "a public space between the state, the market and the ordinary household, in which people can debate and tackle action,"[14] it becomes obvious that subtitlers' work should be perceived in such a way. It is definitely a set of activities located between state- and market-driven actions. The definition of the civil society, however, has a hidden assumption, and every civic activity

[10] J.-F. Noubel, *Collective Intelligence: The Invisibile Revolution*, 2004, 19, http://www.thetransitioner.org/Collective_Intelligence_Invisible_Revolution_JFNoubel.pdf (accessed April 20, 2010).

[11] Ibid., 2–15. In the "gift economy" (as opposed to the competition-based economy) we are not individually paid (usually in money) for our work, but we benefit as the members of the community. Alain Caille, who investigates "new media," states directly that "the Internet relations are the relations of a gift." See Filiciak et al., *Obiegi kultury*, 24.

[12] J.-F. Noubel, *Collective Intelligence*, 9.

[13] Ibid., 8.

[14] R. Sarnaik, "What Is Civil Society?," *BBC World Service*, http://www.bbc.co.uk/worldservice/people/highlights/010705_civil.shtml (accessed May 2, 2013). See V. Perez-Diaz, "The Possibility of Civil Society: Traditions, Character and Challenges," in J. R. Hall (ed.), *Civil Society: Theory, History, Comparison* (Wiley 1995); M. Kaldar, "The Idea of Global Civil Society," *International Affairs* 3 (79) (2003): 583–593.

must serve the community. The cultural phenomena related to crowdsourcing and/or file sharing also meet this requirement. It is worth noticing that today's civil society, at least in developed countries, is different from the civil society of the 1980s or 1990s. Today, most civic actions take place on the internet. A prime example of this is Wikipedia—an encyclopedia written by internet users.[15]

Paradoxically, Wikipedia was a pretext to the formulation of a critique of free sharing of knowledge and other content on the internet. Commenting on the phenomenon of Wikipedia, in 2005 Nicholas Carr coined the term "the cult of the amateur," which was popularized by Andrew Keen.[16] The main topic of his work is the participation of amateurs in creating different types of content, which, in the author's opinion, should be done by professionals. Keen thinks that:

> the free, user-generated content spawned and extolled by the Web 2.0 revolution is decimating the ranks of our cultural gatekeepers, as professional critics, journalists, editors, musicians, moviemakers, and other purveyors of expert information are being replaced by amateur bloggers, hack reviewers, homespun moviemakers, and attic recording artists.[17]

His criticism is, however, aimed at Wikipedia as the main result of the work of internet users, "where anyone with opposable thumbs and a fifth-grade education can publish anything on any topic from AC/DC to Zoroastrianism."[18] In his book, Keen sarcastically "foretells" that those "noble amateurs would democratize the dictatorship of expertise."[19] The question, which we would like to pose, concerns the correctness of this diagnosis in the context of the work done by members of the Polish subtitles scene. Does the fact that subtitles available on sites such as Napiprojekt.pl or Podnapisi.net are free mean that they are of poor quality?

---

[15] J.-F. Noubel, *Collective Intelligence*, 31.

[16] A. Keen, *The Cult of the Amateur: How Blogs, MySpace, YouTube, and the Rest of Today's User-Generated Media are Destroying our Economy, our Culture, and our Values* (New York: Doubleday, 2007), 32.

[17] Ibid., 36–37.

[18] Ibid., 27.

[19] Ibid., 52.

## Research Tool and Sampling

Respondents who filled out the questionnaire did so without any financial incentive in response to the invitation extended by the researchers. The research method was chosen due to the fact that there is no other possibility to make contact with respondents in which we were interested (e.g. there are no rallies of subtitles creators). The questionnaire consisted of 47 questions, of which 7 were open-ended.

The procedure of sampling consisted of three stages. In the first, researchers, using the e-mails available on webpages and Facebook, contacted the representatives of the most popular groups of Polish-language subtitles creators: the KinoMania SubGroup, the DarkProject SubGroup, Project Haven, and the NewAge SubTeam oraz Hawaii SubTeam. In the letter, which presented our research, we placed a link to an online survey along with a request to disseminate news about the study among the members of the group. We got 14 questionnaires back. Searching for other respondents, we used the Polish section of the portal Podnapisi.net. This choice was dictated by the availability of a list of users who have posted on subtitles, which allowed us to make contact with them. The invitation was sent to those persons who submitted at least one set of subtitles.[20] At this stage we also received 14 questionnaires. During the next one we used the limited possibilities of making contact with subtitle creators (e.g. names of authors of the most popular subtitles, the newest and recommended ones) offered by the portal Opensubtitles.org. In this way we got three questionnaires. In the last stage, the invitation was sent to the users of less popular subtitles websites,[21] thanks to which we received 10 questionnaires.

Finally, 41 respondents took part in the online research. Our analysis concentrates on 40 results, because one respondent turned out to be a professional translator. The majority of respondents did not belong to any of the aforementioned groups. Among those affiliated, there were members of the Hatak Group (15%), Project Haven (10%), Kinomania.org and NAPIerce-SQUAD (each 2.5%).

The sample size, although not very large, seems sufficient to perform exploratory research due to the four independent factors. Firstly, it can be

[20] The letter also contained information that respondent can send the questionnaire to other known subtitles creators.

[21] They were: (1) http://animesub.info/uzytkownicy.php
(2) http://subtitlesbank.com/pl/subtitles/language/pl/
(3) http://v2.subscene.com/subtitles/polish.aspx
(4) http://www.nast.ws/profile.php?lookup=14519 (all accessed May 2, 2013).

assumed that the investigated community is very limited in number. Reviewing all the websites devoted to Polish subtitles we often encountered the same nicks, suggesting that the same authors publish on various sites. This preliminary hypothesis was confirmed by the results obtained in the questionnaires. Moreover, it appears that many users of websites with subtitles only post subtitles, but do not create them. Secondly, subtitles creators may have been reluctant to express their opinions because they make subtitles for illegal materials, despite assurances from the researchers that the survey has scientific goals only, and is completely anonymous. Thirdly, by deliberately not placing the questionnaire on internet forums (in order to find people actively creating Polish-language subtitles), we probably limited the range of potential participants in the survey. However, it seems that the most important is the fourth reason, which is the spread of invitations to fill questionnaires seemingly similar to ours, made for the purposes of students' essays and theses. Unfortunately, those questionnaires, in each case examined by us, were negligent and contained a large number of methodological errors, and logical or technical problems. Mostly, they were questionnaires consisting of several yes/no questions. Conducting such "research" is a textbook example of respondents becoming disheartened.

The respondent who receives such a poorly designed questionnaire has sound reasons to be discouraged from participating in similar research. Hoping to weaken this effect, in the letter to the respondents we underlined that the questionnaire was created by an experienced researcher affiliated to the Institute of Sociology at Jagiellonian University, and we sent a link to the website where his identity could be verified. Moreover, we guaranteed that respondents would receive the article based on the results of the research.

## Who Are the "Subtitlers"?

In sampling there were twice as many men (27) as women (13). The oldest respondent was born in 1966, the youngest in 1998. Therefore, the youngest respondent was 15 years old on the day of the research, and the oldest 47. The average age was 27. Most frequently, the respondents were 24. Receiving a median value of 25 years (lower than the mean), we can say that the oldest respondents slightly overstated the mean age of the person creating the subtitles. Most people in the sample indicated work (52.5%) or studies (42.5%) as their main occupation, and two people currently did not study or work. Half of the respondents identified the situation of their household as average ("It is sufficient for every day, but we need to save"), and 30% described it as good ("We can afford much without a special need to save"). The other answers, "We live modestly" and "We live very well," were indicated by two and one person, respectively. More than half of the respondents (52.5%) lived in a house or apartment owned by the family (parents, grandparents, etc.), 17.5% had their own apartment, and almost one third of respondents (30%) rented an apartment.

The average household comprised three people. As many as 62.5% of respondents were not currently in a relationship and, interestingly, the distribution of these responses was not related to the ages of the respondents. While the data gathered by the Central Statistical Office say that nearly 60.0% of the population in Poland was in a stable relationship (54.6% married, 2.4% in non-formal), compared to 27.2% single people, the respondents seem to contradict the existing model of the family.[22] Moreover, as many as 92.5% of the respondents did not have children. The three people who did have children were 40 years old. These data allow us to conclude that subtitles creators are mainly people carrying out a so-called new family model.

Almost half of the respondents (52.5%) defined themselves as religious believers (but half of this group does not participate in religious ceremonies), while 35% are atheists or agnostics. As many as 40% of respondents said that they are not interested in politics, or do not have definite political views, and almost one third (27.5%) did not want to answer this question. The views of other people were divided more or less equally between right-wing, left-wing and liberal.

Almost all respondents lived in Poland (95%). Two people lived in England and Australia. Only one person, who lived in Poland, had stayed abroad for more than six months. Therefore, these data allow us to conclude that the subtitles creators are, in general, young or middle-aged, affluent persons, connected to their home country. However, they neglect the religious and other cultural patterns of traditional Polish culture.

The level of education of respondents was high. Half of them had a university degree, almost half had a medium education, and the only respondent with a primary education was born in 1998. Those who got a university degree graduated in technical, exact or natural sciences (50%), with slightly less in humanities (45%), and relatively few in foreign philology (5%). Among those still learning were one junior high school student, two high school students, four university students of humanities

---

[22] *Rocznik demograficzny 2012*, 157, http://www.stat.gov.pl/cps/rde/xbcr/gus/rs_rocznik_demograficzny_2012.pdf (accessed April 21, 2013).

(other than foreign philology), one student of foreign philology, seven students of natural sciences, and one student whose field of study was difficult to classify. The great majority of graduates studied only in Poland (90%), and the rest spent a few semesters abroad.

We did not ask about the place of residence because we expected (and, as it turned out it, this was a good supposition) that the majority of respondents would be students or people with a university degree. Such persons, regardless of where they came from, had cultural contact with a big city. The collected data (we asked about the city in which the respondent studied), indicate that members of the Polish subtitles scene are mainly associated with the largest Polish metropolitan areas: 25% studied in Warsaw, 15% in Krakow, and 10% in Wroclaw.

Nearly 70% of respondents knew more than one language; 62.5% of respondents knew two languages in a communicative degree; 2.5% knew three languages, and another 2.5% four.[23] The most popular foreign language was English, which all respondents knew. As many as 77.5% of respondents knew it at the B2 or C1 levels (according to the classification of the Council of Europe, which measures the knowledge on the six levels from A1 to C2), which corresponds to the second step in the level of independence and the first step of linguistic proficiency. The second most popular language was German, the knowledge of which was declared by 65% of respondents, but the degree of knowledge of German was very diverse. The situation with Russian was similar, and 32.5% of respondents knew it, but the fluency varied greatly in this case. French language (17.5%) and oriental language speakers (15%)[24] were less fluent (A1-B2), while 25% of respondents also knew another European language.

The profile of a typical subtitles creator proved to be consistent with our assumptions—a relatively well-off young person (much more often men than women), with a university degree, who knows several foreign languages. Translators' occupations were more difficult to predict. As it turned out, amongst them there were production workers, office workers, salespeople (sales representatives, advisors in a media store), middle managers, professionals (a researcher, journalist, software developer, a self-employed person, a coach), as well as an officer of the prison service.

One of our detailed research questions was whether such individuals constitute an online community, or whether they are individuals. We know that as many as 52.5% of respondents get to know other subtitles creators via the internet ("there were no subtitles for the TV series I watch, and

---

[23] One person declared that he or she does not know any language on the communicative level.

[24] Half of them were manga fans.

after contacting a person who translated it previously, I stared to collaborate with her"), 17.5% knew such people before they started creating subtitles ("I was encouraged by a friend," "my colleague e-mailed me, because he searched for some help in creating comics and cartoons"), and 7.5% of respondents got to know them in another way. This shows that only one third of respondents have no contact with other subtitles creators.

Some of the questions were constructed in such a way that we were able to investigate the attitude of respondents toward the issue of potential copyright infringement. Respondents did not have a clear opinion concerning the statement that downloading movies from the internet with violation of copyright is a crime, but rather reluctantly agreed with it (the average score on the five-point scale was 2.33).[25] What is interesting is that they would like to protect the effect of their work, and the statement "Subtitles made by me are my intellectual property and cannot be changed (corrected) without my permission" was supported by a large part of the respondents (3.53).

## How Do Subtitles Creators Participate in Culture?

It should not surprise anyone that respondents actively use the internet. According to their declarations they do it daily for about 6 hours (median).[26] Subtitles creators were also active in social media. As many as 82.5% had a Facebook account,[27] 37.5% had a Google+ account, and 22.5% each had an nk.pl (Polish social networking servis) and Twitter account. Furthermore, more than 45% had an account at Chomikuj.pl (a popular file sharing service, considered by many as the main pirate site in Poland). Only three respondents (7.5%) did not have an account at any of these services.

Almost three quarters of respondents had an account on websites related to creating subtitles: 57.5% of respondents had an account at Napisy24.pl, 42.5% at NapiProjekt.pl, 32% at Kinomania.org, 27% at Opensubtitles.org, 25% at service Grupahatak.pl, and 22% at Napisy.info. As the best sources of Polish language subtitles, respondents indicated

[25] Respondents could assess statements on a 1–5 scale, where 1 referred to "I strongly disagree" and 5 "I strongly agree." The more the average score (given in brackets) is closer to 5, the more respondents accepted this claim.

[26] The median is equal to the mode. The average (8.5 hours) was overstated by some extreme results.

[27] The fact of having an account on this website was not associated with age.

napisy24.pl, napisy.info, podnapisi.net, grupahatak.pl, animesubinfo, and OpenSubtitles.

Respondents go to the movies relatively often—57.5% do it once a year, 17.5% at least once a month, and 5% at least once a week. Significantly fewer respondents buy movies on DVD or use video on demand services. Half of the respondents do it less than once a year (52.5%), while only 15% say that they do it at least once a month. When we compare data concerning watching TV and purchasing DVDs with data concerning time spent watching films and TV series by the respondents, it turns out that subtitles creators mostly watch films downloaded from the internet. On average, during the week the respondents devoted 12 hours to watching films. However, many of them (55%) do not watch TV at all.[28]

The respondents can be described as active participants in culture (in the broadest sense). A significant part of respondents declared that they read books regularly. As many as 35% read a book at least once a week, 27.5% at least once a month, 25% several times a year, and 5% once a year. Only 7.5% of respondents read a book less than once a year. In comparison to data gathered by the National Library and TNS Poland, in 2012 this ratio seems to be low because this research shows that 61% of Poles had not read a book in the last year. Moreover, 34% of Poles with a university degree did not read a book during the previous twelve months.[29] Readership of magazines is similar, with 35% of subtitles creators reading them at least once a month, 22.5% less frequently (several times a year), another 22.5% more frequently (once a week), and 20% once a year or less. Meanwhile, 60% of subtitles creators go to a pub or restaurant at least once a month, 25% several times a year, and 15% once a year or less. Some respondents actively participate in club life, with 20% of respondents declaring regular visits to clubs (at least once a month), 37.5% several times a year and 10% once a year. One third of respondents go to a club less often than once a year. The frequency of visits to theatres is much lower. As many as 75% of respondents go less than once a year, 10% once a year, and only 15% more often. This result is consistent with

[28] Those who watch TV do it traditionally (TV set, aerial, decoder), or with official players made available by broadcasters (IPLA, TVN Player), or internet streaming (Weeb.tv, Polsky.tv). These three options were chosen by 35.0%, 17.5% and 7.5% of all respondents, respectively. Some of them choose more than one way to watch television.

[29] R. Chymkowski, *Społeczny zasięg książki w Polsce w 2012 r.*, 2–3, http://www.bn.org.pl/download/document/1362741578.pdf (accessed April 21, 2013).

the national average. In 2011 all Polish drama theatres were visited by only 7 million people.[30] Respondents also sporadically participated in sport events (77.5% at once a year or less).

In order to complete the portrait of Polish-language subtitles creators, we also asked them about the electronic devices they own. The largest part (80%) have a TV and radio set, while 60% also have a DVD player, 47.5% a TV decoder, 30% a game console, 20% e-book readers, and 10% a tablet. These statistics show that those people are generally open to new technologies. What is interesting is that almost all respondents (92.5%) use Windows, and the others use Linux. We can infer from this that creators of subtitles are not Mac users (in Poland, Mac computers are popular among affluent urban youths and companies, or people who want to create a "modern and dynamic" image). Thereby, it can be assumed that subtitles creators do not belong to any of these categories. The question about the computer operating system the respondents use at home can be considered a secondary indicator of their level of wealth (we assume that more wealthy people use up-to-date devices). Among Windows users, 67.5% used a new version (Windows 7 or 8) in comparison to 32.5% using older versions (XP and older).

## How Are Polish-language Subtitles Created?

Subtitles creators use specialized dictionaries while they are working, with 57.5% of respondents using them "often" and another 20% "from time to time." Only 12.5% of respondents do not use them at all. More than half of the respondents use Google Translator in creating subtitles, 37.5% of them do it "often" and 15% do it "always." Other translators are used by a little less than half of the respondents (27.5% "sometimes," 17.5% "often"). Half of the respondents look for help on the websites dedicated to foreign languages, and 7.5% of respondents do it often; 20% of respondents additionally seek a native speaker's help (but none of them do it often). Much more often, respondents consult the effects of their work with non-native speakers—20% of respondents ask people from their social surroundings, and another 35% ask other people. So in total we have 55% of respondents who consult with others, while another 30% do not but take into account the amendments submitted by other users. Only 15% of respondents never improve the primary effect of their work.

---

[30] *Kultura w 2011 roku* (Warszawa: GUS, 2012), 451, http://www.stat.gov.pl/cps/rde/xbcr/gus/kts_kultura_w_2011.pdf (accessed April 21, 2013).

We were also interested in the general method of creating subtitles. We asked respondents whether they use subtitles in foreign languages or make translations based on listening. It turned out that more than half the respondents (55%) use both methods but prefer to base their translations on foreign subtitles, while 40% translate only on the basis of foreign subtitles. So, in total we have 95% who give preference to this technique. This can be explained by the fact that translating based on listening comprehension is much more difficult and time consuming compared to translating a foreign text. The two remaining respondents were in favour of translations based on listening comprehension, one arguing that: "I do not tolerate translating texts. Scenes should be translated." However, such utterances were very rare.

The average respondent has created subtitles for three years. Long-serving subtitles creators have not done it for longer than 8 years. If we keep in mind the fact that an average member of the subtitles scene has created 30 sets of subtitles (median), we can state that respondents create subtitles relatively often. However, it should be pointed out that respondents differ very much in this regard—some have created a few sets of subtitles, while some have created a few hundred. When asked to assess the regularity of work on the subtitles the respondents said that they do it not so regularly (the average score on a five-point scale was 3.00.)

Creating subtitles is, according to respondents, a difficult and time-consuming activity. A great part of respondents openly admitted that translating subtitles creates some difficulties (the average score on a five-point scale was 3.00). Creating subtitles for a 40-minute film takes, on average (median), 5 hours. Only 25% of respondents declared that they are able to do it in less than 3 hours. So, respondents generally agreed that making subtitles takes a lot of time and is tiring. Therefore, this brings us to the crucial question—why do they do it?

## What Motivates Subtitles Creators?

In order to answer this question we asked respondents to take a stance on a series of statements, allowing us to evaluate in a measurable way their attitudes towards the results of their work. Respondents definitely agreed with the first statement ("When I make subtitles I feel that I do something useful"). Their answers were close to absolute agreement (average 4.47). The majority of respondents admit that they took pleasure in creating subtitles (4.18). The reliability of this question is also confirmed by the open-ended question ("I really enjoy it," "It's my hobby," "I do love language"). Respondents are sometimes driven by the need to deepen their understanding of a film ("to understand the film better, to enjoy a film").[31] At the same time, none of the respondents claimed that he or she does not like to create subtitles. Some of them treat it as their favourite form of spending leisure time (2.90), although opinions on this matter were divided. Some of the respondents find creating subtitles to be the best way to cure boredom or kill time ("Finding an activity during job search," "The way to kill free time," "I've started making subtitles basically out of boredom"). A significant number of respondents also agreed (4.63) with the statement that subtitling helps them to raise their linguistic skills. It also turned out that respondents usually chose to translate those films and TV series which they had already planned to watch (4.15). This result is confirmed by the answers to open-ended questions ("I'm a fan of British films and TV series and I translate mostly them"). Respondents were also asked to say if "they create subtitles at somebody's request." The average score on this (2.73) contrasts sharply with the answers given to the previous question. This result, analyzed in the context of a selfish choice of TV series and recognizing subtitling as a chance to polish language skills, can be treated as an argument against the theory of collective intelligence. Those results indicate that motivations related to own interests are more important for respondents than motivations oriented toward other people. Moreover, very often, even if respondents pointed to some other people, they were younger brothers, wives and girlfriends; that is, persons closely attached to the translator. In some responses ("I am pleased when I see that my subtitles are popular") we can observe a discourse of self-realization.[32] Respondents expected at least slight gratitude for their work ("It is about just some simple thanks in the form of comments on subtitles"). In some responses we can see associations with the ideology expressed in the slogan "Do It Yourself," which demands taking matters into one's own hands and condemning passive expectation ("[I've started to create subtitles] Because I used to complain at the lack of them"; "No one else wanted to translate this TV series, so I decided to try it by myself").

A few respondents, however, spoke about their selfless helping of unknown people ("I did something for others who weren't able to do it

---

[31] This idea is consistent with the theory of translation, which says that only in the act of translation—not the reading or listening even with a good knowledge of the language—do we appropriate the meaning of the work. See U. Dąmbska-Prokop, *Warsztat tłumacza i jego pułapki* (Kielce: Wyższa Szkoła Umiejętności, 2005), 9–10.

[32] See M. Olcoń-Kubicka, *Indywidualizacja a nowe formy wspólnotowości* (Warszawa: Wydawnictwo Naukowe Scholar, 2009), 39–41.

without me"; "Some people do not know English/German and it would be difficult for them to understand a TV series in the original language version"; "I would like to allow people who do not speak the English language to watch films which I translate," "TV series/films, which are unavailable in our country are often very interesting," "Korean cinema, which is not well known in Poland, is very good, and it can be a great antidote to the flood of American crap. It is also a form of protest and rebellion against moronic pap served by Polish television"), on the basis of which such projects as Wikipedia are founded. Clearly, community-oriented motivations were seen only among manga fans and fans of Far East movies, who emphasized that they create for a certain community: "I translate in 100% South Indian cinema, that is Telugu, Tamil and Malayalam, in order to have someone with whom I can talk about it"; "Willingness to expand among a Polish audience the interest in anime series that I liked, but that are not translated."

Additionally, in the questionnaire there was an open-ended question concerning motivations to create subtitles. The most commonly cited reason was a desire to develop language skills ("Free language training," "I find it a good way to polish the language," "to polish my English"). It confirms the information obtained by multiple-choice questions. For respondents it is very important that thanks to translating subtitles they learn languages, which does not come from a textbook ("Creating subtitles to films and TV series gives me the opportunity to have contact with language expressions, vocabulary etc. which are spoken in reality, and not how they are taught in school"). It is worth noting that the respondents usually mentioned "polishing" language rather than "studying" it. The high language skills declared by respondents allow for capturing not only errors, but also inaccuracies in the translation ("I decided [to start subtitling] when I knew English good enough—I came to the conclusion that the subtitles have a lot of mistakes and do not reflect the exact point in the dialogue, so I wanted to try my hand"). At this point it is useful to recall the theory of translation, which stresses that the (correct) translation of the text requires not only extensive knowledge of the vocabulary, but also different shades of meaning of words, phraseology, proverbs, idioms and above all the cultural context. Without knowledge of the connotations of different expressions it is easy to distort the meaning of translated dialogues.[33] The interpreter should, however, also have a highly developed competence in the native language. Translated sentences should be conveyed in accordance with the logic of the Polish language and in a

[33] See U. Dąmbska-Prokop, *Warsztat tłumacza i jego pułapki*, 149–150.

manner appropriate for the Polish cultural context.[34] It seems that this is a reason why respondents often pointed to the improvement of their Polish language as a motivation to create the subtitle ("for training a foreign language and mother tongue," "training English as well as Polish").

If the subtitles creators point out that one of their goals is the development of language skills, it is justifiable to describe them as amateurs (as Andrew Keen suggests). However, in light of the collected data the case seems to be more complicated. Many authors have pointed out that the distinction between professionals and amateurs has become increasingly vague and perplexing. For this reason, it seems more efficient to make a division between formal and informal elements of the media industries we have used so far.[35] Moreover, the subtitles scene is very diverse and it is difficult to label all its members "amateurs" or "professionals." Many subtitle creators reveal, in spite of the lack of formal qualifications, a consciousness typical of professional translators, emphasizing the quality of their subtitles ("Subtitling is definitely not for everyone. It is a work that should be done diligently, without haste. Each subtitle is important. According to the respondents, someone who knows a foreign language at a basic level should not take it, because he or she will mainly use automatic translators and fail to notice blatant and often basic errors in their subtitles. It is also necessary to know Polish spelling rules, punctuation, and syntax"). The unsatisfactory quality of subtitles is often indicated as the reason for taking an interest in translation ("I was not satisfied with the quality of the subtitles to one of my favourite TV series," "I was motivated to create my first subtitles, because of the terrible quality of subtitles to the show that I wanted to watch," "Because there were no good subtitles for the series/movie," "Well, I do not get headaches seeing spelling mistakes and translation errors"). On the basis of these comments one can argue with Keen's thesis. It seems that in the light of these statements, as well as knowledge of some effects of the respondents work, it can be stated that one does not have to be a professional to ensure a high standard of content that is placed on the internet for free. It should also be noted that, although the immediate cause of creating subtitles is usually a personal interest or close relation with someone who has asked for them, these are not the only motivations. Quite often, a selfish motivation constitutes an impulse to create subtitles for a wider audience. Respondents presented their reasoning as follows: "And if I've already translated [subtitles for my friend], why not to share the effects of my

---

[34] Ibid., 8–90.

[35] See Filiciak et al., *Obiegi kultury*, 20.

work with the others?"; "Then [after translating subtitles for the brother] I came to the idea of publishing them."

## Summary

Contrary to Keen's theory, it is difficult to describe the creators of Polish-language subtitles as "incompetent amateurs." Although they are usually not professional translators (not having a philological education nor jobs related to art), they take their work seriously. In many cases they have undergone transformations from being a consumer of pop culture to becoming a contributor to it. Thanks to their work, products of Western culture which, due to corporate policies in the entertainment industry, are unavailable in Poland can be viewed by others.

It is worth noting, however, that altruism is often not the main motive inducing respondents to undertake unpaid work. For this reason, they are not typical representatives of "collective intelligence." Nevertheless, many people enjoy the results of their work. In this case, the second element of the definition of civil society, which we have already mentioned, is fulfilled. Subtitling is obviously an activity that helps many people, providing access to the texts of culture which, as a result of economic decisions, remain unavailable in many non-English speaking countries (or they at least come with a significant delay). By saying that, we also touch on the first element of a common-sense definition. The subtitle scene is distinctive both from the state and economy. In our opinion, it is actually a brilliant realization of the postmodern civil society because it goes beyond traditional participation. It is a postmodern civil society—a civil society online.[36]

This chapter is an introduction to the basis for a more detailed research on the issue, through which we can examine the postmodern civil society regarding other examples. But, even in our field, further research is needed. For example, in the study we did not ask about issues concerning the technical preparation of subtitles, which can also be an interesting research topic. Creating subtitles requires not only linguistic competence but also some technical knowledge of how to synchronize them with a film. Furthermore, it would be desirable to compare the results obtained by us with some foreign research. Unfortunately, to date such studies have not been conducted. A tool created by us allows for the replication of the

---

[36] C. Farrington, *Models of Civil Society and their Implications for the Northern Ireland Peace Process* (Dublin: Institute for British-Irish Studies, University College Dublin 2004), 14.

study in other countries. We perceive a comparison of two groups of countries as particularly important—Central and Eastern Europe (where presumably we will see similar motivations for creating titles) and the countries of Western Europe (where the motivations of the members of the subtitle scene may be completely different, because of the shorter distance to the world "centre").

Kamil Łuczaj is a PhD student at the Institute of Sociology at the Jagiellonian University. His scientific interests are the sociology of culture and visual sociology.

Magdalena Hoły-Łuczaj is a PhD student at the Institute of Philosophy at the Jagiellonian University. Her scientific interests are contemporary philosophy and philosophical anthropology.

# PART THREE

# QUALITY OF REGIONAL AND LOCAL IDENTITY AS A DEMOCRATIC PATTERN OF EFFICACY OF CIVIL SOCIETY

# CHAPTER TWELVE

# THE GOVERNANCE MODEL IN THE POST-SOCIALIST CITY: NECESSITY OR NATURAL DEVELOPMENT?

ADAM JAROSZ

## Introduction

Nowadays, local governments all over the world are searching for new methods of governing and managing. The new challenges to local governments, together with the globalisation processes, budgetary problems and the growing conscience of societies force the new relations of power at the local level to be defined. The cities are the centres of growth on the one hand, and a complex sphere of different actors on the other. The governance concept, which combines the influences and potential of different actors, is one of the solutions to the new challenges. This also concerns post-socialist countries and their local governments, which after the period of transition have redefined their ways of formulating policies.

The systemic transformation had a great influence on cities, and social, economic, spatial as well as political changes can be observed, influencing the development of cities both positively and negatively. This chapter follows these changes and presents not only the restructurings but also the great challenges appearing after fifty years of communist rule.[1]

The main aim of this chapter is to present the possibilities of introducing the idea of governance within the conditions of a post-socialist city. The specifics of the post-socialist transition on the level of cities, the

---

[1] J. Friedrichs, H. Häußermann, "Die Entwicklung der Städte in den neuen Bundesländern," in H. Bertram, R. Kollmorgen (eds.), *Die Transformation Ostdeutschlands: Berichte zum sozialen und politischen Wandel in den neuen Bundesländern* (Opladen: Leske & Budrich, 2001), 315.

creation of new structures, the main areas and dimensions of modernization and prospects for future developments will be outlined. The second aim is to research if and how the ideas of governance can be introduced in the cities of former communist countries, as the development of a representative democracy and market economy brought about phenomena known in the Western European countries, but also some specific fields of activities and demands. The final aim is to draw a comparative perspective from two countries—Germany and Poland—where the post-socialist transition had a different scenario.

The former GDR was dissolved as a state and five new *Länder* were incorporated into the well-established system of West Germany. This meant the transfer of institutions, law and economic systems, as well as capital and financial support on the one hand, and on the other the necessity of adjusting the structures to the new situation. The Polish method of transformation had a more evolutionary character and was done at a slower pace, using the Western European (mostly German) experiences and referring to the systemic solutions adapted in the Second Polish Republic in the interwar period.[2]

---

[2] K. von Beyme, "Die Transformation Ostdeutschlands im Vergleich der postkommunistischen Systeme," in M. Benkenstein et al. (eds.), *Politische und wirtschaftliche Transformation Osteuropas: Chancen und Potentiale für die neuen Bundesländer* (Wiesbaden: Deutscher Universitäts-Verlag, 2001), 9–12; H. Wollmann, "Die ostdeutschen Kommunen: Organisation, Personal, Orientierungs- und Einstellungsmuster im Wandel," in H. Naßmacher et al. (eds.), *Politische Strukturen im Umbruch* (Berlin: Akademie Verlag, 1994), 267–269; H. Wiesenthal, "Die Transformation Ostdeutschlands: Ein (nicht ausschließlich) privilegierter Sonderfall der Bewältigung von Transfomation," in H. Wollmann et al. (eds.), *Transformation sozialistischer Gesellschaften: Am Ende des Anfangs* (Opladen: Westdeutscher Verlag, 1995), "Leviathan" Sonderheft 15 (1995): 150–156; A. Pickel, "Das ostdeutsche Transformationsmuster als Paradebeispiel holistischer Reformstrategie: Zur theoretischen Bedeutung des deutschen Falls für die Transformationsdebatte," in J. Wielgohs, H. Wiesenthal (eds.), *Einheit und Differenz: Die Transformation Ostdeutschlands in vergleichender Perspektive* (Berlin: Berliner Debatte Wissenschaftsverlag, 1997), 35; C. Offe, *Der Tunnel am Ende der Lichts: Erkundungen der politischen Transformation im Neuen Osten* (Frankfurt-New York: Campus Verlag, 1994), 255–263; J. Holzer, "Przemiany polityczne w Polsce i NRD w 1989 roku oraz ich tempo i specyfika w latach późniejszych," in J. Holzer, J. Fiszer (eds.), *Przemiany w Polsce i NRD po 1989 roku* (Warszawa: Instytut Studiów Politycznych PAN, 1996), 13–15; A. Sakson, "Wstęp," in A. Sakson (ed.), *Transformacja w Polsce i w Niemczech Wschodnich: Próba bilansu* (Poznań: Instytut Zachodni, 2009), 8–10; H. Baldersheim, "Towards Normalization of Local Democracy in East-Central Europe: A Developmental Approach to Institutional Reform," in H. Baldersheim et al. (ed.),

## The Socialist City

The socialist system, created apart from the centralistic state order, a new type of economy and society, was also the new model of the city. The socialist city was to be a place where the governing party could celebrate, organise demonstrations of support and prove the "geniality" of the architecture of the new system. For these purposes, especially in the 1950s, broad streets and huge squares were created. The parcels were state owned so the planners could order the space much more freely than in the capitalist states, not having to think about the prices or attractive locations. City plans were the realization of ideological assumptions rather than the rational managing of the public space. The historic substance was neglected due to its bourgeois origin, apartments were not well kept and rents were very low. This resulted in poor living conditions, so the city centres were inhabited by people with low incomes and social statuses. The means and resources were invested in the socialist-style buildings.[3]

Another characteristic objective of the creators of socialism was to industrialize the countries which led to big investments in heavy industry. Large state-owned enterprises employing thousands of workers where constructed and led to a huge flow of people from rural areas to cities to cover the workforce demand. This led to a great housing demand and significant failures in the infrastructure. Because investments were often made only in one branch, many cities became homogenous in both their economic and social structures. In this respect, urbanization lagged behind industrialization and had an industrial character, as the industry generated urban development.[4]

Huge districts comprising blocks of flats at the city peripheries were founded so that the workers of the industry could have a place to live. The multi-storey buildings were constructed from the prefabricated elements, which after only a short period turned out to be of very low quality and generating high costs, as the objective was to construct the highest number of flats in the shortest time and at the lowest cost possible. Also, the

---

*Local Democracy in Post-Communist Europe* (Opladen: Leske & Budrich, 2003), 242–244.

[3] H. Häussermann, "From the Socialist to the Capitalist City: Experiences from Germany," in G. Andrusz et al. (eds.), *Cities after Socialism: Urban and Regional Change and Conflict in Post-Socialist Societies* (Oxford-Cambridge: Blackwell, 1996), 216–222; I. Szelenyi, "Cities under Socialism—and After," in G. Andrusz et al. (eds.), *Cities after Socialism*, 294–307.

[4] D. Szymańska, A. Matczak, "Urbanization in Poland: Tendencies and Transformation," *European Urban and Regional Studies* 9 (1) (2002): 42–45.

surrounding infrastructure, comprising schools, shops and parklands, was neglected. The distribution of apartments often had a political motivation. There were no typical social divisions based on incomes or financial statuses, as the social equality was a priority for the socialist economy and state. Another problem was the central distribution of flats, which led to a situation where whole districts were inhabited by people of the same age, causing disturbances in generation exchange and a demand for specific services. Both factories and new socialist districts were built in the peripheral parts of the city. The result was the artificial spilling-over of cities, leaving empty spaces in the central parts, a phenomenon called under-urbanization. The socialist cities were developed unsustainably, irregularly and artificially, and the plans were often realized only partially. This resulted in many disturbances in the building substance and social structure.[5]

## The Post-Socialist City and the Transformation Period

The system transformation, introduction of the market economy, re-establishment of local governments and changes in management turned socialist cities into post-socialist ones. Intensive urbanization, migration and concentration of people on a massive scale were stopped, and the space and resources management in the cities changed. Restructurings in ownership, privatization, restitution of property and marketization of ground prices caused the filling and development of empty spaces in the central parts of the cities. The ground rent rules, non-existent before, started to influence the developments. Space became a value and a commodity, which could be bought and sold for a good price. The central parts became attractive localities for services of a higher order like solicitors, banks, tourist agencies, luxury shops and restaurants. Many attractive parcels were sold to private investors and huge shopping malls were established both in the suburbs and the city centres. The city centres, especially those of historic value, have been gradually revitalized and are now attractive places for tourists as well as the most representative parts of the cities.[6]

The systemic transformation led to the development of the middle class, combined with a foundation of districts of single-family houses in

[5] H. Häussermann, *From the Socialist to the Capitalist City*, 216–222; I. Szelenyi, *Cities under Socialism*, 294–307.

[6] D. Bogdanov, "Problemy lokalizacji wielkopowierzchniowych obiektów handlowych," in J. Słodczyk (ed.), *Przemiany bazy ekonomicznej i struktury przestrzennej miast* (Opole: Wydawnictwo Uniwersytetu Opolskiego, 2002), 387.

the suburban areas. This also caused negative phenomena like suburbanization through the moving of persons and firms to the peripheries and depopulation of the city centres, as well as gentrification, which is a rapid change in the social structure of districts.[7] Social changes were connected to the degradation of former industrial areas due to bankruptcy or the restructuring of factories. This resulted in the unemployment of many persons (almost unknown in a communist society) and many pathological phenomena. City inhabitants also started to use individual transportation on a massive scale as cars became more widely available, forcing changes in public transport and leading to traffic intensification. Numerous problems with traffic jams and the limited capacities of streets and car parks created great investment demands. Although many of these problems can be observed in the cities of countries that have never been socialist, the post-socialist city is characterized by the huge dynamics of these processes.[8]

The post-socialist city is a form of postindustrial and post-fordist city. The collapse of heavy industry factories forced changes in the economic profile from production to services in the sectors of trade, education, science, culture, telecommunications and information technology. In the postindustrial city, small and middle enterprises overtake the economic leading position and diversify the local economy, and the development of districts of buildings produced from prefabricated elements has stopped.[9]

The post-fordist concept was invented on the basis of postindustrial changes. The main assumption is a departure from massive production to the development of services delivered by small and medium enterprises, and labour becomes more flexible and specialized. The stock is produced in smaller series with a higher diversity, using advanced technologies,

---

[7] M. Löw et al., *Einführung in die Stadt und Raumsoziologie* (Opladen-Farmington Hills: Budrich, 2007), 111.

[8] K. Stanilov, "Taking Stock of Post-Socialist Urban Development: A Recapitulation," in K. Stanilov (ed.), *The Post-Socialist City: Urban Form and Space Transformations in Central and Eastern Europe after Socialism* (Dordrecht: Springer Verlag, 2007), 6–11; J. Słodczyk, "Wielkość miast i ich struktura przestrzenna w świetle kryteriów rozwoju zrównoważonego," in J. Słodczyk (ed.), *Przemiany bazy ekonomicznej i struktury przestrzennej miast*, 330; H. Häussermann, "Von der 'sozialistischen' zur 'kapitalistischen' Stadt," *Aus Politik und Zeitgeschichte* 12 (1995): 8–13.

[9] D. V. Shaw, "The Post-Industrial City," in R. Paddison (ed.), *Handbook of Urban Studies* (London-Thousand Oaks-New Delhi: Sage, 2001), 285–286; J. J. Parysek, "Wewnętrzne i zewnętrzne uwarunkowania transformacji przestrzenno-strukturalnej i rozwoju miast polskich w końcu XX wieku," in J. Słodczyk (ed.), *Przemiany bazy ekonomicznej i struktury przestrzennej miast*, 19–20.

mass communication and de-concentration of production. Competition, prevalence of knowledge and means of communication support the cooperation and create the network structures. The post-fordist city results from heterogenic construction, with a polarized and individualized society and living styles. The transition from the socialist industrial city to a postindustrial and post-fordist one had a much more dynamic form than in the capitalist countries, where these developments had an evolutionary character.[10]

At the beginning of the post-socialist transformation, cities in the former communist countries were in very bad conditions. City infrastructure such as roads, streets, public transport, sewerage network, schools, hospitals, cultural, sport, leisure facilities and other public buildings needed either renovation or to be newly built. The buildings were in very bad shape as whole districts had not been refurbished for many years. Not only did the old districts in the city centres need huge capital spending, but also the new ones built during the communist era had degraded due to their very low quality of construction. Even though many new districts were built, still there was a huge housing demand, even a hunger.[11]

Bad management and the generally tragic shape of the economy led to neglecting the necessary investments and creating huge investment demand. The necessity of bringing this under control and overcoming the socialist yoke and longtime negligence became great challenges to the new, democratically elected self-government organs and local elites. Another problem turned out to be lessening city populations due to migration to suburban districts, other towns and other countries, as well as a declining birth rate. Especially in Eastern Germany this happened on a massive scale. As a solution, drastic methods such as tearing down houses were adapted within the program "Stadtumbau Ost." It has also caused problems for sustainable city development, especially where the houses were randomly collapsing, and were without precise planning. The declining number of inhabitants influenced the energy, heating or water and sewage infrastructure, as the lower flows caused blocks and the

---

[10] W. F. Lever, "The Post-fordist City," in R. Paddison (ed.), *Handbook of Urban Studiem*, 273–281; F. Koch, *Die europäische Stadt in Transformation: Stadtplanung und Stadtentiwcklungspolitik im postsozialistischen Warschau* (Wiesbaden: VS-Verlag für Sozialwissenschaften, 2010), 53–61.

[11] H. Sahner, "Zur Entwicklung ostdeutscher Städte nach der Wende: nicht nur 'dem Tod von der Schippe gesprungen'," *Aus Politik und Zeitgeschichte* 5 (1999): 26–29.

declining quality of potable water. This also forced investment in the East German cities.[12]

The re-establishment of local self-government had a great significance for the post-socialist cities. One of the reasons for their bad condition was dysfunctional structures of socialist management. The new organs were elected democratically, and new actors appeared on the local scenes, such as the political parties as well as local initiatives. In Eastern Germany and Poland in the initial period, the system based on the strong position of the city council was established, with the mayor elected by the council members. The local elites became independent subjects, meaning they were to decide on urban development, restructurings and the future in general.[13]

At the later stage, numerous reforms happened in both countries. In Poland the regional and county structures were established in 1998, causing cities with over 100,000 inhabitants to become county cities, fulfilling both commune and county functions. After the reform, new obligations and tasks were distributed to the cities and their administrations. Another important change was strengthening the position of mayors in 2002 after introducing direct elections. Since then, the mayor could be recalled only in the local referendum and not by the council, as it was in the old regulation.[14] In Germany the main reforms were finished by 1994 and each of the five new federal states had overtaken the elements of the partner Länder, which supported adjustment and institutional transfer to the new structures. In addition, local peculiarities were taken into consideration with the experiences of the peaceful revolution of 1989. Since then the local governmental systems have differed, but the most popular trend is implementing direct mayor elections. In both cases, and in all of Central and Eastern Europe, the local structures were re-established on the Western patterns. This did not mean "coping" or "transferring" the

---

[12] M. Bernt, "Abriss als Chance? Das Scheitern des 'Stadtumbau Ost'," *Blätter für deutsche und internationale Politik* 4 (2006): 493 and foll.

[13] F. Bafoil, "Systemumbruch in Ostdeutschland und Polen," in H. Wollmann et al. (eds.), *Transformation sozialistischer Gesellschaften*, 597.

[14] P. Swianiewicz, "Reforming Local Government in Poland. Top-down and bottom-up Processes," in N. Kersting, A. Vetter (eds.), *Reforming Local Government in Europe. Closing the Gap between Democracy and Efficiency* (Opladen: Leske & Budrich, 2003), 283 and foll.

institutions, but creating new institutions, using local and Western, democratic experiences.[15]

In the initial period the local political elites have been deeply exchanged. New elites had to learn not only the new roles, such as how to work in democratic structures, but also dependencies between different bodies, assemblies and positions. This led to many conflicts and disappointments of the new councillors. Also, the attitude towards the political parties was generally negative (much more so in Poland), as the "party" was the symbol of the communist governing body. The obligations and competences in the administration had to be newly defined and divided. The were no massive staff exchanges or dismissals, so the old clerks had to learn the new rules and change their habits from the old system. The priority in Germany was to adjust the old communist structures into the West German system. For this purposes the programs of administrative aid were launched, consisting of workshops, seminars and leaflets, as well as sending West German clerks to work for the Eastern administrations.[16]

Therefore, the work of local governments in the post-socialist city in the first years after the breakthrough was determined by four main factors:

(1) "learning while doing" local politics by the actors
(2) necessity of ordering and adjusting administrative structures and communal services to new conditions
(3) necessity of developing the legal-institutional framework and relations between central and local (city) authorities
(4) huge investment and modernization demand.[17]

Even though the local governments gained a broad set of competences and decisive capacities, these barriers limited their activities. Limited support from the state and the lack of possibilities of finding financial sources caused budgetary problems and hindered investment potential. The activities were often a necessity rather than a political vision of parties or

[15] H. Wollmann, "German Local Government under the Double Impact of Democratic and Administrative Reforms," in N. Kersting, A. Vetter (eds.), *Reforming Local Government in Europe*, 91 and foll.
[16] D. Schröder, "Kommunen im Umbruch: Das Beispiel Rostock," in N. Werz, J. Schmidt (eds.), *Mecklenburg-Vorpommern im Wandel: Bilanz und Ausblick* (München: Olzog, 1998), 128–133; F. Berg, B. Möller, "Kommunale Steuerungsprobleme und Interessenrepräsentanz im deutschen Transformationsprozeß," *Deuschland Archiv* 6 (1993): 684–685.
[17] P. Swianiewicz, *Reforming Local Government in Poland*, 283 and foll.

local initiatives. Also, the changes and restructuring at the state level had a significant influence on the development and management of cities. Unstable and rapidly changing law regulations in different areas caused unrest and made the work of local organs much more difficult.

Another point to mention is the position of the local community in the post-socialist city. Symbolic for the transition period was the high engagement of people in the protests and demonstrations against the old regime. Not accidentally, the events of 1989 were called the peaceful revolution. In the GDR it had a much larger character and the protests were organised at the same time in the cities and towns of the whole country. In Poland, workers and the young also protested, but not on such a huge scale and at the same time as Germany. During the local elections many people engaged in the campaign and rallies of Citizens Committees (Komitety Obywatelskie), which overtook the power in most Polish cities after the first democratic elections in 1990.

Paradoxically, this mobilization and self-organisation did not influence the engagement in local politics or even the everyday citizen activities afterwards. Difficulties of the transformation process, especially unemployment, economic problems, the legacy of mistrust towards communist organisations and other forms of activism, as well as general disappointment, significantly lowered the will and interest in local politics. The main indicator of this was low turnouts in the local elections, while another was the lack of dialogue between the local authorities and local communities. Again in Germany, due to institutional transfer, the forms of dialogue have been institutionalized much quicker. District councils (Ortsbeirat) became an important transmitting tool between inhabitants and local politicians. In Poland, although similar bodies exist, and every city has the right to constitute them, they still remain an unexploited change for social participation.[18]

## Modernization as a Main Challenge

As already mentioned, modernization and overcoming the socialist yoke became the main challenges for local politicians and elites. That is why politics and policies in post-socialist cities concentrated on the activities

---

[18] A. Jarosz, "Auxiliary Units of Municipal Governments in Poland: An Unexploited Chance for Social Participation," in R. Schattkowsky, A. Jarosz (eds.), *Questions of Civil Society: Category-Position-Functionality* (Newcastle upon Tyne: Cambridge Scholars Publishing, 2013), 303–307; M. M. Howard, "The Weakness of Postcommunist Civil Society," *Journal of Democracy* 13 (1) (January 2002): 161–163.

aiming at renovation and building infrastructure, refurbishment of buildings, and revitalizing the public space and transport. It all had to be done in conditions of very limited budgets (especially in the initial years) and rapidly growing social problems.

Firstly, the administrative and managing structures had to be newly organised. New legal regulations enforced changes in administrating structures which had stopped working in the hierarchical structure as part of the state administration. The local administration did not have to fulfil the orders of the governing party and instead acted within the frame of legal regulations and defined competences. The main aim was to work on behalf of the local community and serve on the partner and non-paternalistic relations. The legislative organs got real initiative and controlling functions and not just theoretical ones, as was the case in the old system. Local authorities have lost competences in the economic steering (planning and managing local enterprises). The new role is a supportive one and creates good conditions for the development of local businesses.[19]

New management has been introduced to the local finances, and local organs can decide on expenses and shape the budget, and they are able to pose new local taxes and manage incomes from that source. City managers can also take credit from the private banks which enable the necessary financial means for the investments.[20] The result of changes was transition from the real-socialist administration to the classical continental European administration model.[21]

Secondly, better management of resources than the socialist economy, economic growth and the new organisation of the state and local structures enabled numerous investments in the cities, which were necessary due to the new needs of society and the modernization of the neglected infrastructure. Over many years, roads, streets, footpaths, squares, playgrounds, bus stops and schools have been built and renovated. Real milestones were big investments like bridges, tunnels, sport arenas,

---

[19] H. Wollmann, "Kommunalpolitik und—verwaltung in Ostdeutschland: Institutionen und Handlungsmuster im 'paradigmatischen' Umbruch: Eine empirische Skizze," in B. Blanke, S. Benzler (eds.), *Staat und Stadt: Systematische, vergleichende und problemorientierte Analysen "dezentraler" Politik* (Opladen: Westdeutscher Verlag, 1991), 238–240.

[20] P. Swianiewicz, *Reforming Local Government in Poland*, 299–300.

[21] K. König, "Verwaltung im Übergang—von zentralen Verwaltungsstaat in die dezentrale Demokratie," in: *Verwaltung im Übergang—von zentralen Verwaltungsstaat in die dezentrale Demokratie, Cappenberger Gespräche* 25 (1991): 5–6.

cultural buildings (philharmonics, operas, art centres), tram railway networks and waste utilization facilities. It is necessary to stress that many ejected buildings and constructions were planned in the communist times, but were not realized due to limited means and the bad economic situation.

This broad process, touching almost every aspect not only of local governments' competences but also every inhabitant, has also been much more dynamic in the new German federal states. Solidarity support, the Unity Fund and other programs from the old federal states have been launched and the former GDR has also become a part of the European Union, bringing extra means in the form of European structural funds. Also, the adopted legal regulations enforced complex planning, broad consulting procedures and information campaigns.[22] This made the processes much more efficient and fluent. In Poland, a similar breakthrough came with the EU enlargement in 2004, when the country became an EU member. Pre-accession and structural funds gave an investment impulse and boosted the modernization processes, and also enforced on the local leaders the preparation of complex plans and strategies so that cities could be developed sustainably, solving problems in the whole range. European procedures also mobilized local authorities to dialogue and consult on the projects and activities with the local community.[23]

Thirdly, another important factor in the post-socialist city modernization was the flow of private capital, a result of deep changes in the city economy. Private investors and foreign enterprises overtook, recapitalized and restructured formerly state-owned enterprises, and as a result many of them managed to survive and continue production. This also brought innovations, new technologies and know-how. The negative phenomena noted in this field are reduction of employment, intentional bankruptcy, and unclear overtaking by the former communist political and economic elite (*nomenklatura*). Privatization also led to protests and conflicts of trade unionists with private investors. The transformation was also a time of creation of many small and middle enterprises which

---

[22] T. Lillig, "Die Finanzierung der deutschen Einheit," *Deutschlands Archiv* 9 (1993): 1076–1083; W. Bayer, E. Horstkötter, "Solidarität statt 'Solidarpakt:' Daten und Kriterien zur deutschen Umverteilungsdebatte," *Blätter für deutsche und internationale Politik* 3 (1993): 303 and foll.

[23] See J. Szlachta, "Fundusze europejskie a samorządy terytorialne," in C. Glinkowski, E. Urbańczyk (eds.), *Samorząd terytorialny III RP w procesie integracji europejskiej: Wybrane problemy. Tom 1* (Kalisz: Wydawnictwo Uczelniane PWSZ, 2003), 24; M. Guz-Vetter, "Schwieriges Geld aus Brüssel: Polen und Strukturgelder der EU," *Osteuropa* 54 (5–6) (2004): 355–359.

gradually became the new basis of the city economy, developing both production and service sectors. Business investors have built shopping malls along with office buildings. Many small companies or simply private owners took care of their houses and estates. This way many single houses, often in the city centres, have been renovated and refurbished, resulting in the significant growth of quality of life and space.[24]

Fourthly, many cities had to define not only their functions but also create a new local identity. The method for this was promoting specific events or periods from the city history, which where newly discovered and brought to light, and part of this was changes in the symbolic landscape. Many street names had to be changed in overcoming the communist past, with some streets given new names and others having their historical names restored. Interestingly, some names were kept as they had become a part of the local tradition in the communist era, or the people and values they commemorated were not controversial. Another argument in the debates was the high costs of such changes. The same story was found with communist monuments, most of which were removed, while others were replaced by the new heroes, and others were kept as they had become significant parts of the local identity.[25]

Fifthly, the post-socialist modernization in the cities resulted in deep ecological change. The new projects were realized with greater care regarding the natural environment. Many facilities like sewage farms and litter utilization facilities have been built, and air pollution has been lowered due to the closure of big factories and innovations in the remaining ones, allowing for gradual changes in the heating systems.[26]

Sixthly, city service deliveries have changed significantly. The new local governments overtook the old enterprises with obsolete facilities and equipment. Most of them had to be restructured into new legal forms (budgetary units, or limited companies), liquidated or merged. Some

---

[24] J. Hardy, "Rebuilding Local Governance in Post-Communist Economics: The Case of Wrocław, Poland," *European Urban and Regional Studies* 11 (4) (2004): 307 and foll.

[25] C. Young, S. Kaczmarek, "The Socialist Past and Postsocialist Urban Identity in Central and Eastern Europe: The Case of Łódź," *European Urban and Regional Studies* 15 (1) (2008): 57 and foll.; A. Leo, "Die Streit um die Name: Straßenumbenennungen als Symptom," *Blätter für deutsche und Internationale Politik* 11 (1991): 1372 and foll; J. Pissowotzki, "Von Kalinin zu Niemöller: Straßenumbenennungen in Schwerin und Rostock zwischen 1990 und 1992," *Deutchalnd Archiv* 5 (2000): 767–768.

[26] H. Sahner, "Zur Entwicklung ostdeutscher Städte nach der Wende: nicht nur 'dem Tod von der Schippe gesprungen'," *Aus Politik und Zeitgeschichte* 5 (1999): 36–37.

facilities like kindergartens had to be overtaken from the state-owned enterprises which provided many social services in the socialist economy. This was combined with modernization and gradual improvement in the quality of services. Also, private capital was engaged when part of the city-owned companies were privatized. In the German case especially, the transfer of law regulations became very helpful. The solutions implemented had already been checked and proven as effective in the Federal Republic. An example of this is the communal enterprises, which from the very beginning could get a proper and functional legal form, allowing them to invest and work on the business and market rules. Another advantage was the possibility of privatization which enabled capital flow and necessary investments. In the Polish case law, regulations were introduced gradually and were changed and corrected many times afterwards. This made the necessary changes longer and less stable. Although it had many successes this was not as complex and dynamic as it was in Germany.[27]

Apart from the unquestionable advantages and positive developments, negative ones also have to be mentioned. After the bankruptcy of some factories and industrial areas, many people lost their jobs and became unemployed. The most destructive effects were seen in the places with homogenized economic structures, or that were dependent on one or a small number of enterprises. This caused deep social inequalities and differentiation in the standard of living. Also, the high mobility and changes in the different social classes within the cities occurred and combined with the symptoms of gentrification, especially in the city centres with historic building substance.[28] Bringing in new investors and companies able to take over the released workforce and equalize the differences in the living standards of broad parts of society became another huge and very difficult challenge. On the other hand, big cities have overcome this problem much quicker than small towns and rural areas.[29]

Another disadvantage is the functional change of the cities. Many of them lost administrative capital status due to the administrative reforms.

---

[27] P. Swianiewicz, *Reforming Local Government in Poland*, 298–299; C. Kleemann, "Festsitzung der Bürgerschaft am 31. Mai 2000: 10 Jahre Bürgerschaft der Hansestadt Rostock," *Neue Demokratie* 6 (2000): 12; K. Lietz, "Wszyscy ludzie prezydenta," *Nowości* (1994).

[28] J. Friedrichs, H. Häußermann, "Die Entwicklung der Städte in den neuen Bundesländern," in H. Bertram, R. Kollmorgen (eds.), *Die Transformation Ostdeutschlands*, 319–320, 324–333.

[29] Ibid.

Even if the administrative or territorial division reforms had a positive impact and made the system function much better, the cities that stopped being regional centres lost many institutions, allowing employment especially for highly educated personnel. The cities which lost their industrial characters not only had to re-branch and diversify their economies to fight unemployment, but also had to get new functional positions and significance for the region and the whole state.[30]

The third disadvantage is the budgetary problems and growing debt of the cities. Broad investment programs, even with the support of external institutions and programs, needed the financial participation of city authorities. This resulted in taking numerous loans as the activities were done at the same time and included many spheres of life. Also, the assigned tasks relegated by the state institutions to the city authorities (e.g. school management) need to be realized with the means of local governments, as the subsidies are not sufficient. The growing deficits can be a significant barrier in city management and development. In the German case the amount of taxes collected have lowered due to the decreasing number of inhabitants and companies registered in the cities of the new federal states. This has caused much lower revenues for the municipal budgets.[31]

The broad operation of city modernization after the socialist period has been set for many years. In Germany, according to financial, institutional and legal transfers in most cities the modernization and adjustment to Western standards happened within approximately fifteen years. In Poland these processes sped up significantly after joining the EU, but are still not finished and will continue for many years more.

## Governance as Necessity?

After addressing the most significant and appalling problems the questions of further development have arisen. The budgetary problems as well as the growing conscience and expectations from the local communities force searching for new methods of governing, administrating and managing the cities.

The answers to these issues are new concepts of managing in the post-socialist cities, which were invented and already "tested" in the Western

[30] B. Hołowiecka, D. Szymańska, "The Changes in the Functional Urban Region in the New Socio-Economic Conditions in Poland: The Case of Toruń," *Bulletin of Geography (Socio-Economic Series)* 9 (2008): 69 and foll.

[31] J. Friedrichs, H. Häußermann, *Die Entwicklung der Städte in den neuen Bundesländern*, 321.

European countries. Mostly, they are based on the cooperative concepts, as is the idea of governance, consisting in the assumption that a large number of actors forming the multi-dimensional networks are involved in the process of managing and solving public issues.[32] The politics should overtake the role of coordinator, moderator and inspiration of activities of different actors. Governing the city should be based on the cooperation between politics/administration-private business sector-local community in different spheres of local issues and problem solving. The evolution in the post-fordist direction enforces flexible and individualized solutions in order to consider the specifics of different communities and their needs. This proceeds together with lowering the role of the state in an overregulated and bureaucratized post-socialist reality, matching the western European standards.[33]

Therefore, the new role of local authorities has to be defined. The mayors have to combine the role of managers and politicians. On one hand the local governments are the arena of political decision-making in different fields, and thus require the skills of consensus building, gaining resources and support for the inhabitants. On the other, the managerial skills are also necessary to run the sphere of local services provision, public companies, etc. The cities are much more complex organisms than enterprises, and the introduction of pure business managing models is impossible , especially in the complicated post-socialist reality. Therefore, the mayor especially has to act as a local leader in a double role, combining the elements of political leadership for the local community through the ability of decision-making and managing the local administration, its units and local service providers, to efficiently realize the investments and provide services of the highest quality. This way, the political sphere can overtake the coordinative role of frame setter for different actors and realize the concept of shifting from "power over" in directing the behaviour of others to "power to," which can provide the

---

[32] J. Pierre, B. G. Peters, *Governance, Politics and the State* (New York: St. Martin's Press, 2000), 1–7, 14 and foll.; R. A. W. Rhodes, *Understanding Governance: Policy Networks, Governance, Reflexivity and Accountability* (Buckingham-Philadephia: Open University Press, 1997), 46 and foll; N. Kersting et al., *Local Governance Reform in Global Perspective* (Wiesbaden: VS Verlag für Sozialwissenschaften, 2009), 14–18.

[33] T. Franke et al., "Soziale Stadt—Stadterneuerungspolitik als Stadtpolitikerneuerung," *Archiv für Kommunalwissenschaften* II (2000): 251–261; P. Żukiewicz, *Przywództwo polityczne: Teoria i praktyka*, Warszawa 2011, s. 307–309.

activation of other actors' potential and gaining a "collaborative advantage."[34]

Is this possible in a post-socialist city? A few years ago many would say "no." After joining the EU as one of eight central and eastern European countries in 2004, and considering the dynamism of the modernization processes in the cities, such a mode of solving problems becomes more and more popular. A large amount of investments in the relatively short period enforced changes in administrative structures to make them more operational. The privatization and outsourcing of public services to private companies or cooperation with social organisations make the activities more efficient and citizen oriented.

One of the means is New Public Management, introduced in Germany as a New Steering Model. After establishing the new administrative structures, cities in the new federal states used the experiences of their Western counterparts to introduce output oriented budgets, overcoming the traditional top-down hierarchy in administration towards a task and service oriented one. This also included the provision of public services, many of which have been marketized, outsourced and privatized. In many cases, the privatization of public services and facilities was combined with modernization projects (mostly infrastructural), enabling capital flow from the private sector.[35]

The development plans have been based on strategic planning. Creating and accepting the development strategies has become a standard in the Eastern German and Polish cities. Such documents introduce a new spectrum and perspective for the local politics in the long term, as decisions made are the result of strategic concepts.

Another important assumption, and the hardest to realize, is the involvement of social partners in the decisive processes, e.g. through

---

[34] D. Sweeting, "Leadership in Urban Governance: The Mayor of London," *Local Government Studies* 28 (1) (Spring 2002): 4–9; L. Habuda, "Wójt—gminny lider polityczny," in S. Wróbel (ed.), *Samorząd miejski: Zadania, instytucje, formy* (Poznań-Chorzów: Wydawnictwo Wyższej Szkoły Bankowej w Poznaniu, 2008), 197 and foll.; L. Habuda, L. Hawrysz, "Polityczny lider," in A. Lutrzykowski (ed.), *Samorząd terytorialny: Ale jaki?* (Toruń: Wydawnictwo Adam Marszałek, 2009), 207–212; R. Berg, "Political Complexity or Managerial Simplicity? Mayoral Norms of Organisational Leadership," in H. Bäck et al. (eds.), *The European Mayor: Political Leaders in the Changing Context of Local Democracy* (Wiesbaden: VS Verlag für Sozialwissenschaften, 2005), 313–315, 328–329.

[35] H. Wollmann, "German Local Government under the Double Impact of Democratic and Administrative Reforms," in N. Kersting, A. Vetter (eds.), *Reforming Local Government in Europe*, 97–100; L. Rajca, "Demokracja lokalna i regionalna w państwach Europy Zachodniej," *Samorząd Terytorialny* 6 (2008): 10.

NGOs, associations and other private initiatives, with which the city managers co-operate more and more intensively. At the beginning of the post-socialist transition, the social engagement was perceived as something unpopular, but gradually inhabitants of the cities became more and more interested in the local issues. The growing number of NGOs creates a potential for cooperation with public authorities, as in many fields social initiatives can have a positive and cheaper input than contracted companies. That is why city authorities support different organisations (also financially), but also begin to perceive them as partners for discussion, e.g. in the realization of different investments (such as consultations with bikers' associations when building cycle paths).[36]

Also, the number of ways inhabitants can engage with their cities is growing rapidly. One of the most important challenges in this field is the development of the legal and administrative infrastructure for social engagement, as the clear rules and easy accessibility encourage people to participate. This can be done through different agencies within the city administration, district councils, participatory budgets, consultations and face-to-face meetings. This way, the city governance can be realized in a citizen-oriented form.[37]

A very important tool with a high potential comprises the auxiliary units and their organs, which are the agents between the local authorities and communities at the lowest possible level of city districts and quarters. Their role is to be close to citizens and maintain communication in an institutional form. The members of the organs are the inhabitants, so they can articulate the needs, concerns and ideas to the city authorities. They work permanently, so they possess a much stronger potential than other forms of dialogue or direct democracy (referendum).[38]

---

[36] G. Stoker, "Comparative Local Governance," in R. A. W. Rhodes et al., *The Oxford Handbook of Political Institutions* (Oxford-New York: Oxford University Press, 2006), 502–503; H. Klages, "Freiwilliges bürgerliches Engagement im kommunalen Raum," *Deutsche Zeitschrift für Kommunalwissenschaften* 2 (2002): 92–104.

[37] Ibid., 94.

[38] A. Jarosz, *Auxiliary Units of Municipal Governments in Poland*, 303–307; D. Maj, "Demokracja bezpośrednia w samorządzie terytorialnym w Polsce jako forma realizacji zasady subsydiarności," in M. Marczewska-Rytko, S. Michałowski (eds.), *Demokracja bezpośrednia w samorządzie terytorialnym* (Lublin: Wydawnictwo Uniwersytetu Marii Curie-Skłodowskiej, 2012), 286; Ł. Jakubiak, "Demokracja bezpośrednia na szczeblu samorządowym w Republice Federalnej Niemiec," in M. Marczewska-Rytko, S. Michałowski (eds.), *Demokracja bezpośrednia w samorządzie terytorialnym*, 135–137; W. Staszczak, "Instytucje demokracji bezpośredniej a wpływ mieszkańców na zarządzanie gminą," in M.

With the growing conscience of inhabitants the voting act becomes insufficient for fulfilling the democratic act. The involvement in the decisive processes needs to be very well planned and concerted to bring about the best effects. This will prevent the NIMBY (not in my backyard), or LULU (locally unwanted land use) syndromes, which often stop or delay investments through protests, social movements or using different legal instruments. This is especially problematic when the investment has reached an advanced level and significant costs have been borne for the post-socialist city. It also has a key importance for the huge demand for instalments and buildings.[39]

To prevent such development a coherent system of local community involvement is necessary. The key factors are communication and the interest of inhabitants in public issues. To make the activities successful broad-scale information campaigns are needed both through administrative channels (websites, meetings with inhabitants, duty hours of city council members etc.), as well as cooperation with local media and NGOs. Coherent activities and policies, using repeatable means of social engagement during different investments and projects, can lead to the stimulation and engagement of local community members. Especially in the post-socialist environment, passiveness and lack of initiative are the hardest things to overcome and last for a very long time.[40]

The most important conditions for the success of such activities are the responsibility and transparency of the local politicians and clerks. As long as people notice that their activities help and bring some input for decisions made, and at the same time activities, policies or investments fulfil the needs and expectations, they will be more and more eager to participate in the local issues. Inoperative administration, long-lasting

---

Marczewska-Rytko, S. Michałowski (eds.), *Demokracja bezpośrednia w samorządzie terytorialnym*, 294–303.

[39] K. Kajdanek, "Podmiotowość społeczności lokalnych w procesach przemian systemu miejskiego," *Samorząd Terytorialny* 12 (2006): 53–54, 57.

[40] D. Fleszer, "Konsultacje społeczne jako forma partycypacji społecznej w procedurze tworzenia jednostek pomocniczych gminy," in M. Marczewska-Rytko, S. Michałowski (eds.), *Demokracja bezpośrednia w samorządzie terytorialnym*, 71–74; J. Kawala, "Funkcja demokratyczna finansów publicznych w gminach," *Samorząd Terytorialny* 7–8 (2006): 35 and foll.; J. Goździewicz-Biechońska, "Partycypacja społeczna w tworzeniu prawa na przykładzie miejscowego planu zagospodarowania przestrzennego," *Samorząd Terytorialny* 7–8 (2008): 39–42; J. A. Rybczyńska, "Partycypacja obywatelska na poziomie lokalnym w III Rzeczypospolitej Polskiej—próba oceny," in S. Michałowski (ed.), *Samorząd terytorialny III Rzeczypospolitej: Dziesięć lat doświadczeń* (Lublin: Wydawnictwo Uniwersytetu Marii Curie-Skłodowskiej, 2002), 120.

procedures, or ignoring the opinions—which characterized the socialist times and are things that have become great challenges in the transition period—will again bring about passiveness and apathy. Only efficient, well-managed and operative administration or services can expect people to help or identify with their work. This will also contribute to the growth of trust in the local authorities and willingness to participate.[41]

The internet possesses a great potential in this field. Citizens cannot only solve important administrative issues through downloading and sending applications for different things, but can also be involved in local issues. An example is online voting (e.g. in participatory budgets), or opinion polls. The internet webpages of the cities are also worthy sources of information, both for important news about a city as well as the work of its administration. The most important documents (development strategies, investment plans, budgets etc.) are available online for every citizen, and this contributes to transparency and has the potential to widen consciousness.

## Summary

The socialist period brought about artificial developments for local administration. The old structures were replaced after the Second World War by the centralistic highly bureaucratic and hierarchic structure. After 1989, within the transformation process the new structures had to be introduced. Not only were the ways of election of decisive organs changed into democratic and pluralistic ones, but also the ways of managing were changed. This meant that some phases of development and "layers" were omitted in the post socialist conditions. When, for example, British local governments were in the phase of New Public Management and developing further concepts of network governance, Central European ones had to establish democratic structures and learn how to work in the new conditions of democratic debate and market economy.[42]

The post-socialist cities have already developed in the direction of post-fordist cities. The next step is the sustainable city; one that is citizen friendly, without barriers, containing ecological and energy efficient solutions in the public sphere.[43] The governance model provides a

[41] D. R. Kijowski, "Partycypacja obywatelska w samorządowych procesach decyzyjnych—zagadnienia ogólne," *Samorząd Terytorialny* 1–2 (2010): 20.
[42] H. Izdebski, "Od administracji publicznej do public governanve," *Zarządzanie Publiczne* 1 (2007): 18.
[43] S. Guy, S. Marvin, "Understanding Sustainable Cities: Competing Urban Futures," *European Urban and Regional Studies* 6 (3) (1999): 268 and foll.

possibility for reaching that. Further research is needed, though, as the new methods of governing at the local level are still underdeveloped especially in the Central European countries. German post-socialist cities could refer to the West German experiences. In Poland, the legal means still have to be introduced which will enable the efficient realization of public-private partnerships without the threat of corruption and unclear relations with business partners. The citizens have to be involved in the processes of governing and cooperate with the representative organs. They have to involved but not necessarily deciders, as too-broad forms of direct engagement can threaten paralysis, manipulation, lack of dialogue or poor decision making.[44]

Therefore, implementing the governance model for the post-socialist city is still a challenge. Some of its elements have already been introduced and have turned out to be successful. In Germany, they are much more popular than in Poland, where many legislative works are still needed to enable the use of the tools (e.g. public-private partnership) which the governance model provides. Should it be introduced through a broad and complex reform? What should this reform look like? These questions need to be addressed in future research.

Adam Jarosz, PhD, graduated in International Relations (German specialisation) from the Nicolaus Copernicus University in Toruń, Poland. He is a researcher and teacher at the University of Zielona Góra, Poland, as well as the scientific secretary of the Copernicus Graduate School. His scientific interests concentrate on local governments with a focus on cities, governance and social participation at the local level, border regions, German history and current issues, German-Polish relations and systemic transformation after 1989, as well as the position of the president in the Polish political system.

[44] J. Błuszkowski, D. Mider, *Demokracja późnej nowoczesności* (Warszawa: Dom Wydawniczy Elipsa, 2012), 107–112.

# CHAPTER THIRTEEN

# PUBLIC-PRIVATE PARTNERSHIP AND CORPORATE PUBLIC SECTOR ORGANISATION: FUNCTIONAL DECENTRALIZATION AND ALTERNATIVE WAYS TO INCREASE SOCIAL PERFORMANCE IN ROMANIA

SIMONA MINA AND FELICIA SURUGIU

## Introduction

Public-private partnership has been presented as an opportunity to improve the input and output legitimacy of global environmental governance. Functional decentralization can generate a considerable improvement in the quality of life of the population and in the functioning of a city and its services. This chapter reports some conclusions regarding externalisation, public-private partnership and improving the quality of life through the correct organisation of public services. We exemplify the well-practiced examples from Portuguese experience, French experience, U.K. private sector participation in governance, and the Romanian case. After an important qualitative analysis of all these results we establish whether the New Public Management regarding the reorganisation of the public services within public-private partnership ideas is correct. Some of the results contradict the New Public Management ideas—mainly that private sector participation through public-private partnerships in the delivery of public services will inevitably lead to a better use of scarce resources, and consequently to lower user prices and a higher quality of goods and services. Our empirical analysis demonstrates that user prices have a stronger relationship with the organisational costs than with property or the adopted management model in the delivery of public services.

## The Romanian Case

The efficient implementation of decentralization is an effective path to raising European standards regarding local governance, as well as improving the administrative activities at the internal level, by offering quality public services for everyone. Who knows best if not the local authorities voted by the citizens, answering to them? What are the development priorities of the local communities and who accepts the obligation to carry them out? We believe in decentralization, not because we have to answer to the European Union's, World Bank's or any other international organisation's requirements, but because we know that a whole series of public services are more efficiently offered at the local level.

Pre-university education, social assistance, public utilities and road infrastructure are only a few of the public services in which the local public authorities are better positioned regarding the administration of the resources and are adapted to that specific community.[1]

Just like the whole public administration process of reforms, decentralization must not be viewed as the sole objective; it must be viewed as achieving clear objectives like improving quality, efficiency and public service equity. Unfortunately, the decentralization policy has for a long time been a constant in the public speeches of the politicians, leaving the impression that interest in this area is only at the declarative level, and is not honest.

The main assignment of decentralization is to consolidate the autonomy of the local governance within the regional administrative units, and this can be achieved by broadening the range of competences as well as the power of decisions regarding the basic public services organised at the local level and the transfer of the indispensable financial resources. The rationales that justify decentralization are, in reality, cutting down public spending, improving efficiency in offering public services by passing them on to the local public administration, bringing the decisional act closer to the beneficiary, and civil society's involvement in the governing process.

There are multiple benefits if the rules of the game are followed, such as decentralized public services, allotted financial resources, transparency and civil society's involvement in the local decisional process, all of which are carried out under the strict observation and control of the central

---

[1] C. Craciun Claudiu, P. E. Collins, *The Management of Public Policies, Transformations and Perspectives* (Iasi: Ed. Polirom, 2008), 329.

public authorities through their regional delegates. We will closely analyze all of these stages to point out the importance of each component and lay out the role for each actor involved in the proper functioning of certain fundamental activities for each community.

Regarding the public services in Romania, many have been decentralized on paper, either totally or in part, and presently the local public authorities exercise three categories of competences according to art. 5 row 1 from Law no. 215/2001 and article no. 2 and no. 19–28 from Law no. 195/2006: exclusive, different and delegated.

The exclusive competences are those attributed by law to the public local administration authorities responsible for achieving them. In accordance with these attributed competences, the public administration authorities have the right to decide and have the necessary resources and means to achieve these competences, respecting the norms, criteria and set standards by the law.

The different competences are exerted by the local public administration authorities jointly with other levels from the public administration (county or central), with a clear separation of financing and decisional power for each one responsible.

The delegated competences are attributed by law to the local public administration authorities simultaneously with the proper financial resources from the central public authorities in order to exercise them on their behalf and implement limits on them. The obligation to assure the total financial support regarding the delegated competences belongs to the central authorities, according to art. 6 row 2 from Law no. 195/2006.

The newly proposed public services for decentralization according to the Governing Program 2013/2017, undertaken by the government, are:

- pre-university education, by transferring competences to the local authorities' level (towns, communes, municipalities and counties) regarding the organisation and functioning of the schools' network, naming/dismissing directors, and at the educational establishment level the dismissal of those involved in the management of human resources
- public health, by transferring the management regarding the commune, town, municipal and county hospitals to the local authorities
- public order, by establishing the commune's police with competences including traffic on the public roads within the townships

- agriculture, by transferring the agricultural attributions of the counties' offices to the counties' counsels, except those for inspection and control
- environment protection, by decentralizing the environment protection counties' offices attributions to the counties' counsels, except those for inspection and control. Regarding decentralization within the cultural sector, it will be continued by transferring the cultural institutions' competences to the National Ministry of Culture and Patrimony, and in the transportation sector, the fluvial ports' decentralization that were left under the subordination of the Ministry of Transportation and Infrastructure, as well as the subway system
- regarding the social assistance that is already decentralized, the objectives are the improvement of the financing framework and monitoring by laying out cost and quality standards
- it needs to be pointed out that the transfer of responsibilities will be assigned to the local authorities simultaneously with the rights on land and buildings still under the administration of ministries or central institutions, as well as businesses with state capital
- increasing the decisional extent of the public administration authorities must involve the demand for accountability on behalf of the deciding players without the possibility of holding other people accountable, except in certain, clearly stated conditions, due to the fact that every authority wants to decide but has the tendency to "run" from responsibilities.

In order to properly evaluate the chances the local public administration has to efficiently achieve the established competences in its tasks, we must objectively evaluate the financial resources available for them.

The most sensitive and difficult part of decentralization is the financial relation that must be established between the state and local communities. Placing the new services in the hands of the local community management will obviously determine a rise in the local public spending, whilst the present tendencies are to reduce this spending. The preoccupation with determining the necessary financial resources to sustain the variety of public services is a characteristic of all the states, mainly because of the unfavourable international financial climate. This does not mean that in more favourable financial times, the problem of financing the public services has not been a priority; it only means that in difficult financial times the solutions entail certain restrictions at the resources level, which will be perceived at the quality level of the services offered.

The main hurdle of decentralization is in fact the financial aspect, representing a hindrance in more ways than one. A defective transfer, with insufficient or non-existent resources, will undoubtedly lead to major imbalances in the local budgets, and the new services will become a burden for the local authorities. The problems are even much more difficult in the poor communities where their own collection sources are limited and dependent on the finances from the state budget. Under these conditions, apart from decentralization's main objective to offer quality public services and bring the community closer to the decisional factor, the situation will worsen.

The financial autonomy of the local communities is the premise for the success of decentralization, and because of that the local communities must have their own adequate financial resources at their disposal to deal with their responsibilities, to freely determine the revenues and spending and not be subjected to inspections except *a posteriori* regarding their financial decisions.[2] The communities' right to financial autonomy must be respected since it is established by the legal dispositions: "the local autonomy is only administrative and financial, being exerted on the basis and within the limits of the law."[3] Furthermore, the provisions of the European Local Autonomy Charter state that "the local public administration authorities have the right to their own, adequate funding, which will be at their disposal freely in order to fulfill their responsibilities," and these resources "must be in direct accordance to the competences stated by the constitution or law" as well as "the protection of the administrative territorial units with an unfavorable financial situation, necessitate[ing] the implementation of balancing financial procedures or corresponding measures, in order to correct the effects of unequal allocation of the potential financing resources" (Article no. 9).

We insist on the importance of establishing a balance among the competences of the local public authorities and the financial resources needed for exerting these competences. Not all local communities have the same financial support due to the fact that the local revenue greatly depends on the degree of economic development of each community. The ability to gain its own revenue from "levies, taxes, contributions, other proceeds, other earnings and share splits from the income tax"[4] determines

---

[2] A. Profiroiu, M. Profiroiu, "Financial Autonomy of Local Communities in Romania–a Premise for the Succes of Decentralization," *The Transylvanian Administrative Sciences Journal* 19 (2007): 78.

[3] Local public administration law nr. 215/2001, Art. 4, Par. 1.

[4] Law nr. 273/2006, regarding the local public finances, amended through E.G.O 63/2010, Art. 5.

disparities at the community level from that territory or even that region, and thus the poorer communities are in a position of not being able to ensure the proper functioning of the decentralized public services. It is important in these situations to make use of the different balancing abilities which represent an indispensable, fundamental mechanism, its objective being the distribution of wealth and decreasing the inequalities among the local communities.[5]

In this respect, the amended Law no. 273/2006 makes important disclaimers regarding the transfer strategy of the decentralized services to the local communities' management and that of the balancing budgets' policies. In order to ensure vertical[6] and horizontal[7] balancing budgets, the territorial administrative units will, in the first case, receive from certain state budget revenues amounts deducted with a specific destination, and secondary amounts deducted for balancing the budgets.

Therefore, according to article no. 6, the government's transferring of the administration and financing of the local public administration authorities for certain public spending, as a result of decentralized activities, as well as other new public spending, will be carried about by the law only if the necessary financial resources for accomplishing these tasks are ensured, as follows:

- in the first year by distinctly encompassing in the budget's law an annex of the deducted amounts with a special purpose, necessary for the financing of the transferred public spending or of the new spending, as well as that of the distribution criteria
- in the following years by encompassing those certain resources in the deducted amounts as a whole, for balancing the assigned local budgets of the territorial administrative units, except those distinctly specified by the state budget's law annex.

Regarding the balancing of local budgets' policies, the law establishes that deducted amounts can be distributed to counties using the following criteria: on one hand, the financial ability determined by the income tax

[5] A. Profiroiu, M. Profiroiu, *Financial autonomy*, 82.

[6] The vertical balance of the local budgets requires the transferring of financial resources from the state's budget revenues to the local budgets to provide the decentralized public services.

[7] The horizontal balance of the local budgets requires transferring from certain state's budget revenues to the local budgets in order to fulfil the differences of the financial capabilities among the administrative-territorial units.

per capita, to the amount of 70%, and on the other hand, on the county's surface area, to the amount of 30%.

Public-private partnership is currently sought by scholars and policy-makers as a tool for overcoming the financial crisis of the state and low performance in public administration. "It is deemed as an opportunity to bring added value to projects and their contents in order to meet new, emerging social demands."[8] Despite the growing attention paid to public-private partnership, international literature has questioned their actual effectiveness and viability. Public-private partnership suffers from a lack of strategy-making and dynamism in the public sector organisation. Public action geared towards public business cooperation requires advanced accounting, management and steering skills that cannot usually be developed. Such issues match the latest developments in the field of urban regeneration and represent a major stake for local governments.

Leaving aside the many facets of public-private cooperation, it is possible to notice two aspects of general interest which can be used mainly to signal the "rise of new tools" for government. Firstly, the discovery of alternate ways for local governments to take advantage of a third part either in the setting of their strategic agendas or the performance of particular tasks.[9] Secondly, the term "public-private partnership" can be referred to "any initiative, entailing the 'pooling' of complementary resources held by several organisations, within a regulatory framework, setting shares of risks and responsibilities among the tires concerned."[10]

Public-private partnership is a solution for implementing financial decentralization, referring to new sources for financing the delivery of public utilities and the chance of loosening the grip on public budgets. It generates innovative solutions for the emerging issues of contemporary society that might ordinarily not be achieved.

## Public Utilities and Private Initiative—the French Model

In France, the economic influence of the state remains strong. The French legal system stimulated network capitalism by establishing a financial and

[8] G. Codecasa, D. Ponzini, "Public-Private Partnership: a Delusion for Urban Regeneration? Evidence from Italy," *European Planning Studies* 19 (4) (2011): 647.

[9] L. Slamon, *The Tools of Government: a Guide to New Governance* (New York: Oxford University Press, 2002), 150.

[10] E. H. Klijn et al., "Public Private Partnerships: a Hybrid Reform Idea? A Comparation of PPP in England and in Netherlands," paper presented at the British Acacdemy of Management Conference (Belfast, September 12–14, 2006).

managerial system allowing for the participation of private capital in the development of major infrastructure projects.[11]

Urban public utilities are divided into four major branches: networks of energy distribution, water distribution and collection, waste collection, treatment and valorization, transport and parking services. Water distribution constitutes the most successful case of the French model of concessionaire capitalism, the main archetypal examples being Compagnie Generale des Eaux and Lyonnaise des Eaux.[12] Indeed, in 2012 private operators were dominant. If we analyze the role of the private sector in distribution from 2006 to 2012, the results are:

- in the domain of treatment and distribution, the number of private operators has grown from 80 to 81, while that of public operators has changed from 20 to 19.
- in the domain of filtering, the number of private operators has grown from 55 to 59, while that of public operators has changed from 45 to 41.[13]

Analysis of the public-private partnership in the water sector in France is a good example of a narrow oligopoly. Since 1996, around 70% of the market was controlled by the three most important groups—almost 40% by Veolia Eau, a subsidiary of Veolia Environment Group, a little over 20% by Lyonnaise des Eaux France, a subsidiary of Suez-Ondeo, one of the main branches of Suez Environment, and around 10% was controlled by SAUR France, a subsidiary of SAUL. Veolia Environment appeared on the defensive facing two independent operators, but SAUR France has the same attitude. The position of the public operators remained stable and significant, comprising almost one third of the market.

The rise of powerful urban corporations in France, specialized in infrastructure and public utilities, constitutes a major characteristic of our

[11] D. Barjot, "Public Utilities and Private Initiative: the French Concession Model in Historical Perspectives," *Business History* 53 (2011): 783, http://www.informaworld.com (accessed March 15, 2013).

[12] H. Bonin, "Le modele francais du capitalisme de l'eau dans la competition europeenne et mondiale depuis les annees 1990," in C. Baron (ed.), *Societe civile at marchandisation de l'eau: Experiences internationals, Science de la Societe* 64 (2005): 55–73.

[13] Ibid. Personal calculation from Ministere de l'Equipment, des Transports et du Logement.

time.[14] The most significant difficulty in implementing private public services in the French case comes, as in Romanian one, from the existence of a specific branch of law—administrative law.[15] There are two definitions of public utility according to this domain of law. From a material point of view, public utilities correspond to a set of human and material means established to realize administrative tasks. Regarding the jurisdictional point of view, however, public utilities refer to an activity of the general interest managed or controlled by the public administration but associated with a regime that falls totally and partially under private law. As a consequence, a private entity can deliver public services, while French administrative jurisprudence has allowed for public utilities to be managed by a private entity within the four major ways of managing:

- leasing them to an entity which does not invest in them but simply manages them
- establishing a contract with an entity which receives payment for services
- directing management by the administrator itself or by an agent
- concession from the public authorities.

The last two modalities are the most common for organising public utilities in France. In the case of direct administration, public utilities are not financed by a specific budget and are not managed to make profit. If deficits are registered the administration is responsible for covering them. The network capitalism and the participation of the private capital in the development of public utilities in France are the main realities for the internalization of the public services.

## Public Private Partnership and Regional Productivity in the UK

The main governmental reason for public-private partnership implementation is to improve service delivery; that is, to create better value for money in comparison to a government delivering the service. However, although private sector participation in public-private partnership frequently contributes to higher levels of efficiency, its participation does not guarantee improvement in service delivery and efficiency. Such improvements

---

[14] D. Barjot, *La trace des batisseurs: Histoire du Groupe Vinci* (Paris: Vinci, 2003).
[15] J. Chevallier, *Le service public* (Paris: Press Universitaires de France, 1987).

depend on a sufficient transfer of risk from the public sector to the private partner.

Similar to the French model, the private financing initiative (PFI) normally involves a concession contract. In the U.K.'s PFI, private consortia enter into long term contracts with the government to finance building and sometimes manage new projects.[16]

Despite the advantages of the public-private partnership and the greater returns offered, there are some disadvantages which should be noted:

- higher prices for public utilities
- financial costs
- reduced competition
- additional time for contract arrangements
- loss of flexibility in the long term
- the rise of a dual labour markets.

As a principle of New Public Management, public-private partnership and its procedures have focused on the need to ensure efficiency improvement "value for money." Public-private partnership offers notable advantages in efficiency and effectiveness when we use traditional procurement as a reference, i.e. a public sector comparator.

The concern for the public deficits was one of the main arguments for implementing New Public Management. Since the 1990s, the effect of public infrastructure on output and productivity has received challenges and alternative solutions from policymakers and scholars.[17]

In the U.K., there is a public controversy over the financing of new assets associated with the delivery of public health services, which is nothing more than a traditional dispute between quality and quantity in priding public health services. The public-private partnership in the UK facilitated a volume of investments in the health sector that from a budgetary point of view will not sustain themselves in the traditional mode of organising public services. The financial burdens on these investments impose on the budgets of current expenditure in the coming years, forcing a decrease in the quantity or variety of benefits. The conclusions of the study based on both micro and macroeconomics perspectives implemented

[16] J. L. Navarro-Espigares, J. A. Marlin-Seguro, "Public-private partnership and regional productivity in the UK," *The Service Industries Journal* 31 (2011): 559–580, www.informaworld.com (accessed March 15, 2013).

[17] D. Aschauer, "Public Investment and Productivity Growth in the Group of Seven," *Economic Perspectives* 13 (5) (1989): 17–25.

in UK is that public-private partnership can be considered an advisable strategy for simultaneously improving public services efficiency as well as the regional aggregate.

**Table 13.1. Regional distribution of PFI projects**

| Region | Total capital value | Number of projects |
|---|---|---|
| London | 25,310.9 | 90 |
| Scotland | 6,125.12 | 98 |
| South East | 5,590.52 | 53 |
| West Midlands | 3,541.34 | 44 |
| North West | 3,342.55 | 55 |
| Yorkshire and The Humber | 3,023.55 | 48 |
| South West | 2,470.29 | 46 |
| East of England | 2,421.53 | 31 |

Source: J. L. Navarro-Espigares, J. A. Marlin-Seguro, *Public private partnership and regional productivity in the UK*, 567.

## The Portuguese Model

New Public Management has been determined in the Portuguese experience by the public budget constraints, and an instability in managing large and complex projects has widened the private sector involvement in providing and managing public services. Portugal's experience in developing public-private partnership projects started in 1994 in the road sector, and the results have been encouraged by expansion to other sectors.

While facing the challenge of increasing public deficit, the Portuguese government applied public-private partnership. This resulted in some well-practiced models; for example, when in the 1980s the British Government was looking for "quick wins" to allow capital flow, the British Airport Authority (BAA) and several utilities in related industries, such as telephone, electricity, gas and water, were sold. In the 1990s, as described earlier, also in the U.K., the Public Finance Initiative (PFI) was developed as an innovative model for service provision and financing.[18] Between 1999 and 2001, several public-private partnership contracts were signed in Portugal: 9 for highway construction/financing/operation and 2 for railways (heavy and light rail system only in the transportation sector,

[18] C. Oliveira Cruz, R. Cunda Marques, "Revitalizing the Portuguese Experience with Public-Private Partnership," *African Journal of Business Management* 5 (11) (2011): 4023–4032, www.academicjournals.org/AJBM (accessed March 15, 2013).

extending seaports). This was an intense period of public-private partnership development and *a posteriori* it is possible to claim that the Portuguese government went too far in launching so many projects in such a short period. There are authors[19] who maintain that there was not enough time to consolidate know-how to improve new tenders with the experience acquired in the past projects, and second that there was no legislative framework to guide new contracts or a structured civil servant group to manage the projects.

In the drinking water and wastewater collection, several public-private partnership arrangements were launched at the retail level through concessions granted by local authorities, and over time the contracts have been renegotiated with the rise in tariffs.

Another important case study for Portuguese practices in implementing public-private partnership is contract extension in the Alcântara concession.

Alcântara Terminal is the largest container terminal in Portugal, placed in the Lisbon Port. The concession was granted in 1985 ending in 2005, when it was extended for 10 years (two periods of 5 years) to allow for the depreciation of additional investments. In 2009, six years before contract termination, the contract was extended for an extra 27-year period. The argument was that capacity increases where necessary, and it was not possible to wait until 2015, when the contract expired (with high investments required). In addition, as a result of the bilateral negotiations, changes were made in the risk-sharing agreement, transferring significant commercial risk to the Public Port Authority—if, in the period between 2009 and 2013, demand is lower than 20% (compared with the business model) then the concessionaire can ask for the financial re-equilibrium of the concession. To illustrate the optimism bias behind traffic forecasts, the real traffic, in 2009, was already 24% below the business model scenario.

This example also shows the problems of having concessions, which imply a large investment in public works. This type of concession became more interesting to construction companies, since most of the project capital is devoted to investment funding; that is, for a profit maximization strategy a construction company has the incentives to lowball its offer for the concession (predatory prices) because it will probably get free-of-charge and directly-awarded, multi-million construction projects, where large profit margins can be applied well above the market, since no competition exists. The public-private partnership project of highways in Portugal provides evidence of this type of behaviour, and the same

[19] R. C. Marquest, "Comparing Private and Public Performance in Portuguese Water Services," *Water Policy* 10 (1) (2008): 25–42.

happened with the privatization of Argentinean airports. In order to finance the large investment program necessary to upgrade the infrastructure, the government launched a concession for airport management and operation, and the winning bid was unrealistically low.[20] Several investments were planned, but as economic performance downgraded traffic decreased, and the concessionaire faced financial problems. In 2007, the government decided to renegotiate the contract, replacing the annual royalty fee with a variable 15% fee on aeronautic and non-aeronautic revenues.

## Conclusions

Public-private partnership is a well-researched solution of implementing financial decentralization. It refers to new sources for financing the delivery of public utilities and the chance for loosening the grip on public budgets. It generates innovative solutions for the emerging issues of contemporary society.

To many, the recent global crisis has been the midwife for the return of the "Leviathan" of "big government" that interferes with markets and economy efficiency. But a question rarely asked is "What kind of government?," because throughout the past 25 years, advanced industrial governments have made substantive reforms. Today, the private sector—because of privatization and contracting out—provides more than 40% of public goods. Public sector reforms have led to the widespread introduction of market competition throughout departments and governmental agencies. It is uncertain how these will reinforce market strategies for wage restraint and boost service or export growth or provide opportunities for parties and labour movements to explore alternative models.

On the one hand, public private partnership allows users to increase their consumption benefits through lower prices and higher quality services, due to higher efficiency levels. On the other hand, municipal corporations offer another possibility in public services delivery. These corporations should be run as businesses, just like private firms. Nevertheless, their main aim is still linked to non-commercial goals.

The statistical interpreted regarding the Portuguese Water Sector showed that the municipal corporations are related to a higher social performance in comparison to private firms. For instance, user prices and the quality of goods and services are positively correlated with municipal

---

[20] G. Lipovitch, "The Privatization of Argentine Airports," *J. Air Transport Manage* 14 (1) (2008): 8–15.

corporations rather than private firms. One of the avenues for future research is that even municipal corporations did not prove they had better social performances than bureaucracies. A first reflection is that the sector providing the service shaped social performance even when private sector participation benefits were not proved. For example, in the Portuguese water sector, with higher prices and the same quality, the new theoretical public management reasons for public-private partnership's usage were not proven (due to the difficulty in promoting competition under natural monopolies).

The second reflection for future research has arisen from recent literature questioning whether post-bureaucratic organisations perform worse than traditional bureaucracies. Since public bureaucracies can internally share their costs they can lower user prices, thus benefiting from them.

Simona Mina, PhD is a lecturer at the University Ovidius of Constanţa, Romania, Faculty of Law, Administrative Sciences and Sociology. She is also an associate PhD at the Maritime University of Constanţa, Romania. Her issues of interest are organisational behaviour, conflict management, communication and public relations.

Felicia Surugiu, PhD, graduated in doctoral studies in 2006 at the Economic Studies Academy. She coordinates the Department of Managing in Transportation at the Constanţa Maritime University, Romania.

# CHAPTER FOURTEEN

# ADMINISTRATIVE SUPERVISION OF LOCAL SELF-GOVERNMENT IN THE CONTEXT OF GOOD GOVERNANCE: THE CASE OF LITHUANIA

VIOLETA KIURIENĖ

## Territorial Administrative Division of Lithuania and the Peculiarities of Government

Lithuania is a unitary state, and is not divided into territorial state formations. The territory is divided into administrative units which consist of residential areas. The territorial administrative unit is a part of the territory, and the governing thereof is organised by the Government of Lithuania or the institutions of local authorities. The country is divided into 10 counties, which are subdivided into 60 municipalities.[1]

The county is the higher territorial administrative unit, the governing of which shall be organised by the central government pursuant to the Law of the Republic of Lithuania on the Government and other laws. The cabinet organises governance in the counties through ministries, institutions of government, offices of ministries, and other directly subordinated and accountable public administration entities of the government. The county is formed from the territories of the municipalities that have common social, economic, ethnic and cultural interests.[2]

---

[1] *The Law of the Republic of Lithuania on the Territorial Administrative Units of the Republic of Lithuania and their Boundaries*, http://policy.mofcom.gov.cn/english/flaw!fetch.action?id=C80160FB-EED1-493F-9950-02060D6FA3F8 (accessed April 1, 2013).

[2] *The Law of the Republic of Lithuania on the Government*, http://www.litlex.lt /Litlex/eng/Frames/Laws/Documents/172.HTM (accessed March 20, 2013).

The municipality is a territorial administrative unit of Lithuania, which is governed by institutions of local authorities elected by the local community pursuant to the Law of the Republic of Lithuania on Local Self-Government and others. In article 119 of the Constitution of the Republic of Lithuania, the right for self-government has been guaranteed for the law-defined administrative units of the state territory and is implemented through the appropriate municipal councils.[3]

In article 3 of the Law of the Republic of Lithuania on Local Self-Government, the municipality is described as an administrative unit of the territory of the state, defined by law. Its community has the right to self-governance guaranteed by the constitution and implemented through a municipal council, elected by the permanent residents of that unit and an executive institution as well as other institutions and establishments of a municipality, which are formed by the latter and are accountable to it.[4] The same has been defined in article 2 of the Law of the Republic of Lithuania on the Territorial Administrative Units and their Boundaries.[5]

Summing up the conceptions of public administration institutions acting within the territorial administration units of Lithuania, we may draw the conclusion that all these institutions must follow the Constitution of the Republic of Lithuania, the laws, and substatutory legal acts.

## Legal Regulations of the Administrative Supervision of Municipalities in Lithuania

One of the main conditions of the implementation of public administration is the rule of law. In this way, the institutions of local self-government are not exceptional. They, like the institutions of state public administration, have to follow the constitution and the laws both in enacting legal acts and in their daily work. Such an attitude is based by the conception of local self-government. In article 3 of the European Charter of Local Self-Government, the local self-government is defined as the local authorities,

---

[3] *The Constitution of the Republic of Lithuania*, http://www3.lrs.lt/home /Konstitucija/Constitution.htm (accessed April 1, 2013).

[4] *The Law of the Republic of Lithuania on the Local Self-Government*, http://www.litlex.lt/Litlex/eng/Frames/Laws/Laws.htm (accessed April 1, 2013).

[5] *The Law of the Republic of Lithuania on the Territorial Administrative Units of the Republic of Lithuania and their Boundaries*, http://policy.mofcom.gov.cn /english/flaw!fetch.action?id=C80160FB-EED1-493F-9950-02060D6FA3F8, (accessed April 1, 2013).

[6] *European Charter of Local Self Government*,http://conventions.coe.int/Treaty /en/Treaties/Html/122.htm (accessed April 1, 2013).

within the limits of law, which have a right and ability to regulate and manage a substantial share of public affairs under their own responsibility and in the interests of the local population.[6] As mentioned, a valid concept of local self-government in Lithuania is identical to the conception given in the Charter. Such content of local self-government corresponds the idea of the legal state. According to E. Kūris, "the legal state is the state, where freedom of actions is limited by the law."[7]

The legal basis for administrative supervision over local authorities in Lithuania derives from the European Charter of Local Self-Government, the Constitution of the Republic of Lithuania and other legislative acts such as the Law of the Republic of Lithuania on Local Self-Government, the Law of the Republic of Lithuania on the Government and others.

The European Charter of Local Self-Government provides that the administrative supervision of local authorities may only be exercised according to the procedures provided by the constitution or by law and that it should ensure compliance with the law and constitutional principles. According to the charter, any administrative supervision of local authorities may be exercised and organised according to the constitution or statute only.[8]

The Constitution of the Republic of Lithuania specifies that the observance of the constitution and the laws as well as the execution of decisions of the government by municipalities shall be supervised by the representatives appointed by the government. The constitution also declares that the powers of the government representative and the procedure of their execution shall be established by law.[9] The same attitude is embedded in the Law of the Republic of Lithuania on the Government.[10]

The Law of the Republic of Lithuania on Local Self-Government also states that the compliance of local authorities with the constitution, other laws and decisions of the government shall be supervised by the government representative. This law also states that one of the main principles on which the local self-government is based is the legality principle of adopted decisions by the municipalities' actions and its institutions. Following this principle, the activities of local authorities and

---

[7] E. Kūris, *Legal State, Variety of Legal Systems and the Tradition of West Laws*, in M. Glendon, M. Gordon, Ch. Osakwe, *The Traditions of West Laws*, (Vilnius: Pradai, 1993), XXIII.

[8] *European Charter of Local Self Government.*

[9] *The Constitution of the Republic of Lithuania.*

[10] *The Law of the Republic of Lithuania on the Government.*

other public administration entities of a municipality, as well as decisions taken on all the issues related to their activities, must meet the requirements of laws and other legal acts.[11]

The main provisions of the administrative supervision of local self-government are regulated by the Law of the Republic of Lithuania on the Administrative Supervision of Local Authorities. This law implements the provisions laid down in the constitution and specifies powers of the officers appointed by the government who exercise administrative supervision on local authorities. They act in compliance with the constitution and other laws, and carry out the decisions of the government. The analysis of legal acts states that the action of local authorities is supervised by the central government.[12]

## Legal Status, Forms of Realization of Powers and Rights of Representative of the Government in the County

As far as the municipalities act within their own sphere of activity they are subject to legal supervision. Here, legal supervision is restricted to supervising the performance of public law tasks and the obligations of the municipalities as laid down by law and adopted, as well as the legality of their administrative activity. Thus, the state may not interfere in the exercise of discretion where the municipalities have been given discretion by law and where they act lawfully.[13] However, where the institutions of municipalities act illegally, the officers, who execute the administrative supervision, must interfere. In Lithuania that is the government representatives in the counties, whose power, rights and duties, and offices are defined by the Law of the Republic of Lithuania on the Administrative Supervision of Local Authorities, which also states that one representative of the government is assigned to each county.

A representative of the government exercises administrative supervision of local authorities, i.e. supervises the local authorities that act in compliance with the constitution and laws of the Republic of Lithuania, and carries out the decisions of the government.

---

[11] *The Law of the Republic of Lithuania on the Local Self-Government.*

[12] *The Law of the Republic of Lithuania on the Administrative Supervision of Local Authorities*, http://www3.lrs.lt/pls/inter3/dokpaieska.showdoc_l?p_id =369278&p_query=&p_tr2=2 (accessed February 20, 2013).

[13] J. Harbich, "State Supervision on Local Government Authorities," http://fwww.fu.uni-lj.si/uprava/clanki/Letnik2009/2009-4-December-3-Harbich.pdf (accessed February 20, 2013).

The government representative is a civil servant—the manager of the institution organised by the government—who is appointed for these duties for four years in a competitive way. The representative is subordinated to the government and is accountable to the Prime Minister. A person having university education and with at least five years' experience in the field of public administration, or having university legal education or public administration education and with at least three years' experience in the field of public administration, may be appointed to this position.[14]

The territory of Lithuania is divided into 10 counties, which are subdivided into 60 municipalities. Each representative of the government has an office established by the government. There is one office for each county, so that the number of municipalities supervised ranges from 4 to 8. Each office has a number of staff ranging from 3 to 9[15] (see Table 14.1 below). This office helps the government representative to implement their authorities and rights.

As can be seen from Table 14.1 below, the ambits of administrative supervision of municipalities executed by the government representatives are very big. The amount of civil servants working in the offices of the government representatives in the counties is very small compared to the amount of supervised municipalities and the number of people living in these municipalities. The municipal entities adopt legal acts, but as we know, the legal acts adopted by municipal entities are not always lawful. A government representative in the county, with the intention to defend the interests of the municipality's and state's people, must react to the violation made by the municipal entities. According the constitution of Lithuania, the powers of the government representative and the procedure of their execution are established by law.

[14] *The Law of the Republic of Lithuania on the Administrative Supervision of Local Authorities.*

[15] Government of the Republic of Lithuania, www.lrv.lt (accessed February 1, 2013).

**Table 14.1. The objects and offices where the government representatives in the counties implement the administrative supervision of municipalities**

| County | Population in 2013 (thousands)[16] | Name of the Government Representative | Number of staff in Office of Government Representative | Number of municipalities in county |
|---|---|---|---|---|
| Alytus | 152,505 | in Alytus | 4 | 5 |
| Kaunas | 594,087 | in Kaunas | 7 | 8 |
| Klaipėda | 332,488 | in Klaipėda | 6 | 7 |
| Marijampolė | 156,795 | in Marijampolė | 4 | 5 |
| Panevėžys | 242,837 | in Panevėžys | 4 | 6 |
| Šiauliai | 291,357 | in Šiauliai | 5 | 7 |
| Tauragė | 106,672 | in Tauragė | 3 | 4 |
| Telšiai | 148,185 | in Šiauliai | 3 | 4 |
| Utena | 146,080 | in Utena | 3 | 6 |
| Vilnius | 808,304 | in Vilnius | 9 | 8 |

Source: Author's own research.

[16] *Population*, http://db1.stat.gov.lt/statbank/selectvarval/saveselections.asp ?MainTable (accessed February 1, 2013).

**Table 14.2 Implementation forms of the authorities of the Government Representative**

| Implementation forms of the powers | The content of implementation forms of the powers | The conditions, under which such implementation form of power is applied | The subject, to which is applied implementation form of powers |
|---|---|---|---|
| **Reasoned motion** | The proposal to discuss the question of abolition or change of legal acts | Applicable, when the legal act initiated by the municipal administration entity does not comply with the constitution, laws, the decisions of government. | (1) Collegiate municipal administration entity (the municipal council).<br>(2) Other municipal administration entities (mayor of municipality, the director of administration, warden and likewise). |
| **Written request** | The request to implement the law, to execute the decision of government immediately | Applicable, when the municipal administration entity does not execute the law, does not execute the decisions of government. | (1) Collegiate municipal administration entity (the municipal council).<br>(2) Another municipal administration entities (mayor of municipality, the director of administration, warden and likewise). |
| **Advance control of the drafts legal acts** | Advanced review of the drafts of legal acts | Applicable, when the drafts legal acts do not comply with the constitution, laws and decisions of government | Collegiate municipal administration entity (the municipal council) |

| | | | |
|---|---|---|---|
| **Decree** | The execution of legal acts is suspended | Definable, if:<br>(1) Initiated legal act, by which a contract can be made on illegality and violating the public interest;<br>(2) Initiated legal act can violate the public interest. | (1) Collegiate municipal administration entity (the municipal council).<br>(2) Other municipal administration entities (mayor of municipality, the director of administration, warden and likewise). |
| **Application to the administrative court regarding legality of legal act** | The appeal to the administrative court with abstract application to investigate the legality of the standard administrative act. | Applying to the administrative court when there is doubt over when a standard administrative legal act (or its part) adopted by the collegiate municipal administration entity corresponds with the law or decision of the government. | Administrative court |
| **Application to the administrative court regarding defending the public interest** | The appeal to the administrative court with application, that the public interest would be vindicated | The administrative court applies when the representative of the government thinks that the legal acts or actions (inaction) adopted by the municipal administration entity violate the public interest. | Administrative court |

| | | | |
|---|---|---|---|
| **Claim to the court of general jurisdiction regarding defence of the public interest** | Application of claim to the court of general jurisdiction regarding public interest | Application to the court of general jurisdiction is made when:<br>(1) Following the legal act of the municipal administration entities, which conflicts the constitution and laws, a contract was made in the name of municipality which violates the public interest;<br>(2) There are other bases of contract invalidity foreseen in the laws. | Court of general jurisdiction |
| **Application to the administrative court regarding abolition of legal act or regarding obligation to execute the law or decision of government** | The appeal to the administrative court with a request to abolish the legal act (or its part) or oblige the institution of municipality to execute the law or decision of the government. | Application to the administrative court is made when:<br>(1) The municipal administration entity, after revolving the presentation of the representative of government, refuses to change or abolish the questionable law act;<br>(2) The municipal administration entity, after revolving the request of representative of Government, refuses to execute it. | Administrative court |

Source: Author's research on the basis of the Law on Administrative Supervision of Local Authorities of the Republic of Lithuania.

The government representative, fulfilling their authorities, controls the legitimacy of action of municipal institutions and officers. For this purpose they are empowered by law to react if illegal solutions are adopted or decisions of the government are not executed. That administrative supervision of municipalities executed by the representatives of government is important and useful, and confirmed by 27 of 35 municipalities; 3 municipalities have indicated that this supervision is not useful.[16]

The government representative in the county, in the implementation of their powers, has rights established in the Law on Administrative Supervision of Municipalities[17]:

(1) To access the legal acts within the field of public administration adopted by units of the administration of municipality.
(2) To request from municipal administration entities copies of the adopted legal acts as well as copies of the minutes of meetings of municipal collegial administration entities. This requirement must be fulfilled not later than within five working days after the receipt thereof.
(3) To apply to municipal administration entities for the provision of information about their activities in the course of the implementation of laws and execution of decisions of the government.
(4) Upon the disappearance of the circumstances which served as the grounds for the suspension of a legal act, the submission of a proposal to amend or repeal a legal act, or the request for the immediate implementation of a law, the execution of a decision of the government, to revoke such a proposal or request with a reasoned ordinance, provided that the proposal or the request has not been executed.
(5) To set a different time limit for fulfilling the actions of the government representative subject to the receipt of a reasoned request to extend this time limit, submitted by a municipal administration entity within its remit.
(6) To attend sittings of the government in accordance with the procedure laid down by the rules of procedure of the government,

---

[16] *State Audit Report*, http://www.vkontrole.lt/pranesimas_spaudai.aspx?id=16250 (accessed February 1, 2013).
[17] *The Law of the Republic of Lithuania on the Administrative Supervision of Local Authorities.*

as well as in the events organised by state institutions where issues of activities of municipalities are considered.

(7) To apply to state institutions according to their competence with a request to explain the procedure for applying resolutions of the government, if this is directly related to activities of municipalities, their relations with state institutions and activities of the government representative.

Government representatives are entitled to access the legal acts adopted by units of the municipal administration, and to request copies of the adopted legal acts and the protocols of meetings of municipal collegial administration entities. Other rights include applying for the provision of information about their activities in the course of the implementation of laws and the execution of decisions of the government, as well as the right to attend their meetings, and where there are reasons for this to inform the municipal councillors that drafts under consideration do not comply with the laws or decisions of the government. The government representative may authorize a state servant of their office.

## Conclusions

Good governance is transparent, participatory, consensus-oriented, accountable, effective and efficient, responsive and inclusive, and follows the rule of law. Good governance requires fair legal frameworks that are enforced impartially.

Improved governance requires an integrated, long-term strategy built upon cooperation between government and citizens, involving both participation and institutions. Institutions must act under the rule of law, which is a technical and legal issue at the local self-government level, but also necessary to build up local self-government that it is legitimate, effective and widely supported by citizens, as well as a civil society that is strong, open and capable of playing a positive role in politics and self-government.

In democratic countries the local self-government is controlled by the state government; i.e., in the implementation of the constitution, the requirements of the laws and other legal acts in which the local government is not absolutely independent. The main aim of the administrative supervision of municipalities is to ensure that the principle of the rule of law and the constitutional prescriptions are followed.

In the Lithuanian constitution, local self-government is solidified as a system of local public administration acting within the bases of self-activities. This system is not directly subordinated to the institutions of state government. The Constitutional Court of the Republic of Lithuania has stated that self-government supposes the particular freedom of activity and independence from the institutions of state government. However, this freedom is not without limits and the independence does not mean the possibility to ignore the interests of state. Therefore, the harmonization principle of interests of municipalities and state is very important. In one case, this is indicated for the state in various ways and forms in supporting the municipalities, while in another case, in the coordination of common actions, when seeking important social aims, and in a third case for the state by the forms, which are defined by the law, in the supervision of municipal activities.

The legal basis for administrative supervision over local authorities in Lithuania derives from the European Charter of Local Self-Government, the Constitution of the Republic of Lithuania and other legislative acts, such as the Law of the Republic of Lithuania on Local Self-Government, the Law of the Republic of Lithuania on the Government, and others.

The constitution specifies that observance of the legal acts as well as the execution of decisions of the government by municipalities shall be supervised by the representatives appointed by the government.

The purpose of the government representatives in Lithuania is to control the legality of the activities of municipal entities and officers. To implement this aim the government representatives have a right to react in the ways defined by laws, if adopting decisions in municipalities are illegal or the laws and government decisions are not executed.

The government representatives implement their activity by executing the advance control of legal acts of municipal entities, giving reasoned presentation or written request, and appealing to the court when municipal entities do not satisfy the presentations and requirements, as well as defending the public interest.

Violeta Kiurienė, M.A. is a lecturer at the Department of Public Administration at the Faculty of Social Sciences the Šiauliai University in Lithuania. Her research interests concentrate on local self-government, administrative law and administrative supervision.

# CHAPTER FIFTEEN

# THE ROLE OF NON-GOVERNMENTAL ORGANISATIONS WITHIN HOUSING POLICY FORMATION AND IMPLEMENTATION: THEORETICAL APPROACHES AND MAIN CONCEPTS

DILOROM AKHMEDZHANOVA

The connection between good governance and NGO activities in the housing sector is pretty clear, as for any other sectors of policy. It is common sense to link these two phenomena, and as many studies show there is a direct correlation between the quality of public administration and non-governmental organisations' development. This tie is a consequence of the functions that NGOs are called on to serve in the society. Among these functions are the following: to neutralize lack of social services, community building and civil society improvement, expert support, advocacy, control and monitoring. Success in carrying out these functions provides a ground for positive change and development in society. However, this ideal view is a more complex process depending on many variables, including basic institutional conditions (legal rules for NGOs operation, participation level, general economic conditions) and unique factors which are characteristic for the concrete situation and the sector where a NGO operates.

This chapter is part of doctoral research with the wider title of "The Role of Non-government Organisations within Post-socialist Housing Reforms in Poland and Russia—Between Civic Activity and State Regulation." Its main aim is a consideration of the current concepts and theoretical approaches in an examination of the housing policy and realization of the NGO's role within housing policy. Such analysis is necessary for further operationalization of concepts and field research design.

The presented topic refers to the two macro-contexts of housing policy and nongovernmental organisations, both of which are full of different concepts and theories. But it is important to select, inter-connect and analyze particular concepts from two contexts from the perspective of one theoretical scheme. Thus, the goal of the chapter is identifying, establishing and proving the theoretical scheme which will have an explanatory power for the role of NGOs within housing policy.

## Non-Governmental Organisations in Housing Studies

Regarding the state of the field of housing NGOs studies, it is necessary to say that this topic is not completely new for social scientists, and there are several significant texts in this research area that could be revisited. The first is the thesis by Ramya Ramanath about housing NGOs in India,[1] and another is about NGO networks in the South African housing sector by Asrtid Ley.[2] Both texts deal with NGOs' roles in the developing countries, mostly considered cases dealing with the so-called operational NGOs which are profitable for housing policy action implementation.

The key puzzle informing the current chapter is the absence of an examination of housing NGOs in the implications of the current housing regime and provision of advocacy activities within significant housing reforms. There are several studies of the housing reforms in the post-socialist space. In general, these investigations deal with a process of privatization and housing system transition. The Polish housing policy is commonly compared to policies in the new EU countries such as Slovakia, Slovenia, the Czech Republic and Hungary. Martin Lux has conducted a number of such studies, in which he also analyses the general trends in their housing policies and the problem of social housing.[3] Housing reforms in Eastern Europe and the problems of social housing have also been

---

[1] R. Ramanath, *From Conflict to Collaboration: Nongovernmental Organizations and their Negotiations for Local Control of Slam and Squatter Housing in Mumbai, India* (Blacksburg, Virginia, 2005), 445.

[2] A. Ley, *Housing as Governance. Interfaces between Local Government and Civil Society Organizations in Cape Town, South Africa* (Berlin: Technische Universitat, 2010), 365.

[3] See M. Lux, "Social Housing in the Czech Republic, Poland and Slovakia," *European Journal of Housing Policy* 1 (2) (2001): 189–209; M. Lux, "Efficiency and Effectiveness of Housing Policies in the Central and Eastern Europe Countries," *European Journal of Housing Policy* 3 (3) (2003): 243–265.

studied by Sasha Tsenkova.[4] She examines the general course of reforms and their results, mostly concentrating on the situation in the countries of southeastern Europe. A number of other studies have also examined post-socialist housing reforms in Eastern Europe. However, there is still no research which would estimate the NGOs' roles or their absence in this part of the transition process. Another reason evoking interest in this topic is the lack of a conceptual tie between the housing system specifics, especially housing regimes, their transformations, and non-governmental activities in the housing sector.

This text is an attempt at the rather ambitious goal of finding conceptual links and tools for further estimation of NGO roles within a post-socialist housing transformation, with special respect to the features of the housing sector itself and characteristics of the housing regimes' transformations.

But first of all it is necessary to define what housing policy is and how it conceptualized within this chapter. Housing policy is a kind of state policy aimed at the regulation of all or part of housing system elements. This policy is directed to the provision of an essential human need and reduction of the negative effects of the housing system operation. Brian Lund shapes housing policy with a more narrow approach: "Housing policy is about state attempts to make corrections to the housing market."[5] Thus, in laissez faire markets, the regulation of the services market is not in the sphere of state responsibility. However, even in such conditions, housing policy could not be outlined only by attempts of housing market regulation. As in any area of human activity, housing is a highly interconnected system either internally or externally. Housing policy deals not only with the housing market but also with the market of communal services, banking, taxation regulation and social policy of the state in general. However, for measuring the housing policy it is instrumental to apply the concept of housing regime.

## Housing Regime Concept and Classifications

In discussing the housing property rights and the level of state intervention on housing system regulation, we have to deal with the concept of the housing regime, which concerns administration and operation, mostly

[4] S. Tsenkova, *Housing Policy Reforms in Post-Socialist Europe: Lost in Transition* (Heidelberg: Physica-Verlag, 2009), 262.

[5] B. Lund, *Understanding Housing Policy* (Bristol: The Policy Press, University of Bristol, 2011), 20.

caused by the combination of property rights to housing stocks and the level of state intervention in their operation. In this narrow sense, the housing regime may vary from the full state property rights for housing stocks to full private property for dwellings. These two kinds of property rights regimes are poles in the wide scale of different combinations of property for dwellings.

There are two general classifications of housing regimes: enabling/non-enabling, with a welfare policy character (applicable for developed countries only).

Angel singles out five lines for distinguishing enabling or non-enabling housing regimes:

(1) Special cases of government interventions in the economy as a whole
(2) Systems where housing needs are met by markets and governments overseeing markets and correcting market failure, versus systems where governments are directly responsible for meeting housing needs
(3) Systems governed by the rule of law versus systems governed by decree
(4) Pluralist versus centralized systems, allowing multiple visions to coexist rather than advancing a single shared vision
(5) Situations consisting of two different sets of government interventions, each being enabled or non-enabling itself.[6]

Centralization and pluralization of the housing system in general are also one dimension for the measurement of the housing regime. It is very important to realize that decisions about the level of centralization or pluralisation of housing systems have grown from there. Within an enabling regime we have a self-regulating system which is adaptive and based on strong mechanisms of feedback, designed to prevent crises of system management. Therefore, enabling order intended for a more variable and sensitive housing system aims at providing the satisfaction of different kinds of housing needs and is adaptive for various challenges.

The character of the housing regime has a direct impact on five elements of the housing sector regulation: (1) property rights, (2) housing finance, (3) housing subsidies, (4) residential infrastructure, and (5)

[6] Sh. Angel, *Housing Policy Matters: a Global Analysis* (New York: Oxford University Press, 2000), 12.

regulation of land and housing development constraining the character of the housing regime and housing policy in a particular country.

Property rights for housing can vary from full state property to absolute private property through mixed forms when housing is partially a property of the state but a significant part of it is privately owned.

A housing finance regime may be presented within a continuum between conditions of mortgage finances to a lack of any crediting and constructing by owners' resources of the state finances. This regime has a strong influence on the speed and volume of new construction and renovations of already existing housing stock.

Housing subsidies in the form of the co-financing of housing construction and state subsidies for communal service companies influence the housing market development in general and cause housing system variety. In an enabling regime, housing subsidies are absent or exist at a paltry scale. Within a non-enabling regime, housing subsidies may have a substantial role in the housing sector formation and operation. This phenomenon became a basis for the vulnerability of communal services markets when such markets depend on state subsidies and the population is not able to estimate the real price for services.

Residential infrastructure also directly depends on the kind of housing regime. It mostly deals with the character of investments for infrastructure development and the manner of regulation of this infrastructure. In the additional impact of the state, we may observe this in the situation of the existing and operating state subsidies for infrastructure.

Regulation of land and housing development depends on the form of the housing regime because the speed of housing development and construction is directly connected with land regulation—the easier the granting of permission for construction, the greater the volume of house building in the particular country.

Paul Balchin and Maureen Rhoden classify housing regimes through the estimation of the welfare regime. There are three types of welfare states defined: social democratic, corporatist and liberal.[7]

The social democratic regime is oriented to high standards of social needs provision and tends to construct the universal provision system. This group of countries have a housing policy promoting "various forms of rented housing as an alternative sector available to all, and on a long-term basis."[8] The second, corporatist-type states deal with the removing of social needs provision to the market, also provided by the principle of

[7] P. Balchin, M. Rhoden. *Housing Policy: An Introduction* (London, New York: Routledge, 2005), 4.

[8] Ibid.

profession and class attachment. These kinds of states provide both private and rented sectors of housing. Another category is the liberal type of welfare state, which provides needs for a low-income class in a standard higher than that necessary "to survive." These countries tend towards private ownership housing. The possibility of state interventions in this sector is very low and is concentrated on the provision of the affordable housing for groups deprived from the housing market.

Understanding the particular housing regime and its reforming provides an opportunity for outlining the interest groups within housing policy-making and implementation, opportunities and limitations for NGOs' performance in the housing sector, It constitutes the general conditions for different NGO types in the housing sector development. The type of housing regime also forms the agenda for NGOs, especially at the moment of regime transformation.

## Non-Governmental Organisations as Objects of Research

A huge mass of different scientific researches, conceptual schemes and classifications of NGOs have been accumulated, and selection of the most applicable becomes a separate research task. However, is it important to select the most significant and measurable concepts for the NGO considerations.

To avoid a long discussion about methods for NGO definition it is important to operationalize this concept in a more concrete and applicable way. The most productive, in my opinion, is the definition proposed by David Lewis:

> The definition proposes that a non-profit organization has the following five key characteristics: it is *formal*, that is, the organization is institutionalized in that it has regular meetings, office bearers and some organizational permanence; it is *private* in that it is institutionally separate from government, though it may receive some support from government; it is *non-profit distributing*, and if a financial surplus is generated it does not accrue to owners or directors (often termed the "non-distribution constraint"); it is *self-governing* and therefore able to control and manage its own affairs; and finally it is *voluntary*, and even if it does not use volunteer staff as such, there is at least some degree of voluntary participation in the conduct or management of the organization, such as in the form of a voluntary board of directors.[9]

[9] D. Lewis, *The Management of Non-Governmental Development Organizations: an Introduction* (London and New York: Routledge, 2001), 37.

This set of characteristics is universally applicable for practice-oriented research and suggests clear features of organisations, not only for their definition but also for the case selection during field research.

Therefore, NGOs can be defined as formally registered, acting, private and constitutionally separated from the state (earning its support), with the non-profit organisation dealing with particular aspects of political or social life. Such organisations may be directed not only at solving the problems of disadvantaged people, but also at the presentation and elaboration of interests of different social and professional groups.

Non-governmental organisations' classifications are based on different characteristics that depend not only on a scientific point of view but are also outlined by national legislatures which regulate the practice of NGO activities. The basics for NGO classifications are the following: legal status, orientation, level of co-operation and the character of activities.

The legal status is provided by national and international law, and it is possible to distinguish four NGO family groups:

(1) Unincorporated and voluntary association
(2) Trusts, charities and foundations
(3) Not-for-profit companies
(4) Entities formed or registered under special NGO or non-profit laws.[10]

These types could be presented in different combinations. Very often, the legal form of an NGO depends on the organisation's orientation. There are four main types of orientation in NGO activities:

(1) Charitable orientation. These NGOs operate towards the organisation and provision of different kinds of support to disadvantaged groups and those in need.
(2) Service orientation. NGOs with service orientation provide a range of services for various groups on the basis of its program: "... people are expected to participate in its implementation and receiving the service."[11] These services could be delivered in the form of educational projects or oriented to the solving of concrete social problems.

---

[10] G. Stillman, *Global Standard NGOs: The Essential Elements of Good Practice* (Geneva: Lulu, 2007), 13–14.

[11] T. McPhail, "The Role of Non-Governmental Organizations (NGOs)," in T. McPhail (ed.), *Development Communication: Reframing the Role of the Media* (Oxford: Blackwell Publishing Ltd, 2009), 69.

(3) Participatory orientation. NGOs of this type operate through the involvement of people at the local level in the realization of concrete activities towards self-help projects. These NGOs engage people to participate in voluntary work, funding and help to perform a project through other resource contributions.
(4) Empowering orientation. NGOs of this kind operate in the field of delivering a clear understanding of factors which are affecting citizens' lives. This knowledge about citizen potential in the political sense opens up prospects for their impact on a current policy: "Sometimes, these groups are developed spontaneously around a problem or an issue."[12]

Of course, these presented types should be mostly considered as "ideal types," and in many cases NGOs may have mixed orientations.

The level of NGO operation is categorized into three dimensions:

(1) Local, when an NGO's activities are realized on the level of a settlement or region. In some cases, this level is divided into another two levels: community-based and city-wide organisations.[13]
(2) National, on which level operate NGOs are oriented to a particular country.
(3) International, at which level a small amount of representative organisations operate.

One more important classification of NGOs is proposed by the Asian Development Bank based on the NGOs' principal focus and types of interaction. There are two types of NGO: operational and advocacy. This distinction is constructed around "operational cooperation and collaboration versus policy dialogue."[14] Operational NGOs exist on all levels, from local to international. These organisations are oriented to delivering services to the population through the realization of different programs. Referring to concepts of NGO orientation, these are organisations with charitable, service and participatory orientations. Advocacy NGOs are seeking to impact on policies and practices of governments to raise political issues and present and lobby different

---

[12] T. McPhail, *The Role of Non-governmental Organizations*, 69.

[13] P. Rogers et al., *An Introduction to Sustainable Development* (London: Earthscan, 2008), 124.

[14] A. Jha et al., *Safer Homes, Stronger Communities: A Handbook for Reconstructing after a Natural Disaster* (New York: The World Bank, 2009), 212.

groups' interests, operating on national and international levels. In terms of orientation, these organisations are empowering.

David Lewis distinguishes six strategies for advocacy work: negotiations, lobbying (i.e. influencing key individuals), gaining membership of government bodies, building networks and coalitions, using the media and conducting campaigns.[15] These strategies constitute activities of any advocacy NGO, and it is important to define them within NGOs' activities for further estimation of their roles within policy re-shaping. In a strong sense, advocacy NGOs do not have to deal with policy implementation, but are oriented to the policy changes and launching of new programs. Participation in an already-made decision could not be considered an advocacy activity.

Additional important characteristics for NGO classifications are the following: organisation size, character and volume of funding, or sector of activities.

Independently, the level of operation, orientation, type of communication and legal forms of all types of these organisations might be presented in the housing sector. It is important to underline that operational-type organisations are mostly oriented to the political decisions implementation, while advocacy-type NGOs tend to participate in the policy formation on the national level.

If the research issue is oriented to the evaluation of the NGOs' role within housing policy, there are two basic research strategies on the level of case selection. The first strategy is selection of a so-called "operational" type of NGO which actively participates in the process of the local, regional or state administration task implementations. In this sense, it is only possible to estimate the level of NGO involvement in the housing sector performance.

The kind of NGO in the housing sector causes its level of activities, character and main orientations. Apart from the conventional classification of NGOs there is one more typology applicable not for NGOs in general, but also for NGOs in the housing sector.

Two types of housing NGOs were selected from all the general formal characteristics. The first is resident movements oriented on common problem solving, and assisting "others in eviction cases … actively lobby[ing the] government in order to force it to promulgate policies that will help to resolve the problems of urban poor."[16] Very often, such

[15] D. Lewis, *The Management of Non-Governmental Development*, 124

[16] S. Kiu Ha, "Urbanization, Low-income Housing and Urban Governance in South Korea," in K. Ho Mok, R. Forrest (eds.), *Changing Governance and Public Policy in East Asia* (New York: Routledge, 2009), 334.

organisations appear because of visible disadvantages and pressure of residents' interests. This kind of housing NGO has an instrumental character and is oriented to concrete problem solving.

The second kind of NGO dealing with housing issues is the so-called "intellectual movement," more oriented to the preparation and lobbying for political proposals for significant economic and social changes. This kind of organisation has a stronger ideological orientation and is attuned to more general values, such as the redistribution of public goods, active citizenship and the increase of public administration efficiency. Sometimes, housing issues are not the only field of activity for such organisations.

Actually, this typology could be combined with the classification of NGOs from the point of view of NGO orientation and the character of interaction. Residents' movements are intended to be more operational and to provide services, while the so-called "intellectual movement" in housing tends to work as an advocacy embedded NGO.

From the types of movements, all housing NGOs have deliberate missions to mediate between the governors and citizens. This important role has several measures. The mediating position includes expression of citizens' positions in particular questions, interpreting legislative and administrative changes.

For the estimation of advocacy (or empowering) activities, it is necessary to select national or international level organisations, since regional and local ones usually have no sufficient resources for active participation in the process of policy formation and re-shaping. This strategy allows for the clarifying of concrete NGO activities and estimating of their role in the process of housing policy making. But there are more factors with direct impacts on the character of NGOs' role within housing policy, concentrated around two macro-parameters: the character of NGO-GO[17] relationships and the character of the housing regime itself. These parameters will be considered further in this text, but in this part it is important to clarify two concepts designed for NGO activities examination: empowerment and participation.

Simply put, empowerment is the ability to influence a process or phenomenon, and the constitutional part of this concept is a concept of power. Rowlands argues that it is possible to distinguish "power over" (control or influence) and "power to" (stimulating activity), and empowerment implies gaining the "power to" to resist or challenge

---

[17] Governmental Organisations.

"power over."[18] The level of empowerment of an NGO is one of the major factors providing successful activities. Considering the nature of empowerment in the sense of "power to," it is possible to conclude that this characteristic is more applicable to advocacy NGOs than operational ones.

For the applied research this concept is useful and measurable in its connection with characteristics of NGO activities such as participation. This connection is emphasized by Lewis: "the concept of empowerment is linked to that of participation, which speaks of involvement rather than passivity, and a role for people in decision making instead of being 'acted upon' in the name of progress or development."[19]

The concept of participation in the sense of civic and NGO activity is rooted in the reaction to the inability of governments to promote social development in the 1960s to 1970s.[20] The active involvement of ordinary citizens was called upon for the creation of projects which served their local communities, and there are four forms of participation[21]:

- Nominal participation arises when government-formed groups are created, but these groups have a symbolic display as their main purpose.
- Instrumental participation is a way to provide jobs through a structural social agreement when the costs of these working places are moved to local communities.
- Representative participation consists of gaining planning committees or other governmental bodies for the expression of citizen's interests.
- Transformative participation is the strongest form since it supposes the decisions and actions of citizens without outsider involvement. This form of participation is the most empowering in the political sense.

As Lewis argues: "… top-down interests in participation are different from bottom-up interests, and participation is therefore a 'site of conflict' which

---

[18] J. Rowlands, "Empowerment Examined," *Development in Practice* 15 (1995): 103.

[19] D. Lewis, *The Management of Non-Governmental Development*, 115.

[20] J. Migdley, *Social Development: The Development Perspective in Social Welfare* (London: Sage, 1995), 36.

[21] S. White, "Depoliticizing Development: the Uses and Abuses of Participation," *Development in Practice* 6 (1) (1995): 9.

might have positive or negative outcomes for the poor."[22] In this sense, participation is a process which involves resources and could be stopped in the case of dissatisfaction with its results.

## Non-Governmental Organisations' Relationships

It is evident that any formally registered organisation is immersed in its relationships with the official authorities. The characters of these relationships can vary from only following the necessary formal requests to active cooperation and collaboration with authorities on different levels. The type and character of NGOs' relations with the state (presented by the authorities in different levels and sectors) depend not only on the particular NGO's specifics and intentions, but also from a multitude of factors including the general social and economic context and state policy towards NGOs, or sectors where NGOs operate.

The general state attitudes towards NGO activities have a direct impact on these activities. A continuum of such attitudes is defined, ranging from supportive to facilitative to neutral to regulative to repressive.[23] The attitudes of the government towards NGOs are under the influence of the general political context and the level of democratization, and additional factors also have a meaning here. Among these factors are those specific to the NGO itself, the field of the NGO performance, and the condition of this field. This typology is a good starting point for the contextualization of an applied research but not sufficient for a deeper understanding of the NGO-GO relationships. Therefore, the "Four Cs" model is more productive for these purposes.

Adil Najam created the Four Cs model for the estimation of the NGO-GO relationships character. This model's continuum lies between cooperation and co-optation to confrontation and complementarity.[24] The characters of these relationships depend on the relationships between the goals and strategies of both sides—NGOs and GOs—in particular policies. It is possible to summarises this as in Table 15.1 below.

---

[22] D. Lewis, *The Management of Non-Governmental Development*, 118.

[23] C. Commuri, "State Repression and the Limits of Voluntary Action: Case Study of the 'Save Narmada movement' in India," paper presented at the 1995 Annual Association for Research on Nonprofit Organizations and Voluntary Action (ARNOVA) Conference, Cleveland, Ohio, November, 1995.

[24] A. Najam, "The Four-C's of Third Sector-Government Relations: Cooperation, Confrontation, Complementarity, and Co-optation," *Non-profit Management and Leadership* 10 (4) (2000): 383.

**Table 15.1. NGO-GO relations based of the Four Cs model**

| | | Goals (ends) | |
|---|---|---|---|
| | | similar | dissimilar |
| Preferred strategies (means) | similar | cooperation | co-optation |
| | dissimilar | complementarity | confrontation |

Source: A. Najam, *The Four-C's of Third Sector-Government Relations*, 383.

The cooperative relationship is characterized by similar goals and strategies used in obtaining these ends. Confrontation is the contrasting situation when there is a disparity in both goals as well as means. Complementarity and co-optation are situations where the government and NGO have the same goals but no agreement about the strategies for achieving them.

Goals and strategies from two sides (GO and NGO) are determined by the area of policy in which they are implemented. Simultaneously, NGOs possess their own strategies not only within concrete actions but for the NGO performance in general, and these strategies involve different tactics. A combination of NGO strategies and tactics is presented in Table 15.2 below.

**Table 15.2. NGO strategies and tactics**

| Strategies | Tactics |
|---|---|
| Acquiesce | Habit, Imitate, Comply |
| Compromise | Balance, Pacify, Bargain |
| Avoid | Conceal, Buffer, Escape |
| Defy | Dismiss, Challenge, Attack |
| Manipulate | Co-opt, Influence, Control |

Source: C. Oliver, "Strategic Responses to Institutional Processes," *Academy of Management Review* 16 (1991): 156.

The issue of the operationalization of these tactics and strategies for field research is a question for a separate article, but it is important to point out that all these tactics can be found during the analysis of a particular NGO's activities, documents and project evaluation documents.

## NGO Participation in the Housing Policy—Practical Implications

It is important to clarify the methods of NGO participation in housing policy and the tools for this participation estimation. This part of the chapter is dedicated to these issues with respect to further field research design.

The NGOs' roles may be notable during the urban planning processes and performed within public hearings, which are usually provided by the state law as a form of participation. This is recognized as "the most common form of public participation, from the local to the national levels."[25] Public hearings are an inexpensive form of joint decision-making, are a rapid form of participation and also provide an opportunity to present opinion from all sides. However, this form of participation is criticized as insufficient in the aspect of influence on the provided decisions and policy.[26] However, in the analytical sense the participation in public hearings, checking possible and accepted proposals as well as their inclusion in further official decisions are informative data for an NGOs' evaluation role.

Having a good initial idea during public hearings is a form of citizen impact on policy, and this form of citizen and NGO participation is considered a "trigger of citizen frustration, anger and even conflict."[27] This unflattering characteristic of public hearings is strengthened by the statement that public hearings "were more effective in legitimating agency decisions that had already been made."[28] Therefore, the main function of public hearings is substituted by the legitimating of proven decisions.

Another form of participation in the policy-making process is expertise work, which is slower and more expensive for NGOs than public hearings. Expertise work is an important part of a general process of lobbying during political decision adoption. This form of participation provides an argument for NGOs during public discussion about particular governmental proposals.

---

[25] S. Senecah, "The Trinity of Voice: the Role of Practical Theory in Planning and Evaluating the Effectiveness of Environmental Participatory Process," in S. Depoe et al. (eds.),*Communication and Public Participation in Environmental Decision Making* (Albany: State University of New York Press, 2004), 27.

[26] Ibid., 27.

[27] Ibid., 29.

[28] D. Fiorino, "Citizen Participation and Environmental Risk: A Survey of Institutional Mechanisms," *Science, Technology, and Human Values* 15 (2) (1990): 232.

The legislative initiative is probably the most influential form of participation in policy making, but requests massive and powerful resources from the NGO side. These requirements are not only about the professional level of political proposals and provided expertise, but also include the direct access for initiative consideration. Another important condition for such a form of political impact is a particular law which regulates the rights for legislative initiatives for citizens, their organisations and NGOs.

Some NGOs (especially with services and operational orientations) are working in the field of housing policy provision. Their activities in the policy implementation could be realized in the form of educational programs, consultations and supporting feedback mechanisms due to policy realization. The role of these organisations on the advocacy level is not noticeable due to the character (operational) and level (local or regional) of activities.

The type of NGO constitutes the level of involvement in the decision-making processes and stages where NGOs may participate. It is apparent that empowering or advocacy NGOs tend to take part in more of these processes than operational, or services providing organisations.

## Conclusions

The connection between housing systems with housing regimes and the level of NGO performance in this sector is evident. The character of the housing regime in both enabling and non-enabling senses or on a welfare basis shapes the set of groups of interests in the housing policy formation, target groups, limitations and opportunities for the participation and empowerment of housing policy in the particular country.

The general political environment for any kind of NGO activity, including political regime and governmental attitudes towards NGOs, provides the type of relationships between governmental and non-governmental organisations which also have an influence on the level of NGO involvement and role within housing policy.

For the estimation of this role it is necessary to evaluate not only general institutional conditions for different types of NGO development and performance but also the dynamic of housing regime changes. The character of the housing regime determines types of housing NGOs acting in the particular system. It is possible to conclude that enabling the housing regime broadens opportunities for advocacy NGOs, but this conclusion would not be sufficient without one important assumption—that the level of mobilization depends on the scale of disadvantage. If the system works well there are few reasons for a strong political struggle. Therefore, from the point of view of the NGOs' role in the housing policy estimation, housing systems in transition are representative cases for such analysis.

The general conditions for NGO development are important variables for the research, but it is important to respect the specifics of housing policy itself, which is oriented to the entire population of the country, providing one of the basic needs and dealing with very specific markets, real estate and communal services.

There are two strategies for cases selection for such research goals. The first is an analysis of particular NGOs and their activities, and the second is consideration of points of passage when the system has been changed.

Two worlds—the housing system and NGOs—meet in at least one critical moment—the so-called state intervention when the government takes the role of reforms initiator, and these reforms are sometimes oriented to the improvement of the state domination in the housing sector. These interventions form the main field for the advocacy of NGO performance, and such cases carry large amounts of data and open wide research opportunities for further analysis.

Dilorom Akhmedzhanova has an M.A. in Sociology and is a graduate of the European University in Saint-Petersburg, as well as being a PhD student at the Institute of Political Science at the University of Wrocław.

# CHAPTER SIXTEEN

# THE ANTI-CIVIC ETHOS OF THE CREATIVE CLASS

ALICJA PALĘCKA

Ten years ago, the American economist and urban studies theorist Richard Florida announced "the rise of the creative class."[1] Not only did his book of the same name become a best seller, but city governments worldwide also started to rely on it as a basis for effective development policies. This chapter presents a short introduction to this powerful and widely-discussed concept, as well as a critique of some of its elements. We will consider the ethos of the subject drawing from Florida's notion of the creative class, and relate it to the concept of civil society, especially in its local dimension.

Creative class is strictly bound with city and urban culture, and therefore its activism, if performed, may appear to be related to increasingly visible, or even popular, urban social movements. Nevertheless, as will be explained, the creative ethos locates the actors of the creative class in the conservative or neoliberal fraction of those movements. For some critical commentators this position is a contradiction of the values of a self-governing civil society.

## What is Civil Society?

The basic notion of civil society we will start from is Norberto Bobbio's interpretation of Gramsci. In his view, civil society functions contrary to the coercive capabilities of the state as a sphere of freedom, which "represents the active and positive moment of historical development,"[2]

---

[1] R. Florida, *The Rise of the Creative Class: and How It's Transforming Work, Leisure, Community and Everyday Life* (New York: Basic Books, 2002).
[2] N. Bobbio, "Gramsci and the Conception of Civil Society," in C. Mouffe (ed.), *Gramsci and Marxist Theory* (London, Routledge & Kegan Paul, 1979), 31.

therefore being "capable of creating a new history and of collaborating in the formation of a new power."[3] Introducing the third realm, the market, to this notion, one could view civil society as "the arena where the struggle over hegemony takes place and where the societies can defend themselves against the market and the state."[4] Similarly, civil society is defined by Michael Burawoy, who considers Gramsci, as well to Polanyi, in terms of: "For both … (civil) 'society' occupies a specific institutional space within capitalism between economy and the state, but where 'civil society' spills into the state, and 'active society' interpenetrates the market."[5] Also, both authors see historical development as "the subordination of market and state to the self-regulating society."[6]

From this well-defined notion, Burawoy derives the roots and meaning of sociology itself. It:

> was born with civil society in the second half of the nineteenth century, with the rise of trade unions, political parties, voluntary organizations, schools, newspapers, all of which appeared in Europe in reaction to the destructiveness of the market. Just as economics takes the standpoint of the economy and the expansion of the market, and politics takes the standpoint of the state and political order, sociology takes the standpoint of civil society and the defense of communicative action.[7]

This view informs our analysis, as criticism towards the concept of the creative class is concurrently a stance against the colonization of the lifeworld by instrumental rationality.

However, Bobbio's and Burawoy's positive project based on Gramsci's notion of civil society is an optimistic one. One could track the "true," more complex relations of civil society and the state, revealing that "in *actual reality* civil society and state are one and the same" [author's emphasis], as is the (non) regulation of the market.[8] Civil society, as Arun

---

[3] Ibid., 36.

[4] G. Piotrowski, "Civil Society, Un-Civil Society and the Social Movements," *Interface* 1 (2) (2009): 168.

[5] M. Burawoy, "For a Sociological Marxism: the Complementary Convergence of Antonio Gramsci and Karl Polanyi," *Politics & Society* 31 (2) (2003): 198.

[6] Ibid.

[7] M. Burawoy, "The Last Positivist," *Contemporary Sociology* 40 (4) (2011): 403–404; See also I. Wallerstein, *Open the Social Sciences. Report of the Gulbenkian Comission on the Restructuring of the Social Sciences* (Stanford: Stanford University Press, 1996), 19.

[8] A. Gramsci, *The Gramsci Reader: Selected Writings 1916–1935*, D. Forgacs (ed.) (New York: New York University Press, 2000), 210.

Patnaik explains, "receives class instincts, class interests, class struggle and tries to normalize them through family, religious associations, cultural groups, and networks of social capital."[9] It is, therefore, a sphere of a hegemonic struggle, where consent over ideological and political matters is achieved or imposed (as opposed to the state, where it is coerced).

As we will see, both Bobbio's and Patnaik's notions are productive in analyzing the ethos of the creative class in terms of civil society.

## What is the Creative Class?

The power of Florida's argument may be its simplicity—he noticed that certain groups of workers are a fly-wheel of urban and regional economic growth, and the reinforcement of this growth may be achieved by attracting those groups to live and work in cities that aspire to become regional leaders. It can be said that, according to Florida, the concept of the "knowledge economy" is outdated, being replaced by its next level—an economy based on creativity. Therefore, the categories of workers desired in the cities are: "scientists, engineers, university professors, poets and novelists, artists, entertainers, actors, designers and architects, as well as the thought leadership of modern society: nonfiction writers, editors, cultural figures, think-tank researchers, analysts and other opinion makers."[10] Creatives are also those who "work in a wide-range of knowledge intensive industries such as high-tech sectors, financial services, the legal and health care professions, and business management."[11] They produce knowledge or are required to resolve problems using knowledge produced by the creative core, and higher education is therefore usually one of the essential characteristics of the creative class members.

As mentioned above, according to Florida the first task on the way to regional economic growth is to draw on specific groups of professionals, and not necessarily to attract big business—"The companies follow the people," says Florida,[12] the people are "not slavishly following jobs to places. Instead, it appeared that highly-educated individuals were drawn to places that were inclusive and diverse."[13] Mobility is another attribute of creatives, as they easily relocate from their initial abode to places that are

[9] A. Patnaik, "The Contemporary Significance of Gramsci's Critique of Civil Society," *Working USA* 15 (2012): 579–580.
[10] R. Florida, *Rise of the Creative Class*, 69.
[11] Ibid.
[12] Ibid., 37.
[13] R. Florida, "Cities and the Creative Class," *City & Community* 2 (1) (2003): 7.

liveable, vibrant, have rich urban cultures, have amenities enabling the active spending of free time (green parks, sports clubs, cafes, pubs and clubs supporting the artistic scene) and, last but not least, a high proportion of bohemians, immigrants and homosexuals as three factors showing the openness and tolerance of non-standard, non-traditional ways of living, which are distinctive for highly individual members of the creative class. City governments should therefore create conditions for creative class growth by reinforcing those factors.

From Florida's suggestive description one can easily infer a "typical member" of the creative class as a person who is "fortunate enough to be paid to use their creativity" at work.[14] Therefore, his or her paid work becomes a way to express themselves. It is easy then to extend working hours long into the traditionally free time of evenings or weekends. Indeed, creative workers never stop working, just as they never cease to be creative. Such a person is flexible, mobile, active and does not bind his or herself to an employer, rather searching for a change and the next step in a career horizontally, in new environments, than on the vertical path of promotion. Such a person looks for challenges, novelties and thrills both at work and during leisure time, and has high expectations towards themselves as well as working and living environments.

## Creatives as a Class

One may ask a relevant question—is the creative class indeed a social class? Whichever approach is used, Marxist or Weberian, Florida's concept does not match them accurately. It is enough to leave this inconvenience with Tomasz Kukołowicz's remark: "How can one criticize Florida for imprecise use of the term of class, when the class borders are so blurred now?"[15] Regardless of the opinion on the distinctness of class measures nowadays, it may be useful to surpass the discussion about those borders and treat class as a political idea rather than a theoretical or analytical one. Social classes exist:

> only inasmuch as all sorts of historical agents … have succeeded in transforming what could have remained an "analytical construct" into a

[14] Ibid., 8.

[15] T. Kukołowicz, "Ponowoczesność oczami geografa," *Studia Socjologiczne* 3 (206) (2012): 167; See also A. Mo, "Why Put 'Class' in the Creative Class?," *Quaestiones Geographicae* 31 (4) (2012).

> "folk category," that is, into one of those impeccably real social fictions produced and reproduced by the magic of social belief.[16]

Departing from Bourdieu's assertion, Piotr Płucienniczak proposes reaching for a practical understanding of class, instead of a theoretical one. "Economic class determined on the basis of objective measures and relations is not necessarily a political subject … (For) class identity competes with other means of self-realization and expression … Most of those means lead to various kinds of alienated and dependent existence,"[17] which perhaps accurately describes the position of the creative class. To arise as a political subject, a class requires some shared experience, as well as a belief in the community.

If the creative class can become a "practical" one by recognizing itself as a coherent group with common interests, how would it mobilize and act in the sphere of civil society? And if, on the other hand, civil society is an arena of economic class struggle, who would be the foe of the creative class?

## The Anti-Civic Ethos Theoretically

The concept of creative class, although popular and appealing, has attracted considerable criticism from varied perspectives. Some progressive sociologists point out the exclusive and excluding character of the creative class, its ideology reinforcing the social status quo and leading to self-exploitation, or its dependency on the underemployment of service class members.[18] These characteristics are relevant when considering creative class members as potential participants in civil society, understood as a society defending itself against the state and, above all, the market.

Florida's book can be read as a handbook for urban and regional policy planners, but its impact may be even stronger as a means of the creative class identity and ethos construction. Analyzing the concept from this perspective, Fougère and Solitander use a helpful tool of Foucault's governmentality: "The semantic linking of 'government' with 'mentality'

---

[16] P. Bourdieu, "What Makes a Social Class? On The Theoretical and Practical Existence Of Groups," *Berkeley Journal of Sociology* 32 (1987): 9.

[17] P. P. Płucienniczak, "Praktyczna uniwersalność: Wprowadzenie do klasotwórstwa," paper presented during the conference *Po kapitalizmie: Od egoizmu do wspólnoty*, Kraków, December 7–8, 2012.

[18] See footnotes 26 and 34, as well as Florida's own concerns in *The Rise of the Creative Class*, Chapter 13.

implies a fusion of new technologies of government with a new political rationality."[19] In the case of the creative class, economic growth stands for political rationality, and therefore the creative ethos may be a technology of government. Referring again to the aforementioned authors, "governmentality aims to create common sense making frames wherein people voluntarily delegate moral autonomy and responsibility to a moral force external to the self."[20] As Nikolas Rose puts it: "power also acts through practices that 'make up subjects' as free persons."[21]

It has been noted by many of Florida's commentators that his concept of creativity is a perfect tool for governing a whole new class of workers to be workaholics subordinated to the capital. According to himself, they also do not expect capital to assure their social security. "Their only real job-security comes from their capabilities and continued productivity."[22] A creative person is rewarded by the work itself, when realizing individual identity as, for example, a copywriter, an academic teacher, a performer or a surgeon. It makes a perfect stakeholder of new capitalism.

What also emerges from Florida's description is the extreme individuality of a subject. "The creative class is constructed as one that is characterized by its freedom ... freedom of acting as an individual, freedom to aim for the top, and freedom of mind." Members of the creative class are thus "governed through (their) freedom"[23] and individuality, as those privileges or features (like creativity) are realized mainly on the market and are yoked by capital. Florida's concept of creativity can therefore be analyzed in terms of colonization of the lifeworld by instrumental rationality.

Consumerism, besides work, is another way to realize freedom and creativity. A model that one could call "the creative consumption" is relatively new. It is distinctive from the passive reception of entertaining content, like watching movies or sports. A creative consumer needs to be active and to participate, so he or she chooses to play football instead of watching it, to go to the concert, mingle with people and dance, instead of just listening to the music at home, or combining extreme sports with tourism instead of programmed, steady sightseeing. An ethos of the active

---

[19] M. Fougère, N. Solitander, *The Rise of Creative Governmentality—And How It's Transgressing Working Hours, Job Security, Politics and Everyday Strife*, 2007, 3, http://www.mngt.waikato.ac.nz/ejrot/cmsconference/2007/proceedings/apolloanteportas/proceedings_apolloanteportas.asp (accessed June 2, 2013).
[20] Ibid.
[21] N. Rose, *Powers of Freedom* (Cambridge: CUP, 1999), 95.
[22] R. Florida, *The Rise of Creative Class*, 110.
[23] M. Fougère, N. Solitander, *The Rise of Creative Governmentality*, 11.

consumer emerges, as well as a whole new active entertainment industry to satisfy these demands.

The social context for the creative class comprises two other classes identified by Florida, namely the service and working classes. The relation between the service and creative classes is the most direct and symptomatic. The service class enables a creative style of living, uniting people with "low-end, typically low wage and low-autonomy occupations,"[24] meaning ancillary workers in health care, administration and offices, low-end retailers, occupations related to teaching (up to high-school level) and care, social and council services, food preparation and serving, guarding, building and land cleaning and maintenance. As Florida himself notes, the growth of the creative class is related to the increase in the number of low-wage positions, as well as the expansion of economic inequality. Moreover, if the city is designed for the creative class, as Florida recommends, living in attractive neighbourhoods becomes "reserved" for its housing and leisure. Economic inequality and gentrification is one of the main issues of the creative class politics pointed out by a number of commentators.[25] As Kukołowicz humorously notes, Florida "restricts his task to elucidate to creative class members the reasons for which they occupy privileged position."[26] This relation of creative class members to fellow citizens positions them at the top of the social hierarchy in the terms of economic, cultural, political and social capital.

According to Fougère & Solitander, Florida implicitly praises the apoliticism of the creative class, pointing out that in creative centres people are less likely to get politically involved. Indeed, some excerpts of his book are designed to convince readers that the domain of politics is "naturally" remote from, for example, art and culture:

> Many cultural theorists like to see cultural forms such as graffiti art and rap as political movements expressing the voices of the oppressed—Florida observes—this absurd notion does a disservice to both politics and art. True political movements, from the civil rights movement to the grassroots organizing of the right wing, are serious entities, laboriously put together

---

[24] R. Florida, *Rise of the Creative Class*, 71.

[25] See J. Peck, "Struggling with the Creative Class," *International Journal of Urban and Regional Research* 29 (4) (2005); J. Zimmerman, "From Brew Town to Cool Town: Neoliberalism and the Creative City Development Strategy in Milwaukee," *Cities* 25 (2008); E. J. McCann, "Inequality and Politics in the Creative City-Region: Questions of Livability and State Strategy," *International Journal of Urban and Regional Research* 31 (1) (2007).

[26] T. Kukołowicz, *Ponowoczesność oczami geografa*, 166.

> and directed to specific political ends. These movements sometimes adopt art forms but are not generated by them.[27]

This narrow definition of politics relieves the "average citizen" of political responsibility and organising in civil society. In this view, a privileged position is bound to the lack of an explicit political stance, as governing is delegated to some professional "political directors."

Recapitulating the creative ethos, one should state that the subject emerging from it is highly individualistic and focused on realizing his or her identity. Using the dominated service class to achieve it makes the creative subject alienated from the society. Moreover, such a person is mobile and, according to Florida, looking for quasi-anonymity and loose, weak social bonds which may be easily abandoned instead of linking them to a place, group or political views and ideas. Finally, he or she is apolitical and willing to realize freedom and creativity on the market.

## The Anti-Civic Ethos Practically

The notion of civil society described above assumes that it has been antithetical from the very beginning and opposed to the state and the market. Here, we focus on the second relation, as it appears to be the most urgent. However, Florida's concept sets the creative class on the side of capital. With his simple theoretical move, the creative class becomes excluded from civil society.

Adding that the creative class, due to its superior status, is an aspirational group for service class members, we may find Florida's concept dangerous and threatening to civil society. One can, however, believe that being a creative individual is something more than Florida suggests, as the market does not give enough space for creativity to fully flourish. Creatives would therefore search for spheres independent from the market to realize their potential, namely alternative culture and civil activism. Most probably, due to its special relation with the city, the creative class could be related to urban movements which have lately become very visible in North America and Europe, as well as in Poland.

Marcin Galent and Paweł Kubicki, who studied the "new middle class" (which overlaps with the creative class) in Polish cities, describe urban activity as cultural and strongly connected to specific patterns of consumption:

---

[27] R. Florida, *The Rise of the Creative Class*, 201.

> cities are perceived not as dehumanised places as before, but rather as places which are conducive to living in, where everybody can fulfill themselves, not only in terms of their professions but, above all, by entertainment, lifestyle, hobbies, etc. Today it is consumption which to a large extent locates individuals in a social structure and influences the construction of identity, hence urbanism as a way of life becomes desired and a much appreciated value and constitutes significant grounds for defining the identities of generations of the "new urban middle class."[28]

This notion of urban living steers creative class activism towards identity building and preserving heritage and aesthetic aspects of the city.[29] It is focused on cultural, "soft" issues and subjects, while accessibility to social services or building an inclusive policy extending "the right to the city" to every group of the urban population is left to radical groups recruited from outside the creative class.

In accordance with this observation, Przemysław Pluciński[30] categorizes Polish urban movements into two main groups based on their pragmatic activities. Protest movements are grassroots, radical, anti-systemic and focused on social problems. On the other hand, "middle class movements" are reformist, pro-systemic, working in the framework of law and available legal options, often in NGOs, renouncing politics and using the rhetoric of meritocracy instead. They sometimes explicitly lobby for middle-class interests in the city.

Going further in this characteristic, Jarosław Ogrodowski, an urban activist from Łódź, explicitly reproaches some middle class movements for being conservative, antisocial, fighting for gentrification and supporting city governments in the implementation of excluding and exclusive policies.[31] He notes that urban policies are favourable to the creative class at the expense of non-affluent ones.

---

[28] M. Galent, P. Kubicki, "An Invisible Revolution. How the Urban Way of Life is Transforming the Identities of Poles," in M. Góra, Z. Mach (eds), *Collective Identity and Democracy The Impact of EU Enlargement* (Oslo: ARENA Centre for European Studies, University of Oslo, 2010), 222.

[29] P. Kubicki, *Nowi mieszczanie w nowej Polsce* (Warszawa: Instytut Obywatelski, 2011), 84–85.

[30] P. Pluciński, "Miejskie (r)ewolucje. Radykalizm retoryki a praktyka reformy," *Praktyka Teoretyczna* 3 (9) (2013), http://www.praktykateoretyczna.pl/czasopismo/miejskie-rewolucje/ (accessed April 25, 2014).

[31] J. Ogrodowski, *Dobry car i nowi mieszczanie*, 2013,

## Defending the Civic

The defeatist conclusions of this analysis are somewhat tendentious and biased in their static and mostly theoretical approach. Still, a concern about the anti-civic ethos within civil society should be considerable and productive in terms of proposing an opposition.

According to Florida's research, the presence of the creative class correlates with GDP increase and should be drawn by regional governments to boost economic development. However, the opinion that GDP is not an accurate measure for assessing standards of living gains considerable attention.[32] Developing new approaches to this kind of assessment has a civic dimension, as it works for the inclusion of various groups of the population.

Some critiques, as well as positive projects and propositions, are being employed from within the creative class by members who feel it is not accurately described by Florida's overwhelming concept.[33] As suggested above, the market does not give satisfying recognition to some creative activities. The core meaning of the term exceeds any possibilities given by the narrow economic entrepreneurship. There is a visible link between creativity, lifeworld and civil society, thus defending creativity against the market is one of the tasks lying ahead of creatives themselves. Bringing the term back to its roots, where it is not reserved only for the privileged, would thereby be a civil activity. It would serve the inclusion and cooperation of groups for which the access to market-based creativity is denied.[34]

---

http://nowyobywatel.pl/2013/03/24/dobry-car-i-nowi-mieszczanie/ (accessed June 2, 2013); See also J. Grzegorczyk, *Kwestia mieszkaniowa w dobie globalizacji*, 2009, http://recyklingidei.pl/grzegorczyk-kwestia-mieszkaniowa-w-dobie-globalizacji (accessed June 2, 2013).

[32] See J. E. Stiglitz et al., *Report by the Commission on the Measurement of Economic Performance and Social Progress*, 2009, www.stiglitz-sen-fitoussi.fr (accessed June 2, 2013).

[33] See *Creative Class Struggle*, http://creativeclassstruggle.wordpress.com (accessed June 2, 2013); I. Lorey, *Governmentality and Self-Precarization. On the normalization of cultural producers*, 2006, http://eipcp.net/transversal/1106/lorey/en/ (accessed June 02, 2013); G. Raunig et al. (eds.), *Critique of Creativity Precarity, Subjectivity and Resistance in the "Creative Industries"* (London: MayFlyBooks, 2011).

[34] See T. Rakowski, *Łowcy, zbieracze, praktycy niemocy. Etnografia człowieka zdegradowanego* (Gdańsk: Słowo/Obraz/Terytoria, 2009); T. Rakowski (ed.),

Alicja Pałęcka is a PhD student at the Sociology Institute, the Jagiellonian University in Kraków, Poland. She is working on a thesis entitled "Alienation of Creative Work: an Extended Case Study."

# CHAPTER SEVENTEEN

# IMPLEMENTATION OF THE PRINCIPLES OF CIVIL SOCIETY AND PUBLIC GOVERNANCE IN THE CASES OF CAUCASIAN COUNTRIES

KACPER NOWAK

## The Difficult History of Countries in the Caucasus Region

The "Caucasian Region" refers to the area extending from the Caucasus Mountains through the territories of Armenia, Azerbaijan, Georgia and a part of Russia; however, only three of the countries mentioned above can be called Caucasian countries. The main issue raised in this chapter is whether it is possible to create a Civil Society and to implement the Principles of Public Governance in the countries with such a difficult history, and what methods can be applied to this.

The three Caucasian countries in question are connected by their history and current problems. However, it is also the history which divides them, concerning mutual ethnic and territorial disputes. They somehow share their history since they were a part of the Tsarist Russian Empire and the Soviet Union. Their USSR heritage includes *homo sovieticus* citizens, i.e. citizens accustomed to a lack of freedom and living in a country where the state made all decisions for them and encompassed them from all sides. However, if one considers the theoretical and official characteristics of the social education of that time, greatly different from the reality of everyday life, *homo sovieticus* should have been prepared to live in the civic society, since "a Soviet man is the best leading type of the man of modern era."

Firstly, "a Soviet man" knew voluntary work, i.e. they actively participated in voluntary actions (in the USSR called a *subotniki*); secondly, he or she was a member of various organisations, since they were a responsive member of a society in which, if he or she did not want to be alienated and wanted to study or pursue their professional career, for example, they had to belong to an appropriate organisation, starting from scouting (*pionier*), followed by membership of a youth political organisation (*konsomolec*) and finally crowning their endeavours with membership of the Soviet Union Communist Party. Moreover, the Soviet Union citizen was not a nationalist and for seventy years (between 1921–1991 in Azerbaijan and Georgia, and 1920–1991 in Armenia), they were brought up as an internationalist. Although nationalism in its extreme form, as an armed conflict revealed even before the disintegration of the Soviet Union, the battle between Azerbaijan and Armenia for Nagorno-Karabakh started in 1988.

## Civil Society and the Communist Past

Patriotism in the social class aspect was highly estimated, but vigilance was warranted, since it might have been close to nationalism. On the other hand, nationalism was a synonym of wrong attitudes, hostile to the Soviet society. According to the *Short Dictionary of Philosophy*: "Relics of nationalism, if not radically opposed, become a medium for pests sent by a foreign secret service and saboteurs … scheming against the Soviet Union."[1] *Nota bene*, the accusation of "scheming" by foreign countries, reappeared almost sixty years later, directed at non-governmental organisations operating in contemporary Russia. This time, such activity was conducted by "foreign agents" sponsored by foreign funds.[2]

On the other hand, in all Soviet Union republics, including the three discussed, a "proletarian internationalism" and "Soviet patriotism" were recommended,[3] the more so as national nihilism—disregard for the interests and achievements of their own native countries—was counted among the symptoms of "burgeois cosmopolitism—the poisonous weapon of international reaction." Another common aspect, which still causes suspicion for many citizens who wish to control or even change the authorities, is a conviction that some forces, hostile to the nation and inspired from abroad, lie behind such endeavours. A model of parliamentary democracy, with competing parties and opposition having access to the media, would to many citizens seem a dangerous anarchy, and far from traditional. It is particularly important in the countries that never experienced even a short period of sovereignty and democracy

[1] M. Rozental, P. Judin, *Krótki Słownik Filozoficzny* (Warszawa: Książka i Wiedza, 1955), 436.

[2] "Russia: Controversial NGO Bill Becomes Law," *BBC News*, July 21, 2012.

[3] M. Rozental, P. Judin, *Krótki Słownik Filozoficzny*, 491.

during the period between the First and Second World Wars, as was the case in Estonia, Lithuania and Latvia. Therefore, the present governance model in Azerbaijan and Georgia is a presidential system. In Armenia, the position of the president elected in the general election is also strong, and he can issue statutory instruments and decrees, and is the commander-in-chief appointing the prime minister, who is, however, elected by the parliamentary majority.

The myth of a good ruler (the Tsar or the first secretary) is still alive in the discussed countries. The ruler is obviously good, and only wicked civil servants separate him from the people and deceive them. If the ruler knew what was really going on in the country he would put everything in order. Moreover, if any difficulties occur they are only temporary, so if someone is criticising the authority, the question of who is behind the criticism arises. Anyway, the authority should be neither controlled nor watched too closely, nor criticised. It is obvious that such criticism would only challenge the authority and serve the native country enemies, so it is inspired from the outside. The NGO activists operating in Moscow in 2012 learned this truth the hard way.[4]

Accepting such reasoning is a considerable weakening of the attitude favouring creating the civic society through, among other things, the right to control and criticise the authority, the right to undertake activities not initiated on the central level, and the right to protect local values which are not always equal as seen from the central perspective. No ruler, such as a strong all-controlling Tsar, first secretary or president, likes social organisations which are independent from the state and created as a result of bottom-up initiatives.

## Urbanisation of NGOs

Another potential threat for creating a civic society and local social initiatives realised by non-governmental organisations may be the excessive urbanisation of NGO locations.

[4] D. Sandford, "Russia NGO law: Election watchdog Golos fined," *BBC News*, April 25, 2013.

**Table 17.1. Share of population of the largest Georgia cities in total population number and share of non-governmental organisations operating in the largest cities, Georgia (2012)**

| | Georgia | Tbilisi | Zugdidi | Kutasis | Gori | Ozurgeti |
|---|---|---|---|---|---|---|
| **Population** | 100% | 24.4% | 2.1% | 4.4% | 1% | 0.4% |
| **NGOs** | 100% | 65.5% | 9.8% | 7.2% | 3.1% | 2.8% |

Source: http://www.friends-partners.org/partners/georgia/sub/dbsa.htm (accessed April 2, 2013).

Table 17.1 above shows the phenomenon of NGO concentration in the biggest cities of Georgia. A comparison of the city dwellers' share of the country population and share of NGOs located in the cities to the total number in the country clearly shows an over representation of urban NGOs. Such domination of NGOs established in the largest cities (82.5% of the NGOs are established in the three biggest cites) may lead to further marginalisation of rural communities, which constitute almost half (47%) of the total population of Georgia.[5] Moreover, even among the urban NGOs the organisations located in the capital prevail. This is not a proper way to de-centralise the social life or equalise the citizens' chances, irrespective of their place of residence, and it does not diminish the risk of social exclusion. In this case, the needs of rural dwellers will be identified far more poorly, and hardly articulated.

Moreover, the country image, created from the city dweller's perspective, as an idyllic place where at most rural tourism with elements of a rural museum provide the main aim of economic activity, may become a reality. The issues of environmental protection and ethnography will dominate. In such a situation, the real needs of rural dwellers, including economic development targeting the creation of new jobs or the development of technical infrastructure, will be minimised. If the rural inhabitants' interests are not represented by NGOs, the bases of sustainable development elements are threatened, i.e. maintaining the balance between economic and social development and environment protection. The centralised location of NGOs is not a good method of decentralisation of the state authority, creating mechanisms of joint governance and the handover of power outside the capital.

[5] http://www.friends-partners.org/partners/georgia/sub/dbsa.htm (accessed April 2, 2013).

## Methods of Implementing NGO Activities in the Caucasus

Creating a civic society is a notion requiring the implementation of programmes which reach the society directly, not in a general or total sense, but by targeting each person, individual family or local group. The first step to implementing the principles of civic society should be launching programmes which, being non-controversial, would give people a sense that their activity counts and is important. The awareness of a possibility to act considerably influences the development of social capital and consequently civic society, as well as attitudes for the implementation of good governance. It is important that this type of programme should be non-controversial and unopposed to public authority. Caucasian countries face the problem of a deficiency of democracy, and their authorities reveal a tendency for autocracy, being averse to civic activities, seeing them as a threat. Frequently, NGOs are perceived as critical parties, without any constructive elements but only as the organisers of protests, etc.[6] On the other hand, the governments wish to be perceived positively by the Western countries, and therefore need NGOs to prove that they act democratically and develop the principles of a democratic state. A compromise and at the same time a tremendous power of NGOs may be based on non-controversial programmes addressing local communities, such as promoting pro-ecological behaviours, development of rural women's organisations, promoting local tourism, development of renewable energy generation systems or monitoring river pollution.

Activities related to the development of citizenship and civil society can be divided into those supported by local NGOs and those supported by international organisations and the governments of foreign countries. As an example of local, non-controversial programmes of NGOs targeting local communities in Armenia, the projects organised by the Green Lane Agricultural Assistance NGO may be indicated. Among others it implemented the programme "Women Can Run the Country: Support for Gender Sensitive Local Governance," which includes empowerment of women centres in Armenia through providing business promotion opportunities and outreach.[7] The same organisation is responsible for the programmes aiming at making people aware of the key issues of ecology and how to counteract the threat of extinction of some local plant and

---

[6] A. Peters, "Dual Democracy," in J. Klabbers (ed.), *The Constitutionalization of International Law* (Oxford: Oxford University Press, 2009), 315.
[7] http://www.greenlane.am/index.htm (accessed April 3, 2013).

animal species. Such a programme was implemented in 2011, targeting children and youths from rural areas.[8]

The development of civil society is also supported by international organisations, an example of which is the activity of UNDP in Georgia. Strengthening the role of women in social life and better local governance is also one of the objectives for the Georgian NGOs. For instance, in Tbilisi the UNDP supports the realisation of similar project as in Armenia: "Women Can Run the Country: Support for Gender Sensitive Local Governance," owing to financial support from Sweden within the framework of a wider program, "To Enhance Gender Equality in Georgia." A meeting of 180 women, who are councillors in their native regions, was held on May 20, 2013, where they formed the Women Councilors' Forum. In her presentation, Jamie McGoldrick, Georgia's representative in UNDP, stated:

> Women better understand everyday issues. They can influence decisions at the municipal level and advocate for better policies that affect their communities. The Women Councillor's Forum is a powerful platform which will help Georgian women to play more active role in local governance.[9]

"The Black Sea—Silk Road Corridor" is an example of the action supported and financed by Western countries, since this project is supported by the European Union and the U.S. Agency for International Development. What makes the project even more interesting is the fact that it presents another positive aspect of NGO activity. The strength of non-governmental organisations also lies in the fact that they are able to unite people inhabiting warring countries.[10] The project unites the inhabitants of Turkey, Greece, Georgia and Armenia, and it should be noted that the Turkish-Armenian relationships are exceptional. Therefore, it shows that mutual relationships may be based on history, but on the fragment of history which joins rather than separates. The legendary Silk Road is associated positively both on the international arena and in the individual countries, through which the caravans passed many years before.

---

[8] http://www.greenlane.am/Education.htm (accessed April 3, 2013).

[9] J. McGoldrick, *To Enhance Gender Equality in Georgia* (Tbilisi: Caucasus Environmental NGO Network [CENN], 2013).

[10] USAID, EDMC, *Black Road Silk Road Corridor Project*, www.blackseasilkroad.com (accessed April 5, 2013)

In the Caucasian region, programs directly connected with introducing the good governance principles are developed. An example of such a program is the "Good Governance in Georgia Project (3G),"[11] targeting the development of good governance principles both on the local and state levels. Its objectives on the national level include[12] improving the quality of public administration, and improving the public sector using human and institutional capacity development approaches. On the local level these are developing a responsible, professional and involved local governance and supporting citizen participation in the public life in ten cities in Georgia. The 3G program is supported by the U.S. Agency for International Development.

## Main Problems Related to Non-Governmental Activity in the Caucasus

Caucasian countries face numerous problems of social and economic life, which are characteristic for this region of the world. In Armenia the problem of issuing false invoices has been reported, wherein one may get an invoice even though no commodity was purchased. For this reason, numerous frauds are committed and no honest project account settlements is presented, which moreover offers an opportunity to actually not realise the projects. At the same time, money is allocated but accounts are settled using unreliable invoices. Fortunately, this is not a rule, yet it remains a very significant problem since it undermines the integrity of the NGOs, regardless of the fact that only some of them practice such things.

Another problem is a lack of democracy within the NGOs themselves. They operate based on charismatic leaders but not on the whole structure or mass of people.[13] The problem of a deficit of democracy is therefore also usual in NGOs and leads to criticism of their operational methods, particularly when focusing on their own needs and self-appointments are added.[14]

Another danger for a development of efficient civic activities is corruption, a phenomenon common in all post-socialist countries.

---

[11] http://georgia.usaid.gov/search/node/NGO (accessed April 5, 2013).
[12] http://georgia.usaid.gov/programs/economic-growth (accessed April 5, 2013).
[13] Transparency International Anticorruption Center, *Risks and Opportunities for the NGO Sector in Armenia* (Yerevan: Transparency International, 2011), 12.
[14] A. Peters, *Dual Democracy*, 316.

**Table 17.2. Corruption Perception Index and Human Development Index in Armenia, Azerbaijan and Georgia, 2012**

| Country | Corruption Perception Index rank | Human Development Index rank |
|---|---|---|
| Armenia | 105 | 87 |
| Azerbaijan | 139 | 82 |
| Georgia | 51 | 72 |

Sources: Transparency International, 2012; United Nations Development Program (UNDP), Human Development Reports, 2012.

Table 17.2 above shows the positions of the countries of the Caucasus region in the Corruption Perception Index rank and Human Development Index rank (HDI). It is clear that from among those countries it is Azerbaijan that has the biggest problem with corruption, and in comparing the HDI one comes to the conclusion that in terms of life quality the situation in Azerbaijan is similar to the situation in Armenia. Georgia takes the top positions from among the Caucasian countries in both rankings.

In this country, corruption is a barrier to private initiatives and development. In Georgia, the issue of ineffective NGO activities and their concentration in the capital city is the most acute problem. NGO activities target local communities insufficiently, and therefore do not solve their problems or aid improvement of the quality of local community living standards, or the development of their civic attitudes.[15]

Georgia may be proud of its greatest success in controlling corruption. Under the USSR regime, corruption in this country was plainly proverbial, and in 2002 Georgia placed 85 in this ranking, Azerbaijan 95 (2002) and Armenia 78 (2003). As may be seen, Georgia improved its position in the ranking by 34 places, whereas Armenia declined by 27 places, whereas Azerbaijan, which declined by 44 places, belongs to the countries where corruption is the highest. Considering the former USSR states, corruption is currently worse only in Ukraine (144), Kyrgyzstan (150) and Uzbekistan (170).

NGOs in Azerbaijan work in very specific circumstances, even when compared to other countries of the Caucasus, namely Armenia and Georgia. Corruption has been a problem in the country for years, and even

---

[15] http://yerevanblog.europeanmovement.eu/?p=144#comment-12426 (accessed: April 7, 2013).

President Aliyev has spoken about the need for a national effort[16] to eliminate it or at least substantially reduce it for a number of years, yet the progress in this domain has been relatively inconsiderable. For example, in 2013, in the ranking of The Corruption Perceptions Index 2013 Transparency International, Azerbaijan was 127 out of the 177 evaluated countries of the world, while 10 years earlier (2003) it was 124. During the same period, other countries of the Caucasus region discussed in this document handled the problem of corruption much better. In the case of Armenia, it was 94 in 2013 and 78 in 2003, while Georgia was 55 in 2013 and 124 in 2003 (as in the case of Azerbaijan). Thus, despite the declarations and support of the President, Azerbaijan has moved up by three places, while Armenia has improved its position by 16 places in a period of ten years. Georgia, having moved up 69 places, is a decisive leader in this domain. In Azerbaijan, corruption of such a considerable size lasting for years is a major obstacle in building a civil society.

According to Ms Khadija Ismail, an investigative journalist and Radio Liberty Azerbaijan Bureau correspondent, the reason for the difference between the declarations of the government and the real lack of progress in limiting corruption is a deliberate government policy: "The government could easily turn bribery into taxes, but argues that while envelopes make people grateful, taxes turn them into demanding citizens."[17] This observation is particularly important, as the building of civil society consists in, *inter alia*, the activity of citizens who care about the interests of the society and creating social relations based on cooperation and trust between the state authorities and citizens. Another feature defining the specific character of the conditions of NGOs' actions are legal barriers. Compared to other countries of the Caucasus region, the NGOs in Azerbaijan have the biggest problems with the registration of their activity. The government of Azerbaijan has repeatedly lost lawsuits in the European Court of Human Rights for refusing the registration of NGOs, recognised by the international forum as an unjustified limitation of civil rights.

In the initial period, after Azerbaijan gained independence in 1991, the development of NGOs was promising. After decades of shaping a "Soviet man," one could hope it possible to create civil society, of which the NGOs would be a significant element. This hope is still justified, despite

[16] F. Gurbanov, "Azerbaijan and the World," *The Economist*, November 26, 2011.
[17] K. Ismail, "Azerbaijan: A Small Country Grows Drunk on Oil Wealth," *The Economist*, November 12, 2011.

all the problems. In this country of 9.3 million inhabitants,[18] there are 2,600 working NGOs. The estimated number of unregistered organisations is about one thousand.[19] In Azerbaijan, the NGOs wishing to work legally must register at the Ministry of Justice. According to the Organization for Security and Co-operation in Europe, the main obstacles used by the Ministry when registering NGOs include[20]:

(1) Lack of any formal decision
(2) Illegally issued refusals
(3) Requirement of submitting extra documentation not required by law
(4) Exceeding deadlines for registration or refusal to register
(5) Additional criteria applied
(6) Repeated requests for correction in documents
(7) Unclear internal procedures within the registration department
(8) Non-availability of public information about the NGOs register.

Many of the problems of NGOs do not result from the substantive law itself, but from its statutory interpretation and procedural law. The interpretation of law applied in this country is used to the citizens' disadvantage, and the expanded bureaucracy is also a problem. On the one hand it gives hope because the problem lies within the execution of law and the officials' actions. On the other hand, it is often easier to change the law than to apply it and modify a clerical way of acting.

## Conclusions

Summing up, it should be noticed that the way chosen by NGOs in Caucasian countries positively influences the changes occurring in these countries, particularly considering their democratisation. Realisation of the programs accepted by both the society and the authorities may prove a proper method of developing social capital, creating a society aware of its rights and potential. The progressive implementation of programmes focussed on developing the activities of local groups may provide bases for creating civic society and implementing the principles of good governance. This is particularly important in the post-Soviet countries,

---

[18] The State Statistical Committee of the Republic of Azerbaijan, *Population*, 2013.
[19] http://www.icnl.org/research/monitor/azerbaijan.html (accessed April 12, 2013).
[20] http://www.osce.org/baku/42386 (accessed April 12, 2013).

such as the countries of the Caucasus region, since the activity of NGOs may influence the change in perception of the state by the citizens as well as the perception of the citizens by the state authorities. The model of the society created with *homo sovieticus* therefore turns into civil society.

The activity of NGOs may also affect stabilisation in the region. The programs connecting feuding countries of the Caucasus region can become an alternative to thinking filled with hate, resulting from difficult and bloody histories. The NGOs bring new, democratic and peaceful values, much needed for the countries discussed in this chapter.

Kacper Nowak is a Law student at the Faculty of Law and Administration at the Jagiellonian University in Kraków and a graduate of Public Administration at the Faculty of Economics and International Relations at the University of Economics in Kraków. His research interests concentrate on constitutional law and public governance.

# PART FOUR

# ECONOMY AS REGULATOR OF SOCIO-POLITICAL RELATIONS IN MODERN SOCIETIES

# CHAPTER EIGHTEEN

# INTEREST GROUPS AND THEIR INFLUENCE ON THE CZECHOSLOVAKIAN AUTHOR'S RIGHTS ACT

HANA BERÁNKOVÁ

## Introduction

This chapter builds on previous research confirming that the system of author's rights emerged due to interest groups. The chapter aims at treating one aspect of creation of a new legal environment for authors, identifying the particular organisations involved in the process of drafting the act and how these interest groups exerted their influence. In 1926, the new modern Author's Rights Act (hereafter "the Act"), n. 218/1926 Coll. was approved in Czechoslovakia. The legislative process had begun in 1920. For more than six years, interest groups had been influencing the wording and the content of the law, and took part in the related debates and subsequently shaped its practical application.

This chapter focuses mainly on the Czechoslovakian legislative process. For the sake of completeness, it is worth explaining that international treaties as a result of international negotiations also had important impacts on Czechoslovakian law. Although Czechoslovakian authors also contributed to the results of international diplomatic meetings, their activity in Czechoslovakia is mostly examined in this chapter.

One may raise an objection that the impact of Czechoslovakian interest groups is negligible, as the necessity of adopting the new Author's Rights Act stemmed from the Berne Convection. The Convention was a part of the Treaty of Peace of Saint-Germain-en-Laye from 1919 signed by Czechoslovakia after World War I, but the Berne Convention provides only for a minimum standard, which was overcome by the Czechoslovakian legislation.[1]

## Identification of Interest Groups

Although many clubs and associations existed in Czechoslovakia during the 1920s and 1930s,[2] they were important only from a local point of view and did not influence the drafting of the new Author's Rights Act. Nevertheless, the influence of other organisations can be easily identified as activities of interest groups evident in all sources used.

A list of concrete organisations which proudly presented how successfully they contributed to the copyright debate is as follows: Společnost spisovatelů, skladatelů a nakladatelů (The Society of Writers, Composers and Publishers); Společnost hudebních skladatelů v Praze (The Society of Musical Composers in Prague);[3] Unie čsl. hudebníků (The Union of Czechoslovak Musicians); Jednota hudebních stavů (The Association of Music Occupation); Deutscher Musikerverband (German Unions of Musicians);[4] Literární odbor Umělecké Besedy (The Section for Literature of Art Forum) and Syndikát československých spisovatelů a hudebních skladatelů (The Syndicate of Czechoslovak Writers and Musical Composers),[5] the last being one of the most important interest group representatives. There were other important institutions like the Association for Protection of Authors (collective rights management company) and the Czechoslovakian Department of the International Association for Literature and Art.

The Syndicate of Czechoslovakian Writers and Musical Composers frankly presented[6] its goals and how it reached them. As an agent of the

---

[1] J. Löwenbach, *Novela k zákonu o právu autorském: zákon ze dne 24. dubna 1936, č. 120 Sb. z. a n., s výkladem a materialiemi, nové znění zákona o právu autorském s judikaturou a římský text bernské úmluvy z r. 1928 s dodatky* (Praha: Československý Kompas, 1937), 1, 212.

[2] M. Lašťovka, *Pražské spolky: soupis pražských spolků na základě úředních evidencí z let 1895-1990*, Ed. 1 (Praha: Scriptorium, 1998), 742.

[3] "Tisk 227—důvodová zpráva: Historické senátní tisky z 1. volebního období, 2. zasedání," *Senát národního shromáždění*, 1920, http://senat.cz/informace/z_historie/tisky/1vo/tisky-2zas.php?ke_dni=27.12.2012&O=8 (accessed December 27, 2012).

[4] J. Löwenbach, *Hudba v samostatném Československu* (Praha: Státní nakladatelství, 1931), 22–23.

[5] "Zprávy spolkové," *Soutěž a tvorba* (1927): unnumbered pages.

[6] "Zprávy," *Soutěž a tvorba* I (1928): 76.

whole interest group, it protected the rights of its members and contributed to the improvement of their social status, despite the fact that in those days the public concentrated rather pragmatically on politics. It negotiated collective contracts between authors and publishers on minimum royalties for authors, promoted the adoption of the Author's Rights Act and the Publisher Act, mediated copyright protection for Czechoslovakian authors in the USA, and achieved the granting of state subsidies for the pension insurance of authors, but the idea originated from Bohumil Zahradník Brodský, a ministry executive. The Syndicate managed a fund for supporting ill and disabled authors. Its member Adolf Červinka provided free legal advice for authors, advocating the interests of authors abroad and at the same time influencing Czechoslovakian legislators. For example, the Syndicate prevented the adoption of so-called compulsory licensing, i.e. a provision in the Act stating that any producer of a phonographic record had to be granted with permission to use an artistic work. This unsuccessful proposal for prohibiting exclusive licensing aimed to strengthen the competition in the phonographic industry. The Syndicate was supported by the ministries of education, foreign affairs and justice. Legislators also showed a lot of understanding of the needs of the Syndicate.

Other important representatives of interest groups, Ochranné sdružení autorské československých skladatelů, spisovatelů a nakladatelů, spol. s r. o. (OSA Association for Protection of Authors, ltd., a collective rights management company), emerged in 1919[7] as a common project of the Club of Czechoslovakian Composers, the Club of Publishers and the Club of Lyricists. This form of limited liability company conducting business for the benefit of its members (the OSA was not a cooperative)[8] contrasted with its current status as a non-profit civic association.

The OSA needed the new Author's Rights Act, as before 1926 there were no legal grounds for collecting royalties from users on behalf of authors. Users, e.g. owners of restaurants and cafes, were reluctant to pay the royalties and made complaints.[9] The role of the OSA and obligations for users were introduced into the proposal of the Act shortly before the law was finally approved by legislators in 1926.[10] The royalties were set

---

[7] J. Löwenbach, *Hudba v samostatném Československu*, 23.

[8] J. Hora, *Filmové právo: Výklad s autentickými texty všech nařízení a doplňujících výnosů, oběžníků, vyhlášek a pod., judikatura nejvyšších soudů a nejdůležitější formuláře* (Praha: V. Linhart, 1937), 409–412, 516.

[9] J. Löwenbach, *Autorskoprávní abeceda* (Praha: Orbis, 1948), 115.

[10] "Tisk 447: II. volební období, 2. zasedání," *Společná česko-slovenská digitální parlamentní knihovna*, 1926, http://www.psp.cz/eknih/1925ns/ps/tisky

either by the Ministry of Education or by mutual agreements between the OSA and groups of entrepreneurs, e.g. cinema operators.[11] These rates were generally lower than those determined by the Ministry's regulation.[12]

The monopoly power of OSA over Czechoslovakian users rose significantly after the entry into force of the amendment of the Author's Rights Act from 1936, but still the monopoly was not absolute. The amendment provided an exclusive right for the OSA to grant licenses for using an author's work in the domain of Czechoslovakia (so that no other management company could compete with the OSA). However, the possibility to ask an author not directly represented by the OSA remained. This was related to small performing rights in public non-theatre performing, mechanic reproduction of works with or without a text, producing mechanic recordings, and using works in film and radio broadcasting.[13]

## Personalities Interconnecting Particular Organisations and the State

There was a commonly accepted standard that legislators had to know and respect the opinion of representatives of authors and related experts and that they had to satisfying their demands. The cooperation of the state and interest groups was perceived as desirable and necessary, and nobody worried about potential conflicts of interest. Lawyers closely linked to copyright interest groups were established as experts, e.g. Jan Löwenbach[14] and Karel Hermann-Otavský.[15] University professors Frankl

/t0447_01.htm (accessed December 28, 2012).

[11] J. Hora, *Filmové právo*, 420, 516.

[12] A. Čejka, *Ochranné sdružení autorské* (Praha: Ochranné sdružení autorské, 1940), 38.

[13] Today, this kind of author's right is compulsorily managed collectively. That means that when using a work, for example in broadcasting, a user has to ask a collective rights management company. They are not allowed to obtain a licence directly from individual authors. According to article 96 of the law n. 121/2000 Coll., the Author's Rights Act as amended by later acts, a user also has to contact the OSA when he or she uses works of authors not represented by a collective rights management company.

[14] Attorney Jan Löwenbach played an important role in the process of drafting, negotiating and adopting the Act. He was a member of domestic and foreign interest groups, active both formally and informally. Thanks to his authority, he represented Czechoslovakia at international meetings. He led the journal *Soutěž a tvorba* (*Competition and Creation*) from its beginning in 1928 to World War II, when he emigrated to the USA. His activities arose possibly from his interest in

and Miřička[16] were also appointed as consultants in the Chamber of Deputies.

The contemporary journal *Soutěž a tvorba* (*Competition and Creation*) describes the interconnection of lawyers and other personalities that operated in several organisations in detail, and how they used to meet on various occasions;[17] e.g. the chairman of the OSA J. B. Foerster and director of OSA Karel Balling[18] are frequently mentioned. Literární odbor Umělecké Besedy (The Section for Literature of Art Forum) organised debate evenings on copyright both in 1927 and 1928, where Viktor Dyk (his activity is described later), Adolf Červinka, Jan Löwenbach, Karel Hermann-Otavský, Rudolf Medek (writer), Burda (representative of Ministry of Posts) and Daneš (representative of Ministry of Education) made speeches. Evidently, ministry officials were also involved.

Another event, a congress of lawyers,[19] took place in Bratislava in 1930, where the issue of the 1928 Rome revision of the Bern Convention was discussed. There, for the purpose of examining how to introduce new elements of copyright protection into the Czechoslovakian law, a new radio committee was established by the Czechoslovakian Department of the International Association for Literature and Art. Its members, also active on other platforms, were Karel Hermann-Otavský, Jan Löwenbach, Otakar Šourek, Karel Balling and Karel Scheinpflug.

But the activity of Viktor Dyk, a senator, the chairman of The Syndicate of Czechoslovakian Writers and Musical Composers and chairman of The Section for Literature of Art Forum, is one of the most exemplary cases of the interconnection of interest groups with the state. In

---

music as he created librettos under the pseudonym J. L. Budín and wrote articles on music. V. Reittererová, J. Löwenbach, "Centrum Hudební Lexikografie, Ústav hudební vědy Filozofické fakulty Masarykovy university," *Český hudební slovník osob a institucí*, 2008, 2010 http://www.ceskyhudebnislovnik.cz/slovnik /index.php?option=com_mdictionary&action=record_detail&id=6281 (accessed Novermber 11, 2012).

[15] He was the first chancellor of the Charles University in Prague after 1918, and a consultant during the Author's Rights Act legislative process. He represented Czechoslovakia at international meetings on copyright and contributed to the journal *Soutěž a tvorba* (*Competition and Creation*).

[16] "Tisk 447: II. volební období, 2. zasedání," *Společná česko-slovenská digitální parlamentní knihovna*.

[17] "Zprávy spolkové," *Soutěž a tvorba* (1927): unnumbered pages.

[18] J. Löwenbach, *Hudba v samostatném Československu*, 23.

[19] Z. Morávek, "Ochrana autorů a rozhlas," *Soutěž a tvorba* III (1930): 170–174.

the debate of the senate[20] on the proposal of the new Author's Rights Act, he openly made demands on behalf of his profession. He used arguments about social justice to prolong the duration of protection for authors as a means to promote their social statuses, advocated the introduction of moral rights, i.e. provisions that prevent or punish prospective degradation of work, and tried to ensure the protection for literary works broadcast on the radio. However, this kind of protection was introduced later, after the amendment of the Act in 1936 which was a reaction to the Rome revision of the Berne Convention in 1928. He criticised a provision that allowed the use of a work freely on the condition that a new original work eligible for copyright protection had been created, because he worried about plagiarism.

Another case showing the interconnection of interest groups concerns special advisory committees established by the government. Their role was to provide on-demand expert opinions of a technical character to judges in author's rights litigation, but they could not interpret the law.[21] The following list presents that members of advisory committees for judges were representatives of lobbyists for author's rights,[22] gathering names of members of the advisory committee for musical works and members of the Czechoslovakian Department of the International Association for Literature and Art.

The advisory committee[23] comprised chairman Dr. Jan Branberger (executive of Ministry of Education) and members Karel Balling (director of OSA), J. B. Foerster (professor at the conservatory, music composer and chairman of OSA), Dr. Vladimír Helfert (university professor in Brno and writer), Antonín Hromádka (inspector of private music schools), Frico Kafenda (director of the music academy in Bratislava), Jan Kunc (composer, director of music and dramatic conservatory in Brno), Rudolf Prochaska (retired government official and composer), Dr. Erich Steinhard (editor of the journal Auftakt), Otakar Šourek (chief magistrate councillor and music critic, who made a speech in 1930 at the congress of lawyers in

[20] Rozprava 50, schůze: Historické senátní tisky z 2. volebního období, 3. zasedání. *Senát národního shromáždění*, November 24, 1926, http://senat.cz/informace /z_historie/tisky/2vo/schuze-3zas.php?ke_dni=27.12.2012&O=8 (accessed December 28, 2012).

[21] J. Löwenbach, *Autorskoprávní abeceda*, 106, 115.

[22] "Znalecké sbory pro obor autorského práva," *Soutěž a tvorba* (1927): unnumbered pages.

[23] "Zprávy spolkové," *Soutěž a tvorba* (1927): unnumbered pages.

Bratislava on the revision of the Bern Convention),[24] and Dr. Václav Štěpán (composer).

The Czechoslovakian Department of International Association for Literature and Art[25] comprised Chairman Karel Hermann-Otavský and members Dr. Hanuš Jelínek, prof. Dr. V. Tille (member of advisory committee for literature), Jan Löwenbach (also very active also elsewhere), Karel Balling (also very active elsewhere), E. Weinfurter (a member of the advisory committee for literature), K. M. Čapek-Chod (a famous writer), Dr. Otto Gellner (also very active elsewhere), prof. Dr. K. Kadlec, Ing. Fr. Khol (Dramatický svaz [Dramatic Union]), Karel Scheinpflug (a member of the advisory committee for literature), prof. Dr. O. Sommer (who made a speech in 1930 at the congress of lawyers in Bratislava on the revision of the Bern Convention),[26] J. Štolovský (Chairman of the Syndicate of Fine Arts, and a member of the advisory committee for fine arts), arch. O. Novotný (a member of the advisory committee for fine arts), prof. Dr. Frant. Weyr, Miroslav Rutte (Dramatický svaz [Dramatic Union]), and J. Riedl.

From the two lists, the typical profile of an author's rights lobbyist could be given as a lawyer or an attorney, usually a teacher at a university or an artistic high school, actively publishing books or articles in journals, a member of at least one important organisation, and participating in social life and thus contributing to the copyright discussions as consultants of the government, experts and members of advisory committees. Often, such personalities represented Czechoslovakia abroad, as explained later.

## Exertion of Influence of Interest Groups

The interconnections of organisations by a specific group of personalities provided a good basis for execution of their influence, and the interest groups were able to replace the representatives of the government (for example, officials of ministries) at international diplomatic meetings on the Bern Convention. As regards the Rome conference in 1928 on the revision of the Bern Convention, Czechoslovakia was represented by Dr. Vojtěch Mastný and Karel Hermann-Otavský.[27]

---

[24] Z. Morávek, *Ochrana autorů a rozhlas*, 170–174.

[25] "Zprávy spolkové," *Soutěž a tvorba* I (1928): 25–26.

[26] Z. Morávek, *Ochrana autorů a rozhlas*, 170–174.

[27] K. Hermann-Otavský, "Římská revize Bernské úmluvy o ochraně děl literárních a uměleckých," *Soutěž a tvorba* I (1928): 77–80.

International meetings organised by the Confederation of Collective Rights Management Companies in 1927 and 1928 were attended by representatives of the OSA (Jan Löwenbach a Karel Balling) and by representatives of Dramatický svaz [Dramatic Union] (Engel-Müller, Fr. Kohl, Dr. E. Konrád, Dr. Miroslav Rutte). It is worth recalling that Jan Löwenbach and Karel Hermann-Otavský were established as experts providing advice to the government on how to draft the proposal of the new Author's Rights Act.

The text of the proposal changed during the legislative process. The reason for introducing various changes was clearly stated in explanatory memorandums or openly admitted by members of Parliament in their debates,[28] and they adjusted the law according to the interest groups' wishes. The examination of the drafting of the law shows that new amendments brought benefits for authors, but not for users of their works.

Practical implementation of the law was also dependent on the work of advisory committees, as they influenced the jurisprudence. Since members of these committees were strongly interested in the strict enforcement of the law, their advices could be biased in certain directions and, according to cases published in the journal *Soutěž a tvorba* (*Competition and Creation*), it seems that they were.

## Conclusions

The 1920s and 1930s were extremely favourable periods for the activity of interest groups. The government was open to the opinions of organisations whose interest were at stake. Deputies and senators were ready to regulate many spheres of life[29] and they did not recognise the potential conflicts of interest that emerge when interest groups can heavily influence policy-makers. On the one hand, Czechoslovakia was obliged to follow the rules stated by the Berne Convention, but on the other authors were allowed to set up their own rules that overcame the level of protection according to this international treaty stating a minimum standard only.

This chapter illustrates how the interest groups were interconnected and the links between their members and the state. They actively influenced Czechoslovakian legislature and ministries and participated in

[28] "Tisk 227—důvodová zpráva: Historické senátní tisky z 1. volebního období, 2. zasedání," *Senát národního shromáždění*, 1920, http://senat.cz/informace/z_historie/tisky/1vo/tisky-2zas.php?ke_dni=27.12.2012&O=8 (accessed December 27, 2012).

[29] A. Doležalová, "Ekonomická tvářnost 'nové' Evropy," in *Zrod nové Evropy* (Praha: Historický ústav AV ČR, 2011), 391–413.

international meetings on behalf of the state. They were able to organise themselves to provide advice to the state and control the practical implementation of the law thanks to advisory committees. Viktor Dyk, who personally persuaded his colleagues—senators—that authors needed appropriate protection as they were critically important for the Czechoslovakian cultural life, is the most striking example of the linkage between the state and authors' organisations.

Hana Beránková is a PhD Student in the Department of Institutional Economics at the Faculty of Economics, the University of Economics, Prague.

# CHAPTER NINETEEN

# GOOD GOVERNANCE IN THE DEVELOPMENT OF THE ABSORPTIVE CAPACITY: CAN IT PROMOTE A NATIONAL INNOVATION SYSTEM?

VITA JUKNEVIČIENĖ

## Introduction

This chapter reveals, through a new approach, the relevance and novelty of the perfection of the absorptive capacity development implementation, enabling the practice of good governance and strengthening the national innovation system (NIS). It explains that governmental institutions, being part of the system, directly impact on the absorptive capacity's development processes through the implementation of public policy. How, though, to do it in a good way? There emerges a scientific problem—how could and should good governance promote the NIS by participating in the process of absorptive capacity development?

The aim of the chapter is to reveal the interfaces of good governance and the absorptive capacity development, identifying and analyzing ways in which governmental institutions could promote the national innovation system. For the purpose of implementation, the following objectives were used:

(1) identify the absorptive capacity's concept in the context of a national innovation system
(2) reveal the role of public administration organisations in the national innovation system
(3) establish the importance of good governance for the development of the absorptive capacity.

## Assumptions in Looking for Better Ways of Acting in the National Innovation System

Modern society is facing contemporary challenges determined by globalization, rising economic competitiveness, social and political unrest, and technological change. It is necessary to look for new methods, measures and techniques, enabling the national innovation system to work successfully. One such method would be the development of absorptive capacity as the essential specification for innovative processes, proceeding in organisations, regions and countries. Therefore, the author of this chapter emphasizes the idea that absorptive capacity is an integral part of the public governance institutions because of its being the primary functional assumption for institutions, an innovation management coordination unit, and a performance efficiency and high-scoring assumption for institutions as separate entities, liable to develop this capacity. And public administration organisations, as participators of the national innovation system, should operatively react to global knowledge management tendencies, trying to use all good practice for the common society's and institutions' aim of better wellbeing. Despite that, some national innovation systems still feel the shortage of knowledge, and its participants' (especially agents of governmental sector) contribution to processes of the national innovation system's strengthening. The scientific literature, dealing with the innovativeness and the development of absorptive capacity issues, has until now been oriented to the capacities of individuals, organisations or regions, with little emphasis on the role of governmental institutions. Besides, studies of good governance are more focused on public management's changes, intending little attention to issues of innovations and competitive development of a country or region. According to the necessity to innovate (as the only way to become competitive and enhance the economic, social, individual, organisational, regional and national welfare), more attention needs to be focussed on the economic, social and environmental problems. Moreover, the focus is on the implementation of a state policy and the requirements for the activities of public administration organisations (such as new ways of thinking and acting [such as good governance], more effectiveness, new forms of activity, betterment of activity's indicators, etc.). The economic and social wellbeing of a country builds on its capacity to innovate. The innovativeness of the country is mainly due to the efficiency and level of the whole national innovation system which is associated with new public governance because, first of all, it is described as the network of public and private sector institutions. The perception of innovative determinants and processes manages objectives of the national development and measures development strategies.

The objective of less-developed countries is to reach the social and economic levels of the EU countries. In order to evolve rapidly, it is necessary to innovate, learn quickly, adapt and embrace the best international practices. This perceives the increasing importance of innovation creation, diffusion and transformation as processes of the knowledge-based economy which provide the result, reflecting society's expectations and value for an organisation, a country or even the whole world. This can be done when the private and public sectors collaborate and introduce organisational and structural changes, when new public programs and projects are launched, state-of-the-art technologies are created and applied, appropriate funding is provided, and human resources are skillfully managed.[1] Necessary for the success of innovations are (in all institutions of the national innovation system, including public administration organisations) political will, time (for institutional reforms to take effect), flexibility of financial resources, stakeholders' support, investment in technologies and support of all sectors of society.[2]

It is necessary to look for new methods, measures and techniques, enabling the national innovation system to work successfully. One such method would be the development of an absorptive capacity as the essential specification for innovative processes, proceeding in organisations, regions and countries. Therefore, this chapter emphasizes that absorptive capacity is an integral part of public governance institutions. This is the primary functional assumption for institutions as innovation management coordination units, as well as for their performance efficiency. It also works as a high-scoring assumption for institutions as separate entities liable to develop this capacity. Public administration organisations, as participators in the national innovation system, should operatively react to global knowledge management tendencies, trying to use good practice for the common society's and institutions' aims of better wellbeing.

The scientific literature, dealing with the innovativeness and development of absorptive capacity issues, has until now been oriented to the capacities of individuals, organisations or regions, with little emphasis on the role of governmental institutions. Studies of good governance are more focused on public management's changes, placing little attention on

---

[1] S. Puskorius, A. Raipa, "Teoriniai viesojo sektoriaus veiklos modernizavimo aspektai," *Public Policy and Administration* 2 (2002): 9.

[2] A. Alberti, *The Critical Role of Innovation in Public Administration in Promoting Economic and Social Development*, http://unpan1.un.org/intradoc/groups/public /documents/unescwa/unpan010862.pdf (accessed November 12, 2009).

issues of innovation and the competitive development of a country or region. There emerges a *scientific* problem—how could good governance promote the national innovation system by participating in the process of the absorptive capacity development? This chapter reveals its relevance and novelty through a new approach to the perfection of the absorptive capacity development's implementation, enabling the practice of good governance to work for strengthening the national innovation system.

## Conception of the Absorptive Capacity in the Context of a National Innovation System

The current processes of innovation creation and deployment allow for the assumption that "absorptive capacity" and "development capacity" are fundamental for building the knowledge-driven economy. The ability to create and apply knowledge is the source of sustainability and superiority for organisations,[3] and the assumption of precise organisational learning and transformation is the absorptive capacity.[4] This construct includes individual (organisational) abilities to learn and acquire new knowledge, as well as the motivation to do so[5] and share best practices.

Different authors emphasize various aspects of the absorptive capacity concept. It can be understood as a consequence of an existing organisation's resources, tacit and explicit knowledge, internal practices, managerial skills and culture,[6] its capacity to identify, assimilate and exploit information from the organisational environment,[7] and its ability to identify, assess and absorb new knowledge (development capacity to use

---

[3] K. Alisauskas et al., *Inovacijos ir projektai* (Šiauliai: Press of Šiauliai University, 2005), 94.

[4] S. E. A. Dixon, M. Day, "Leadership, Administrative Heritage and Absorptive Capacity," *Leadership & Organization Development Journal* 8 (28) (2007): 728.

[5] V. Mahnke et al., *The Impact of Knowledge Management on MNC Subsidiary Performance: The Role of Absorptive Capacity*, http://openarchive.cbs.dk/bitstream/handle/10398/6495/01-2004-3.pdf?sequence=1 (accessed April 02, 2012).

[6] C. Gray, "Absorptive Capacity, Knowledge Management and Innovation in Entrepreneurial Small Firms," *International Journal of Entrepreneurial Behaviour & Research* 6 (12) (2006): 347.

[7] H. Welsh et al., *Organizational Absorptive Capacity and Firm Responsiveness: an Empirical Investigation of Growth-Oriented Firms*, http://usasbe.org/knowledge/proceedings/proceedingsDocs/USASBE2001proceedings-095.pdf (accessed March 09, 2013).

that new knowledge).[8] The modern conception of absorptive capacity declares three main components: the capacity to access international networks of knowledge and innovation, the capacity to anchor external knowledge from people, institutions and firms, and the capacity to diffuse new innovation and knowledge in the wider economy.[9]

The extent to which absorptive capacity (hereafter AC) and development capacity (hereafter DC) are used to create added value differs by economy sectors as well as by organisations, regions and countries. Therefore, the author predicates that the possibilities for the adaptability of the model are different in each country (national innovation system), and that there are no identical development processes, methods and instruments for opportunity measurement. Not only a practical, but also a scientific problem arises in how the model should be implemented. Other questions emerge over how actors of the system should be involved in the processes of absorptive capacity development, how the system would be crowded with high innovation rates, and whether it is possible to instigate the appropriate conditions for the processes of value creation and growth of competitive advantage.

The ability to innovate depends on internal and external knowledge sources complementing each other. It is important to attract good ideas from elsewhere (innovation AC) and exploit them to develop new products or services (innovation DC). These are conditions for prosperity and enhancement of operational efficiency for organisations (institutions, regions, cities, or states). The modern innovation model is shown in Fig. 19.1 below.

Fig. 19.1. Model of absorptive capacity and development capacity

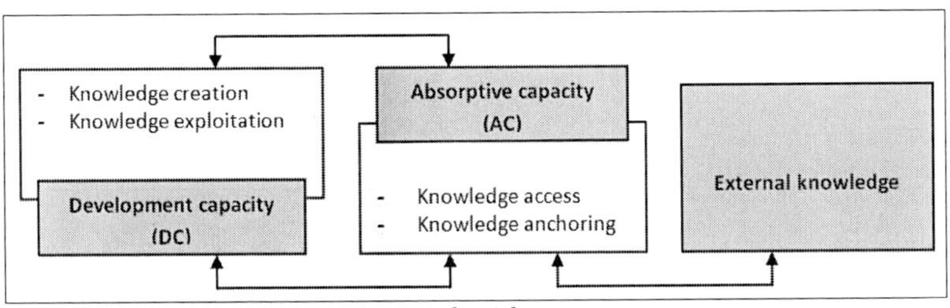


Source: S. Mahroum et al., *Innovation by Adoption.*

---

[8] S. Mahroum et al., *Innovation by Adoption: Measuring and Mapping Absorptive Capacity in UK Nations and Regions*, http://www.nesta.org.uk/assets/Uploads/pdf /Research-Report/innovation_by_adoption_report_NESTA.pdf (accessed March 20, 2013).

[9] Ibid.

The concept of absorptive capacity was analyzed through various aspects, but the most important is the level of a concept's application. In early studies it was examined on two levels (individual and organisational), but according to the latest intelligence three levels of absorptive capacity are highlighted:

(1) Organisational absorptive capacity concerns the directions of organisational activity (policy) and procedures, promoting individual absorptive capacity.[10] The capacity of the organisational unit to aggregate its knowledge with innovativeness and learn from external knowledge resources depends on its absorptive capacity.[11] Studies of this level substantiate the role of the institutional dimension in the national innovation system.

(2) National absorptive capacity is defined as the ability to learn about and exploit technologies concerning developed countries' practices.[12] A national absorptive capacity is not just the aggregation of domestic enterprises or industries, but also reflects the country's ability to create value and competitiveness in the global economy.

The author emphasizes that absorptive capacity could be analyzed not only vertically (through organisational levels), but also horizontally (according to the following areas):

(1) the industry's internal knowledge absorptive capacity (needed to attract the knowledge contained in the industry)
(2) the knowledge absorptive capacity among industries (knowledge created in other industries)
(3) the scientific knowledge absorptive capacity (knowledge arising from interactions with universities and research institutes)[13]

---

[10] Ch. W. Soo et al., *The Process of Knowledge Creation in Organizations*, http://www2.agsm.edu.au/agsm/web.nsf/AttachmentsByTitle/A04_Paper_RB005_CSoo_KnowInnov.pdf/$FILE/A04_Paper_RB005_CSoo_KnowInnov.pdf. (accessed November 12, 2009).

[11] W. Tsai, "Knowledge Transfer in Intraorganizational Networks: Effects of Network Position and Absorptive Capacity on Business Unit Innovation and Performance," *The Academy of Management Journal* 5 (44) (2001): 996–1004.

[12] R. Narula, *Understanding Absorptive Capacity in an "Innovation System" Context: Consequences for Economic and Employment Growth*, http://www3.druid.dk/wp/20040002.pdf (accessed April 11, 2010).

[13] M. Abreu et al., *Absorptive Capacity and Regional Patterns of Innovation*,

(4) the institutional knowledge absorptive capacity (knowledge, transformed by public policy and administration institutions, determines the national innovation system and its viability; knowledge created and transformed by business support structures enabling the promotion of an innovation system's actors; and knowledge created, transformed and diffused by formal and informal education organisations giving a foundation for the traditions of knowledge base building.

All four types are important in developing the absorptive capacity in the national innovation system, because they determine the scale, intensity, speed and empowerment options of the total national absorption capacity.

The national absorptive capacity could be developed by enhancing, strengthening and promoting any of the three components of access to knowledge, knowledge anchoring and knowledge diffusion. This can be done only by knowing the structure of the national innovation system and identifying its actors, especially organisations of public administration as the essential agents representing the state in the model of the national innovation system.

## Role of Public Administration Organisations in the National Innovation System

A national innovation system comprises all important economic, social, political, organisational, institutional and other factors, influencing innovations' development, diffusion and exploitation.[14] The national innovation system can be understood as the network of public and private sectors' institutions whose activities and interactions initiate, import and disseminate new technologies.[15] The main functions of the national innovation system are knowledge generation and its dissemination and exploitation, innovation commercialization, training of scientific and technical personnel, management of innovative processes, coordination, legal regulation, and financial support. The structure of a national innovation

---

http://www.dcsf.gov.uk/research/data/uploadfiles/DIUS-RR-08-11%20%282%29.pdf (accessed March 10, 2013).

[14] C. Edquist, "Systems of Innovation: Perspectives and Challenges," in J. Fagerberg et al. (eds.), *The Oxford Handbook of Innovation* (Oxford: Oxford University Press, 2004), 182.

[15] E. Bergman, S. Usai, *Knowledge Diffusion in European Regions*, http://www.iareg.org/fileadmin/iareg/media/papers/IAREG_WP4.8_final.pdf (accessed December 10, 2012).

system can be analyzed in two ways: in the aspect of institutions (institutional approach) and their implementing functions (functional approach), and in the aspect of their interaction at different levels (hierarchical approach). The institutional approach of the national innovation system proposes the model of institutions and organisations where the role of public administration organisations as important agents in the system could be identified (see Fig. 19.2 below). The role of public administration organisations in the management of innovation (the activities of the national innovation system) occurs in the following aspects:

(a) disseminating information, providing training and workshops on new technologies' potential for innovation management
(b) providing financial support, creating funds and supporting innovation management methodologies and techniques
(c) facilitating research cooperation between the business and academic sectors, seeking to determine business needs
(d) developing policies and legislation, promoting innovations and forming a favourable legal environment for their development
(e) contributing to the development of innovation management technologies and supporting ongoing innovation activities by small and medium businesses.[16]

The institutional approach to a national innovation system can be defined as a set of different institutions either individually or collectively involved in the development of new technologies and diffusion processes, as well as the formation of a structure which allows for the governance and executive policy to affect innovation processes. This is a system of interconnected organisations that create, accumulate and transfer knowledge and skills, describing the new technology. An element of nationalism manifests itself not only in technology policy, but also in the language and culture (joining the system), as well as in other accents of national policies, laws and regulations, creating an environment for innovation.[17] In the contemporary competitive world it is necessary to develop new types of innovation policy focused on the systematic identification of possible failures and improvement of the absorptive capacity of organisations and networking. Schemes of networking highlight the interaction between different actors

[16] *Innovation Management and the Knowledge-Driven Economy*, http://www.inovacijos.lt/index.php?-1742732791 (accessed July 18, 2009).
[17] B. Carlsson, "Internationalization of Innovation Systems: A Survey of the Literature," *Research Policy* 35 (2006): 58.

and organisations in the national innovation system, increasing the importance of joint research or other technical co-operations between businesses and public sector institutions. In this context, schemes promoting research and advanced technology partnering with the authorities become important and useful.

Fig. 19.2. Institutional structure of a national innovation system

| *Level* | *Type of the institution* | ***NIS*** |
|---|---|---|
| **Strategic level** | *Political institutions* | Ministries, national councils of science and technology |
| **Programmable level** | *Bureaucratic institutions* | Public agencies and institutions involved in the implementation of innovation policy |
| | *Regulating institutions* | Institutions, responsible for standards, norms and certification |
| **Coordination, and support level** | *Intermediary institutions* | Institutions, linking science and technology with industry: innovation centers, industry associations |
| | *Knowledge-oriented, non-profit organisations* | National laboratories of special activities, non-profit organizations |
| | *Social institutions* | Academies and professional associations |
| **Implementation level** | *Education institutions* | Universities and schools |
| | *Profit-oriented enterprises* | R&D companies, joint ventures, consortia |
| | | National human resources |

Source: Author's own research based on M. Meeus, L. Oerlemans, "National innovation systems," in S. Casper, F. Van Waarden (eds.), *In Innovation and Institutions: A Multidisciplinary Review of the Study of Innovation System* (USA: Edward Elgar, 2005), 55.

Consequently, innovations affect public administration organisations, and in turn the country's innovative processes. Innovations become important aspects of national and international activities, affecting governmental and administrative institutions, their activities and organisational processes, as well as influencing the development of the public administration paradigm in the conception of good governance.

Good governance is based on the interpretation of international organisations' positions (such as the World Bank and the International Monetary Fund). The essential argument is that developing countries are facing economic and social problems because they lack good governance, the new public management empowerment ensuring the justification of political, social and economic priorities under the inclusive public consensus, and that the needs of the poorest and most vulnerable are respected in decision-making processes with regard to the allocation of development resources.

According to the United Nations Development Program, ten principles of good governance are highlighted: citizens' participation, legal authority, transparency, responsiveness, consensus principle, justice and fairness, efficiency and effectiveness, accountability, and strategic vision. In the context of good governance, public administration organisations face three major challenges. First, they must operate and provide high quality services with receding resources and limited operational capacities. This encourages institutions to use resources and develop skills not only more efficiently but also more creatively, for example by involving the private sector and citizens in public services. Second, public authorities must become more accountable, responsible and efficient and increase orientation towards the needs of citizens. Third, it is necessary to respond adequately to citizens' demands, seeking greater cooperation. Citizens must become a part of the process, pursuing the resolution of problems and responding to changes in the environment.[18]

However, the question of whether (and to what extent) public administration organisations are prepared to adapt to the needs of knowledge and encouragement of innovation is still relevant. Innovation, unsuccessful in the private sector, can damage a company's reputation and, as a result, its responses to owners. The effects of failures in the public sector would be felt by all citizens. Successful public sector innovation is less conspicuous than failure, and innovation in the public sector is a tender question. The current system of public service management discourages

---

[18] *Innovations in Governance and Public Administration: Replicating What Works*, http://unpan1.un.org/intradoc/groups/public/documents/un/unpan021963.pdf (accessed February 1, 2013).

innovation, being more in favour of foreseeing defined actions. However, bureaucratic organisations in the transformation of the "learning" and "minded" organisation failures can lead to new and better ways of performing their missions. Essential directions for the development of modern public administration are considered to be the public authorities' attempts for efficiency, the ratio of public institutions with democratic values and traditions, and trends of innovation and modernization in the public sector (also strengthening of the good governance implementation).

## The Role of Good Governance in Developing a National Absorptive Capacity

Analyzing the role of good governance in the process of national absorptive capacity development, and public administration organisations' activities in the implementation and promotion of the processes of the national innovation policy, should be emphasized. Attention must be paid to several aspects:

(a) the commercialization of new technologies (technological innovation) is a long-term process requiring a stable political and legal environment (which could be promoted by good governance principles like justice and fairness, or legal authorities)
(b) it is important to disseminate new knowledge and to establish and expand the network, helping to commercialize new technologies and organise conditions for such transfer
(c) it is important to develop a favourable business and research environment, which could ensure the fruitful functioning of innovation centres and technology parks
(d) it is important to create a common network of governmental, administrative and business structures and an academic community, which could establish a creative and supportive environment for innovation
(e) the forward-looking production of innovative products and knowledge, competitive in the global market, is the most important goal of public and private sectors' cooperation in the area of innovations.[19]

---

[19] A. Jakubavicius et al., "Inovacijos versle: procesai, parama, tinklaveika," http://www.inovacijos.lt/index.php?-1742732791 (accessed July 18, 2009).

According to such assumptions, innovation policy should be consistent with the macroeconomic environment, the legal and administrative environment, the educational system, information and communication structures, values and the cultural environment as well as the market demand structure of the elements to influence the innovative activities and promote interactions between the main subsystems of the national innovation system. Therefore, innovation policy should be focused on the creation of assumptions for the development of innovativeness.

Public and private sector cooperation should be based on different mechanisms, underlying the favourable situation for economic development, ensuring rapid anchoring of new technologies, seeking to increase the competitive advantage of the country. As noted earlier, the competitive advantage could be in promoting and developing the absorptive capacity under the AC/DC model, which works through networks of information and cooperation. Public administration organisations, as agents of the national innovation system, are associated with other governmental and administrative institutions, international organisations, foreign partners, the business sector, non-governmental organisations, and citizens' associations. A significant role falls on scientific institutions and international organisations conducting research, publishing studies and forming trends of public management change. In trying to develop the national absorptive capacity, all its components should take part in the implementation processes of the innovation policy, amplifying knowledge access, and its anchoring and diffusion aspects.

Access to the knowledge enhances creativity, development and usefulness, but it is a fairly complicated process, based on the four different components of the knowledge economy:

(a) access to human knowledge (education, know-how, human capital development through the learning of new skills)
(b) access to information (a particular field of knowledge information, data or reports)
(c) access to knowledge-embedded goods (whose production costs include significant scientific and technical knowledge, often protected by intellectual property rights)
(d) access to facilities for the production of integrated knowledge production (scientific and research tools, materials and components of experimentation, computer software and hardware).[20]

[20] F. Noronha, J. Malcolm (eds.), *Access to Knowledge. A Guide for Everybody* (Kuala Lumpur: Consumers International, 2010), 113.

National access to external knowledge capacity is developing through public and private investment in the connectivity through its infrastructure and legal systems, facilitating a knowledge transfer processes in trade and investment measures. Particular national innovation systems (especially with low scientific, economic and social potential) can increase their access to external knowledge through:

(a) the concentration of institutions, generating intellectual property (universities, technical research opportunities, knowledge centres, etc.), and accelerating and making more effective processes of learning and knowledge transfer. A particular country's capacity to access global knowledge flows is closely connected with the density of large companies (specialized, knowledge-intensive) and universities (supported by infrastructures, and characterized by large flow volumes)
(b) the local culture (level of confidence, social cohesion)
(c) the economic activity, reflecting the practices of strong cooperation (trade, foreign investment, integration into global value chains, leading subdivisions of global networking companies). A variety of efforts and investments must be used for strengthening and availability (especially in international relations). Developing countries especially should use opportunities to access external knowledge (of new technology and innovation) through such measures as foreign investment, international partnerships and importing.

Knowledge anchoring is an organisation's or area's capacity to access external knowledge and use it in any way (e.g. through application, economic utilizing, recombination, recycling etc.).[21] According to various authors' research data, it is possible to distinguish the following three knowledge-anchoring levels: personal, organisational and regional (see Fig. 19.3 below), influencing the level of anchoring the national innovation system and possible directions for its development. Despite the anchoring capacity, embodied in all three mentioned levels, it must be emphasized that its development processes and specifics will depend on the direction of the knowledge flow. Knowledge can be anchored from the internal environment on the individual, organisational and national levels through national clusters or networks (see Fig. 19.3 a and b clusters below), as well

[21] H. Halkier et al., *Knowledge Dynamics, Regional Development and Public Policy* (Denmark: Aalborg University, 2010), 60.

as the external environment through interpersonal, organisational or network relations (see Fig. 19.3 c and d clusters below).

Regarding the development of the national innovation system's absorptive capacity (depending on the possibilities of improving the anchoring process), it is necessary to identify the specifics of each level of expression to assess their contribution to the promotion of innovation, the development direction, and the trends of quantity-quality.

Knowledge diffusion is a process of perception, beginning with the transfer of knowledge, which is characterized by unpredictability, and its success is determined not only by knowledge transfer. The diffusion is necessary so that transferred knowledge can be absorbed and converted into local actors (groups of innovators and imitators). In this process, new knowledge complements existing knowledge, but at the same time, the latter gives validity for the new knowledge (requiring motivation, resources and the abilities of actors).[22] The diffusion of innovation creates preconditions for the improvement or similar innovation activities, which create additional value for the innovation. The importance of public administration organisations is revealed through a hard-measurable social capacity (including such indicators as the law and public order, judicial independence, property rights protection, business regulation mechanism, anti-corruption activities, democracy [autocracy] degree, the political system of balance and control, the level of competition in legislative and executive powers division, and the scales of political rights and civil liberties).[23] According to the diffusion sources, methods and operating mechanisms, the most important task for innovation policy is to implement a variety of mechanisms facilitating the local and external knowledge, the anchoring and assimilation, and the exploitation of technology and knowledge across the country.[24]

---

[22] E. Zhuang et al., "Network Model of Knowledge Accumulation through Diffusion and Upgrade," *Physica A* 390 (2011): 2582.

[23] J. Fagerberg, M. Srholec, *National Innovation System, Capabilities and Economic Development*, http://www.tik.uio.no/InnoWP/0710_TIKwp_FagerbergSrholec.pdf (accessed October 20, 2012).

[24] C. Autant-Bernard et al., "Knowledge Diffusion and Innovation Policies within the European Regions: Challenges Based on Recent Empirical Evidence," *Research Policy* 42 (2013): 196.

Fig. 19.3. Interfaces of a national innovation system's levels and directions of knowledge flow

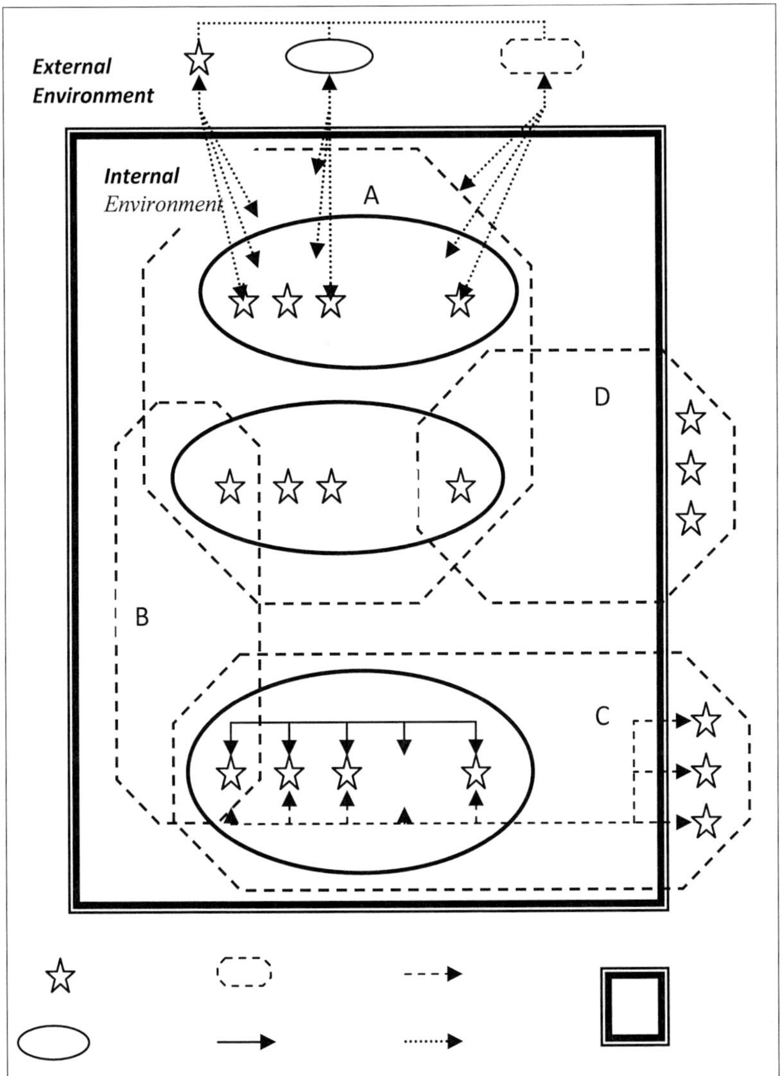


Source: Author's own research.

Public administration organisations, following the principles of good governance in their activities, could be actively involved in the development processes, developing a national absorptive capacity (in the areas of knowledge access, anchoring and diffusion), and properly accomplishing their mission in the national innovation system, if they would actualize such recommendations. First of all, better conditions should be allowed for organisations, cities, regions and countries to access relevant national and international sources of new ideas, knowledge and innovations. Schemes for supporting and inducement should be created, creating improved opportunities to access sources. Second, more should be done for attracting the knowledge of such organisations and universities which adapt their acquired knowledge outside the organisation or the region. These market actors should be identified, or even created; they should also be supported for the purpose of enhancing their relationships with external partners. Thirdly, there should be greater investments in the development of such organisations with the ability to disseminate knowledge in a given economic space. Promotions and awards should be designed with the aim of supporting the open exchange of knowledge between different types of organisations, regardless of the area, sector or industry boundaries. Finally, the strategy of innovation should be based on organisations and regions of a country's strengths and weaknesses.[25]

Governance and management should provide additional value, staying directly related to the needs of citizens. The management structure is changing, as it has to coexist with ideas and innovation, and search for better ways to implement the mission. The suitable environment for innovations and the absorptive capacity can be created through a number of measures (where the contribution of public administration organisations is needed in the implementation process), such as legal and administrative environment adaptation, facilitating the support for business start-ups and innovations, and facilitating innovation funding.[26]

The opportunity to participate in networking opens up chances not only for the exchange of knowledge and for organisation development (through relationships with partners to gain access to otherwise inaccessible technological and market knowledge), but also allows a certain stability and for the development processes of the innovation system. However, the

[25] S. Mahroum et al., *Innovation by Adoption: Measuring and Mapping Absorptive Capacity in UK Nations and Regions. Research Report*, http://www.nesta.org.uk /assets/Uploads/pdf/Research-Report/innovation_by_adoption_report_NESTA.pdf (accessed September 8, 2009).

[26] A. Jakubavicius et al., *Inovacijos: procesai, valdymo modeliai, galimybes*, http://www.inovacijos.lt/index.php?-1742732791 (accessed October 20, 2012).

extent of benefit depends on the organisations', regions' and countries' abilities to identify, interact, assimilate and exploit new sources of knowledge for the absorptive capacity.[27]

Therefore, a country's innovative activities that are influenced by public administration organisations and the principles of good governance should be characterized with certain cooperation, networking and support for innovation development. In order to make the public administration organisations flexible and innovative, looking for the best ways to carry out agreements, and creating new and adopting existing ideas to work, the needs can be met only by providing the preferred environment (conditions for the good governance implications). This is needed to provide greater freedom of self-determination for the heads of institutions seeking to implement new technologies, adapt innovative management and search solutions, promote public-private cooperation and the institutional and societal needs of the area.

## Conclusions

The changing role of innovations throughout the world (including public administration organisations) challenges the changes in all areas of life. Innovations, differing in their nature and results, are of fundamental importance in public administration. They develop base factors in scientific innovation linked to the progress of management and administration science, technological innovation for methods and measures in public service improvement, managerial innovation, introducing new organisation and management techniques, and optimizing performance.

The innovative performance of public administration organisations and the state is impacted by those organisations' innovative activities related to the development of innovation policy and management processes, as well as shaping the innovation environment in the context of the national innovation system. An absorptive capacity creates assumptions to attract good ideas from elsewhere, thereby enabling the creation and development of new improvement provisions for a national innovation system's performance. Under the development capacity those provisions are being implemented in practice.

---

[27] S. Mahroum, B. Poirson, *UK Global Opportunities, Local Challenges: Absorbing Innovation from Above and Below*, http://www.nesta.org.uk/assets /Uploads/pdf/Working-paper/UKglobalopportunitiesworkingpaperNESTA.pdf (accessed October 20, 2009).

Public administration organisations should be based on participation and cooperation concepts. Therefore, the public administration has to be transformed into tools that respond to the needs of citizens. To achieve this it is necessary to innovate the public administration organisational structures, practices, skills and a system for mobilizing human, material, information, technological and financial resources.

Vita Juknevičienė, M.A. is a PhD student at the Kaunas Technology University and a lecturer at the Department of Public Administration at the Faculty of Social Sciences of the Šiauliai University (since 2005). Her scientific interests concentrate on the modernization of public administration.

# CHAPTER TWENTY

# CIVIL SOCIETY AND ECONOMIC OUTCOMES IN THE TRANSFORMATION OF POLAND: PUSHBACK—ONE COMPANY'S STRUGGLE TO SURVIVE POLAND'S MASS PRIVATIZATION PROGRAM; A CASE STUDY

CHRIS O'NEILL

This is the story of the demise of Krakowska Fabryka Aparatów Pomiarowych—KFAP—and a struggle between two sides: KFAP's employees and the management firm of the Vth National Investment Fund. It is illustrated with examples of this management firm's methods of control and of realization of financial returns. The case study is preceded by a discussion of the two main reasons for the failure of the mass privatization program: the content and application of commercial law, and weakened trade unionism.

## Introduction

It is an enduring aspect of human history that prevailing political conditions and powerful forces in society both shape the law and its application. Thus law, ostensibly meant to regulate and serve the common good, is often a tool that promotes the interests of powerful groups in society and acts against the interests of others. If civil society can be defined as the "… ability of society to take action upon itself,"[1] then the passivity of society can be seen as its antithesis. It is passivity that allows the powerful to utilize law to their own benefit. It was this passivity that ultimately led to the failure of Poland's mass privatization program with

[1] To utilize Alain Touraine's definition of "historicity": in A. Touraine, *Samotworzenie się społeczeństwa* (Cracow: Nomos, 2010), 20.

its negative economic outcomes for society—passivity both in terms of one of civil society's traditional modes of expression of self-organised groups that is the union and, even more so, passivity from one of the most important outcomes of civil society—the *politeia*[2]—or state.

This chapter focuses on an aspect of an economic experiment that was part of Poland's economic transformation from a command to free-market economy. This was the National Investment Fund program (NIF) and was Poland's version of the mass privatization programs that took place in over half of the countries of the former Soviet bloc. This experiment was an economic failure that resulted in a markedly smaller economy for Poland than would have been the case had the experiment not taken place.

This chapter focuses on two specific aspects of the demise of the economic assets in the NIF program: (1) how aspects of commercial law that paradoxically arose in Communist Poland in explosions of social unrest, becoming tools of the workers for the preservation of the economic viability of their SOEs, were transformed into weapons of short-term aggrandizement by newly empowered groups in post-1989 Poland; and (2) how a weakened trade union movement, though its passivity in protecting these SOEs, contributed to this economic demise. It needs to be stressed that research by this author has shown the correlation between participation in the NIF program and negative economic outcomes.

The first part of this chapter is devoted to a discussion of commercial law and trade unionism in Poland and their roles in the NIF program, while the second part backs up this discussion with a detailed case study of one particular company's struggle to survive the NIF experiment, replete with examples of both the usage of commercial law as a tool of "company control and economic depletion" by this particular NIF management company, and unsuccessful attempts by an isolated company union—unsupported by its union on the national or regional levels—to defend its company from economic destruction.

---

[2] *Politeia*—in Greek thought meaning both "rights of citizens" and "form of government." See Henry George Liddell, Robert Scott, *A Greek-English Lexicon*, http://www.perseus.tufts.edu/hopper/text?doc=Perseus%3Atext%3A1999.04.0057 %3Aentry%3D%2384506&redirect=true (accssed August 18, 2014).

# Part I—How Polish Commercial Law and Weak Trade Unionism Contributed to the Failure of Poland's Mass Privatization program

## Mass Privatization in Poland

Poland's mass privatization program (also known as the National Investment Fund program) was an economic experiment that did not work. While Poland's industry as a whole—measured in terms of the real value of sold production—rose by 60% between 1995 and 2005, the real value of sold production of the 11% of Poland's industrial assets placed in the MP program in 1995 decreased over this same period by 58.2%.[3]

Seventeen of the twenty-two nations that arose from the former Soviet bloc had mass privatization programs, and their negative economic and social outcomes have been the subject of numerous studies.[4] The main criticisms and reasons given for the failure of these programs were the speed in which they were executed and, more importantly, the lack of institutional infrastructure surrounding their implementation.[5] Poland's program, however, was unique in that it was planned as a gradual program and equipped with an institutional infrastructure that included privatizing agents contracted by the state, several layers of oversight and, most importantly, formal state control over the assets in the program for its first three years. Nevertheless, the program was a failure. Although imperfect, the infrastructure created for the Polish MP program could have brought a measure of success, specifically in the amount of participant programs that

---

[3] Based on a database compiled from the financial data collected on the entire population of Poland's MP program, 512 firms, for the years 1995/1996, 2004/2005, from financial reports published in *Monitor Polski B, Dziennik Urzędowy Rzeczypospolitej Polskiej (Monitor Polski B, Official Journal of the Republic of Poland)*, Warsaw. This database is hereafter known as the O'Neill MP database.
Data on Poland's general industrial output based on the author's composite of data from various issues of the *Rocznik Statystyczny Przemysłu (Annual Industrial Yearbook)*, Warsaw; Główny Urząd Statystyczny (Chief Statistical Office), 1996, 2006.

[4] For a partial listing see C. O'Neill, "Poland's Mass Privatization Programme: Institutions and Market," in L. Czechowska, K. Olszewski (eds.), *Central Europe on the Threshold of the 21st Century, Interdisciplinary Perspectives on Politics and Society* (Newcastle Upon Tyne: Cambridge Scholars Publishing, 2012), 320.

[5] Ibid., see, for example J. Nellis, *The World Bank, Privatization and Enterprise Reform in Transition Economies: A Retrospective Approach* (Washington DC, The World Bank, 2002), 50.

survived, their financial health and the value of their sold production. However, it did not, because the state, upon creating the program, purposely took a passive role, instead putting its trust in the market mechanisms supposedly built into the program—namely the self-interest of the privatizing agents (known as the management firms)[6] that prepared their MP charges for secondary privatization. The legal construction of the program, however, was ambiguous and its manner of remuneration of the management firms was flawed. These drawbacks in the context of the passivity of the state seemed to inexorably draw the privatizing agents toward avenues of least resistance in realizing short-term benefits for themselves, instead of towards the development of the long-term potential of their charges, which would not only have brought greater benefit to the Polish economy but also to themselves.[7]

## Route of Least Resistance

There were, of course, success stories, and some companies were successfully bought out by workers and management, some found Western branch investors, and some became success stories in their own right and maintain it today. Others had no chance of surviving and disappeared as expected, some became owned by insiders and others were cannibalized for their assets or the land on which they were located. My general conclusion, however, is that a great number of companies could have survived but did not, and they did not survive because the funds' management companies were generally not interested in developing their long-term potential, instead focussing on short- and mid-term returns. If a company was "survivable" but too problematic in terms of effort and time, it was a ripe candidate to be "quickly squeezed" and discarded, usually at very low prices and to persons or entities also not interested in development but in assets.

---

[6] Of the 15 national investment funds that made up the program, private management firms governed at first 14 and then all of the funds.

[7] Against the general backdrop of state passivity in terms of program oversight, I have identified several reasons for the failure of Poland's mass privatization program, which are ideology, resource limitations (oversight personnel), ambiguities in the NIF law, weakened trade unionism and commercial law. There is no room in this article for an examination of each of these reasons; instead the significance of just two of them, weakened trade unionism and commercial law, will become evident as we examine the case of the demise of the KFAP.

Examples of how short-term returns could be engendered are selling the company for the value of its real estate,[8] liquidating the company after transferring its assets, debt and most employees to specially created "receiving companies," by draining the company of cash (or creating debt that could later be traded for company equity) through forcing it to hire expensive consultant companies affiliated with the management firms, by lowering the company's book value to sell at a profit that would positively affect the fund's balance sheet and thus impact on the management firm's remuneration, and by forcing the company to finance undertakings or new companies that had nothing to do with its development.

## Control Needed to Obtain Short-Term Benefits

This process of short-term return could be called "short-term company utilization." Control was needed in order to reap these short-term returns. In terms of the individual companies, the most obvious and effective form of control resulted from the simple fact that the management firms could replace—through control of the company's supervisory board—members of the company's management board, including presidents. This was a factor of the *de facto* owner-employee relationship built into the program between the management firm and its MP charges, and in most cases was sufficient. A company's management board, out of concern for their positions, submitted to the will of the management firm. In cases where the management board resisted it was replaced. Whether in respect to a new or existing management board, management firms would sometimes force a change in the company's statute to allow the amount of members of management boards to be as little as one or two (instead of the average of four or five) since it was easier to control one or two persons rather than five. Control over a company's management board was not always sufficient to control the company, particularly if the latter had a union ready to proactively resist changes it felt were detrimental. In that case the management firm might, through its control of the company's supervisory board, threaten union leaders through economic pressure, either through potential loss of their jobs or even company apartments, if such were held by them.[9]

---

[8] Poland in the 1990s was undergoing a construction and real estate boom, and many factories that found themselves in the MP program were located on prime pieces of urban real estate, attractive, for example, for shopping malls.

[9] Although the jobs of a company's union officials were legally protected, employers sometimes fired them anyway, often during attempts at unionizing non union workplaces, like hypermarkets; See D. Ost, *The Defeat of Solidarity, Anger*

## Role of Commercial Law

The application of this control over MP companies was greatly facilitated by the legal context in which the program took place, namely the status of MP companies versus commercial law (both in the legal construction of the MP program and commercial law in general), as well as by the inability of the companies to effectively resist this control—an inability due in no small part to a weakened trade unionism.

## Civil Society Paradoxes in Communist Poland

While law is ostensibly meant to regulate and serve society and individuals, it is an enduring aspect of human history that prevailing political conditions and powerful forces in society shape both the law and its application. The same is true in law regulating the economic entities of post-Second World War Poland. Laws nationalizing enterprises and creating a command economy were quickly implemented by Poland's communist party after 1945.[10] The lip service paid to worker input in this system remained empty propaganda[11] until the political upheaval by the workers in 1956 breathed life into the slogans of worker self-management that were real and revolutionary in character.[12] This was short-lived,

---

*and Politics in Postcommunist Europe* (Ithaca: Cornell University Press, 2005), Chapter 6; though the threat itself of depriving a union representative of his or her job was also used as a tool of control (see the case study below).

[10] See "Ustawa z dnia 3 stycznia 1946 r. o przejęciu na własność Państwa podstawowych gałęzi gospodarki narodowej" ("Law of January 3rd, 1946 on the assumption of ownership by the state of the main areas of the national economy"), *Dziennik Ustaw (Dz. U.) (Journal of Laws)*, 1946 no. 3 item 17; "Dekret z dnia 26 października 1950 r. o przedsiębiorstwach państwowych" ("Decree of October 26, 1950 on state enterprises") *Dz. U.* 1950 no. 49 item 439, and its amended version *Dz. U.*, 1960 no. 18, item 111, these laws (and all others cited in this article) can be accessed at the Internetowy System Aktów Prawnych database (Internet System of Legal Acts) at http://isip.sejm.gov.pl/prawo/index.html (accessed April 15, 2013).

[11] An example is the unimplemented degree that each SOE was to possess a "Council of Social Supervision" as an independent body with supervision, control and opinion functions, "Dekret z 3 stycznia 1947 r. o tworzeniu przedsiębiorstw przemysłowych, handlowych i górniczych" ("Decree of January 3, 1947 on the creation of industrial, trade and mining enterprises"). See link above for access.

[12] Workers councils were created that were to be elected by respective SOE workforces through secret ballot. The given workers council would "govern the enterprise in the name of the workforce" and have the right to approve yearly production plans, approve operation plans, establish the structure and organisation

however, and as the political forces unleashed by the worker upheaval subsided in the face of the institutionalized force of the Polish communists and their allies, economic control of state-owned enterprises (SOEs) once again returned to the state.[13]

A second worker upheaval had, however, more lasting impact on commercial law. Pressure by the Solidarity union and the weakness of the party in 1980–81 saw the passage of two key laws that introduced enduring worker control over SOEs: the law on state enterprises and the law on worker self-government in state enterprises.[14] These laws were written and passed during Solidarity's period of strength—that of a legal union of ten million members not yet outlawed by martial law. Not only were workers councils now involved in the selection of the directors of most SOEs,[15] but Solidarity was also successful in its stipulation that

---

of the enterprise, set the enterprise's direction of development, set efficiency guidelines in the area of production, technology, quality and usage of materials, approve yearly balances, sell un-needed fixed assets (based on the director's opinion), set pay schedules, decide whether part of the enterprise's profit should be used by the enterprise and how the part of the profit (if) earmarked for the workers should be divided; see "Ustawa z dnia 19 listopada 1956 r. o radach robotniczych" ("Law of November 19, 1956 on workers' councils"), *Dz. U.* 1956 no. 53 item 238, particularly points 1 to 11 and art 7 par. 4.

[13] The 1956 law was first undermined in practice and then formally rescinded in 1958: "Ustawa z dnia 20 grudnia 1958 r. o samorządzie robotniczym" ("Law of December 20, 1958 on worker self-government"), *Dz. U.* 1958 no. 77 item 397. Workers Councils were retained in name but greatly reduced in terms of real power by both placing them within the structure of other organs and by the statutory inclusion within these structures of party activists and SOE directors.

[14] "Ustawa z dnia 25 września 1981 r. o przedsiębiorstwach państwowych" ("Law of September 25, 1981 on State Enterprises"), *Dz. U.* 1981, no. 24, item 122 and "Ustawa z dnia 25 września 1981 r. o samorządzie załogi przedsiębiorstwa państwowego" ("Law of September 25, 1981 on the self-government of the workforce and the state enterprise"), *Dz. U.* no. 24, item 123; see link above for access.

[15] The government did not want to allow the workers council of an SOE to have the right to select the director of the enterprise. See M. Bałtowski, *Przekształcenia własnościowe przedsiębiorstw państwowych w Polsce* (Warsaw: Wydawnictwo Naukowe PWN, 2002), 47.

A compromise was reached in which the workers could exercise this right except in SOEs considered strategic for the national economy. In 1983 the government decreed that 1,372 SOEs were of strategic importance (to put this into perspective, a total of 8,453 SOEs existed in 1990). See G. W. Kołodko, *Post-Comunist Transition The Thorny Road* (Rochester, 2000), 6–7; "Rozporządzenie Rady Ministrów z Dnia 5 lutego 1983 w sprawie ustalenia listy przedsiębiorstw o

SOEs were to be independent, self-governing and self-financing. These blows to the principles of central planning and control not only weakened the party and central administration presence in these important centres of societal organisation that were SOEs, but also manifested a sense of concern for the economic status of national assets. The levels of SOE autonomy and worker influence on company affairs introduced by these laws were probably unknown in any other country of the world. The language of these acts reflects the mutual responsibility felt towards the economy both by Solidarity and most of the population, stating that the enterprise was "… a unit of the national economy meant to meet the needs of society …."[16]

## Workers as Proxy Owners of SOEs

Historical events in communist Poland had thus precipitated a situation in which control of economic entities moved in the direction deemed most desirable by classical economists and proponents of privatization, i.e. towards concentrated ownership. The workers were not owners of their factories but, like the NIF management firms (though to a lesser extent), they could exercise significant control over factory management. This worker influence over the factories was considered a nonsensical aberration by vocal proponents of privatization that arose post-1989 and criticized even by those alarmed by the economic damage that a doctrinaire approach to privatization could engender.[17] Indeed, examples could undoubtedly be found to confirm the classic fear that worker control would lead to wage inflation to the detriment of the company.[18] On the other hand, numerous examples exist of worker forbearance concerning economic demands, and even a long-time manager of the World Bank

podstawowym znaczeniu dla gospodarki narodowej" ("Regulation of the Council of Ministers of February 5, 1983 Concerning the Setting of the List of Enterprises of Fundamental Significance for the National Economy") *Dz. U.* 1983, no. 9, item 47, see above link for access.
It should also be mentioned that some doubt has been expressed about the extent of the realization of the right of workers' councils to elect company directors during the 1980s. See M. Wyczałkowski, *Transformacja systemu ekonomicznego w Polsce: Uwagi krtyczne, Zeszyt 7* (Warsaw: Instytut Badań Społecznych i Międzynarodowych, 2001), 22.

[16] *Ustawa z dnia 25 września 1981 r. o przedsiębiorstwach państwowych*, Article 1.

[17] See M. Wyczałkowski, *Transformacja systemu ekonomicznego w Polsce*, 22–23.

[18] Case of the Prima company in Łódź, *Elite* Interview, Management Board, Polmo Łódź, January 9, 2012.

responsible for private sector development realized, in hindsight, the beneficial character of workers councils.[19] It is also probable that the economic results of companies governed by workers councils compared favourably with those of MP companies.[20]

## NIF Management Firms as Proxy Owners of SOEs

The companies that participated in the MP program found, however, that the wind of commercial law was changing direction, and now blew not at their backs but in their faces. The first step to joining the MP program was to undergo commercialization; that is, to be transformed into a joint stock company, with 100% of the stock held by the state. As SOEs, the law on worker self-government had guaranteed them the right to "… appoint and dismiss the company director and those that perform management functions in the enterprise …,"[21] and the 15-person workers council itself acted as a kind of supervisory board. Workers in SOEs, commercialized in preparation for their inclusion in the MP program, saw this control significantly diluted by commercialization, which according to the privatization law of 1990 gave the employees the right to elect one third of the make-up of the supervisory board[22] (which appoints the management board). It is important to mention that commercialization frequently took

---

[19] "… one also has to admit that the workers' councils, so worrisome to both bank staff and external advisors in 1990, ultimately proved to be a positive force in Polish SOEs. In other transition economies, like Bulgaria and Ukraine, where the old centralized state structures and sectoral [*sic*] ministries crumbled, where firm managers took over the control of assets, and where privatization was accepted in principle but not extensively carried out in practice, but where workers' councils were weak or non-existent, the result was asset stripping and deterioration of firm quality on a large scale … [In Poland] … the workers' councils were keeping an eye on managers, and checking if not totally preventing them from asset-stripping and 'spontaneous' privatization." J. Nellis, *The World Bank, Privatization and Enterprise Reform in Transition Economies: A Retrospective Approach* (Washington DC: The World Bank, 2002), 16–17.

[20] The author of this article is preparing a comparative economic analysis (over a 10-year period) of MP companies and SOEs governed by workers' councils.

[21] *Ustawa z dnia 25 września 1981 r. o samorządzie załogi*, article 24, passage 2.

[22] "Ustawa z 13 lipca 1990 o prywatyzacji przedsiębiorstw państwowych" ("Law of July 13, 1990 on the Privatization of State Enterprises"), article 17, *Dz. U.* 1990 no. 51 item 298; see link above for access.

place on the initiative of the workers[23] who often felt that privatization was the most rational way of developing their enterprises.[24]

An examination of commercialized firms fully owned by the state indicates that in practice they enjoyed broad autonomy, with the representatives from the relevant government ministry (usually the ministries of industry and ownership transformation and then the ministry of the treasury) performing a passive oversight role.[25]

When in the MP, companies found themselves subject to much more active control of the management firm/proxy owner. Although for the first three years of the program the state had control of 85% of the equity in each firm—25% directly and 60% through 100% ownership of the funds' equity—the state treasury had only one representative on each five-person MP company supervisory board.[26] This was in proportion to its 25% direct equity in each company. The given fund, via its management firm representatives, had two or three representatives for its 33% equity share and, through a gentleman's agreement, the additional 27% held by the remaining "minority" funds, and the company workers, who received 15% of equity in their given companies as part of the program, had one

---

[23] In the case of SOEs commercialized via the 1990 law (as were the MP firms), agreement by the workers was necessary (article 5.1).

[24] David Ost examines in detail the complicated—sometimes enthusiastic, sometimes ambivalent—attitude of Polish workers towards privatization. D. Ost, *The Defeat of Solidarity*.

[25] The ministry of treasury (SP), for example, had three instruments of "mechanical" oversight and control in relation to entities that had state equity: (1) company-prepared quarterly reports—lengthy documents detailing the economic condition of the entity; (2) voting instructions for SP representatives at shareholder meetings, and (3) post-meeting reports on votes taken—based on a review of documents by this author concerning SP oversight of 14 selected NIF companies and a smaller amount of non NIF but state-owned commercialized companies from 1995–2005; Archiwum Ministerstwa Skarbu Państwa (Archives of the Ministry of Treasury, herein known as AMSP).

The nature of this state oversight as well as the fact that commercialized companies had a month in which to prepare and submit their quarterly reports, meant that the SP had information *post factum*, often too late to effectively respond to crisis situations. *Elite Interview with head of the NIF department in the ministry of treasury*, April 2011.

Another indication of the passivity of state oversight is the fact that amongst Polish firms, changes in management occurred least frequently in SOEs and state-owned commercialized firms: M. Bałtowski (ed.), *Przedsiębiorstwa sprywatyzowane w gospodarce polskiej* (Warsaw: Wydawnictwo Naukowe PWN, 2002), 251.

[26] Except for the cases in which an investor also purchased the state treasury's equity during secondary privatization.

representative. This active control by the management firms was in keeping with the aim of the program in which the funds, via their management firms, were to actively prepare MP firms for successful secondary privatization. As mentioned above, however, this active control in practice most often led to a demise in the economic potential of the MP companies. We have also seen how this ability to control was a direct result of the shifting legal framework of the MP companies and, as we shall see from the case study below, an MP company was at a decided disadvantage when it tried to use commercial law as a tool in its defence—a disadvantage that was compounded by the pro-privatization political alignment of Poland in the 1990s.

## Instances of Worker "Pushback" in Other Companies

In the absence of effective legal tools for defence against the management firms, some companies that had proactive unions applied various forms of strong-arm tactics. Sometimes, these shows or threats of force were successful, or at least delayed the negative impact of the management firms. A manufacturer of industrial cranes in Mińsk Mazowiecki, that had been forced to take bad investment decisions by its management firm leading it to the edge of bankruptcy,[27] averted that occurrence and instead got its management firm to agree to a business plan to rescue the company only after the management of the crane company ensured the backing of the Warsaw offices of the two main company unions (Solidarity and the "Metalworkers") for its rescue plan. These unions informed the management firm that there would be a lot of commotion (strikes, demonstrations) and bad publicity if the bankruptcy went through, and the

[27] One of the characteristics of this company was that it was active on a limited market, in that the amount of domestic customers for industrial cranes was limited in Poland. The fund management firm noticed that not all the company productive potential was being utilized and forced the company management to accept sales goals that were not in keeping with the reality of its limited core market. The company president had no choice. He was also fearful for his job. The company thus contracted with three large foreign companies (including Rolls Royce and the Finish company Kone) to supply a new line of products outside of its core competence, and thus for which it was not technologically prepared. In addition, the crane manufacturer was not used for large foreign contracts and in effect these contracts were poorly prepared and poorly managed. When the crane company fell behind schedule, it encountered ruinous monetary penalties that led it to the edge of bankruptcy. *Elite Interview with former finance director/MB member of crane company*, August 26, 2010.

management firm backed off.[28] In another case, the union members of a railroad repair factory in Gniewczyń prevented the destruction of their company by a show of force. The Hetman NIF fund had sold a similar railroad repair company in Ostrów Wielkopolski in 2001 to a newly created entity owned by Slovaks and registered in Switzerland. This was a legal entity with no branch experience made up of several persons, including a retired colonel of the Czechoslovakian secret service. It began pumping money out of the rail company using various methods, forcing, for example, all purchases by the rail company to be made via an additional "paper" company the Slovaks set up and which took a commission of between 20% and 40% on each transaction. The new owners also paid themselves for collecting fictitious debts and burdened the company with an expensive monthly contract—paid to their Swiss company—for "marketing services."[29] In January 2002 the Kazimierz Wielki NIF fund sold the rail repair factory in Gniewczyń to two companies, Surfina and Fenix, that were in fact backed by this same group of Slovaks. The unionists quickly realized that this was the same group leading its sister company to destruction and thus wrote to the owners of Surfina and Fenix, threatening to strike and block the company's HQ. The two owners, not wanting to go to the factory full of angry union members, agreed to meet with a four-person union delegation at a neutral location—a roadside restaurant. The delegation came, but with a bus full of angry workers. The workers prevailed on the owners to not only fire four Slovak consultants that the new owners had hired but also to sell their 52% equity holding to another company—the Warsaw Kolmex company.[30]

## Solidarity Does not Step up to the Plate—Lack of Support for Workers at Company Level

Such displays of force were exceptions to the norm, however. The only hope for a company's union to influence the direction of their company

---

[28] Ibid.

[29] J. Tittenbrun, *Z deszczu pod rynnę: Meandry Polskiej Prywatyzacji, vol. 4* (Warsaw: Zysk I S-ka, 2007), 94–95; based on an the article by M. Czekański, "NFI w cieniu afer," *Rzeczpospolita*, June 26, 2004.

[30] Ibid., also two articles by M. Bujara, "Przeglad kadr. Przemysł. W Gniewczynie teraz czas na Kolmex?," *Gazeta Wyborcza*, September 22, 2003; "Dogadali się," *Gazeta Wyborcza (Rzeszów edition)*, September 22, 2003. Before these "company drainers" were stopped, they still managed to draw off 11 million PLN from the company, for which they faced criminal charges in 2004: M. Czekański, *NFI w cieniu afer*.

was to gain the support of the main union force in Poland, Solidarity, on at least a regional scale to apply political pressure in the halls of power or economic pressure through strike actions on a wider scale. Solidarity, however, was not forthcoming with such support. With certain exceptions, in the 1980s the mass actions of Solidarity were basically a thing of the past.

The trade union movement—particularly Solidarity but also the legacy communist-era unions federated in the OPZZ[31]—could have had an impact on the program by forcing the state to take a more pro-active role. The greatest potential for action lay with Solidarity, with its history of activism, protest and accumulated positive societal and political capital. However, despite individual actions and collective meetings at the ministry of treasury, not only did the union movement not effectively impact upon the program, but through its weakness contributed to the program's overall negative outcome.

## Solidarity—Political Liberation but Without the Workers

A number of factors contributed to Solidarity's general ineffectiveness as a trade union despite its presence in all, or almost all, of the 512 companies participating in the program.[32] The primary factor was that of Solidarity's legacy. Although the sparks that began the original strikes were economic, the union that arose became a mass movement, encompassing most of society, whose ultimate aim was political, not economic. Solidarity was a national liberation movement, the goal of which was independence for Poland.[33] It was this political legacy that

---

[31] Ogólnopolskie Porozumienie Związków Zawodowych (National Association of Trade Unions).

[32] In 1998, all (not just Solidarity) union members constituted between 87.5% and 97.6% of the workforce of commercialized firms, including NIF firms. See J. Gardowski, W. Panków, "Część VI Odczarowanie mitu—związki zawodowe w badaniach empirycznych Związki zawodowe w Polsce," in J. Gardowski (ed.), *Rozpad bastionu? Związki zawodowe w gospodarce prywatyzowanej* (Warszawa: Instytut Spraw Publicznych, Fundacja im. F. Eberta, 1999), Table 1, 249. This book is based on empirical research on trade unionism in Poland in 1998, encompassing 200 industrial enterprises, 148 union leaders and 1,225 union and non union employees.

[33] This direction evolved during Solidarity's 1980–1981 "carnival of freedom." See the "Józef and Grzegorz Theories" in A. Touraine, *Solidarity: The Analysis of a Social Movement: Poland 1980–81* (Cambridge: Cambridge University Press, 1983), 87–92, and crystallized during the 1981–1989 period of de-legalization and

stifled Solidarity's effectiveness as a protector of the economic interests of the working class in free-market Poland, and which directed Solidarity toward political instead of trade union activity after 1989.

During the "1980–81 carnival" and afterwards, the articulation of Solidarity's aspirations became increasingly couched in political terms. The source of economic distress was also seen to be political—that of the contemporary command economy. After independence in 1989, as the main political opposition force for the past decade, Solidarity naturally found itself thrust centre stage on the political arena. David Ost argues that post-communism (and thus the arrival of the free market) "set in motion the articulation of class differences that the political world was unable to process ...."[34] Although political parties were in their infancy—particularly those not associated with the former communist party and its satellites—the anti-communist political "pie" emanating from the feelings of a large part of society, including workers, was real and large. As an emotional and thus politically potent force, anti-communism overshadowed worker economic interests, particularly since for most, anti-communism and the free market went hand in hand.[35] Thus, many Solidarity activists (most of Solidarity's elite advisors had already joined the free market bandwagon) gave active support to political parties that emphasized anti-communism and free market reforms but took little notice of worker's economic rights.

It was Solidarity's entrance into politics after 1989 that side lined the economic rights of its members. Specifically, it was the lack of involvement on a regional or national level that enabled the program's proxy owners to utilize the full clout of the commercial law at their disposal.

What this meant in practical terms was that KFAP's union was alone in its struggle to keep its company alive and its attempts to use commercial law to its own advantage were doomed to failure.

---

repression; see S. Ramet, *Social Currents in Eastern Europe: the Sources and Consequences of the Great Transformation* (Duke University Press, 1995), 86.

[34] D. Ost, *The Defeat of Solidarity*, 179.

[35] Ost provides a number of examples of Solidarity activists' and members' beliefs in the benefits of the free market coming from the West: "... as a miner told me, 'if an owner is looking for his own interest, he is looking out for the worker's interest'." D. Ost, *The Defeat of Solidarity*, 157.
Another miner turned automobile worker at the new Opel plant in Gliwice asked, "Why should there be?" when asked about the need for a union in this Western-run corporation. Ibid., 163, 158–169.

# Part II—Case Study

## KFAP—Description of the Company

KFAP was a process-control company in Cracow that entered Poland's transformation with high hopes. It had a motivated engineering cadre and work force, a union consciously interested in securing the company's future and, most importantly, an established economic position that included 40% of its sales as exports, mostly to Sweden and Germany.[36] Three companies were interested in establishing joint ventures with KFAP including the large German company Heraeus and SVM (Svensk Varmematring SVM, a Swedish meter manufacturer), a subsidiary of ABB in Sweden.[37] It had been engaged in an active restructuring program since 1989, including dramatic reductions in its workforce, which went from 1,969 persons in 1989 to 959 in 1991, and 700 by 1992.[38] On the eve of the commencement of the NIF program, in 1995 KFAP had, in Polish zlotys, annual assets valued at 23.5 million, sales of 26.3 million, a very healthy ST debt to receivables ratio (1.85 million/2.86 million), no long-term debt, a gross profit on sales of 6.25 million, a net profit on sales of 2.86 million, a debt of 2.56 million, financial costs of only 326 thousand and a net profit of 1.6 million.[39] It had also further reduced its workforce

---

[36] Archiwum Ministerstwa Skarbu Państwa (Archives of the Ministry of Treasury) (futher: AMSP), *Ogólna informacja o spółce—1992 (General Information on the Company—1992)*, act call no 5370/36, 1992–1994, 3.

[37] AMSP, *various Letters of Intent*, act call no 1449/5, 1990–1992, 22–28, 33–34, 35–36.

[38] AMSP, *Kwestionariusz (Questionnaire), (specifically): Pytanie dodatkowe do kwestionariusza (Additional Questions of the Questionnaire)*, act call no 1449/5, 1990–1992, 39.

[39] It should be mentioned that with sales slightly down (to 25.94 million), employee costs in 1996 (wages and social insurance) rose by 19.9% (from 8.83 million to 10.59 million). This decreased gross P on sales to 4.43 million and was the main factor in the decrease of net P on sales from the 1995 level of 2.86 million to only 112 thousand in 1996. In addition, the level of "other operation costs" (which is a financial statement position after calculating returns on sales and which does not include sales of fixed assets; this was the statement position where management firms placed the costs of the creation of the sizable reserves, which they often imposed upon the MP firms) rose from a modest 569 thousand in 1995 to 2.94 million in 1996. Together, these factors led the company to a net loss of 3.27 million in 1996. See the O'Neill MP database, in this case compiled from *Monitor B*, 23, 1997.

Employment costs are certainly a legitimate management concern, that is, for a management interested in company development, particularly if that company, as

to 637 persons. By 2005 the company had been liquidated, broken up into components, had lost most of its assets, and existed in the form of a legacy company that employed 75 persons, and in nominal terms had assets valued at 6.68 million, sales of 15.59 million, a gross profit on sales of 3.93 million, a net profit on sales of 1.19 million, a debt of 1.22 million and a net profit of 1.19 million.[40] When we take the 1995 results of KFAP and present them in 2005 terms, taking into account inflation, we see the dramatic fall in value of KFAP's output:

**Table 20.1. KFAP output values 1995 and 2005**

| | 1995 values in millions of zlotys | 1995 values in 2005 real values (factoring in inflation[41]) in millions of zlotys | 2005 actual values in nominal terms in millions of zlotys | Percentage of decrease |
|---|---|---|---|---|
| Assets | 23.58 | 41.24 | 6.68 | 83.50 |
| Sales | 26.30 | 46.15 | 15.59 | 62.00 |
| Gross P on S | 6.25 | 10.96 | 3.93 | 64.50 |
| Net P on S | 2.86 | 5.01 | 1.19 | 76.00 |
| Debit | 2.56 | 4.49 | 1.22 | 75.00 |
| Net P | 1.61 | 2.80 | 1.19 | 57.50 |

Source: Author's own research.

## KFAP's Solidarity Union

From the beginning of the transformation period, KFAP was characterized by a proactive Solidarity union. In 1991, this union declared its desire for KFAP to participate in the mass privatization program that the Ministry of

was the case of KFAP, was in relatively good shape. If the management is not interested in development, but rather "short-term company utilization," then employment costs can be a convenient excuse for its actions.

[40] O'Neill MP database; V NIF prospectus 1996.

[41] Główny Urząd Statystyczny (Central Statistical Office), *Miesięczne wskaźniki cen towarów i usług konsumpcyjnych w latach 1989–2010 (Monthly price indices of consumer goods and services 1989–2010)*, http://www.stat.gov.pl/gus/5840_1638_PLK_HTML.htm (accessed May 25, 2013), used for annual inflation rates for Poland for 1996–2005.

Ownership Transformation was preparing.[42] In the union's words: "In the conviction of the personnel … the new form of functioning of the factory should set free those mechanisms and capacity to act in a free market environment, which will bring about clear development to our factory."[43] The real reason seems to be that Solidarity did not feel comfortable with the intentions and ability of the offer to buy the company by private domestic buyers who had the support of the KFAP management board.[44] As the Solidarity union chief at KFAP explains:

> Back in 1990, we accepted the need that we had to privatize, but how? Under communism everything was upside down—not the way it should be. We were afraid, however, of direct privatization. There were not serious buyers. We were not interested in Polish *noveau riche* that made their money in unknown ways and who did not have a reputation we could check. We finally decided to declare our access to the MP program—since we thought it was the safest way.[45]

## Former Proxy Owners Meet New Proxy Owners

The union took an active approach to participation in the program, organising an inter-company union committee within the fund.[46] It organised a meeting with the fund president and the management firm "… where we were assured that … that the main goal of the management company is to develop and improve and not liquidate."[47] Relations, however, soon soured. The union was upset that the management firm "… began with cost-cutting and employment reduction … Either the management firm did not understand the program or it was just doing what

---

[42] AMSP, *Letter to the Ministry of Ownership Transformation from the company's Solidarity union*, July 1, 1991, act call no 1449/5, 1990–1992, 9.
[43] AMSP, *Letter from the company union to the Dep't. of Mass Privatization at the Ministry of Ownership Transformation*, March 11, 1992, act call no 5370/36, 1992–1994, 9–11.
[44] AMSP, *Opinia nt. przekształcenia przedsiębiorstwa* (*Opinion on legal transformation of the enterprise*), *Letter to the Ministry of Ownership Transformaton by then company director and the chairman and vice chairman of the supervisory board*, June 18, 1991, act call no 1449/5, 1990–1992, 12–17; also *Deklaracja Intencji (Letter of Intent signed between the company director and two businessmen interested in buying the factory)*, May 27, 1991, act call no 1449/5, 1990–1992, 20–21.
[45] *Elite interview with the Solidarity union chief of KFAP*, January 5, 2011.
[46] Ibid.
[47] Ibid.

required the least amount of effort."[48] In 1996, KFAP's labour efficiency (amount of revenue generated per employee) was 40,728 PLN and thus about median for the fund's companies.[49] There was room for improvement, though efficiency could also be achieved through increased sales and technological improvements. One of the oft-repeated complaints of the union was that the average salary of KFAP employees was lower than that of the national average, even though the company at this time was profitable and the fund was paying itself dividends.[50]

The union and company president,[51] who was selected through a competition organised in 1994 (before the commencement of the program) by the pre-program supervisory board in which the company workforce had a significant say, came to the conclusion that the company should extricate itself from the fund. First, however, they proposed to the fund that the company should be put on the stock exchange; the fund refused, explaining that the company was not ready.[52] The union now tried to extricate itself from the program.[53] What happened next emerges from the records of supervisory board meetings and other records in the Ministry of Treasury archives and the interview with the union chief.

## Attempt by Workers to Reassert Control

> We tried to disengage ourselves from the fund by increasing our equity and inviting investors to take control. Workers had 15% equity and so enough

---

[48] Ibid.

[49] O'Neill MP database.

[50] Though company profits also generated cash awards for the employees, which the management firm attacked as inappropriate and against a previous decision: AMSP, *Protokół z posiedzeń Rady Nadzorczej Krakowskiej Fabryki Aparatów Pomiarowych S.A. z dnia 4 października 1996 (kontynuowanego w dniu 9 października 1996)* (*Official Record of the session of the supervisory board of [KFAP] from October 4, 1996 and continued October 9, 1996*), act call no 1545/1, 275–276.

[51] KFAP's Solidarity union had lobbied the ministry against its previous company president, AMSP, *Letter from the company union to the Dep't. of Mass Privatization at the Ministry of Ownership Transformation*, March 11, 1992, act call no 5370/36, 1992–1994, 9–11.

[52] AMSP, *Protokół z posiedzeń Rady Nadzorczej Krakowskiej Fabryki Aparatów Pomiarowych S.A. z dnia 4 października 1996 (kontynuowanego w dniu 9 października 1996)* (*Official Record of the session of the supervisory board of [KFAP] from October 4, 1996 and continued October 9, 1996*), act call no 1545/1, 266.

[53] *Elite interview with the Solidarity union chief.*

> to call a general shareholders' meeting[54] during which our president and the unions were to present the fund with our plan. However, we took our time in informing the fund and according to regulations, the shareholders had to respond to the calling of the meeting in order to participate. The fund shareholders—along with the Ministry of Treasury—were late and were thus not allowed to participate in the meeting. We voted to double the amount of company shares to 1,280,000 shares of which 700,000 shares were to be bought by Bank Handlowy in Warsaw (one of the largest Polish banks). Bank Handlowy had agreed to invest and become the majority shareholder.[55]

## Reaction by Management Firm

### Tools of Control
### (1) Supervisory Board Meeting at Proxy Owner Premises
### (2) Initiate Legal Proceedings

This was an attempt by the union to use commercial law to its advantage, and the fund's management firm hit back hard. Within a week a supervisory board meeting was called in Warsaw, instead of Cracow, "... to prevent attempts at disrupting the proceedings ...."[56] The head of the supervisory board and vice-president of both the management firm and fund described how 85% of the shareholders were not able to participate in the extraordinary general shareholders' meeting from the week before, as a result of inappropriate procedural actions by those calling the meeting and thus not providing the other shareholders (main fund, minority funds and state treasury) enough time to submit declarations of intent at the headquarters of the company (which blocks shareholders present at the meeting from acting in the name of the company based on just the equity present). The head of the supervisory board stated that the plan of the company to raise the company's capital was not even discussed with the fund, and added that the fact that the fund's employees were not allowed into the building and had to wait four hours outside in the cold was "... contrary to elementary principles of good behavior and hospitality."[57]

A lawyer retained from the well-known firm McKenna & Co., and who was representing all the funds, cited procedural errors, in particular the fact that the shareholders should have had until midnight of the

---

[54] Which took place on September 27, 1996, AMSP, *Protokół z posiedzeń Rady Nadzorczej*, 266.
[55] *Elite interview with the Solidarity union chief.*
[56] AMSP, *Protokół z posiedzeń Rady Nadzorczej*, 265.
[57] Ibid., 268.

deadline to submit declarations, not 15:00 as set by the organisers, and suggested that KFAP's management board could be prosecuted for "acting against the interest of the company." The head of the supervisory board then added that the sale of 60% of KFAP shares to Bank Handlowy for 30 million PLN was "… at a price 80% less than that recommended by the fund … and that this [price] was a glaring manifestation of poor judgment by the company."[58] Ironically, in just three years the fund would sell its 33% dominant shareholding in KFAP for just under 5 million PLN.[59]

**Tools of Control**
**(3) Management Board Change**
**(4) Seek Support from National Institutions**

The head of the supervisory board then announced that the fund had already submitted a motion to the public prosecutor about "… acting to harm the company's interests,"[60] that a motion had been submitted to the commercial court to invalidate the decisions taken during the September 27, 1996 shareholders' meeting, and that correspondence had been initiated with the national head of the Solidarity union, Marian Krzaklewski, and with Bank Handlowy to "… explain the essence of this conflict."[61] In addition, after the representative of the workers in the supervisory board—the union chief—had left the meeting, the supervisory board voted to recall the president of KFAP with immediate effect.[62]

It is interesting to note how the management fund felt confident enough to reach out to the head of Solidarity—and I imagine not just to inform, but to ask for support. Krzaklewski was head of the just-formed Solidarity Electoral Action, a Solidarity-supported political bloc that was to win the parliamentary elections the following year.

Note that the supervisory board meeting took place far away from the potential source of resistance that was the factory. The practice of holding supervisory board meetings, or more often shareholder meetings, in physically distant places from companies that might be negatively affected

---

[58] Ibid.

[59] A. Maciejewski, "Kalendarium Spółek," *Parkiet* 179 (3) (September 16, 1999): 3; The packet sold on September 14, 1999, just 2 weeks short of three years since KFAP's attempted transaction with Bank Handlowy, included the 27% belonging to the minority funds. All told, the 60% went for less than 10 million PLN. *Elite* interview with the Solidarity union chief.

[60] AMSP, *Protokół z posiedzeń Rady Nadzorczej*, 274.

[61] Ibid., 268.

[62] Ibid., 271–272.

by decisions taken—although understandable in this case—was used from time to by management firms.

Back in KFAP, the union head, in a declaration to the personnel, stated that only the court and not the supervisory board can decide about the legality of the shareholder's meeting, and that "… the representatives of the fund were acting in a way harmful to the interests of the company and its future."[63]

**Tools of Control**
**(5) Threaten Jobs of Union Officials**
**(6) Threaten Company Apartments of Union Officials**
**(7) Deny Bonuses to MB Members**

The counterattack by the fund did not let up during the following supervisory board meetings, and a petition by the workers to reinstate the recalled president[64] to his position had no effect. The union again accused the fund of disregarding the "fundamental interests of the company."[65] The newly appointed acting president of the company, when asked about the union situation, said that OPZZ was peaceful, but that Solidarity was "inciting unrest."[66] The situation in the words of the Solidarity union chief was: "total war."[67] The head of the supervisory board inquired about the status of union officials that were paid employees and obligated the acting president to, by the next meeting, "… put in order matters relating to work time of employees holding union positions."[68] What was potentially more threatening was the request of the supervisory board to the management board to "… determine the legal title of the residents of company-owned apartments." The supervisory board further stated that "… it will **not**

---

[63] AMSP, *Oświadczenie* (*Statement*), October 7, 1996, act call no 1545/1, 280–281.

[64] The former president did not feel up to being interviewed. The union head said that the stress might be too much for him and explained how the former president could not find work, had health problems and still can't really get over what happened; *Elite interview with the Solidarity union chief.*

[65] AMSP, *Protokół z XXXVIII posiedzenia Rady Nadzorczej KFAP S.A. z dnia 14 października 1996* (*Official record of the XXXVIII session of the supervisory board of KFAP S.A. from October 14, 1996*), act call no 1545/1, 283.

[66] AMSP, *Protokół z XXXIX posiedzenia Rady Nadzorczej KFAP S.A. z dnia 13 listopada 1996* (*Official record of the XXXIX session of the supervisory board of KFAP S.A. from November 13, 1996*), act call no 1545/1, 286.

[67] *Elite interview with the Solidarity union chief.*

[68] AMSP, *Protokół z XXXIX posiedzenia Rady Nadzorczej*, 286.

block the management board from selling these apartments."[69] At the next supervisory board meeting in December, the board voted 4-1 to deny the management board III quarter bonuses, to which the board member representing the workers objected and proposed a bonus of 2,000 PLN for the former company president, since he "... should be honored and appreciated ... (for finding) ... a financial investor for the company."[70]

Putting pressure on union officials was another tactic through which the management firm was trying to exercise control over the situation. As has been mentioned, union officials were known to have been fired despite their legal protection. A more serious threat was that of selling company apartments, if indeed this was a poorly veiled attempt to intimidate a union official that lived in a company apartment.

The Solidarity union chief describes the denouement of this stage of KFAP's struggle:

> ... the ministry made such a commotion that Bank Handlowy withdrew from the transaction. The matter made its way to commercial court, which rescinded the decision to raise our company equity since the procedural matter concerning shareholder-meeting attendance is of less importance than equity ownership. I think the court caved in to pressure. We knew, however, that the matter could be struck down in court, but we gambled. If Bank Handlowy—a big player—had not gotten cold feet and had taken the shares, it would have been different.[71]

---

[69] Ibid., 287. It is not clear from the document whether this was related to the conflict with the union. Many workers in Poland lived in apartments originally supplied by the company and although these apartments were theoretically for the time of employment, in practice the agreements were construed in such a manner that the employee would settle in permanently, including after retirement, and be removed only if they were fired at fault. See an example of such an agreement from 1956 between employee Piotr Deresiewicz and the Ministry of Industrial Construction on the basis of which a descendent of the original tenant was still living in housing provided by the company, AMSP, *Umowa (Contract)*, act call no 4255/8, 2001, 290–291.

The security of such apartments was lessening, however, in free-market Poland. The management board of another company in this fund, a construction company in Warsaw, tried to give (!) its company apartments to a private firm, *act call no 4255/8, 2001*, 282–288, 319.

[70] AMSP, *Protokół z XL posiedzenia Rady Nadzorczej KFAP.S.A. z dnia 12 grudnia 1996* (*Official record of the XL session of the supervisory board of KFAP S.A. from December 12, 1996*), act call no. 1545/1, 289–290.

[71] *Elite interview with the Solidarity union chief.*

Thus, the union knew it was at a commercial law disadvantage but it gambled anyway, and without the political clout of Solidarity on the national level it lost that battle.

### Workers Shift from Company Control to Company Survival Mode

The union's struggle for direction of the company's development was dealt a decisive blow. The focus of the struggle now shifted from economic development to economic survival. Shortly after the conflict over equity, economic results began to slow. Sales in the fall of 1996 were lower than expected causing losses for September and October, with costs increasing faster than income. In addition, the unions were pushing hard for the company to respect the wage indexation agreement that had been signed with the previous president, which the acting president said "... would be difficult to respect." Dividends were, however, still paid to the Fund.[72] By the end of 1997 the company had generated a 3,564,722 PLN net loss because of higher costs, lower demand and an unfavourable foreign exchange rate that affected exports. Nineteen ninety-eight brought a clear improvement, however, with end of year losses cut to 1,954,721 PLN, an increase in orders by 15%, and investment in research and development, as well as marketing. KFAP also attained ISO 9001 in 1998.[73]

### Tools of Control
### (8) Reduce Management Board to Pliable Size
### (9) Use of "Hit Men" as Management Board

The fund seemed to be focusing more on control than on development. One method of control was the reduction of the management board to one or two persons directly beholden to the management firm. In April 1997, the company managed to change the company's charter to allow for the management board to be made up from one to seven persons, instead of the previously allowed three to seven members. E. J., the state treasury representative in the supervisory board, recommended that the SP reject this motion:

---

[72] AMSP, *Protokół z XXXIX posiedzenia Rady Nadzorczej KFAP S.A. z dnia 13 listopada 1996*, 285; AMSP, *Protokół z XL posiedzenia Rady Nadzorczej KFAP.S.A. z dnia 12 grudnia 1996*, 290–291.

[73] AMSP, *Memorandum*, May 20, 1999, act call no 5578/2, 51, 55.

> The inordinate subjection of the board to one shareholder—that of the majority fund—exemplified by having only its representative on the board, not only constitutes a threat to the interests of the SP but also could cause a worsening of the "social" situation in the company. The workers of KFAP are very distrustful towards realization of the NIF program and towards the actions of the Vth National Investment Fund.[74] I propose to vote against this motion.[75]

The NIF department, however, overrode its representative's suggestion.[76] The fund did appoint a two-person management board. The fact that these persons, W. T. and G. Ł., later gained notoriety and were arrested as "directing a criminal group" that "… pumped out multi-million (PLN) sums of money …" out of a group of former NIF textile companies that they had gained control over, and that the president of the V NIF fund (who was also president of the management board) became head of the supervisory board of one of these textile companies when he left the fund, give their appointment as KFAP's management team a certain hue.[77] The usage of teams of "hit men" type managers that would move from one company to another performing difficult or unsavoury tasks is another example of how management companies exercised control.

[74] In fact, the union chief had warned the workers in October 1996 of the possibility of the supervisory board's creation of a two-person management board, "… which would be in clear violation of the company charter." AMSP, *Oświadczenie*, 281.

[75] AMSP, *Formularz dla członka rady nadzorczej* (*Form for a Member of a Supervisory Board*), April 16, 1997, act call no. 3670/100, 1997, 41, 45–46. Such a Form which was one of the tools, also called "Instructions," that the SP used to control its reps.

[76] Ibid.

[77] See press articles: A. Domanowska, "Białostockie Fasty na plusie," *Gazeta Wyborcza Białystok*, August 5, 2007, http://wiadomosci.gazeta.pl/kraj/1,34309,4366559.html (accessed May 25, 2013); B. Mikołajewska, "Ty nie masz nic, ja nie mam nic," *Polityka* 7 (2337), February 16, 2002, http://archiwum.polityka.pl/art/ty-nie-masz-nic-ja-nie-mam-nic,372705.html (accessed May 25, 2013);
W. Więcko, "Fasty—Prawie jak Mafia," *Gazeta Wyborcza*, October 19, 2006, http://wiadomosci.gazeta.pl/kraj/1,34309,3693707.html (accessed May 25, 2013).

## Management Firm Moves from Control to Asset-Depletion

### Asset Depletion Method
### (1) Creation of "Recipient" Companies

The fund, of course, was not only interested in control. It also wanted financial benefits from its control over KFAP. Easier than focusing on development was focusing on KFAP's assets, particularly its real estate—prime property in expensive Cracow. In a letter of March 11, 1999, all three KFAP unions sent a letter to the management board in which they complained of the policy of "... breaking the company down into pieces (the creation of the most diverse companies, which constitutes, in our opinion, a camouflaged form of the liquidation of KFAP)."[78] Indeed, the practice of creating external companies that might be tied into the main company (and thus called daughter companies) was used both within the NIF program and without as a means of "pumping out" assets from the mother company.

### Asset Depletion Method
### (2) Liquidation

Events were rapidly coming to a head. The fund intended to liquidate the company. During a supervisory board meeting on May 5, 1999, one of the management board's two members, W. T., stated that because of the rising

---

[78] AMSP, *Letter from (the heads of KFAP's 3 unions) J. Saniternik, Chairman of KZ ZZ Niezależni, J. Ogrodziński, Chairman of NSZZ Metalowcy KFAP S.A. and J. Pogan, Vice Chairman of KZ NSZZ Solidarność KFAP S.A. to the management board of KFAP with a copy to its supervisory board*, March 11, 1999, act call no. 3786/161, 2000, 25. In this letter, the unions also complained of the excessive expenses of the management board—including salaries, administrative costs, travel and living expenses. Indeed, the "general costs of management" ("*koszty ogólnego zarządu*") are so high as to be shocking, at over 10 million PLN for 1997 and 8.5 million PLN for 1998, compared with manufacturing costs (*koszty wytworzenia sprzedanych produktów*) of 16.7 million and 15.8 million respectively, AMSP, *Memorandum*, May 20, 1999, act call no 5578/2, 1999, 55.
Polish accounting methods, which follow European and world norms, define "general costs of management" to encompass the salaries of administrative personnel, office materials, magazine subscriptions and the like, while manufacturing costs, besides materials and energy, also include worker salaries and social insurance. It seems unlikely, however, that such high management costs did not in this case include other costs, otherwise the reaction of the unions surely would have been greater.

liability of the indexation wage dispute, grounds now existed to vote on terminating the company.[79] He added that liquidation could be rescinded if "… we came to an agreement." The union chief, who was the workers' supervisory board representative, responded: "The board does not respond in writing to our successive proposals for agreement."[80] In what could be treated as a warning to the unions or, most likely, a justification for action, the supervisory board presented two alternative resolutions for the upcoming shareholders' meeting. The first was to put the company into liquidation by June 14, 1999 and the second read that this could be avoided if "… a new collective agreement was signed between the unions and the management board by June 30 and if within this time period the wage indexation dispute of December 16, 1996 was resolved." In addition, within this period there had to be agreement for restructuring, group layoffs and "… agreement by the trade unions active in the company to make redundant persons that enjoy particular protection resulting from obligatory regulations."[81] This last phrase is most likely a reference to KFAP's trade union leaders, whose jobs, as mentioned above, were legally protected.

**Workers in Company Survival Mode**
**(1) Attempt to Use Debt/Equity Swap to Create a Worker Controlled Production Facility**
**(2) Attempt to Declare Bankruptcy and have a Union Declared Trustee**

The unions had anticipated this situation and decided to use the company liability caused by the wage indexation dispute to their own advantage by proposing to exchange this debt for equity in the company. This was their

---

[79] AMSP, *Protokół z LXVIII posiedzenia Rady Nadzorczej KFAP.S.A. z dnia 5 maja 1999 (Official record of the LXVIII session of the supervisory board of KFAP S.A. from May 5, 1999), act call no 3670/108*, 2000, 24. Though there is some doubt as to whether the form of this indexation-induced liability could constitute such a basis, since only 2 of the 500 or so employees had the back wages owed to them certified by the court. AMSP, *Letter from Stanisław Kracik Chairman of the Freedom Union, Małopolska Region to Alicja Kornasiewicz, Vice Minister of the Ministry of the Treasury*, May 14, 1999, act call no 3670/104, 1999, 11.

[80] Ibid., 24–25.

[81] AMSP, *Document*, May or June, 1999, probably act call no. 3670/108, 2000, 23–34. Interesting to note that there are two versions of this document in the archives, which were received by fax by the SP—the second has the parts about restructuring, group layoffs and firing of union reps crossed out, which was probably the edited version that the SP was willing to support.

second attempt to use commercial law to their advantage. To this end, they formed a legal entity called SPK (an employee-owned company of KFAP—Spółka Pracownicza SPK). As the Solidarity union chief explained: "We—the workforce—held a sizable asset in the form of 2 million zlotys that the company owed us. This company debt came from unpaid earnings that should have been paid to us resulting from a wage indexation agreement negotiated between the unions and the company when our previous president was still in office."[82] It was mostly likely in response to this proposal for a debt/equity swap that the vice-president of the management firm and fund referred to when he stated, "… the proposals of SPK are impossible to accept."[83] Pressure in this direction was also put on the SP from the union via political representation. In a letter from May 14, 1999, the head of the Freedom Union's (Unia Wolności) Małopolski region, parliamentary deputy Stanisław Kracik, asked the vice-minister of SP to consider allowing the workers to buy equity in exchange for the indexation liability. The Freedom Union was at that time a coalition partner with the governing Solidarity Electoral Action. Kracik added that the workforce was considering declaring KFAP bankrupt (the debt owed to the workers gave them that right) "… as a way of blocking the actions leading to the dissolution of the company by the management board …."[84] The union did indeed ask the court to declare bankruptcy since it saw it as the better of two evils: "We favored bankruptcy over liquidation since under the former procedure the court would appoint a trustee that could give the company to the union [as a holder of company debt] to run." Unfortunately for the union, "… the court rejected our motion for bankruptcy and so only liquidation remained."[85]

---

[82] *Elite interview with the Solidarity union chief.*

[83] AMSP, *Protokół z LXVIII posiedzenia Rady Nadzorczej KFAP.S.A. z dnia 5 maja 1999*, act call no 3670/108, 2000, 24.

[84] AMSP, *Letter from Stanisław Kracik*, May 14, 1999, act call no 3670/104, 1999, 11. There is some confusion as to the amount of this liability—Kracik mentions an indexation-induced debt of 6 million PLN, while in the last quarter of 1999 a reserve of 3.4 million PLN was created to cover "… an indexation agreement." AMSP, *Założenie do rachunku zysków I strat oraz bilansu Krakowskiej Fabryki Aparatów Pomiarowych Spółka Akcyjna za okres od 01 stycznia 2000 do 30 czerwca 2001 roku* (*Basis for the Profit and Loss statement and the balance of [KFAP] for January 1, 2000 to June 30, 2001*), act call no 3670/108, 2000, 21–22.

[85] *Elite interview with the Solidarity union chief.*

**Asset Depletion Method**
**(2a) Liquidation (Criminal Stage), From Passivity to Action—the State Delays Asset Stripping**

The fund, however, wanted to deal with the assets before actual liquidation. It thus began a procedure that was so obvious in its asset-stripping and detrimental effect to the company that the ministry of treasury felt forced to abandon its hitherto-practiced policy of passivity towards KFAP. Before the June 14, 1999 general shareholders' meeting that was to deal with liquidation, the fund called another general shareholders' meeting for May 24. At this meeting, the funds, now as dominant shareholders (it was about this time that the funds, in accordance with the program's timeline, became owners of their own equity and thus the state treasury lost its equity control over the funds, though it still retained a 25% equity share in program companies), passed a resolution allowing "… the management board to vend (dispose of) the factory-related real estate of [KFAP] by means of putting this real estate into [KFAP] dependent companies as contributions in the form of property or to sell this property to these companies, with the final manner of vending of these properties [a list was enclosed] to be decided by the supervisory board."[86] The SP was not passive; it joined the workers in opposing this resolution and in fact submitted a motion to the court (as did the union representatives) to declare this resolution invalid based on the argument that it was economically harmful to the company. In this lawsuit, the Minister of the Treasury Emil Wąsacz called for rescinding this resolution, as it "… violate[d] good commercial practice and harm[ed] the interests of the company." The minister's motion lists the property in question: 22 parcels of land, a total of 6.5 hectares "… constituting 95.6% …" of the company's land, with the value of the company's buildings on these parcels amounting to "… 84.5% of the value of the company's buildings and structures as shown in the balance of accounts for 1998." It is worthwhile quoting at length from the minister's justification for this lawsuit:

> As is apparent from the above, the management board of the company received permission to dispose of almost all of the factory property of the company. This disposal is to occur on behalf of entities that do not yet exist. These entities, described in the charged resolution as "dependent

[86] AMSP, *Uchwała z dnia 24 maja 1999 roku w sprawie zbycia nieruchomości fabrycznych KFAP S.A.* (*Resolution from May 24, 1999 concerning the vending of KFAP's factory real estate*), May 24, 1999, act call no 3670/105, 1999, 40.

companies" are to take over almost the entire activity of [KFAP]. Before the passage of the resolution, however, a plan of the undertaking of this entire transfer was not presented, nor is there a time scale for the vending of these assets and the business plans concerning the creation of these companies do not contain the amount of property, which is to be transferred. Nor was it designated, which of the listed properties are to be contributions in kind and to which company, and which are to be sold; the manner of valuation of these properties was also not defined. The equity share of KFAP in these companies that are to be created was also not designated.

It can be stated with complete certainty that the undertaking of this resolution will … threaten the continued activity … and existence … of the company; the value of its property will be drastically reduced, particularly since it is not known what value in terms of equity the company will receive for its contributions.

As one can notice, the decision to dispose of the company's factory property has as its purpose the removal from the company of as much property as possible and to avoid the need to vend the real estate by public auction, and the need to estimate the value of these properties … The execution of this resolution will cause the reduction of the value of the company and cause difficulties in having the company meet its liabilities ….[87]

## Tools of Control
## (10) Create Procedural Difficulties at Shareholder Meetings

The general shareholder's meeting of June 14, 1999, that was to liquidate the company, was held in Warsaw in the conference centre of the Polish army. The representatives of the SP and the workers had included in the official record that they did not receive materials for the meeting within the required time period, and thus it appears that the fund used the same procedural ploy that the union had back in 1996 when it tried to extricate KFAP from the fund. The SP rep made a motion to adjourn for four weeks while the worker shareholder rep made a motion to adjourn for thirty days and to move the proceedings to the company's headquarters in Cracow. These motions did not pass and as the meeting neared the culminating vote to liquidate the company, the record reveals moments that would resemble "Keystone Kops" scenes if not for the fact they concerned the hopes and

[87] AMSP, *Pozew o unieważnienie uchwały Nadzwyczajnego Walnego Zgromadzenia Spólki Akcyjnej* (*Motion to invalidate a resolution of an Exceptional Shareholders' Meeting*), June 18,1999, act call no. 3670/105, 1999, 96–98.

struggles of persons whose lives had revolved around KFAP's existence. Three times the voting machine broke down, necessitating longer and longer breaks, until finally the dominant shareholders voted to "… dissolve the company and begin the liquidation process[88] as of June 14, 1999," at the same time "… appointing the hitherto-existing management board [WT and GŁ] as liquidators."[89] For the workers, liquidation meant "… the layoff of our 550 employees."[90]

## A Buyer Appears—Secondary Privatization

In the meantime, however, a buyer for KFAP appeared. GH was a colourful Polish businessman with a reputation for successful investment in a wide variety of enterprises including pharmaceuticals, film, the press and even a plantation in Brazil.[91] He expressed an interest in buying both the funds' 60% equity and the 25% belonging to the SP. He apparently realized, however, that it would be best to come to some kind of agreement with the workers, and in a letter from May 21, 1999 to the SP he suggests that the final equity make up of the company could be 60% for his company, 15% for the individual workers and 25% for SPK (the worker created company).[92] According to the union chief:

> The fund wanted to sell our assets to Polish businessmen (who know nothing about our industry) for 10 million PLN … [when] the court rejected our motion for bankruptcy and so only liquidation remained … we negotiated with this expected buyer whereby in exchange for us resigning from our right to the 2 million PLN, [unpaid back wages resulting from wage indexation] he would not object to the workforce purchase of the state treasury's 25% shareholding. If we had that 25%, then we could have created a worker-owned enterprise that could, for example, be responsible for production and the buyer could have managed product sales, for example, through a separate entity—as well as selling off some of the expensive real estate.[93]

---

[88] The process of liquidation often can, and usually does, take a long time.

[89] AMSP, *Akt Notarialny (Public notary act)*, June 14, 1999, act call no. 3670/105, 1999, 102–107.

[90] *Elite interview with the Solidarity union chief.*

[91] See, for example, article by K. Tchórek, "Grzegorz Hajdarewicz: Press Owner Puts his Faith in New Media," *Financial Times*, November 1, 2011.

[92] AMSP, *Letter to director Siejda from GH*, May 21, 1999, act call no 3670/104, 1999, 12–13.

[93] *Elite interview with the Solidarity union chief.*

## The State Refuses to Sell its Equity Share to Workers

On July 5, in response to the workers' lawsuit, the court put on hold the execution of the May 24 resolution about disposal of company assets.[94] On July 20, GH signed a letter of intent with SPK to "... undertake common action to buy [KFAP] equity so as for [GH's company] to have 60% and SPK 25%."[95] In August, the ministry decided to annul the tender process of the sale of its 25% without providing a reason, though an internal document provides the following reason: "... SPK's financing is dependent upon an agreement on wage indexation and thus indirectly dependent upon the conclusion of the transaction between the majority fund and [GH's company] ... which has not yet taken place ... thus the indexation agreement, which was to finance [SPK's] transaction, is under a question mark."[96] The union chief describes the situation somewhat differently:

> The state treasury was willing to sell its shares for 18 PLN per share and we offered 18,01 PLN per share (there were no other buyers—the Polish buyer had agreed not to bid for the state treasury share[97]). But then the department director, Siejda, at the ministry learned that the fund was selling its 33% of shares, plus, by mutual agreement, the 27% that made up the minority fund holdings, to the Polish buyer for 23 PLN per share. So the department director annulled the transaction on the grounds that the ministry could get 5 PLN more per share if the Polish buyer also bought its share.[98] For the state treasury, 5 PLN per share was nothing, for us, it was a big amount—and we would have become a big player in our company—

---

[94] AMSP, *Postanowienie (Decision)*, July 5, 1999, act call no. 3670/106, 1999, 31.
[95] See AMSP, *Letter to director Siejda from GH.*
[96] AMSP, *Notatka Służbowa (Official Note)*, August 18, 1999, act call no 5578/2, 1999, 172.
[97] Though GH's company did apparently offer 18 PLN per share in a non-tender process earlier. AMSP, *Notatka Służbowa*, July 28, 1999, act call no 5578/2, 1999, 165.
[98] Indeed, after its transaction with the funds, GH offered the SP 23.31 PLN per share (November 16, 1999), though by the time this sales agreement with the State Treasury for its 25% holding (160,858 shares) was signed on June 8, 2000, this price per share had risen to 25.41 since the buy offer was indexed to inflation. Thus, at an average exchange rate at the time of 4.2 PLN to the USD, the difference for the SP between the buyer's offer and the that of the workers was between 202,987 USD and 283,416 USD. AMSP, *Umowa Sprzedaży Akcji* (*Contract to sell shares*), June 8, 2000, act call no 3973/164, 2000, 1–5.

along with the Polish buyer. A bit of revenue is one thing, but the societal aspect of the program should have been important as well.[99]

## The Fund Attempts to Indemnify its "Hit Men"

GH's transaction with the funds took place on September 14, 1999.[100] One day earlier, on September 13, the fund held its last general shareholders' meeting during which it proposed to have KFAP cover any costs needed to cover damages that WT and GŁ might have to pay third persons "… as result of the execution of their functions from January 1, 1998 to September 13, 1999, recognizing [that they] acted in good faith and … in the best interest of the company." W. T. and G. Ł.'s activity as liquidators (June 14, September 13, 1999) was to be officially approved by the shareholders, and in addition to their salaries both men were to receive bonuses of 120,000 PLN each.[101] And thus, one of the last acts of the fund in relation to KFAP was to indemnify (at KFAP's cost) its manager "hit team" from costs or legal claims as well as provide them with a generous departure package. The SP opposed all of these resolutions and for bonuses recommended a reduced amount of 85,000 and 65,000 PLN respectively.[102]

## The State Sells its Equity to the New Owner. The New Owner Obtains Right to Dispose of Company Assets

In a letter to the SP of January 28, 2000, KFAP's new management board "… in conjunction with a proposed court agreement between [KFAP] and SP … recognizes the resolution of May 24, 1999 [disposal of assets] to be invalid."[103] KFAP then agreed resolution wording with the SP that "… the price of the sale of the real estate cannot be less than its book value," with "the final conditions and manner of the vending of the property to be confirmed by the supervisory board."[104] The SP then agreed to abstain instead of opposing this resolution at the upcoming shareholders'

---

[99] *Elite interview with the Solidarity union chief.*
[100] A. Maciejewski, *Kalendarium Spółek.*
[101] AMSP, *Projekt Uchwały nr 5 (Draft resolution no 5)*, September 13, 1999, call no 3670/106, 1999, 16–18.
[102] AMSP, *Formularz dla członka rady nadzorczej (Form for a Member of a Supervisory Board)*, September 13, 1999, act call no 3670/106, 1999, 24–30.
[103] AMSP, *Letter*, dated January 26, 2000, act call no. 3670/108, 2000, 7.
[104] AMSP, *Letter*, dated January 27, 2000, act call no. 3670/108, 2000, 6.

meeting.[105] It is interesting to note that the list of KFAP company assets the vending to which SP acquiesced included 25 parcels of land and two office buildings having a total of more than 28,000 cubic metres of space,[106] and thus probably in the range of what was originally proposed eight months earlier. GH thus ended up with a green light to sell KFAP's property, and within six months of this agreement, as mentioned above, he finalized the purchase of SP equity, ending up with 85% of company shares. In 2001, what remained of what the KFAP production facility was moved to a new location and in 2004 sold to a Polish process control company from Toruń.[107]

KFAP's Solidarity trade union chief, who played a key role in the events described above, reflected in 2011:

> There was a point of view that a radical approach had to be taken towards industry since communism was so deeply ingrained in the system (no customer-first culture), I could understand where that point of view was coming from, but what then of the social costs? Why didn't the minister force the management firm to work on developing the companies in the program? Most of the companies in the MP program were the kind of companies that were not "quick return" companies but instead required strategic planning over 10 or more years, to increase technological infrastructure, productivity. Instead we were faced with young, gung-ho managers that wanted results in one or two years. Thus people began to turn against the idea of privatization. I often think that our company was cursed by the fact that we were located on real estate in Cracow that was rapidly going up in value. The land where our company was located is now home to a big shopping center. At the end of our travails … the former head of the supervisory board who was the vice-president of the management firm of our fund told us: "If your company was just 20 miles away, you would now be the owners."[108]

## Conclusion

The national investment funds and the private management firms chosen to govern them were entities brought forth by the state to prepare public property for privatization. The state adopted a passive oversight role

---

105 AMSP, *Letter*, dated January 28, 2000, act call no. 3670/108, 2000, 4.

106 AMSP, *Załącznik A do uchwały w przedmiocie sprzedaży nieruchomości fabrycznych* (*Annex A do the resolution concerning the sale of factory real estate*), January 26, 2000, act call no. 3670/108, 2000, 9.

107 KRS (Commercial Court) records, *Composite*, act call no 203801.

108 *Elite interview with the Solidarity union chief.*

towards these entities that resulted in their deficient, negligent and sometimes criminal management of this public property consisting of 512 mostly industrial firms. The result was a markedly smaller economy for Poland than would have been the case had this mass privatization experiment not taken place. This system of funds and private agents created by the state but bereft of its oversight, instead of using the profit motive to grow the economy and benefit the common wealth, focused on short-term gains to benefit the few and disadvantage the many.

A characteristic of a traumatic transformation is that it engenders many victims. These victims are often neither seen nor heard since a passive citizenry is not vocal. In this sense, the passivity of the state is also a civil society failure, since the state as the *politeia* is a reflection of its citizens.

Not all were passive, however, and this article is about a company's workforce that did not want to submit to economically harmful and societally errant forces. It was an unsuccessful struggle, however. The value of this article is that it identifies, describes and documents the mechanisms used in this process of economic dissolution.

Chris O'Neill is a PhD Candidate in Sociology at Cambridge University. He specializes in economic transformation, its processes and societal outcomes.

# CHAPTER TWENTY-ONE

# CHANGES IN THE CORPORATE ORGANISATION AS A RESPONSE TO GLOBALIZATION (WITH THE APPLICATION OF TRANSACTION COST ECONOMICS)

OSKAR BRASZCZYŃSKI

## Introduction

Changes in the organisational structure of corporations, which are evoked by the set of processes named globalization, constitute the core of this analysis. The argument uses the theory of costs of transaction and parts of institutional economics to highlight the most important factors and their roles in the structural changes.

This chapter analyses the changes that have occurred in the second phase of globalization, and which can be traced back to the early 1970s and marked by the collapse of the Bretton Woods System (1971) and the outburst of neo-liberal policy towards the liberalization of trade. The analysis of the second phase is accompanied by the presentation of different business models with differences in types of transactional costs, and by pathways of development in the structures which are supposed to be determined by transactional costs. The review ends with network enterprise, which could be regarded as an ultimate response to the globalization process.

New organisational forms, similar to those from the outset of the twentieth century, might be seen as determined by the rise of global markets, but in contrast to those previous they encompass a substantially bigger scale and scope. Due to this phenomenon, the corporate strategy followed by its structure is now projected on demand to the degree of its presence in foreign markets, and is closely connected with the different transactional costs inherently involved in each of them.

## Terms

To make the argument clear, the core terms call for precise definitions as they are differently conceptualized by many researchers.

## Globalization

The term "globalization" is as imprecise as it is multidimensional. This phenomenon is widely perceived, which often invites confusion. Manfred Steger, in his book *Globalization: A Very Short Introduction*,[1] provides a complex analysis of it, taking into consideration lots of possible dimensions, e.g. economic, social, political and cultural, but in order to indicate the factors of globalization which affect the corporate organisational structure, it is indispensable to point out only the main forces of this phenomenon, and define only the core of it. Following Steger, globalization can be described as "a set of social processes"[2] which constitutes the pace towards greater integration at various levels and the proliferation of interdependencies. He highlights that these interdependences have social characters and that they undergo constant creation, multiplication, stretching and intensification. These features of globalization lead to profound changes in all business spheres which affect the organisational structure. One can distinguish four kinds of these spheres as highlighted in the recapitulation made by Prechel & Boies: "changing strategies, capital markets, economic conditions and increased size and complexity."[3] All of these dimensions will be present in the following discussion about the roots of corporate change. As mentioned in the introduction, the whole period of globalization was divided into two major phases—the first is marked by the invention of the telegraph, making the world "wired" by 1870.[4] The second is undoubtedly connected with the collapse of the Bretton Woods System (1971), which triggered the unprecedented development of financial markets and coincided with a policy of trade liberalization in many developed countries.

---

[1] M. Steger, *Globalization: A Very Short Introduction* (New York: Oxford University Press, 2003).

[2] Ibid., 13

[3] H. Prechel, J. Boies, "Capital Dependence, Financial Risk, and Change from the Multidivisional to the Multilayered Subsidiary Form," *Sociological Forum* 2 (1998): 322.

[4] K. G. Persson, *An Economic History of Europe* (Cambridge: Cambridge University Press, 2010), 226.

## Foreign Direct Investment (FDI) and Transnational Corporations (TNC)

FDI is a type of investment made to acquire enterprises located and operating outside of the investor's economy,[5] or to build subsidiary from scratch (greenfield investment). In cases of FDI, according to UNCTAD, "the investor's purpose is to gain an effective voice in the management of the enterprise."[6]

Transnational corporations (TNCs) are those incorporated or unincorporated and consist of the parent enterprise and their foreign affiliates.[7] "A parent enterprise is defined as an enterprise that controls assets of other entities in countries other than its home country, usually by owning a certain equity capital stake."[8]

## Organisational Structure

The term "organisational structure" will be used in its basic, essential meaning, which could be described as the set of all functional and hierarchical dependencies between the elements of the organisation which are grouped into cells and units that enable achieving the goals of the whole. At the level of praxis, this term is about who reports to whom or who coordinates whom or what. It implicates that the structure predominantly affects how the information and power connected with responsibilities flow between the agents of the organisation.

## Transactional costs

Transactional costs constitute the key element of the New Institutional Economics or New Economics of Organization. The definition of these costs provided by Kenneth Arrow is the "costs of running the economic system."[9] Moreover, Williamson highlights that these types of costs

---

[5] UNCTAD, *Foreign Direct Investment (FDI)*, http://unctad.org/en/Pages/DIAE/Foreign-Direct-Investment-(FDI).aspx (accessed January 24, 2013).

[6] Ibid.

[7] UNCTAD, *Transnational Corporations (TNC)*, http://unctad.org/en/Pages/DIAE/Transnational-corporations-(TNC).aspx (accessed January 24, 2013).

[8] Ibid.

[9] O. E. Williamson, *The Economic Institutions of Capitalism: Firms, Markets, Relational Contracting*, http://www.sp.uconn.edu/~langlois/Williamson

differentiate from those generally recognized by the neoclassical approach, i.e. the costs of production. He compares transaction costs to "friction in physics"[10] and provides a convincing argument that due to the assumption of absence of friction of air that led to spectacular success in the determination of core elements of complex physical systems, social scientist followed such a pattern. It has reached its exemplification in the Friedman position, stating that real analytical capabilities can stem from not-realistic presumptions. There is no doubt today that these types of costs contribute hugely to the efficiency and performance of the company/organisation in general. Williamson differentiates two types of transactional costs: "*ex ante*" and "*ex post*." Those named *ex ante* are primarily connected with preparing (sketching), negotiating and supervising an agreement, so in general with bringing about a contract. The letters are triggered by the necessity of stating whether the transaction has taken place in accordance with the agreed conditions/contract.[11]

Ronald Coase, in his early but profound analysis of transactional costs "The Nature of the Firm," proved that the main reason for the emergence of a firm as such is the plain fact that the price mechanism generates some costs itself (costs of negotiation, entering into contracts or setting prices). For this reason, an abandonment of the mechanism of prices for administrative coordination in the form of the firm becomes justified.[12]

In this particular meaning, the mechanism of prices (market) and the corporate control constitute alternative forms of the organisation of production. The essence of the firm is therefore derived from relations of exchange between the capitalist agents.[13] Moreover, those agents are "subject to bounded rationality and … at least some agents are given to opportunism."[14]

New institutional economics could be viewed as an interdisciplinary approach towards market phenomena, and transactions in particular. This type of economics is concentrated on the integration of three different fields of science engaged in determining the conditions for doing business: economics per se, theory of organisation and law. The NIE can be divided into two main sub theories: the first is the theory of agency and property,

%20(1985),%20chapter%201.pdf (accessed January 24, 2013).

[10] Ibid., 19.

[11] M. Gorynia, "Przedsiębiorstwo w nowej ekonomii instytucjonalnej," *Ekonomista* 6 (1999): 787.

[12] Ibid., 786.

[13] Ibid.

[14] O. E. Williamson, "The Economics of Organization: The Transaction Cost Approach," *The American Journal of Sociology* 3 (1981): 553.

and the second the theory of transactional costs.[15] For this chapter, the latter is more important. Nevertheless, the theory of agency can also provide an insight into the determinants of the initial changes of corporate structure, so I will start with it.

## Analysis of Changes in the Second Phase of Globalization

Globalization in the mentioned definition is understood as a set of social (for the purpose of this argument, economic only) processes constituting a pace towards greater integration, which results in the proliferation of interdependencies which undergo creation, multiplication, stretching and intensification.[16] Two features of this phenomenon—greater integration and intensified interdependences—are now relevant for the following discussion, as both can be easily used to describe the corporate organisational response to globalization in its second phase which can be traced back to the collapse of the Bretton Woods System in 1971, when the policies towards liberalization of trade and proliferation of financial markets of many countries came together with derivative ones. The complexity of business activities arising in the mentioned processes together with greater flexibility and task specialization in particular geographic regions were the main determinants of new changes in corporate organisational structures. They were, of course, associated with new transactional costs, which had to be minimised by means of the imposition of new structures. It is worth mentioning that this phase of globalization was marked by the previously non-existent proliferation of transnational corporations as their number rose from 7,000 in 1970 to 40,000 in 1995.[17] This made them extremely powerful supranational agents and dramatically increased the competition between them, what also triggered the need for the minimization of transaction costs and structural changes.

In contrast to the first stage of globalization, where the main determinants for structural changes were the type of production and the pattern of its integration-influencing strategy, the new main determinant in the second phase could be named the integration responsiveness

[15] Ibid., 779.
[16] M. Steger, *Globalization*, 13.
[17] See J. Dine, *The Governance of Corporate Groups* (Cambridge: Cambridge University Press, 2000), 152.

framework,[18] which comes not from production but from the need to act both locally and globally.

Nowadays, due to the mentioned complexity of both manufacturing processes and business organisation processes, transnational corporations enter new markets and try to use the local peculiarities of each to boost efficiency and maximize profits. Entering new markets often means employing people with different cultural roots who exercise the general corporate culture, and setting contracts in various conditions (i.e. legal, cultural and societal). In order to maintain both, constructive work must exist among employees and business operations in various local business contexts, which inherently evoke certain new transactional costs connected with negotiations, processing information in various languages under various legal systems, political conditions and informal institutions, and transnational companies (TNCs) must adapt their whole organisational structures.

Making connections between local contexts constitutes the key challenge in gaining a competitive advantage in realising the general company strategy on a global scale.[19] Chandler's finding that structure follows strategy still holds, but the peculiarity nowadays is that, while defining strategy, local conditions and determinants must be considered. Moreover, each strategy is followed by a complementary structure which involves certain types of transactional costs.

The creativity and participation of employees in terms of providing initiatives are now understood as the core points conditioning the overall performance and are regarded as the core assets (e.g. in consulting and financial TNCs). That is why the vertical organisation based on predominant hierarchy is no longer possible. TNCs nowadays are reported to be knowledge-intensive organisations and both processing and inventing knowledge are costly if centrally planned. That is why TNCs are grouping people responsible for creation and making use of knowledge in a more flexible way by establishing units shaped for the local business and cultural environments.[20] Units can effectively minimize transactional costs because they are created for special purposes and engage people who are in a constant process of acquiring knowledge of a particular business environment. This knowledge is indispensable for setting contracts and their servicing is a minimal cost. Moreover, a specific group of people devoted to work in one environment achieves trust from

[18] M. Peng, K. Meyer, *International Business* (London: Cengage Learning EMEA, 2011), 457.
[19] Ibid., 457.
[20] Ibid.

partners/contractors, which also contributes to the minimization of transactional costs. Nevertheless, some *ex ante* and *ex post* costs of transactions are deeply rooted in the nature of each business strategy and structure. It is worth reviewing these structures to identify the mentioned costs and draw more elaborated conclusions about them.

## The Global Models of Business

Before going into an explanation of the change in the structures of today's highly specialised TNCs, it is essential to provide the general international business models. Pankaj Ghemawat, professor of general management at IESE, constructed a special framework for moving towards integration on a global scale, named the AAA triangle, for Adaptation, Aggregation and Arbitrage.[21]

Fig. 21.1 Adaptation, Aggregation and Arbitrage triangle

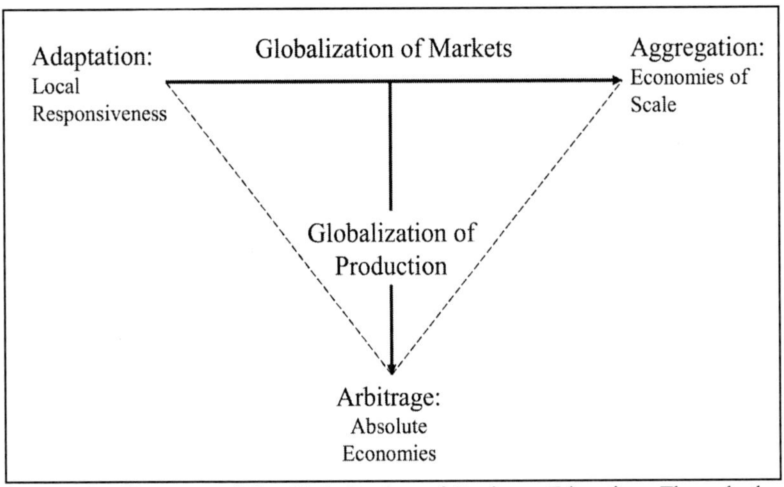


Source: P. Ghemawat, "The Globalization of Business Education: Through the Lens of Semiglobalization," *Journal of Management Development* 27 (2008), http://dx.doi.org/10.1108/02621710810866741 (accessed December 25, 2012).

He argues that the key aim of any global strategy is to cope with the huge differences experienced and observed while crossing borders. By this

[21] P. Ghemawat, "How to Choose Your Global Strategy," *Notes on Globalization and Strategy* 9 (2007): 4.

argument, he doubts whether maintaining balance between benefits from the economy of scale and local responsiveness is a super goal.[22] Moreover, he highlights that by assuming this goal, companies ignore one profitable strategy in the form of arbitrage, which exploits the differences between markets placed in different countries or regions.[23] Adaptation strategy, on the other hand, is focused on providing the market with products shaped and adapted for local customers, taking into consideration both preferences and purchasing power.[24] The last corner of the triangle, aggregation, is primarily engaged in such an organisation of activities in order to achieve the effect of synergy between differently located activities. It could often be made by the means of product standardization or just sharing common resources. Above all, it can be pursued by the regroupment of particular tasks to form aggregated business units (of research and development, production and marketing) at the level of regions sharing the same languages.[25]

The presentation of business models is necessary as each involves different transactional costs, which therefore implicates a different organisational structure. The dominance of adaptation strategy is mainly followed by a country-centred type of organisation as it involves costs of adapting products to specific local needs, such as those of constant gathering and processing information. Aggregation comes paired with cross border units of different types, such as product divisions, regional departments, specific business units, etc.[26]

Certain types of corporate organisational structure, such as matrix or tensor, follow the combination of these types of strategies, which is costly (in terms of transactions costs) as it involves processing knowledge and information at more than one level at the same time, but the potential from the synergy effect could be immense. Gehemwat gives examples of such companies as Procter & Gable pursuing aggregation and adaptation, or Tata Consultancy Service realizing both aggregation and arbitrage.[27] Only between arbitrage and adaptation is there a trade off and that is mainly why the most common framework of management applied to TNS is based on the connection between integration and adaptation and is named the

---

[22] Ibid.

[23] P. Ghemawat, *How to Choose Your Global Strategy*, 5

[24] M. Peng, K. Meyer, *International Business*, 429; P. Ghemawat, *How to Choose Your Global Strategy*, 4.

[25] Ibid.

[26] P.Ghemawat *How to Choose Your Global Strategy, passim.*

[27] Ibid., 5.

integration-responsiveness framework.[28] It makes full use of simple-to-understand profits from the economy of scale,[29] being at the same time locally responsive, and benefits from satisfying the different needs of different customers. A good example of this is the special version of a McDonald's sandwich for Poland named the "WieśMac." But, pursuing both strategies simultaneously is not fully possible, and the capability for TNCs to implement them varies and can take the form of one of four strategies arising from the concentration of different degrees of adaptation and aggregation. All of them can be presented in the form of the matrix in Fig. 21.2 below.

Fig. 21.2 Models of corporate strategies and structures

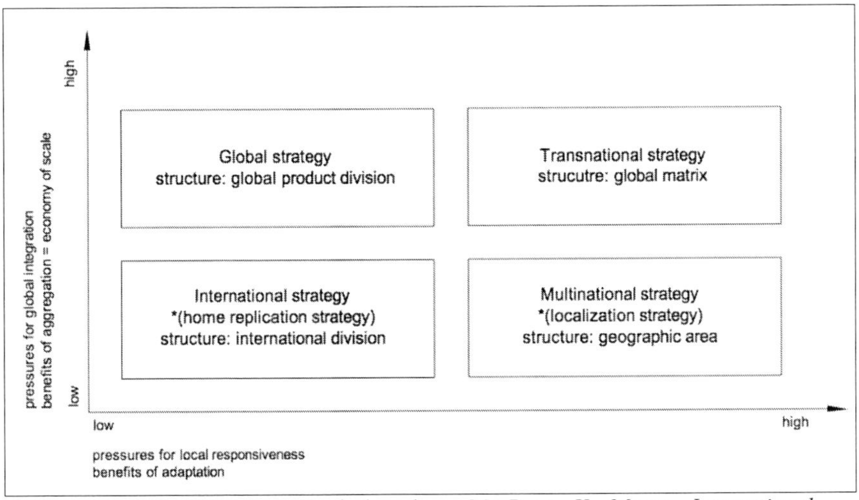


Source: Author's own research based on M. Peng, K. Meyer, *International Business*; B. Swoboda et al., *Preferences and Performance of International Strategies in Retail Sectors: An Empirical Study*, http://dx.doi.org/10.1016/j.lrp.2012.05.002 (accessed January 25, 2013).

## International Strategy and International Division Structure

International strategy assumes the near duplication of home-based features, e.g. level of production output, positioning of a brand, and

[28] M. Peng, K. Meyer, *International Business*, 457.

[29] Ibid.

distribution strategies and channels,[30] so it is based on a transfer of distinct capabilities which constitutes its main advantage. Regarding cons, the main one is the near absence of local responsiveness. This mode of entry is simple and does not demand a lot of experience, and is therefore used by firms for first-time entry.

This strategy is often followed by an international division structure. In this type of structure, all foreign subsidiaries have to report to a main and single international division—the corporate headquarters—and a "top executive at a corporate level is in charge of all foreign operations."[31] This model of organisation is not limited to the second stage of globalization alone, and became widely used in early post-war times as underlined by Bartlett & Ghoshal: "The key task for companies that internationalized then was to transfer knowledge and expertise to overseas environments that were less advanced in technology or market development."[32]

This type of structure arouses two major problems in terms of transactional costs. The first is the not-so-strong position of foreign subsidiary managers in comparison to domestic division managers, which results in a lack of transferring knowledge acquired abroad, therefore increasing costs of transaction. The second is the fact that the activities of international division are not coupled with those in domestic divisions. The performance of contracts made abroad is therefore not compared with the domestic one. In the outcome, the forecasting of trends and market failures is mitigated due to huge transactional costs. These drawbacks make that structure useless for supranational tycoons and were probably the main reason for its change (by large companies with experience in FDI) during the progression of globalization.

International division constitutes the central point in increasing the foreign engagement of firms through foreign direct investments (FDI), gathering international knowledge and experience in one place.[33] Further

---

[30] M. Peng, K. Meyer, *International Business*, 458.

[31] M. Habib, B. Victor, "Strategy, Structure and Performance of U.S. Manufacturing and Service MNCs: A Comparative Analysis," *Strategic Management Journal* 8 (1991), http://www.jstor.org/stable/2486335, (accessed December 28, 2012).

[32] C. A. Bartlett, S. Ghoshal, *Managing Across Borders: The Transnational Solution* (Boston: Harvard Business School Press, 1989), 49.

[33] A. Tobolska, "Strategie globalne a nowe formy organizacji przedsiębiorstw transnarodowych," in Z. Zioło, T. Rachwał (eds.), *Rola przedsiębiorczości w podnoszeniu konkurencyjności społeczeństwa i gospodarki: Seria Przedsiębiorczość—Edukacja vol.2* (Warszawa-Kraków: Akademia Pedagogiczna w Krakowie, Wydawnictwo Nowa Era, 2006), 131–132.

internationalization through FDI comes with the need for more strict control and planning of international activities of domestic corporations[34] in order to minimalize costs of transactions inherent in the international division structure and triggered by the disadvantages mentioned above. In most international organisations this leads to the replacement of international division structures with more global structures, which can be organised on the basis of product, geographical or functional lines of subordination.[35] Change in the strategy leads to change in the structure in accordance with Chandler's pattern.

## Global Strategy and Global Product Division Structure

Global strategy has its roots in Theodor Levitt's famous and provocative article entitled "The Globalization of Markets," in which he said: "Everywhere everything gets more and more like everything else as the world's preference structure is relentlessly homogenized."[36] This strategy is based on the development, manufacturing and distribution of globally standardised products. The approach is aimed at grasping benefits from the economy of scale and shared product creation and development. The best examples of this may be McDonald's or Coca-Cola.

The strategy of global product division follows this structure, in which the organisation is divided according to the developed and offered products. An executive at a corporate level primarily responsible for both international and domestic tasks connected with the particular product heads each of the product departments/divisions. The foreign subsidiaries must report to the heads of product divisions at the top executive level of the structure.[37]

This type of structure allows for minimalizing various costs, such as transactional costs connected with processing the information about the product and *ex ante* type (sketching contracts), and production costs by global consolidation. This structure was adapted by the majority of TNCs involved in multi-line businesses, sometimes with a supplement in the form of regional departments within product divisions.[38]

---

[34] See Ibid.

[35] Ibid.

[36] T. Levitt, "The Globalization of Markets," Boston 1983, reprinted in *The McKinsey Quarterly*, Summer 1984, http://www.lapres.net/levit.pdf (accessed December 28, 2012).

[37] M. Habib, B. Victor, *Strategy, Structure and Performance of U.S. Manufacturing and Service MNCs*.

[38] Ibid.

Despite benefits from consolidation, there are certain drawbacks related to the communication sphere, as product divisions almost separate even if they operate on the same market and could benefit, in the form of minimization of costs of transactions, from exchanging knowledge with other divisions. The synergy effect is therefore lost.

## Localization Strategy and Geographic Structure

The Multinational-Localization strategy relies on a view of each country or region as a separate market worth pursuing in the adaptation of products. The benefits of the economy of scale are diminished but there can be some rooted in satisfying customers, being well-shaped for their needs and wants.

This strategy implicates the geographic-area structure. It is this which divides operations according to specific regions, each being headed by a high executive at the level of the corporation. Foreign subsidiaries must report to the regional heads and are responsible for overall activities.[39]

High transactional costs may arise due to the duplication of *ex ante* costs in multiple countries (sketching contracts, preparing transactions, developing negotiation plans) but they can benefit from the *ex post* costs by having geographic specialization, acquiring the knowledge of how to cope with breaches of contracts (contract failures) in particular legal, cultural and societal environments.

## The Transnational Strategy and Matrix Structure

The step toward greater coordination and integration of global functional, product and geographical responsibilities comes in the form of a matrix structure, which follows a transnational strategy and whose purpose is to grasp the best features of aggregation and adaptation to benefit from the economy of scale, together with cost efficiency and local responsiveness. This strategy is also based on learning and sharing knowledge between worldwide units. The transnational strategy is the most complex of all and therefore not easy to introduce. It requires the sharing and coordination of huge amounts of different types of complex knowledge, affecting the efficiency of the decision-making process and possibly giving rise to *ex ante* transaction costs. Nevertheless, the strategy allows for the exploitation of benefits from the experience curve and the customization of product in not having to resign absolutely from costs efficiency.

---

[39] Ibid.

In the matrix structure one can observe the mixture of global product and geographic area structures; however, this mixture has an emergent character. The middle-level line manager has two roles and must report to two higher entities responsible for the whole extent of two spheres, e.g. product divisions and geographic areas.

The matrix structure is hard and costly to implement, but when implemented well can bring about a huge minimization of transactional costs. Constant processing and sharing knowledge about markets and contacts between various units of a company constitute the most important advantages. There is no simple transferring of knowledge from headquarters to subsidiaries, but this processing is two sided and can also occur on the cross-divisions level. Therefore, it is much easier to gather data to sketch better contracts and create knowledge and skills on how to manage them and foresee what is going on in global market trends, and which spheres are vulnerable to failing.

## Tensor Structure and Network Strategy

The tensor structure is a three-dimensional model of organisational structure involving the same pros and cons as the matrix structure. It stems from the need to combine more than two dimensions, as in the case of a company which implemented a matrix structure combining divisional and functional lines of subordination, eager to involve multi-geographic business activities in its present structure.[40] In this type of structure, and in multidimensional ones in general, organisational units of a lower level are subordinated to a multipoint management system and existing problems and conflicts reach their solutions on the basis of equal partnership by managers responsible for different organisational dimensions.[41] This multi-dimensional structure links benefits from adaptation and flexibility with a consideration of market needs and the conditions of business and integration (economy of scale).[42] Due to this fact it is often implemented by international service firms which are characterized by the necessity of functional and industry-related proficiency in each region.

In the classical view on stages of internationalization, the path is as follows: (a) development of product and domestic sale, (b) export stage,

---

[40] S. Dressler, *Strategy, Organizational Effectiveness and Performance Management: From Basics to Best Practices* (Boca Raton: Universal Publishers, 2004), 95.

[41] A. Tobolska, *Strategie globalne a nowe formy organizacji przedsiębiorstw*, 133.

[42] S. Dressler, *Strategy, Organizational Effectiveness and Performance Management*, 98.

and (c) export is replaced by FDI,[43] which could be viewed as an instrument of minimization of transactional costs, especially *ex post* as it is much harder to manage transaction by just selling abroad than installing a subsidiary in the particular business environment.

## Pathways of Development of Corporate Structure

J. M. Stopford and L. T. Wells, following Chandler's "structure follows strategy"[44] idea, developed the evolutionary path of the structure of international organisations/corporations. They precisely defined development trends coupled with the extent of internationalization. If a company sells only a limited range of products abroad, which constitutes a small percentage of revenue, then it can pursue this using international division.[45] The increase of product diversity implicates, in most cases, structural change in the form of product division,[46] as transactional costs both *ex ante* and *ex post* are elevated due to the necessity of sketching different contracts under different legal and political regimes, negotiating and supervising them, often resulting in lawsuits, posing more costs. These corporations, whose sales increase without extending the range of product lines, often change their structures to those of the geographic area. The evolutionary pattern ends with matrix structure being the one capable of managing transactional and costs of production of TNCs, whose revenue is mainly dependent on selling abroad, and their range of products or services is diverse and wide, which calls for great local responsiveness. The matrix structure following a transnational strategy could be regarded as the ultimate response toward globalization with all its blessings (benefits from the economy of scale) and drawbacks (great costs of managing the structure and implementation). This structure is based on the characteristics of globalization. Following Steger, as mentioned earlier, globalization could be described as "a set of social processes"[47] which constitutes the move towards greater integration at various levels and the proliferation of interdependencies. All of these features at the forefront of complex structures and the internal interdependencies within it are

[43] S. Segal-Horn, D. Faulkner, *The Dynamics of International Strategy* (London: Cengage Learning EMEA 1999), 111.

[44] A. D. Chandler, *Strategy and Structure: Chapters in the History of the American Industrial Enterprise* (Washington, D.C.: Beard Book, 2003).

[45] A. Tobolska, *Strategie globalne a nowe formy organizacji przedsiębiorstw*, 132.

[46] S. Segal-Horn, D. Faulkner, *The Dynamics of International Strategy*, 112.

[47] M. Steger, *Globalization*, 13.

managed by the matrix structure and its extensions in the form of the tensor structure, for example.

Fig. 22.3 Stopford & Wells matrix

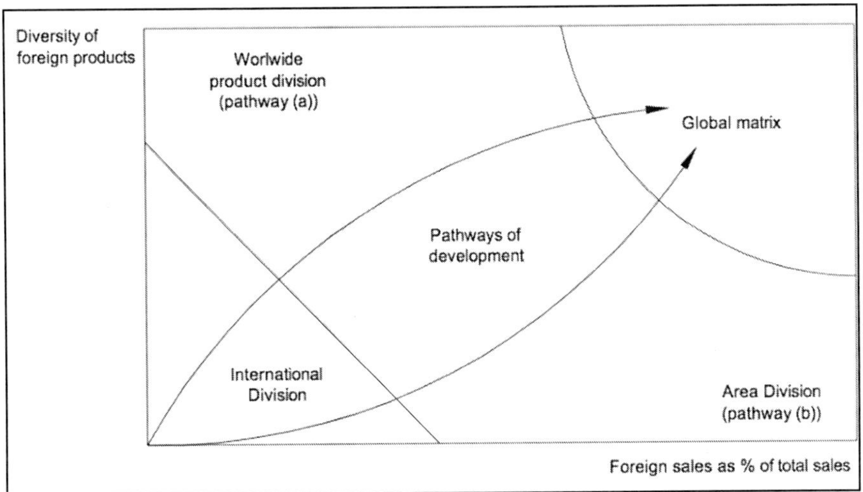


Source: S. Segal-Horn, D. Faulkner, *The Dynamics of International Strategy*, 112.

The presented model has a pure descriptive character and skips an important dimension of the organisation of TNCs. This dimension is well explained by a metaphor developed by Christopher Bartlett, who implied that each organisation has its anatomy (formal structure) but also a physiology (key management processes) and a psychology (ideas, outlooks of their executives and managers).[48] Every analysis should therefore take these other spheres into consideration. For this reason, some researchers outline that while structuring TNC stress should be put on building an organisational culture based on common visions and principles. Competition between TNCs in the second phase of globalization has become overwhelming. Forced to compete, TNCs must simultaneously optimize their efficiency, flexibility and learning processes.[49] Moreover, the recommendation of matching organisational structures to business macro and micro environmental demands totters as

[48] S. Ghoshal, N. Noria, "Horses for Courses: Organizational Forms for Multinational Corporations," *Sloan Management Review* (Winter 1993): 24.
[49] C. A. Bartlett, S. Ghoshal, *Managing Across Borders*, 18.

environments are still not as stable as organisations.[50] These entities are in constant flux, which triggers transactional costs from the mismatch. That is why fit and flexibility are both needed. This need could be partly satisfied in the outsourcing processes comprising a new form of cooperation and management in TNCs. Within globalization, the so-called information revolution, triggered by the unprecedented development of communication technology, enabled the realization of new forms of cooperation called the network.[51] From this time, the economy has undergone the gradual replacement of hierarchical corporate structures by more dispersed ones marking the emergence of network enterprises: "The model became manifested in the form of a network of contracts, opening up new roles for corporate culture and behavioural ethics."[52] This somehow constitutes Barlett's psychology. As an analysis by Stanisław Łobejko outlines, this peculiar type of enterprise is primarily based on contracts set with external entities. This happens not with the application of market mechanisms of the classical type, based on economic equilibrium, but a network market where price is still a determinant, but not the only one.[53] This peculiarity of transactions made inside the network is the main determinant of the lower transactional costs compared to those prevailing on the market *per se*.[54] Moreover, the costs of setting contracts and coordination are much lower in the network due to the higher degree of trust. That is why this type of organisation is fruitful when implicated with transnational corporations in globalised markets when the majority of contracts are complex ones.

## Conclusions

Having analyzed the connections between corporate organisational structure and globalization and their mutual implications on the grounds of the theory of transactional costs, one general conclusion can be drawn. The corporate organisational structure undergoes a change in the moment when transactional costs, both inside and outside of the company, are too high and can be minimized by change in the organisation. This stems from

[50] S. Ghoshal, N. Noria, *Horses for Courses*, 24.

[51] S. Łobejko, *Wykorzystanie kosztów transakcyjnych, jako czynnika rozwoju przedsiębiorstw sieciowych*, http://www.sgh.waw.pl/katedry/karik/Referat20/S._Lobejko_Wykorzystanie_kosztow_transakcyjnychw_przeds._sieciowych.doc (accessed December 28, 2012).

[52] G. Dioguardi, *Network Enterprises Springer* (New York: Springer, 2010), 33.

[53] S. Łobejko, *Wykorzystanie kosztów transakcyjnych*, 18.

[54] Ibid.

the observation that the costs of transaction are inherently connected with the dispersion of information (and processing it), rooted in the complexity and variety of tasks and contracts (in the meaning of New Institutional Economics [NIE]) that the particular company has to deal with. Above all, there is a general strategy of the corporation which determines the dispersion of information, and therefore transactional costs.

The strategy of the corporation is a response to the set of processes towards creating global markets and the liberalization of trade named globalization. That is why the change of structure must be viewed as a response to globalizing markets. It seems that both the natures of the strategic and organisational changes differ between the first phase of globalization that started in the late nineteenth century and the second, which can be traced back to the early 1970s and is marked by the collapse of the Bretton Woods System (1971), followed by the outburst of the neoliberal policy towards the liberalization of trade. The main trigger for the change of strategy and therefore change of structure was connected with the internationalization of production. The ultimate response of corporate structure to economic globalization is the abandonment of the classical hierarchy to be replaced by the emergence of the network enterprise, in which transactional costs are substantially lower if complex contracts and transactions (characteristic to global market) prevail.

Oskar Braszczyński is a student of Interdisciplinary Studies in Humanities at the University of Wrocław and of International Business at the Wrocław University of Economics. His main field of research is connected with the economic and social dimensions of globalization. He likes sailing and skiing.

# CHAPTER TWENTY-TWO

# HOW WALL STREET CHANGED MAIN STREET: UNNOTICED AGENCY PROBLEMS THAT LEAD TO FINANCIAL CRISES[1]

MATEUSZ TRAWIŃSKI

## Introduction

It is commonly said that we are experiencing the biggest recession since the Great Depression in the 1930s. In the present chapter we focus on one dimension of the causes of this crisis—the relations of agency and how they influenced people's choices in various social hierarchy dimensions. The two streets in the title suggest two strong interest groups which seem to be very different. Wall Street represents the financial sector and Main Street is a symbol of the average American—two groups with two different lifestyles, aspirations and possibilities. But in this chapter we show that they have one important thing in common—they both speculated on the assets that they managed. While top managers from Wall Street speculated on securitized mortgage loans, ordinary citizens speculated with the value of their houses.

The analytical perspective of the present chapter is agency theory. It shows what problems are faced by contemporary capitalism and that without proper regulatory policies and individual responsibility we will not be able to end this crisis soon. By focusing on one specific empirical case we show the durability and risks embedded in complex principal-agent relations and how they affect economic and financial systems as a whole. From the perspective of sociology we underline how the Wall

[1] The author acknowledges financial support from the Nicolaus Copernicus University, grant number 328-H.

Street pattern of making money was unintentionally transformed to regular society and how this phenomenon affected people's behaviour. We also identify specific agency problems that arise and that should be regulated at different institutional levels of the contemporary market and society.

## How Wealth is Created

The two main ways to create wealth are soundly described by two prominent researchers, John Foster and Fred Magdoff:

> Marx expressed the accumulation of capital through investment as M-C-M', M(oney) capital is used to purchase raw materials, machines, and labour to produce C(omodities), which are then sold, with the capital receiving back M'—the original money plus Δm, the surplus value produced by labour. In the financial circuit of capital, in contrast, money makes more money directly, represented by Marx as M-M.'[2]

While Wall Street tends to turn money into more money, American society, which is seen as highly entrepreneurial, should create added value with its labour. In the present chapter we will show that a perverted M-M' model leads to excessive risk-taking by bank managers, regulators and mortgage lenders. Even more importantly for sociologists, we will show some indicators that this model was acquired by an American society that speculated with the value of their homes to gain financial benefits. The analysis of the spectacular fall of the Washington Mutual Bank will show how unregulated agency problems contributed to the financial crisis and how the M-M' model of money making reached Main Street.

## Agency Theory

Agency theory, also known as the principal-agent theory, was developed mainly within economics. It describes the primary social relationships existing not only in the economic sphere, but also in almost every area of society that is based on the division of labour.[3] To describe the agency relationship at the most general level it is therefore necessary to build a general social theory. Trying to determine the descriptive scope of the agency theory we can refer to the definition formulated by Stephen Ross, who wrote that:

---

[2] J. Foster, F. Magdoff, *The Great Financial Crisis: Causes and Consequences* (New York: Monthly Review Press, 2009), 45.

[3] E. Durkheim, *The Division of Labor in Society* (New York: Free Press, 1997).

> The relationship of agency is one of the oldest and commonest codified modes of social interaction. We will say that an agency relationship has arisen between two (or more) parties when one, designated as the agent, acts for, on behalf of, or as representative for the other, designated the principal, in a particular domain of decision problems. Examples of agency are universal. Essentially all contractual arrangements, as between employer and employee or the state and the governed, for example, contain important elements of agency.[4]

Agency theory is used to describe situations that involve the delegation of tasks and accountability which are the basic foundations of collective action. Key assumptions of agency theory are presented in a book by Charles Perrow, where he underlines that:

> Three assumptions are at the core of agency theory. The first is the one common to most economists: individuals maximize their own self-interest. The second is more specific to agency theory: social life is a series of contracts, or exchanges, governed by competitive self-interest. The third applies to internal organizational analysis: monitoring contracts is costly and somewhat ineffective, especially in organizations, thus encouraging self-interested behaviour, shirking, and especially opportunism with guile, or to put it more simply—cheating. Contracts will be violated because of self-interest, and can be violated because of the costs and ineffectiveness of surveillance. The theory then attempts to build models, almost always without empirical data, regarding the most effective ways to write and monitor contracts to minimize their violations.[5]

The spectacular development of Western civilization and the success of the free market show that the social system based on a complex division of labour, that is powerful agency relations, is very efficient. The agency theory underlines, however, that every such relationship entails costs. In the literature they are called agency problems. In the literature of the subject, one can highlight many of them—from the perspective of this text we are interested in five:

(1) Adverse selection—the principal almost never sees the real abilities of the agent when they hire them. Hence, the selection of agents must be carried out using indirect indicators. However, the indicators do not reflect the practical competences of agents, and

[4] S. Ross, "The Economic Theory of Agency: the Principal's Problem," *American Economic Review* (1973): 134.

[5] Ch. Perrow, "Economic Theories of Organization," *Theory and Society* (1986): 12.

therefore the selection process is sometimes passed not by the most competent candidates, but by those who did best in the recruitment process.[6]

(2) Agent's Opportunism—no agent is controlled in all aspects of their work and decisions. In the course of performing tasks the agent can take advantage of some upcoming events that give them personal benefits at the expense of their principal.[7] The problem turns out to be very important with regards to the fact that there are no standardized tools to recognize opportunistic individuals in the recruitment process.

(3) Information asymmetries—the agent, being delegated to perform specific tasks, is always better informed about the actual situation in the case of their responsibilities. An informational advantage over the principal can make the agent use their knowledge for the achievement of objectives that are contrary to the formally entrusted role.[8] Information asymmetry is particularly important due to the fact that it is a systemic factor that leads to opportunistic behaviour.

(4) Moral hazard—in the case of agency relation, part of making some decisions is the responsibility of the agent. They may and most commonly do bear their consequences. However, the consequences of an agent's actions do not involve only themselves but also their principal. Moral hazard arises in specific situations where the decision-making entity, at least partially insured (i.e. not bearing all the consequences of their actions), begins to seek more risks than they would without such insurance.[9] The phenomenon of moral hazard is indicated as one of the significant variables that had an impact on the occurrence of the financial crisis.[10]

(5) Conflict of interest—the objectives of the principal and the agent are almost never fully identical. Conflict of interest arises when a

---

[6] K. M. Eisenhardt, "Agency Theory: An Assessment and Review," *Academy of Management Review* (1989): 61.

[7] E. Kiser, "Comparing Varieties of Agency Theory in Economics, Political Science, and Sociology: An Illustration from State Policy Implementation," *Sociological Theory* (1999): 163.

[8] S. Shapiro, "Agency Theory," *Annual Review of Sociology* (2005): 267.

[9] Ch. Perrow, "Economic Theories of Organization," *Theory and Society* (1986): 20.

[10] R. Masera, "Taking the Moral Hazard out of Banking: the Next Fundamental Step in Financial Reform," *PSL Quarterly Review* (2011): 105–142.

> contradiction between the interests of the principal and the agent affects the agent's decision, which does not comply with their formal objectives—representing the interests of the principal.[11]

As we can see from the above definitions, not only are five basic agency problems closely linked with the very existence of the principal-agent relation, but also agents are often so interrelated that it is very difficult to analyze them in isolation. The fundamental challenge of the agency relation that the principal faces is the need to monitor the actions of the agent. However, as already mentioned in the quotation by Charles Perrow, control causes additional costs that are not purely economic. One of them is the increased complexity of the entire system and further development of the agency relations, since the most common controller is not the principal themselves, but another agent. In general, there are three basic methods of solving the agency problems:

(1) Appropriate selection agents—the system of proper selection of agents is crucial for overcoming agency problems.[12] Some researchers underline the informal factors that affect the selection of agents—sometimes principals try to employ individuals who share the same values and are loyal.[13]
(2) Control mechanisms—principals form certain tools (e.g. audit) to verify that the agent behaves according to their interest. Another way is to design incentives that bring together the objectives of an agent and the principal.[14]
(3) Contracts—the very definition of the agency relation points out that the ratio of principal and agent is in the form of a contract. The basic tool to control an agent is therefore to formulate the contract properly. Contracts may take two basic forms:

---

[11] R. Waterman, K. Meier, "Principal-Agent Models: An Expansion?," *Journal of Public Administration Research and Theory* (1998): 187.
[12] T. M. Moe, "The New Economics of Organization," *American Journal of Political Science* (1984): 756.
[13] E. Kiser, "Comparing Varieties of Agency Theory in Economics, Political Science, and Sociology: An Illustration from State Policy Implementation," *Sociological Theory* (1999): 156.
[14] B. M. Mitnick, "Fiduciary Rationality and Public Policy: The Theory of Agency and Some Consequences," paper presented at the 1973 Annual Meeting of the American Political Science Association, http://ssrn.com/abstract=1020859 (accessed June 1, 2013).

Behavior-Oriented Contracts—in cases where the result of the work is difficult to quantify or tasks are highly standardized,[15] such contracts are established where the agent is given a fixed wage for their work (e.g. public officials). A positive consequence of this type of contract is avoiding moral hazard and reducing opportunistic behaviour by agents.[16] As risk-seeking behavior does not involve additional benefits, agents are supposed to be more risk averse. On the other hand, the effectiveness of this type of contract should be supervised by an external control institution, because the principal cannot be sure that the agent is motivated enough to perform tasks soundly.

Outcome-Oriented Contracts—their aim is to make the interest of principal and agent complimentary. Under this contract, the agent is fully or significantly rewarded for the calculated effects of their actions.[17] This solution aims to create a mechanism in which the principal would have to rely largely on an agent's self-regulation without the need for costly monitoring of their activities. In the financial sector, a key element that promotes efficiency is the payment of annual bonuses based in most cases on the financial performance of the company. The main problem here is the increased risk of moral hazard which, among other things, can be manifested in the artificially inflated company results by agents, as was done in the case of the Enron and WorldCom scandals,[18] to obtain undue benefit.[19]

## The Fall of the Washington Mutual Bank

The Washington Mutual Bank (WaMu) was the sixth largest bank in the United States. The numbers presented in this case, even taking into account the scale of the financial sector, are impressive—$300 billion in

---

[15] K. M. Eisenhardt, "Agency Theory: An Assessment and Review," *Academy of Management Review* (1989): 62.

[16] A. Sharma, "Professional as Agent: Knowledge Asymmetry in Agency Exchange," *The Academy of Management Review* (1997): 783.

[17] T. M. Moe, "The New Economics of Organization," *American Journal of Political Science* (1984): 763; K. M. Eisenhardt, *Agency Theory*, 59–60.

[18] C. Culp, W. Niskanen (eds.), *Corporate Aftershock: the Public Policy Lessons from the Collapse of Enron and Other Major Corporations* (New Jersey: John Wiley & Sons, Inc 2003).

[19] S. Shapiro, *Agency Theory*, 279.

assets, $188 billion in deposits, with more than 40,000 employees.[20] However, it was not the bank that was "too big to fail," as an application for bankruptcy was filed on September 25, 2008. The direct cause of this event was the loss of liquidity caused by the classic bank run—customers started to withdraw their deposits on a mass scale. However, the deep causes of this bankruptcy were distributed over time, and some of them lay in the unregulated agency problems. Complex principal-agent relations are shown in Fig. 22.1 below.

Fig. 22.1. Principals and Agents—the Case of Washington Mutual

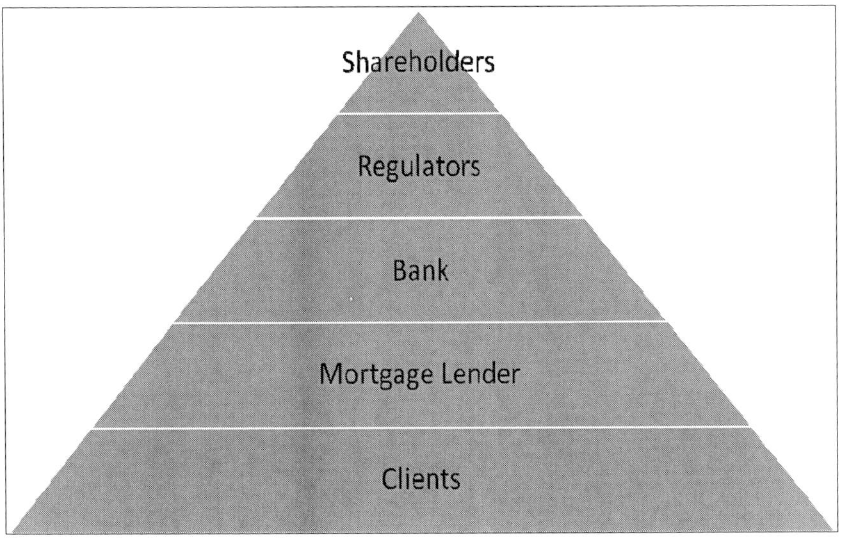


Source: Author's own research.

The primary principal in the WaMu case comprises the shareholders—the owners of the Bank, and ultimately the bearers of consequences of (in)appropriate decisions taken by top managers (Board of Directors). Shareholders' agents are the managers of the bank. However, the mediator between the shareholders and their agents—and their next agent—are financial sector supervisory bodies, who act in the interests of shareholders by controlling the bank. The managers' agent is a Mortgage Lender

[20] Permanent Subcommittee on Investigations—US Senate, *Wall Street & the Financial Crisis—Anatomy of a Financial Collapse* (New York: Cosimo, Inc, 2011), 48.

Company, owned by the bank, that provides clients with mortgages. This is an institution which operates in a situation of double loyalty, and should represent the interests of both clients and its owner—the bank. Here emerges a classic conflict of interest. At the lowest level of agency relation are the clients experiencing the (most) important agency problem in the whole catalogue. In this analysis, we discuss three major areas which, in the case of WaMu, are having problems with the agency-management activities of the Bank and the regulator "Mortgage Lender"—the company granting loans.

## WaMu Top Managers

The Washington Mutual Bank, present in the financial sector since the end of the nineteenth century, historically based its business strategy on lending to customers with a low probability of default. However, in 2003 the WaMu CEO Kerry Killinger announced that the bank intended to enhance its engagement in subprime mortgage loans, granted to people with poor credit scores (subprime). The bank therefore increased its share of subprime loans from 29% in 2003 to 54% in 2007.[21] At the same time, the value of WaMu shares increased by more than 25%, and Kerry Killinger increased his annual earnings from $12 million in 2003[22] to $21 million four years later.[23] In the short term, therefore, there was success in marrying the interests of principals (shareholders) and agents (managers). However, in the middle of 2007 the first effects of the strategy based on risky loans were seen when share prices began to fall steadily. Over a year later, on September 25, 2008, the Washington Mutual Bank was bankrupt. Ten days before this event Killinger resigned, pocketing a $15 million payoff. This example shows that in the long term, the agency problems have not been dealt with in sufficient detail. From the perspective of the relation between the principals—shareholders and agents—there emerge two main problematic areas:

(1) The unregulated problem of information asymmetries. Kerry Killinger's departure just before the collapse of the bank, which allowed him to obtain additional financial benefit, shows how vital the hitherto unregulated agency problems in the financial

---

[21] Ibid., 69.

[22] K. Grind, *The Lost Bank: The Story of Washington Mutual—The Biggest Bank Failure in American History* (New York: Simon & Schuster, 2012), 94.

[23] Ibid., 174.

sector are. One of the axioms of the agency theory is an information advantage of the agent over the principal. The story of the last days of WaMu empirically confirmed the hypotheses that can be derived from provable theory. We can presume that without the creation of an effective system of monitoring agents, similar situations will recur in the future, perverting the agency relations even more.

(2) The ineffectiveness of outcome-oriented contracts. The spectacular success of WaMu after the introduction of the strategy based on providing subprime mortgages, and its equally spectacular fall, shed new light on the legitimacy of the widespread use of outcome-oriented contracts. The problem is that this is a basic tool for the identification of interests of principals and agents. The fact that the principal bares definitive consequences while the agent may at any time leave, keeping their payoff, creates a strong incentive for risk-seeking behaviour. In this context, we conclude that reward managers using result-oriented contracts can contribute to reinforcing the problem of moral hazard.

## Regulator—the Office of Thrift Supervision (OTS)

The task of the regulator in the financial sector is, on the one hand, to ensure compliance with the applicable law, and on the other to provide information to shareholders about the actual condition of the institutions in which they have invested their money. Unfortunately, the Office of Thrift Supervision, the main regulator of the WaMu, failed with both tasks. OTS knew about the risks taken by bank loans with subprime loans, but did not order changes in business strategy.[24] What is more, the same lending violations were repeatedly identified for many years. The OTS claimed a high rating of the bank, pointing out its strong position, until March 2008, as well as the average until September (the month WaMu collapsed, although other institutions were governing the activities of the banks) when the Federal Deposit Insurance Corporation (FDIC) suggested its lowering.[25] In addition, the correspondence between the regulators and the Bank's Management Board points to a large degree of intimacy between them, which questions the professional nature of this relationship.[26] How

[24] Ibid., 223.

[25] Ibid., 274.

[26] Permanent Subcommittee on Investigations—US Senate, *Wall Street & the Financial Crisis—Anatomy of a Financial Collapse* (New York: Cosimo, Inc, 2011), 213.

may the agency's problems have contributed to the occurrence and duration of the above problems?

(1) Behaviour-oriented contracts. The OTS example indicates the long-term inefficiency of this type of contracts in the case of regulators. The state does not have the appropriate tools for rewarding employees effectively—identifying risks and acting on behalf of changes of unauthorized practices. The lack of incentives for efficiency can be a main cause for the failure of the control institutions in general.
(2) Control of opportunistic behaviour. There are known cases of recruitment by former WaMu employees of the OTS.[27] The unregulated problem of a revolving door in the financial sector may lead to strengthening the opportunistic behaviour of the regulatory staff. The prospect of a lucrative contract in the private sector after the completion of the work as a regulator can substantially affect the action not in conformity with the formal mission of the state institution.

## Long Beach Mortgage Company (LBMC)

The LBMC was a company mortgage lender, a separate company owned by WaMu. In this case, managers were rewarded on the basis of behaviour-oriented contracts. The indicator of their performance was the amount of mortgage loans provided. In conjunction with ineffective regulatory institutions this led to a reduction in lending standards. Performance was measured by the volume of mortgages sold rather than their quality. LBMC documentation shows that executives knew about the risks of subprime credit, but did not change the bad practices because they probably did not want to give up their annual bonuses that depended on the amount of loans. In addition, internal control carried out by WaMu indicates that approximately 35% of the credit contract documentation bears the traces of fraud. In 14% of cases one could observe differences in borrowers' signatures.[28] The available data allow for the conclusion that the problem is systemic in nature, and independent of the individual competence of specific managers. After the aforementioned problems, WaMu decided to release the existing management and bring their experienced manager David Schneider to LBMC; however, despite this

[27] Ibid., 223.
[28] Ibid., 78.

treatment he failed to resolve the diagnosed problems.[29] We can hypothesize that the outcome-oriented contracts are very strong incentives promoting more fulfilment of indicators, rather than proceedings in accordance with the mission of the institution. The example of the Long Beach Mortgage Company shows how outstanding and durable two further agency problems are:

(a) Adverse selection. This is an important feature that answers the question of where the inefficiencies of outcome-oriented contracts stem from. In a situation where the outcome is determined by one or more indicators, agents may be more willing to implement the indicators themselves, regardless of their long-term consequences and other essential items not included in the indicators. Focusing on the implementation of indicators replaces the formal mission of the institution, which is sustainable growth with action focused on achieving an indicator alone.
(b) Conflict of interests. Situations where the operation is incompatible with the interests of the principal that bring benefits to the agent, and incentives appear to remain inconsistent with formal standards. Identification of potential conflicts of interest can contribute to a more efficient monitoring of the activities of the agents and reduce the likelihood of agents' opportunistic behaviour.

## Clients/American Households

The agency problems experienced by American households are systemic, the cause laying in the way mortgages in the U.S. are repaid. The scheme is well described by Hans-Werner Sinn in his prominent book on the financial crisis:

> If, in Europe, someone takes out a mortgage to buy a home they know that they must repay it, if necessary until their death. If they become insolvent, the bank auctions off their home to recover the loan. If the proceeds of the sale do not cover the loan, the bank has recourse to other assets and to the future labor income of the homeowner. That is why Europeans are cautious when buying a home and can only sleep peacefully again when the mortgage is repaid. Not so in America. There, only a fool does not incur debt. In the USA, the liability of the homeowner is limited because, as a

[29] K. Grind, *The Lost Bank: The Story of Washington Mutual—The Biggest Bank Failure in American History* (New York: Simon & Schuster, 2012), 137.

> rule, home mortgages are given as so-called non-recourse loans. If something goes wrong, the bank can repossess the house but cannot get hold of other property, let alone the labour income of the debtor. There are special antideficiency laws in eight states that enforce these rules. And in states where there are no anti-deficiency laws, non-recourse loans are nonetheless the common form, maybe because banks are compelled by competition or because in the USA the declaration of private insolvency, which precludes recourse to other assets, is easy anyway. A non-recourse loan means that when the homeowner stops paying mortgage interest, the bank may only claim the home and nothing else. States like California and Arizona, where recourse to other assets of the mortgage holder is legally restricted, report an exorbitantly large number of foreclosures, as many homeowners simply stop payment in the event that the home is over-mortgaged.[30]

The very idea of a non-recourse loan is that the bank is an ultimate risk-bearer of the credit given. The client—a non-professional in the mortgage or financial industries—may be mistaken about their credit score but the bank should account for the risk of the default on its own. Here, two great agency problems that were faced by subprime borrowers emerge:

(1) Moral hazard—while borrowers privatized all the gains of obtaining a mortgage (a better home) they were insured from the risk of repaying the debt in full when they defaulted. This produces a strong incentive to get a mortgage if a bank would provide such a possibility. The mortgage market was based on the belief that the banks would police themselves. However, incentives for short-sightedness perverted the system as a whole.

(2) Opportunistic behaviour—clients took advantage of rising prices in the housing market and could refinance their loans, building their prosperity not on work but on speculation of the value of their homes. Turning to model M -> M' instead of M -> C -> M' made the speculative way of earning money more popular than ever before. This is how Wall Street changed Main Street. The first transferred its business model to ordinary citizens, which resulted in excessive risk that stimulated the financial crisis of 2008.

---

[30] H. W. Sinn, *Casino Capitalism: How the Financial Crisis Came about and What Needs to be Done Now* (Oxford, New York: Oxford University Press, 2010), 94–95.

## Conclusions

The collapse of WaMu reveals one of the hidden causes of the financial crisis, which lies in the unregulated framework of modern capitalism, leading to the essential agency problems. So far, it seems that the outcome-oriented contracts bring together the interests of principals and agents; however, actions taken by banks and mortgage companies, analyzed here through WaMu and LBMC, show that this does not produce incentives to strengthen long-term efficiency in even the most developed economies.

If we cannot rely on this type of contract, control must be carried out by external institutions—market regulators. The action of OTS indicates, however, that they are the same agents as the managers of companies, and the efficiency of their work is subject to the same agency problems.

The biggest challenge might be a social one in estimating to what extent American households build their consumption and prosperity on speculation rather than production. The key aim here is to show how popular the speculative model of earning money, copied from Wall Street, is in American society at present.

Contemporary economic prosperity will depend substantially on the practical ability to regulate and manage existing agency problems, and part of an institutional settlement should be geared towards solving them. Anti-crisis action refers only to purely economic tools (packages to stimulate the economy, lowering interest rates, etc.), and apart from the dimension of regulating agents behaviour, the production of a solution to the problems of contemporary capitalism may prove a lot harder than is commonly thought.

Mateusz Trawiński is a PhD candidate at the Institute of Sociology at the Nicolaus Copernicus University in Toruń. His current research addresses the social causes of financial crisis.

# CHAPTER TWENTY-THREE

# SOCIAL ENTERPRISES AS CIVIL SOCIETY ORGANISATIONS: A POLISH PERSPECTIVE

MARTA CISEK

## Introduction

The diagnosis of civil society's position in CEE countries is often of a negative nature. This is visible through, among other things, low levels of social capital and social trust, low levels of civil participation, low engagement in non-governmental organisations (NGOs), and lack of confidence in the ability to influence public affairs. Often, the condition of civil society is linked with the quality of the third sector. However, in Poland there are inconsistent trends in this area, for example increasing the number of NGOs with a small percentage of voluntary activities. Due to this, new solutions are required. Clearly, it is not only NGOs that are responsible for the quality of civil society. In this context, it is worth looking at the other entities that may have an impact on the quality of civil society.

Therefore, the subject of this chapter is the social enterprises present in the current public debate and their role in the development of civil society in Poland. Firstly, the classification of social enterprises into groups of institutions of civil society is interesting. Those entities are connected with the three areas of country state/public area, market and the third sector, and they are benefiting from three kinds of initiatives: public, economic and social. However, the following questions arise: are they still independent entities in their activity or are some of them merely an extension of the public administration at the moment? Also, does the fact that they are closer to the business environment as they perform regular business activities deprive them from a social initiatives title?

The main purpose of this chapter is to present Polish social enterprises that can be considered as new institutions of civil society. Undoubtedly, their social missions, goals and values are close to the idea of civil society. In this chapter, the innovative aspect will be presented as a willingness to establish business activities and associated risk, in which respect they differ from traditional civil entities.

## Civil Society Organisations

The idea of civil society still remains one of the most popular and broad categories of social sciences. In the narrative sphere, this type of social self-organisation is created by specific solutions, formal procedures, attitudes, rights, and civil liberties such as freedom of expression and association. Due to the fact that the subject of this chapter is related to some aspects of institutional functionality in civil society and not the theory of civil society as such, we will not discuss the theoretical concepts of it here.

For the purposes of the chapter it seems reasonable to adopt a definition of civil society which allows us to analyze the specific institutions and their practical roles in social life. Therefore, the empirical perspective which identifies civil society as the third sector will be applied here. In this context, civil society is created by all kinds of individual initiatives and associations with public aims.[1] As per Jerzy Szacki, the idea of civil society undermines the public-to-private dichotomy and assumes the existence of the intermediates.[2] This is called the third sector, alternatively the non-governmental sector, the civil sector, the social sector, or the non-profit sector. Certainly, NGOs confirm the existence of civil society. The question here is whether the scope of the latter concept can be extended by other entities such as the social economy entities, i.e. social enterprises which are not so obviously taken into consideration, and their importance for the functioning of civil society. The social economy is not only undermining the diversity of public-to-private, as social enterprises are located between country, market and non-governmental sector. What makes them different from the traditional non-governmental organisations is the fact that their revenues are partly generated by

---

[1] J. Szacki, Wstęp: "Powrót do idei społeczeństwa obywatelskiego," in *Ani książę, ani kupiec: obywatel. Idea społeczeństwa obywatelskiego w myśli współczesnej* (Kraków: Znak, 1997), 52–57.

[2] Ibid.

business activities, i.e. sales of services and products, thanks to which they are not so dependent on donations and grants from the state.

## An Ideal Model of Social Enterprises as a Subject of Social Economy

Social enterprises are nothing more than the entities of the new social economy. Deliberately, the adjective "new" is used here to stress the renewed interest in this issue in Poland. Despite the pre-war tradition and examples of social projects, the idea of the social economy in Poland depreciated during the time of Communism. For this reason, the term "*ekonomia społeczna*" is often used in Poland, rather than "*gospodarka społeczna*," which recalls a negatively perceived, centrally planned socialized economy. The renaissance of the social economy in Poland results from the increase of the unemployment rate linked with social exclusion, and the reorientation of the social policy model from a protecting policy to an active, multi-sector and civic policy. At the micro level, the development of the social economy is caused by changes in the third sector, like the economization and professionalization of NGOs. Despite the production of goods and delivery of public services, the social economy takes actions towards social and professional integration and the re-integration of people at risk of social exclusion. A low capacity in delivery and implementation of social services has increased the role and importance of the social economy. Therefore, in recent years the need to support the sector through financial instruments, legality and programming has been recognized. Also extremely important was the Polish accession to the European Union, which allowed Polish social entrepreneurs to gain opportunities to finance their activities from the structural funds. Increasing interest in the social economy of the European Union institutions is also visible, and the European Commission in particular is taking action to promote this area. The European Commission defines social entrepreneurship as:

> an operator in the social economy whose main objective is to have a social impact rather than make a profit for their owners or shareholders. It operates by providing goods and services for the market in an entrepreneurial and innovative fashion and uses its profits primarily to achieve social objectives. It is managed in an open and responsible manner

> and, in particular, involves employees, consumers and stakeholders affected by its commercial activities.[3]

Researchers from the Emergence of Social Enterprises in the Europe European Research Network (EMES) outline three groups of indicators that define a social enterprise.[4] These are economic indicators such as: continuous activity in the production of goods and/or services, a significant level of economic risk, and a minimum amount of paid work. Social indicators are: a clear aim to bring benefits to the community, initiatives launched by a group of citizens or civil society organisations, as well as limited profit distribution. Participatory indicators are: a high level of autonomy, a decision-making authority not directed by ownership, and the participatory nature of the various parties involved.

It is worth underlining that the social enterprises which do not meet the above criteria will not be excluded from the set of those entities. Indicators describe an ideal type which is an abstract construction and does not exist in practice. It is worth verifying how Polish social enterprises meet those criteria of the ideal model in the meaning of EMES.

## Social Enterprises in Poland—Law vs. Practice

In this chapter a social enterprise will be considered as comprising new social economy participants operating in the following legal forms: non-governmental organisations operating in business, social co-operatives (spółdzielnie socjalne), Centres for Social Integration (Centra Integracji Społecznej), clubs for social integration (kluby integracji społecznej), Professional Activity Workplaces (Zakłady Aktywności Zawodowej), and therapy workshops (warsztaty terapii zajęciowej). As the concept of social enterprise is different from the socially engaged companies, another aspect of corporate social engagement, social corporate responsibility, and the framework of the concept of social marketing will not be analyzed here. Social enterprises operating in Poland will be briefly presented below, mainly through the perspective of law and practical aspects. It should be noted that the legal situation of the types of entities in Poland is not fully covered by law regulations. In contrast to other European countries, the

---

[3] *Social Economy and Social Entrepreneurship: Social Europe Guide vol. 4* (Luxembourg: European Commission European Research Institute on Cooperative and Social Enterprises, 2013), 31.

[4] *Social enterprise*, http://www.emes.net/about-us/focus-areas/social-enterprise (accessed August 20, 2013).

functioning of different types of organisations are regulated by separate legislation, and works on the legal act were started in 2008.

## Non-Governmental Organisations Engaged in Business Activities

The issue of non-governmental organisations is an opening point for discussions about social enterprises. There is general consensus that NGOs including associations and foundations are institutions of civil society. The Polish legislator defines an association as:

> a voluntary, self-governing, durable non-profit association which itself determines its goals, programs, activities and organizational structures and shall adopt internal rules for its activities. The Association's activity is based on the work of its members, can hire employees to conduct its affairs.[5]

The following types of associations are in the Polish legislation: an incorporated association created by a minimum of 15 members, an ordinary association which has no legal personality and has at least 3 members, and the union of associations made up of at least three associations or other legal entities.

In accordance with first article of the Act on foundations, a foundation is formed for the "implementation consistent with the fundamental interests of the Polish social purposes or are economically useful, in particular, such as health care, economic development, science, education and upbringing, arts and culture, health and social welfare, environmental protection and preservation of historic monuments."[6]

Systematic surveys about polish NGOs conducted by the Klon/Jawor Association indicate 11,000 foundations and 72,000 associations registered in 2012. In the context of the social enterprise, we are interested in those organisations that undertake business activities. Evolution from NGO to the social enterprise and, therefore, a matter of professionalism and economization of Polish NGOs comes from NGOs that do not fit into the traditional formula of a NGO. Often for the purpose of survival of the organisation or the independence of the state authorities, business activities are being taken which at the end are also in opposition to the

---

[5] "Ustawa z dnia 7 kwietnia 1989 roku prawo o stowarzyszeniach," *Dz. U.* 2001, nr 79, poz. 855 ze zm.

[6] "Ustawa z dnia 6 kwietnia 1984 roku o fundacjach," *Dz. U.* 1991, nr 46, poz. 203.

mission of the third sector. In the European Union the reasons for interest in social entrepreneurship, not only in the non-governmental sector but also in public institutions, are linked to the crisis of the welfare state, the change of the state's role in providing public services, the promotion of resourceful people, the processes of modernization of public administration targeted to good governance and public-to-private partnerships.[7] But, as stressed by expert Jan Jakub Wygnański, the economic involvement of NGOs on the international level is not extraordinary, and the profits from the sales of services in the area of representing the interests of professional, cultural, development, education, environmental protection and advocacy are the largest financial source for the sector.[8] In Poland, though, the economic activity is at the twelfth position of the popularity of sources of financing, represented by 9% of the organisation, and for half of them it is the dominant source.[9]

In addition, the economic activity excludes other ways of raising funds and is equal to the high economic risk. Created by the web portal www.ekonomiaspoleczna.pl, the Atlas of the Best Practices of Social Economy[10] includes a number of examples of non-governmental organisations engaged in economic activities, such as the Mutual Aid Association "Flandria" from Inowrocław, whose aims are its members' health protection and increase of the availability of medical services and professional nursing care.

These aims are being reached by shop ownerships and the rental of medical equipment, pharmacies and Private Health Care (NZOZ). Another example is the Association for Community Development Balts "Balt," undertaking touristic and economic activities such as JuraPark Balts, a ski slope and horse races. Due to the fact that these organisations spent their profits on statutory aims, they conduct continuous business activities based on economic instruments, take risks and employ paid staff, and therefore are included in the group of social enterprises.

---

[7] J. J. Wygnański, *Ekonomizacja organizacji pozarządowych. Możliwość czy konieczność?* (Klon/Jawor Association, 2008), 15–16.

[8] Ibid., 12.

[9] *Podstawowe fakty o organizacjach pozarządowych. Raport z badania 2012* (Klon/Jawor Association, 2013), 111.

[10] *Atlas dobrych praktyk ekonomii społecznej*, http://atlas.ekonomiaspoleczna.pl/ (accessed August 20, 2013).

## Social Cooperatives

The functioning of cooperatives in Poland is regulated by the Social Cooperatives act, which lists the two main goals of these subjects: a social reintegration of members understood as an activity which aims to restore and maintain the skills for participation in community and social roles in the workplace—residence or domicile—and the professional reintegration of members, understood as an activity aimed to restore and maintain the ability for self-provision on the labour market.[11] These objectives are achieved from business, however the profit gained is not distributed between them, but allocated to increase the resource fund, the mutual fund and socially useful activity. The act also contains a catalogue of people entitled to establish cooperatives. At least half of the members of the cooperative must be unemployed, disabled and subjected to social exclusion which is preventing or limiting their participation in professional, social and family life. The last group includes homeless people involved in the program of leaving homelessness, alcoholics who have finished treatment at the plant treatment centres, drug addicts at the end of their therapeutic program in a health care institution, the mentally ill in respect of the act on the protection of mental health, people released from prison having difficulties in social reintegration, and refugees pursuing individual integration programs in respect of the act on social welfare.[12]

Currently in the catalogue of the Polish Association of Social Cooperatives (Ogólnopolski Związek Rewizyjny Spółdzielni Socjalnych) there are 712 registered cooperatives.[13] The Ministry of Labour and Social Policy (Ministerstwo Pracy i Polityki Społecznej), which monitors social cooperatives, is reporting that the number of Polish social cooperatives is steadily increasing. In 2009 there were only 187, but by 2011 there were 402.[14] These cooperatives are primarily concerned with providing various services, and few are engaged in production. The main areas of their activities are home and garden, construction (electrical, electronic, hydraulic,

---

[11] "Ustawa z dnia 27 kwietnia 2006 r. o spółdzielniach socjalnych," *Dz. U.* 2006 Nr 94, poz. 651 z późn. zm.

[12] "Ustawa z dnia 13 czerwca 2003 r. o zatrudnieniu socjalnym," *Dz. U.* 2003 Nr 122, poz. 1143.

[13] *Katalog Spółdzielni Socjalnych,* http://ozrss.pl/katalog.htm (accessed August 20, 2013).

[14] *Informacja o funkcjonowaniu spółdzielni socjalnych działających na podstawie ustawy z dnia 27 kwietnia 2006 roku o spółdzielniach socjalnych za okres 2010-2011r.* (Warsaw: Departament Pożytku Publicznego, 2012), 8.

maintenance, painting, repair, welding, carpentry, metalwork and masonry services), and catering (catering services, events organisation and dining), wherein 80% of respondents intend to expand the scope of their business activities.[15] Furthermore, the majority of cooperatives are leading activities in social, cultural and educational areas, and more than a half of them are in charitable activities.[16] Among others are: Social Cooperative Warsaw, the owner of the Emma hostel in Warsaw; the advertisement agency Doozo from Szczecin, founded by graphic designers and photographers; the cooperative Nasz Dom Bydgoszcz running a home for seniors with a choir, theatre, science, foreign languages; and Spółdzielnia Socjalna Usługowo-Handlowo-Produkcyjna from Byczyna, dealing with construction and printing services.[17] Social cooperatives tempt young people by working without hierarchies, having equal salaries and running businesses in accordance with their own interests.[18]

## Social Integration Centres

Social Integration Centres operate through the act on social employment. According to this, the goal of reintegration of society is defined as:

> activities, including a self-help, designed to restore and maintain a person participating in activities at the centre of social integration, social inclusion and the club hired by the employer, skills for participation in community and social roles in the workplace, residence or domicile and to re-integrate or actions to restore and maintain a person participating in activities at the centre of social integration and social inclusion club capacity to perform the work in the labour market.[19]

These activities, as well as cooperatives, are aimed at people who are excluded or at risk of social exclusion, but in contrast to the cooperative they cannot be the founders of the centre. The intention of the legislature is social reintegration, which means the creation of the further ability to perform social roles and the achievement of social positions available to non-social exclusion, and the acquisition of vocational skills and apprenticeships, retraining and improvement of vocational qualifications,

---

[15] Ibid., 43–44.
[16] Ibid., 54.
[17] A. Lewińska, "Spółdzielnie socjalne kręcą młodych," *Gazeta Wyborcza* 264 (2012): 7.
[18] Ibid.
[19] *Ustawa z dnia 13 czerwca 2003 r. o zatrudnieniu socjalnym.*

ability to plan lives and to meet the needs through own efforts, particularly by increase of salary or profits from business, and the ability to manage wealth.

The discussed entities cannot run businesses, but the participants can work in commerce, service or manufacturing, for which integration benefits should be granted. According to the official statistics for 2004–2011, the number of these units increased from 24 to 74, wherein 20 were created by the government and 54 by the third sector.[20] An example of a well-functioning centre is the Centrum Integracji Społecznej Piątkowo, founded in 2006 by the Association of School "Barka" named Hans Christian Kofoed.[21] The partner association was the Poznań Housing Association, which opened new opportunities for the residents of housing estates who had overdue rent amounting to 5 million PLN. People in Centrum had the chance to acquire skills, return to the labour market and consequently pay the rent.[22]

## Social Integration Clubs

Social integration clubs operate on the same normative basis as the Social Integration Centres (Centra Integracji Społecznej), and their activities are also addressed to people subjected to social exclusion. Clubs' activities are carried out through the following forms: actions taken to find a job for a specified or non-specified period of time, service on the basis of civil law contracts, preparation for starting employment or undertaking an activity in the form of a social cooperative, socially useful works, public works, legal advice, self-help activities in finding employment, housing and social services, and internships subjected to the regulations on employment promotion and the labour market institutions act. Clubs may also be established by local government units (Ośrodki Pomocy Społecznej) and NGOs, and these are smaller and less formal than the Social Integration Centres. People are often directed to clubs by social workers under a

---

[20] *Informacja o funkcjonowaniu Centrów i Klubów Integracji Społecznej dla Sejmu i Senatu Rzeczypospolitej Polskiej* (Warszawa: Ministerstwo Pracy i Polityki Społecznej, Departament Pomocy i Integracji Społecznej 2012), 24.

[21] J. Koral, *Podmioty Ekonomii Społecznej vol 2. Centra Integracji Społecznej* (Warszawa: Fundacja Inicjatyw Społeczno-Ekonomicznych, 2009), 7.

[22] Ibid.

contract entered into with the customer. The number of registered clubs in 2010 was 286, including 223 which were running business.[23]

## Professional Activity Workplaces

The legal frameworks for the functioning of Professional Activity Workplaces are created by the Act on vocational and social rehabilitation and the employment of disabled persons.[24] The entities eligible for the establishment of Vocational Rehabilitation Works are municipalities, counties, foundations, associations and other social organisations whose statutory role is a professional and social rehabilitation of the disabled. They lead dual activities in the social and vocational rehabilitation of people with disabilities defined in the provisions as rehabilitation and service, and a maintenance business. The registration procedure is difficult and takes about two years. Zakład Aktywności Zawodowej status is given to the governor. Professional Activity Workplaces can benefit from a favourable system of funding from the State Fund for Rehabilitation of Disabled Persons (Państwowy Fundusz Rehabilitacji Osób Niepełnosprawnych), and from local government. Income from business and tax exemptions must be devoted entirely to the company's activity fund, which may finance the improvement and additional instrumentation of job unit supporting standalone operations, improvement of working conditions, purchase of equipment and supplies to support the independency of disabled people, participation in social life in the local community by preparing to work off site and equalization of opportunities in the new workplace, further education, training and retraining, assistance in the preparation, construction, renovation and equipment of individual and collective forms of protected housing, recreation and participation in cultural life, and meeting other social needs and the associated social rehabilitation of disabled employees.[25] In the second half of 2012, there were 69 Professional Activity Workplaces employing 3,524 people, including 2,651 disabled people.[26]

[23] The obligation to keep a register of clubs was imposed by the Ministry of the Governors in 2012. Further official statistics on the operation of clubs are forthcoming.

[24] "Ustawa z dnia 27 sierpnia 1997 r. o rehabilitacji zawodowej i społecznej oraz zatrudnianiu osób niepełnosprawnych," *Dz. U.* 1997 nr 123 poz. 776.

[25] "Rozporządzenie Ministra Pracy i Polityki Społecznej w sprawie zakładów aktywności zawodowej z dnia 17 lipca 2012 r.," *Dz. U.* 2012 nr 0 poz. 850.

[26] *Dane od wojewodów dotyczące ZAZ*, http://www.niepelnosprawni.gov.pl

## Therapy Workshops

Another form of activity supporting the process of the social and vocational rehabilitation of people with disabilities is occupational therapy workshops, which are formed on the same legal basis as the previously mentioned organisations. Workshops function as separate organisational and financial institutions whose activity is to acquire or restore the necessary skills to start employment for people with disabilities. Workshops can be organised by foundations, associations or other entities. The expenses from its creation, activities and other things resulting from an increase of the number of participants in the workshop are co-funded by the Państwowy Fundusz Rehabilitacji Osób Niepełnosprawnych and grants from county authorities. Social and professional rehabilitation is carried out by using techniques of occupational therapy which, according to legislators, should aim at developing the ability to perform activities of daily living and personal resourcefulness, mental fitness, and basic and specialized skills in order to participate in vocational training or starting work. For participants, individual rehabilitation programs are created that include, among others, the form, scope and effects of the planned rehabilitation. These programs are reviewed by the evaluation program of the workshop participants' abilities to start employment. The activities of the workshop are non-profit, and any eventual profit from the sales of products and services provided by the workshop participants during their rehabilitation and therapy program is to be spent, after consultation with the participants, on their expenses. Therapy workshops are the most numerous projects in the field of social economy in Poland. In the Klon/Jawor Association, 670 entities are registered.[27]

## Conclusions

The above-mentioned entities do not comprise a complete ranking of social enterprises, in which private health care, work cooperatives and non-profit corporations could be also included. However, the presented organisations build a picture of the social economy in Poland. It seems that among the above-mentioned entities, the closest to the ideal model of social enterprise within the meaning of EMES is the social cooperative.

---

/niepelnosprawnosc-w-liczbach-/rynek-pracy/dane-od-wojewodow-dotyczace-zaz/ (accessed August 20, 2013).

27 *Portal Organizacji Pozarządowych*, http://bazy.ngo.pl/ (accessed August 20, 2013).

The answer to the question of whether there is a place for projects in the field of social entrepreneurship in the space of civil society seems to be the affirmative. They are based on the values of co-operation, collective action, social capital, solidarity and participation. There is no doubt that they meet social functions such as the social and professional reintegration of the unemployed and the disabled. Though many of them are still far from the ideal model of social enterprise within the meaning of EMES, we should say that they do a good job.

Marta Cisek holds a Masters in Political Science with a specialization in political marketing, is an employee of the University of Wrocław, and a PhD student at the Department of Social Policy and Economics at the Institute of Political Science of the University of Wroclaw. She is preparing a doctoral thesis on the influence of instruments supporting social economy and social enterprises in Lower Silesia, and is a member of the Polish Society of Social Policy. Her research interests are social economy, social entrepreneurship, the non-governmental sector, active citizenship and multi-sectoral social policies.